EASY

1001 Slow Cooker Recipes

Come home to dinner – it's ready!

Barbara C. Jones

Cookbook Resources, LLC
Highland Village, Texas

1000 Slow Cooker Recipes
Come home to dinner – it's ready!

Printed September 2011

International Standard Book Number: 978-1-59769-108-6

Library of Congress Conrol Number: 2011936333

Library of Congress Cataloging-in-Publication Data:

Cover and illustrations by Nancy Griffith

Edited, Designed, Published and Manufactured
in the United States of America by
Cookbook Resources, LLC
541 Doubletree Drive
Highland Village, Texas 75077

Toll free 866-229-2665

www.cookbookresources.com

cookbook resources® LLC
Bringing Family and Friends to the Table

Introduction

Convenient slow cookers make life easier for anyone who uses them. Put your food inside, cover the pot, turn the switch to "on" and come home after hours of errands, soccer games, meetings, work or play and dinner is ready! Meals are simple, convenient and much better than any fast-food, drive-through-window meal.

1001 Slow Cooker Recipes provides recipes for beef, chicken, seafood, vegetables, soups and casseroles that are great as one-dish meals or as accompaniments to a main dish.

These recipes are family tested and used everyday by moms, dads, seniors, teens and college students. They are packed with nutritious ingredients and are economical, wholesome and practical.

The recipes are easy, simple and everyday cooking that everybody loves. They are ones families grow up on and ones we remember long after adulthood. They are recipes that give you a warm and fuzzy feeling and let you know someone cares about you.

These recipes should never be taken for granted or passed by because they are too simple or too "normal". They are the recipes that strengthen our families and bring us the happiness and satisfaction of being together for a homecooked meal.

Contents

Snacks, treats and dips are especially good cooked and served warm from a slow cooker. Check out the hearty meat dips – everyone loves them!

Soups, stews, chilis, chowders, gumbos and jambalayas are at their best with blended flavors developed through slow cooking.

There is no better way to create tender, juicy sandwiches than with meat and sauce cooked the slow and easy way!

Contents

Dedication

With a mission of helping you bring family and friends to the table, Cookbook Resources strives to make family meals and entertaining friends simple, easy and delicious.

We recognize the importance of a meal together as a means of building family bonds with memories and traditions that will be treasured for a lifetime. It is an opportunity to sit down with each other and share more than food.

This cookbook is dedicated with gratitude and respect for all those who show their love with homecooked meals, bringing family and friends to the table.

More and more statistical studies are finding that family meals play a significant role in childhood development. Children who eat with their families four or more nights per week are healthier, make better grades, score higher on aptitude tests and are less likely to have problems with drugs.

Appetizers

Dips & Spreads

Snacks & Munchies

Artichoke Blast

1 (16 ounce) package frozen chopped spinach, thawed	455 g
1 (14 ounce) can quartered artichoke hearts, drained, chopped	395 g
1 (4 ounce) jar diced pimentos, drained	115 g
¾ cup mayonnaise	170 g
1½ cups shredded mozzarella cheese	175 g
1 teaspoon seasoned salt	5 ml
Baguette chips	

- Squeeze spinach between paper towels to completely remove excess moisture and place in sprayed slow cooker.

- Stir in artichoke hearts, pimentos, mayonnaise, cheese, seasoned salt and a little pepper.

- Cover and cook on LOW for 1 hour 30 minutes to 2 hours. Keep on LOW while serving or for as long as 3 to 4 hours. Serve with chips. Yields 3 cups (750 ml).

Hot Bean Dip

2 (15 ounce) cans refried beans	2 (425 g)
1 (15 ounce) can pinto beans, rinsed, drained	425 g
1 small onion, finely chopped	
1 (4 ounce) can diced green chilies	115 g
1 (2 pound) box Mexican Velveeta® cheese, cut into chunks	910 g
1 (1 ounce) packet taco seasoning	30 g

- Combine refried beans, black beans, onion, green chilies, cheese and taco seasoning in sprayed slow cooker. Stir to mix ingredients well.

- Cover and cook on LOW for 3 to 4 hours and stir after 2 hours. Dip may be held on LOW for up to 3 hours. Yield: 9 cups (2 L).

Lazy Daisy Broccoli Dip

¾ cup (1½ sticks) butter	170 g
2 cups thinly sliced celery	200 g
1 onion, finely chopped	
3 tablespoons flour	20 g
1 (10 ounce) can cream of chicken soup	280 g
1 (10 ounce) box chopped broccoli, thawed	280 g
1 (5 ounce) garlic cheese roll, cut in chunks	145 g
Wheat crackers or corn chips	

- Melt butter in skillet and saute celery and onion, but do not brown; stir in flour. Pour into sprayed small slow cooker, stir in remaining ingredients and mix well.

- Cover and cook on LOW for 2 to 3 hours and stir several times. Serve with wheat crackers or corn chips. Serves 6 to 8.

Hot Broccoli Dip

1 (16 ounce) box Mexican Velveeta® cheese, cubed	455 g
1 (10 ounce) can golden mushroom soup	280 g
¼ cup milk	60 ml
1 (10 ounce) box frozen chopped broccoli, thawed, drained	280 g

- Combine cheese, soup and milk in sprayed slow cooker, stir well and fold in broccoli.

- Cover and cook on LOW for 1 to 2 hours. Stir before serving. Serves 8 to 10.

Hot Southwest Dip

1½ pounds lean ground beef	680 g
2 onions, finely diced	
1 (10 ounce) can diced tomatoes and green chilies	280 g
1 (8 ounce) can tomato sauce	230 g
2 (16 ounce) packages shredded Mexican Velveeta® cheese	2 (455 g)
Tortilla chips	

- Cook beef and onions in large skillet until onions are translucent. Drain and transfer to sprayed slow cooker. Add tomatoes and green chilies, tomato sauce and cheese; stir until they blend well.

- Cover and cook on LOW for 2 hours, stirring every 30 minutes. Use chips for dipping. Serves 12 to 14.

TIP: This dip is great served over baked potatoes.

Hearty Bean Dip

1 (15 ounce) can baked beans with liquid	425 g
1 (15 ounce) can pinto beans with jalapenos, rinsed, drained	425 g
1 pound lean ground beef	455 g
1 small onion, finely chopped	
½ cup packed brown sugar	110 g
⅓ cup ketchup	90 g
Chips	

- Place baked beans and pinto beans in sprayed slow cooker. Mash about half the beans.

- Brown ground beef in non-stick skillet, drain and spoon into sprayed slow cooker. Stir in onion, brown sugar and ketchup.

- Cover and cook on LOW for 4 hours or on HIGH for 2 hours. Serve hot with chips. Yields 6 cups (1.4 L).

Whiz Bang Dip

1 pound lean ground beef	455 g
1 small onion, very finely chopped	
2 (16 ounce) package cubed Velveeta® cheese	2 (455 g)
2 (10 ounce) cans diced tomatoes and green chilies	2 (280 g)
1 teaspoon minced garlic	5 ml
Tortilla chips	

- Cook beef in skillet on low heat for 10 minutes and break up large meat chunks. Transfer to sprayed slow cooker and add onion, cheese, tomatoes and green chilies, and garlic.

- Stir well, cover and cook on LOW for 1 hour. Serve with tortilla chips. Serves 6 to 8.

He-Man Hamburger Dip

Men love this meaty, spicy dip.

2 pounds lean ground beef	910 g
2 tablespoons dried minced onion	30 ml
1½ teaspoons dried oregano leaves	7 ml
1 tablespoon chili powder	15 ml
2 teaspoons sugar	10 ml
1 (10 ounce) can tomatoes and green chilies	280 g
½ cup chili sauce	135 g
2 (16 ounce) packages cubed Mexican Velveeta® cheese	2 (455 g)
Chips or crackers	

- Brown ground beef in large skillet, drain and transfer to sprayed slow cooker.

- Add remaining ingredients plus ½ to 1 cup (125 to 250 ml) water and stir well.

- Cover and cook on LOW for 1 hour 30 minutes to 2 hours. Stir once or twice during cooking time. Add a little salt, if desired. Serve hot with chips or spread on crackers. Serves 8 to 10.

TIP: This dip makes a full supper when spooned over baked potatoes.

Snappy Quick Dip

1 (10 ounce) can fiesta nacho cheese soup	280 g
2 (15 ounce) cans chili beef soup	2 (425 g)
1 (4 ounce) can chopped green chilies	115 g
1 (8 ounce) package shredded Velveeta® cheese	230 g
Tortilla chips	

- Combine cheese soup, chili beef soup, green chilies and cheese in sprayed slow cooker; gently stir to mix.

- Cover and cook on HIGH just until dip is hot and cheese melts. Serve with tortilla chips. Yield 5 cups (1.2 L).

Hot Spot Southwest Dip

1½ pounds lean ground beef	680 g
2 onions, finely diced	
1 (10 ounce) can diced tomatoes and green chilies	280 g
1 (8 ounce) can tomato sauce	230 g
2 (16 ounce) packages shredded Mexican Velveeta® cheese	2 (455 g)
Tortilla chips	

- Cook beef and onions in large skillet until onions are translucent. Drain and transfer to sprayed slow cooker. Add tomatoes and green chilies, tomato sauce and cheese; stir until they blend well.

- Cover and cook on LOW for 2 hours, stirring every 30 minutes. Use chips for dipping. Serves 12 to 14.

Indian Corn Dip

1 pound lean ground beef	455 g
1 onion, finely chopped	
1 (15 ounce) can whole kernel corn, drained	425 g
1 (16 ounce) jar salsa	455 g
1 (1 pound) package cubed Velveeta® cheese	455 g
Tortilla chips	

- Brown and cook beef in skillet on low heat for about 10 minutes and drain. Transfer to sprayed slow cooker and add onion, corn, salsa and cheese.

- Cover and cook on LOW for 1 hour, remove lid and stir. Serve with tortilla chips. Serves 6 to 8.

Muy Bueno Chili con Queso

2 pound lean ground beef	910 g
1 (2 pound) box Mexican Velveeta® cheese, cut into cubes	910 g
1 (10 ounce) can diced tomatoes and green chilies	280 g
1 teaspoon ground coriander	5 ml
2 teaspoons ground cumin	10 ml
¼ teaspoon hot pepper sauce, optional	2 ml
1 bunch fresh green onions, sliced	

- Cook ground beef in non-stick skillet for about 5 to 10 minutes; drain and spoon into sprayed slow cooker. Stir in cheese, tomatoes and green chilies, coriander and cumin.

- Cover and cook on LOW for 2 to 3 hours. Add hot sauce and garnish with green onion. Yield 3 cups (750 ml).

The Big Dipper

2 (15 ounce) cans chili	2 (425 g)
1 (10 ounce) can tomatoes and green chilies	280 g
1 (16 ounce) package cubed Velveeta® cheese	455 g
1 bunch fresh green onions, chopped	

- Place all ingredients in sprayed slow cooker. Cover and cook on LOW for 1 hour to 1 hour 30 minutes.

- Serve right from slow cooker. Stir before serving. Serves 6 to 8.

Hot Reuben Spread

1 (8 ounce) package shredded Swiss cheese	230 g
¾ cup drained sauerkraut, rinsed, drained	110 g
1 (8 ounce) package cream cheese, softened, cubed	230 g
2 (2.5 ounce) packages sliced corned beef, chopped	2 (70 g)
Rye bread	

- Combine Swiss cheese, sauerkraut, cream cheese and corned beef in bowl and spoon into sprayed, small slow cooker.

- Cover and cook on LOW for 1 hour. Serve on slices of 3-inch (8 cm) rye bread. Serves 4 to 6.

Hot Chipped Beef Dip

1 (8 ounce) package cream cheese, softened	230 g
¾ cup shredded Monterey Jack cheese	85 g
2 tablespoons finely chopped onion	20 g
2 tablespoons mayonnaise	30 g
¼ teaspoon garlic powder	1 ml
2 chipotle chilies (smoked jalapeno chilies) chopped	
1 (2 ounce) package dried beef, finely chopped	60 g
⅓ cup chopped pecans, toasted	40 g
Assorted crackers	

- Combine cream cheese, Monterey Jack cheese, onion, mayonnaise, garlic powder and chiles in bowl and beat until mixture is creamy. Stir in dried beef and spoon into sprayed slow cooker. (It is easier to "chop" the dried beef if you use your kitchen scissors.)

- Cover and cook on LOW for 1 hour 30 minutes to 2 hours. When ready to serve, sprinkle pecans over top. Dip can be kept warm in slow cooker for up to 1 hour. Serve with assorted crackers. Yields 1½ cups (375 ml).

Chicken-Enchilada Dip

2 pounds boneless, skinless chicken thighs, cubed	910 g
1 (10 ounce) can enchilada sauce	280 g
1 (7 ounce) can diced green chilies, drained	195 g
1 small onion, finely chopped	
1 large red bell pepper, seeded, finely chopped	
2 (8 ounce) packages cream cheese, cubed	2 (230 g)
1 (16 ounce) package shredded American cheese	455 g
Tortilla chips	

- Place chicken, enchilada sauce, green chilies, onion and bell pepper in sprayed slow cooker.

- Cover and cook on LOW for 4 to 6 hours. Stir in cream cheese and American cheese and cook for additional 30 minutes. Stir several times during cooking. Serve with tortilla chips. Serves 8 to 10.

Ranch Chicken Dip

2 (12 ounce) cans chicken breast, drained	2 (340 g)
2 (8 ounce) packages cream cheese, softened, cubed	2 (230 g)
2 (12 ounce) packages shredded cheddar cheese	2 (340 g)
1 (16 ounce) bottle ranch dressing	500 ml

- Place all ingredients in sprayed slow cooker. Cook on LOW 3 hours; stir occasionally. Serves 6 to 8.

TIP: This dip is also great on hot baked potatoes.

Cheesy Bacon Dip

2 (8 ounce) packages cream cheese, softened	2 (230 g)
1 (16 ounce) package shredded Velveeta® cheese	455 g
1 (8 ounce) carton whipping cream	230 g
¼ cup finely chopped onion	40 g
1 tablespoon mustard	15 ml
1 tablespoon Worcestershire sauce	15 ml
¼ teaspoon hot pepper sauce	1 ml
1 (4 ounce) package cooked bacon, crumbled	115 g
Chips or crusty bread	

- Combine cream cheese, Velveeta cheese, cream, onion, mustard, Worcestershire sauce, hot sauce and a little salt in sprayed slow cooker.

- Cover and cook, stirring occasionally, on LOW for 1 hour. Stir to make sure cheeses melt. Stir in crumbled bacon. Serve with chips or crusty bread. Yields 1 quart (1 L).

Crowd-Pleasing Bacon Dip

2 (8 ounce) packages cream cheese, softened	2 (230 g)
1 (8 ounce) package shredded colby Jack cheese	230 g
2 tablespoons mustard	30 ml
2 teaspoons marinade for chicken	30 g
4 fresh green onions with tops, sliced	
1 pound bacon, cooked, crumbled	455 g
Rye or pumpernickel bread	

- Cut cream cheese into cubes and place in slow cooker. Add colby Jack cheese, mustard, marinade for chicken, green onions and ¼ teaspoon (1 ml) salt. Cover and cook on LOW for 1 hour and stir to melt cheese.

- Stir in crumbled bacon. Serve with small-size rye bread or toasted pumpernickel bread. Serves 6 to 8.

Firecrackers and Bacon

1 (16 ounce) package cubed Mexican Velveeta® cheese	455 g
1 (10 ounce) can tomatoes and green chilies	280 g
1 tablespoon dry minced onion	15 ml
2 teaspoons Worcestershire sauce	10 ml
½ teaspoon dried mustard	2 ml
½ cup whipping cream or half-and-half cream	40 g
16 slices bacon, cooked, crumbled, divided	

- Combine cubed cheese, tomatoes and green chilies, onion, Worcestershire, mustard and half-and-half cream to sprayed small slow cooker. Cover and cook on LOW for about 1 hour, stirring several times to make sure cheese melts.

- While cheese is melting, place bacon in skillet, fry, drain and crumble. Fold three-fourths of bacon into cheese mixture. When ready to "dip", sprinkle remaining bacon on top and serve from slow cooker. Serves 4 to 6.

Great Balls of Fire

1 pound hot sausage	455 g
1 (10 ounce) can diced tomatoes and green chilies	280 g
1 (2 pound) box Velveeta® cheese	910 g

- Brown and cook sausage in skillet, drain and place in sprayed small slow cooker. Stir in tomatoes and green chilies and mix well. Cut cheese into chunks and add to sausage-tomato mixture.

- Cover and cook on LOW for 1 hour or until cheese melts. Stir when ready to serve and serve hot in slow cooker. Serves 4 to 6.

TIP: This works best with large tortilla chips.

Sausage-Hamburger Dip

1 pound bulk pork sausage	455 g
1 pound lean ground beef	455 g
1 cup hot salsa	265 g
1 (10 ounce) can cream of mushroom soup	280 g
1 (10 ounce) can tomatoes and green chilies	280 g
1 teaspoon garlic powder	5 ml
¾ teaspoon ground oregano	4 ml
2 (16 ounce) packages cubed Velveeta® cheese	2 (455 g)

- Cook sausage and ground beef in large skillet for 15 minutes and drain. Place in sprayed slow cooker.

- Add salsa, mushroom soup, tomatoes and green chilies, garlic powder and oregano; stir well. Fold in cheese. Cover and cook on LOW for 1 hour or until cheese melts. Stir once during cooking time. Serve from cooker. Serves 8 to 10.

Peppy Pepperoni Dip

1 (6 ounce) package pepperoni	170 g
1 bunch fresh green onions, thinly sliced	
½ red bell pepper, finely chopped	
1 medium tomato, finely chopped	
1 (14 ounce) jar pizza sauce	395 g
1½ cups shredded mozzarella cheese	170 g
1 (8 ounce) package cream cheese, cubed	230 g
Wheat crackers or tortilla chips	

- Chop pepperoni into small pieces and place in sprayed small slow cooker. Add onion, bell pepper, tomato and pizza sauce and stir well. Cover and cook on LOW for 2 hours 30 minutes to 3 hours 30 minutes.

- Stir in mozzarella and cream cheese and stir until they melt. Serve with wheat crackers or tortilla chips. Serves 4 to 6.

Creamy Crab Dip

1 (8 ounce) and 1 (3 ounce) packages cream cheese, softened	230 g/85 g
⅔ cup mayonnaise	150 g
1 tablespoon marinade for chicken	15 ml
1 tablespoon sherry or cooking sherry	15 ml
3 fresh green onions with tops, chopped	
2 (6 ounce) cans crabmeat, drained, flaked	2 (170 g)

- Combine cream cheese, mayonnaise, 1 teaspoon (5 ml) salt and marinade for chicken in bowl and mix well with fork. Stir in sherry, onions and crabmeat and spoon into sprayed small slow cooker. Cover and cook on LOW for 1 hour 30 minutes to 2 hours and stir once. Serves 6 to 8.

Tasty Crab-Artichoke Spread

1 (6 ounce) can crabmeat, flaked	170 g
½ cup grated parmesan cheese	50 g
1 bunch fresh green onions, sliced	
1½ tablespoons lemon juice	22 ml
1 (15 ounce) can artichoke hearts, drained, finely chopped	425 g
1 (8 ounce) package cream cheese, cubed	230 g
Toasted bagel chips	

- Combine all ingredients in sprayed small slow cooker and stir well.

- Cover and cook on LOW for 1 hour to 1 hour 30 minutes. Stir until cream cheese mixes well. Serve on toasted bagel chips. Serves 4 to 6.

Mind-Blowing Crab Dip

1 (6 ounce) can white crabmeat, drained, flaked	2 (170 g)
1 (8 ounce) package cream cheese, softened	230 g
½ cup (1 stick) butter, sliced	115 g
2 tablespoons white cooking wine	30 ml
Chips or crackers	

- Combine crabmeat, cream cheese, butter and wine in sprayed small slow cooker.

- Cover and cook on LOW for 1 hour and gently stir to combine all ingredients. Serve from cooker with chips or crackers. Serves 4 to 6.

Company Crab Dip

1 cup mayonnaise	225 g
1 (8 ounce) package cream cheese, softened	230 g
½ teaspoon garlic salt	2 ml
2 eggs, hard-boiled, mashed	
1 (4 ounce) can diced green chilies	115 g
3 fresh green onions, finely chopped	
1 tablespoon cooking sherry	15 ml
2 (6 ounce) cans crabmeat, drained	2 (170 g)
1 (4 ounce) can chopped pimento	115 g
Chips or crackers	

- Beat mayonnaise, cream cheese and garlic salt in bowl until smooth and spoon into sprayed slow cooker. Gently stir in eggs, green chilies, onions, sherry, crabmeat and pimento.

- Cover and cook on LOW for 1 hour 30 minutes to 2 hours. Serve with chips or crackers. Dip can be held for 3 to 4 hours on LOW. Yields 2½ cups (625 ml).

Hot Meatball Appetizers

2 (18 ounce) packages frozen cooked meatballs, thawed	2 (510 g)
½ cup packed brown sugar	110 g
1 (1 ounce) beefy onion soup mix	30 g
2 tablespoons tomato paste	30 ml
1 (12 ounce) can beer, (not lite beer)	355 ml

- Place meatballs in sprayed slow cooker and sprinkle on brown sugar and onion soup mix. Combine tomato paste and beer in small bowl and pour over meatballs.

- Cover and cook on LOW for 5 to 6 hours. Before serving, gently stir mixture to coat meatballs. Remove meatballs with slotted spoon and serve hot with wooden toothpicks. Yields about 66 meatballs.

TIP: Meatballs can be kept in slow cooker on LOW for about 1 hour.

Sausage-Pineapple Bits

The "sweet and hot" makes a delicious combo.

1 (1 pound) link cooked Polish sausage, skinned	455 g
1 (1 pound) hot bulk sausage	455 g
1 (8 ounce) can crushed pineapple with juice	230 g
1 cup apricot preserves	320 g
1 tablespoon white wine Worcestershire sauce	15 ml
1½ cups packed brown sugar	330 g

- Slice link sausage into ½-inch (1.2 cm) pieces. Shape bulk sausage into 1-inch (2.5 cm) balls and brown in skillet.

- Combine sausage pieces, sausage balls, pineapple, apricot preserves, Worcestershire sauce and brown sugar in sprayed slow cooker. Stir gently so meatballs do not break up. Cover and cook on LOW for 1 hour 30 minutes to 2 hours. Serves 8 to 10.

Party Smokies

1 cup ketchup	270 g
1 cup plum jelly	320 g
1 tablespoon lemon juice	15 ml
2 (5 ounce) packages tiny smoked sausages	2 (145 g)

- Combine all ingredients in sprayed small slow cooker. Cover and cook on LOW for 1 hour. Stir before serving. Serve right from cooker. Serves 4 to 6.

Spicy Franks

1 cup packed brown sugar	220 g
1 cup chili sauce	270 g
1 tablespoon red wine vinegar	15 ml
2 teaspoons soy sauce	10 ml
2 teaspoons dijon-style mustard	10 ml
2 (12 ounce) packages frankfurters	2 (340 g)

- Combine brown sugar, chili sauce, vinegar, soy sauce and mustard in sprayed small slow cooker and mix well. Cut frankfurters diagonally in 1-inch (2.5 cm) pieces. Stir in frankfurters.

- Cover and cook on LOW for 1 to 2 hours. Serve from cooker using cocktail picks. Serves 4.

TIP: The kids would love these franks served over seasoned spaghetti.

Bubbly Franks

1 (1 pound) package wieners	455 g
½ cup chili sauce	135 g
⅔ cup packed brown sugar	150 g
½ cup bourbon	125 ml

- Cut wieners diagonally into bite-size pieces. Combine chili sauce, brown sugar and bourbon in sprayed small slow cooker.

- Stir in wieners. Cover and cook on LOW for 1 to 2 hours. Serve in chafing dish. Serves 6 to 8.

Teriyaki Wingettes

2½ pounds chicken wingettes	1.1 kg
1 onion, chopped	
1 cup soy sauce	250 ml
1 cup packed brown sugar	220 g
1 teaspoon minced garlic	5 ml
1½ teaspoons ground ginger	7 ml

- Rinse chicken and pat dry. Place chicken wingettes on broiler pan and broil for about 10 minutes on both sides. Transfer wingettes to sprayed large slow cooker.

- Combine onion, soy sauce, brown sugar, garlic and ginger in bowl. Spoon sauce over wingettes.

- Cover and cook on HIGH for 2 hours. Stir wingettes once during cooking to coat chicken evenly with sauce. Serves 8 to 10.

Wingettes in Honey Sauce

1 (2 pound) package chicken wingettes	910 g
2 cups honey	680 g
¾ cup soy sauce	175 ml
¾ cup chili sauce	205 g
¼ cup canola oil	60 ml
1 teaspoon minced garlic	5 ml
Dried parsley flakes	

- Rinse chicken, pat dry and sprinkle with a little salt and pepper. Place wingettes in broiler pan and broil for 20 minutes (10 minutes on each side) or until light brown. Transfer to sprayed slow cooker.

- Combine honey, soy sauce, chili sauce, oil and garlic in bowl and spoon over wingettes.

- Cover and cook on LOW for 4 to 5 hours or on HIGH for 2 hours to 2 hours 30 minutes. Garnish with dried parsley flakes, if desired. Serves 8 to 10.

Honey Wings

16 - 18 chicken wings (about 3 pounds)	1.4 kg
2 cups honey	680 g
1 cup barbecue sauce	270 g
1 teaspoon minced garlic	5 ml
¼ cup soy sauce	60 ml
¼ cup canola oil	

- Cut off and discard wing tips and cut each wing at joint to make two sections. Sprinkle wings with a little salt and pepper and place on broiler pan. Broil for about 10 minutes; turn wings and broil for additional 10 minutes. Place wings in sprayed slow cooker.

- Combine honey, barbecue sauce, garlic, soy sauce and oil in bowl and mix. Pour mixture over wings. Cover and cook on LOW for 2 to 3 hours. Yields 32 to 36 wings.

Condensation forms on the inside of the lid and creates a "seal" while cooking with a slow cooker. This is why it is important not to lift the lid during the cooking period unless the recipe gives instructions to do so. It's also why the lids are usually glass - just so we can take a peek without removing the lid!

Good Time Snacks

3 cups Corn Chex® cereal	95 g
3 cups Quaker® oat squares	95 g
4 cups Crispix® cereal	95 g
2 cups pretzel sticks	110 g
1 cup salted peanuts	150 g
1 (16 ounce) can cashews	455 g
1 teaspoon seasoned salt	5 ml
1 teaspoon garlic salt	5 ml
1 teaspoon celery salt	5 ml
¾ cup (1½ sticks) butter, melted	170 g

- Place cereals, pretzel sticks, peanuts and cashews in sprayed slow cooker and sprinkle with seasoned salt, garlic salt and celery salt. Drizzle mixture with melted butter and gently toss.

- Cover and cook on LOW for 3 to 4 hours. Uncover last 45 minutes. Yields 2 quarts (1.9 L).

TIP: You may mix and match other cereals in the same amounts.

Sweet and Sour Meatball Delights

1 (10 ounce) jar sweet and sour sauce	280 g
⅓ cup packed brown sugar	75 g
¼ cup soy sauce	60 ml
1 teaspoon garlic powder	5 ml
1 (28 ounce) package frozen cooked meatballs, thawed	795 g
1 (20 ounce) can pineapple chunks, drained	565 g

- Combine all ingredients in sprayed slow cooker and mix well. Cover and cook on LOW for 5 to 6 hours; stir occasionally. Serves 6.

TIP: This can be served as an appetizer or served over seasoned spaghetti.

Cranberry Twist Meatballs

1 (1.2 ounce) envelope brown gravy mix	30 g
1 (28 ounce) package frozen meatballs, thawed	795 g
1 (16 ounce) can whole cranberry sauce	455 g
2 tablespoons whipping cream	30 ml
1 tablespoon dijon-style mustard	15 ml

- Make gravy according to package directions. Place meatballs, cranberry sauce, cream, mustard and gravy in sprayed slow cooker; mix well. Cover and cook on LOW 4 to 5 hours; stir occasionally. Serve with toothpicks. Serves 20 to 25.

Soups & Stews

Soups • Stews

Chilis • Chowders

Gumbos • Jambalayas

Country Cheddar Cheese Soup

½ cup (1 stick) butter, melted	115 g
2 ribs celery, thinly sliced	
1 small onion, chopped	
1 green bell pepper, seeded, chopped	
½ cup shredded carrots	55 g
1 (14 ounce) can chicken broth	395 g
1 (12 ounce) package shredded sharp cheddar cheese	340 g
½ cup flour	60 g
1 quart milk	1 L

- Combine butter, celery, onion, bell pepper, carrots, broth and cheese in sprayed slow cooker. Cover and cook on LOW for 4 to 6 hours.

- Mix flour with about 2 tablespoons (30 ml) milk in bowl until mixture is smooth; stir in remaining milk.

- Stir in milk mixture, cover and cook for additional 20 to 30 minutes or until soup is thoroughly hot. Serves 4 to 6.

The Ultimate Cheddar Cheese Soup

1 onion, finely chopped	
1 red bell pepper, seeded, finely chopped	
½ cup (1 stick) butter, melted	115 g
1 (16 ounce) package shredded extra sharp cheddar cheese	455 g
1 cup finely grated carrots	110 g
1 (14 ounce) can chicken broth	395 g
½ teaspoon minced garlic	2 ml
2 tablespoons cornstarch	15 g
1 (1 pint) carton half-and-half cream	500 ml

- Combine onion, bell pepper, butter, cheese, carrots, broth, garlic and a little pepper in sprayed slow cooker. Cover and cook on LOW for 5 to 7 hours.

- Mix cornstarch with about 2 tablespoons (30 ml) half-and-half cream in bowl until mixture is smooth; stir in remaining cream.

- Stir in cream mixture, cover and cook for additional 15 to 20 minutes or until soup is thoroughly hot. Serves 6.

Old-Time Cheese Soup

¼ cup (½ stick) butter, melted	60 g
1 small onion, finely chopped	
2 ribs celery, thinly sliced	
½ cup shredded carrots	55 g
2 (14 ounce) cans chicken broth	2 (395 g)
1 (12 ounce) package shredded Velveeta® cheese	340 g
1 tablespoon dried parsley	15 ml
2 tablespoons cornstarch	15 g
4 cups milk	1 L

- Combine butter, onion, celery, carrots, broth, cheese, parsley and ½ teaspoon (2 ml) salt in sprayed slow cooker. Cover and cook on LOW for 4 to 6 hours.

- Mix cornstarch with about 2 tablespoons (30 ml) milk in bowl until smooth. Stir in remaining milk. Add milk mixture to cooker, cover and cook for additional 30 minutes or until soup is thoroughly hot. Serves 6.

Rich and Hearty Cheese Soup

5 slices bacon, fried, crumbled	
1 small onion, finely chopped	
2 ribs celery, sliced	
1 medium leek, halved lengthwise, sliced	
3 (14 ounce) cans chicken broth	3 (395 g)
1 potato, peeled, cut into small cubes	
⅔ cup quick-cooking oats	55 g
1 cup shredded Swiss cheese	115 g
1 (8 ounce) carton whipping cream	230 g

- Set crumbled bacon aside. Combine onion, celery, leek, broth, potatoes and oats in sprayed slow cooker. Cover and cook on LOW for 5 to 7 hours.

- Cool slightly and place half soup in blender and process until smooth. Repeat with remaining soup and return to slow cooker.

- Add cheese and cream and stir until cheese melts. Cover and cook for additional 20 to 30 minutes or until soup is thoroughly hot. Sprinkle crumbled bacon over each serving. Serves 4.

For easier cleanup, it is best to always spray a slow cooker with a cooking spray or rub the inside with a little oil. Another option is using disposable liners.

Capital Cheese Soup

1 (10 ounce) can cheddar cheese soup	280 g
1 (10 ounce) can cream of celery soup	280 g
1 (16 ounce) package shredded cheddar cheese	455 g
1 teaspoon paprika	5 ml
1½ cups half-and-half cream	375 ml

- Combine soups, cheddar cheese, paprika and a little pepper in sprayed slow cooker. Cover and cook on LOW for 2 to 3 hours.

- Stir in half-and-half cream, cover and cook for additional 20 minutes. Serves 4.

TIP: If you don't like black specks in your dish, try white pepper.

Special Asparagus Soup

¼ cup (½ stick) butter, melted	60 g
3 (14 ounce) cans chicken broth	3 (395 g)
½ teaspoon minced garlic	2 ml
1 bunch green onions with tops, diced	
1 large potato, peeled, cubed	
1 (8 ounce) package shredded Velveeta® cheese	230 g
2 (15 ounce) cans cut asparagus with liquid	2 (425 g)
1 (8 ounce) carton sour cream	230 g

- Combine butter, broth, garlic, green onions, potato and cheese in sprayed slow cooker. Cover and cook on LOW for 4 to 6 hours. Stir in asparagus and sour cream and serve immediately. Serves 6 to 8.

Thick Asparagus-Cream Soup

1 onion, finely chopped	
1 red bell pepper, seeded, finely chopped	
¼ cup (½ stick) butter, melted	60 g
2 (15 ounce) cans cut asparagus, drained	2 (425 g)
2 (10 ounce) cans cream of chicken soup	2 (280 g)
1 (14 ounce) can chicken broth	395 g
1 teaspoon lemon juice	5 ml
¼ teaspoon dried tarragon	1 ml
1 (1 pint) carton half-and-half cream	500 ml

- Combine onion, bell pepper, butter, asparagus, soup, broth, lemon juice and tarragon in sprayed slow cooker. Cover and cook on LOW for 3 to 4 hours.

- Stir in half-and-half cream, cover and cook for additional 30 to 40 minutes or until soup is thoroughly hot. Serves 6.

Enticing Broccoli-Rice Soup

1 (6 ounce) package chicken-flavored rice mix	170 g
1 (16 ounce) package frozen chopped broccoli, thawed	455 g
2 teaspoons dried chopped onion	10 ml
1 (10 ounce) can cream of chicken soup	280 g
1 (8 ounce) package cream cheese, cubed	230 g

- Combine rice mix, seasoning packet, 6 cups (1.4 L) water, onion, soup and ½ teaspoon salt in sprayed slow cooker. Cover and cook on LOW for 4 to 5 hours.

- Add cream cheese cubes. Cover and let stand for about 10 minutes for cream cheese to melt. Stir again before serving. Serves 4 to 6.

Parmesan-Spiked Broccoli Soup

3 (14 ounce) cans chicken broth	3 (395 g)
3 ribs celery, sliced	
1 onion, finely chopped	
1 medium potato, peeled, chopped	
1 (16 ounce) package frozen chopped broccoli, thawed	455 g
1 (1 pint) carton half-and-half cream	500 ml
1 (5 ounce) package grated parmesan cheese	145 g

- Combine broth, celery, onion, potato, broccoli, half-and-half cream and 1 teaspoon (5 ml) salt in sprayed slow cooker. Cover and cook on LOW for 6 to 8 hours.

- Spoon soup in individual soup bowls and top with a little parmesan cheese. Serves 6.

Saucy Broccoli Soup

1 (16 ounce) package frozen broccoli florets, thawed	455 g
1 (12 ounce) can evaporated milk	375 ml
1 (1 ounce) packet white sauce mix	30 g
1 (1 ounce) packet vegetable soup mix	30 g
1 (14 ounce) can chicken broth	395 g
1 (12 ounce) shredded Velveeta® cheese	340 g

- Combine broccoli, evaporated milk, white sauce mix, vegetable soup mix, broth, 1 cup (250 ml) water and cheese in sprayed slow cooker.

- Cover and cook on LOW for 7 to 8 hours. Stir soup about 1 hour before planning to serve. Serves 6.

Incredible Broccoli-Cheese Soup

1 (10 ounce) package frozen chopped broccoli, thawed, drained	280 g
¼ cup (½ stick) butter, melted	60 g
½ onion, very finely chopped	
2 (14 ounce) cans chicken broth	2 (395 g)
⅛ teaspoon cayenne pepper	.5 ml
1 (12 ounce) package shredded Mexican Velveeta® cheese	340 g
¼ cup flour	30 g
1 (1 pint) carton half-and-half cream	500 ml

- Combine broccoli, butter, onion, broth, cayenne pepper, cheese and ½ teaspoon (2 ml) salt in sprayed slow cooker. Cover and cook on LOW for 4 to 6 hours.

- Mix flour with about 2 tablespoons (30 ml) half-and-half cream in bowl until mixture is smooth; stir in remaining cream.

- Stir cream mixture into cooker, cover and cook for additional 20 to 30 minutes or just until soup is thoroughly hot. Serves 4 to 6.

Creamy Broccoli Soup

½ cup finely chopped onion	
2 (10 ounce) cans cream of broccoli soup	2 (280 g)
1 cup milk	250 ml
1 (8 ounce) package cubed Velveeta® cheese	230 g
1 (10 ounce) package frozen chopped broccoli, thawed	280 g
1 (14 ounce) can chicken broth	395 g

- Combine all ingredients in sprayed slow cooker. Cover and cook on LOW for 3 to 5 hours. Serves 4 to 6.

Surprise Broccoli Soup

1 (6 ounce) package chicken-flavored wild rice mix	170 g
1 (10 ounce) package frozen chopped broccoli, thawed	280 g
3 ribs celery, sliced	
1 (1 ounce) packet onion soup mix	30 g
1 (10 ounce) can cream of chicken soup	280 g

- Combine wild rice mix, 6 cups (1.4 L) water, broccoli, celery, onion soup mix and chicken soup in sprayed slow cooker. Cover and cook on LOW for 5 to 7 hours. Serves 4 to 6.

Neighborly Broccoli Soup

¼ cup (½ stick) butter, melted	60 g
2 onions, finely chopped	
3 (14 ounce) cans chicken broth	3 (395 g)
1 (16 ounce) package frozen chopped broccoli, thawed	455 g
1 cup grated carrots	110 g
1 (10 ounce) can cream of chicken soup	280 g
3 tablespoons flour	20 g
1 (5 ounce) can evaporated milk	150 ml

- Combine butter, onions, broth, broccoli, carrots and chicken soup in sprayed slow cooker. Mix flour with evaporated milk in bowl, stirring until blended well and add to slow cooker. Cover and cook on LOW for 6 to 8 hours. Serves 6.

Tantalizing Broccoli Soup

5 slices bacon, fried, crumbled	
1 small onion, very finely minced	
3 medium potatoes, peeled, cut in small cubes	
1 (10 ounce) package frozen chopped broccoli, thawed	280 g
¼ cup (½ stick) butter, melted	60 g
3 tablespoons flour	20 g
1 (1 pint) half-and-half cream	455 g

- Set crumbled bacon aside. Combine onion, potatoes, broccoli, butter and 1 teaspoon (5 ml) salt in sprayed slow cooker. Cover and cook on LOW for 5 to 7 hours.

- Stir flour into about 2 tablespoons (30 ml) half-and-half cream in bowl and mix until smooth. Add remaining half-and-half cream and stir in slow cooker; cover and cook for additional 30 minutes or until soup in thoroughly hot. Sprinkle 1 tablespoon (15 ml) crumbed bacon over each serving. Serves 4.

Cream of Carrot Soup

1 (10 ounce) package frozen chopped bell peppers and onions, thawed	280 g
¼ cup (½ stick) butter, melted	60 g
1 (16 ounce) package shredded carrots	455 g
3 (14 ounce) can chicken broth	3 (395 g)
1 (10 ounce) can cream of chicken soup	280 g
1 (8 ounce) carton whipping cream	230 g

- Combine bell peppers and onions, butter, carrots, broth, soup and ½ teaspoon (2 ml) salt in sprayed slow cooker. Cover and cook on LOW for 5 to 7 hours. Stir in whipping cream, cover and let stand for about 10 minutes. Serves 4 to 6.

Silky Cauliflower Soup

1 (10 ounce) package frozen chopped bell peppers and	
onions, thawed	280 g
½ teaspoon garlic powder	2 ml
3 (14 ounce) cans chicken broth	3 (395 g)
1 large cauliflower, cut into small florets	
1 (1 pint) carton whipping cream	500 ml

- Combine bell peppers and onions, garlic powder, broth and cauliflower in sprayed slow cooker. Cover and cook on LOW for 3 to 5 hours.

- Process soup in batches in blender until smooth and return to cooker. Stir in cream, ½ teaspoon (2 ml) salt and pepper. Cover and cook for additional 1 hour or until soup is thoroughly hot. Serves 6.

Cheesy Cauliflower Soup

1 (16 ounce) package frozen cauliflower florets, thawed	455 g
2 ribs celery, sliced	
1 cup grated carrots	110 g
1 onion, finely chopped	
3 (14 ounce) cans chicken broth	3 (395 g)
½ teaspoon lemon pepper	2 ml
1 (8 ounce) carton whipping cream	230 g
1 (12 ounce) package shredded Monterey Jack cheese, divided	340 g

- Combine cauliflower, celery, carrots, onion, broth, 1 cup (250 ml) water, lemon pepper, ½ teaspoon (2 ml) salt and cream in sprayed slow cooker. Cover and cook on LOW for 4 to 6 hours.

- Stir in about three-fourths cheese; cover and let stand for about 10 minutes for cheese to melt. Spoon into individual soup bowls and sprinkle remaining cheese over each serving. Serves 6.

Cauliflower-Potato Soup

1 cup instant mashed potato flakes	60 g
3 (14 ounce) cans chicken broth	3 (395 g)
½ cup finely chopped scallions, white part only	80 g
½ teaspoon caraway seeds	2 ml
1 (16 ounce) package frozen cauliflower florets, thawed	455 g
1 (8 ounce) package shredded cheddar cheese, divided	230 g

- Combine potato flakes, broth, scallions, caraway seeds, cauliflower, 1½ cups (375 ml) water, ½ teaspoon (2 ml) salt and a little pepper in sprayed slow cooker. Cover and cook on LOW for 4 to 6 hours.

- Stir in half cheddar cheese and let stand for about 10 minutes for cheese to melt. Spoon into soup bowls and sprinkle a little cheese over each serving. Serves 6.

Corn Soup Olé!

2 tablespoons flour	15 g
2 (14 ounce) cans chicken broth	2 (395 g)
2 (15 ounce) cans whole kernel corn	2 (425 g)
1 (15 ounce) cream-style corn	425 g
½ onion, chopped	
¼ cup (½ stick) butter, melted	60 g
1 (1 pint) carton half-and-half cream	500 ml
1 (7 ounce) can chopped green chilies	200 g
1 (8 ounce) package shredded cheddar cheese	230 g
1 - 2 cups crushed tortilla chips	55 - 100 g

- Mix flour and about ½ cup (125 ml) broth in bowl, stir until mixture is smooth and place in sprayed slow cooker. Add remaining broth, corn, cream-style corn, onion, butter, half-and-half cream, green chilies and cheese. Cover and cook on LOW for 4 to 6 hours. Sprinkle about 1 heaping tablespoon (15 ml) crushed tortilla chips on each serving. Serves 6.

Quick-Fix Corn Soup

2 (15 ounce) cans whole kernel corn	2 (425 g)
2 (10 ounce) cans cream of potato soup	2 (280 g)
2 (14 ounce) cans chicken broth	2 (395 g)
1 (8 ounce) carton whipping cream	230 g
⅛ teaspoon cayenne pepper	.5 ml

- Combine all ingredients in sprayed slow cooker. Cover and cook on LOW for 3 to 4 hours. Serves 6.

Choice Corn Soup

¼ cup (½ stick) butter, melted	60 g
1 (16 ounce) package frozen bell peppers and onions, thawed	455 g
1 (16 ounce) package frozen corn, thawed	455 g
1 (15 ounce) can cream-style corn	425 g
1 (10 ounce) can diced tomatoes and green chilies	280 g
2 (14 ounce) cans chicken broth	2 (395 g)
¼ cup flour	30 g
1 (1 pint) carton half-and-half cream, divided	500 ml

- Combine butter, bell peppers and onions, corn, cream-style corn, tomatoes and green chilies, broth and ½ teaspoon (2 ml) salt in sprayed slow cooker. Cover and cook on LOW for 6 to 8 hours.

- Mix flour with ½ cup (125 ml) half-and-half cream in bowl and stir until mixture is smooth; stir in remaining cream and add to slow cooker.

- Cover and cook for additional 30 to 45 minutes or until soup thickens and thoroughly hot. Serves 6 to 8.

Mellow Mushroom Soup

3 (8 ounce) packages fresh mushrooms, cut in half	3 (230 g)
1 small onion, chopped	
2 ribs celery, chopped	
¼ cup (½ stick) butter, melted	60 g
3 (14 ounce) cans chicken broth	3 (395 g)
1 teaspoon dried tarragon	5 ml
¼ cup flour	30 g
1 (1 pint) carton half-and-half cream, divided	500 ml
¼ cup dry white wine	60 ml

- Combine mushrooms, onion, celery, butter, broth, tarragon and a little salt and pepper in sprayed slow cooker. Cover and cook on LOW for 4 to 6 hours.

- Mix flour with about ½ cup (125 ml) half-and-half cream in bowl and stir until mixture is smooth; add remaining cream and stir into cooker. Cover and cook for additional 30 to 45 minutes until soup thickens and thoroughly hot. Stir in wine just before serving. Serves 6.

Tempting Mushroom-Rice Soup

1 (16 ounce) package whole mushrooms, halved	455 g
½ cup brown rice	95 g
8 baby carrots, cut in half	
1 (1 ounce) packet onion mushroom soup mix	30 g
1 (32 ounce) carton beef broth	910 g
1 (10 ounce) package frozen sugar-snap peas, thawed	280 g

- Layer, mushrooms, rice, carrots, mushroom soup mix, broth and 1 cup (250 ml) water in sprayed slow cooker. Cover and cook on LOW for 6 to 8 hours.

- Gently stir in sugar-snap peas, cover and cook for additional 15 minutes. Serves 6 to 8.

Quick Onion Soup

8 yellow onions, thinly sliced	
¼ cup (½ stick) butter, melted	60 g
2 (32 ounce) cartons beef broth	2 (910 g)
8 slices French bread, crust trimmed, toasted	
8 slices Swiss cheese	

- Combine sliced onion, butter and broth in sprayed slow cooker. Cover and cook on LOW for 4 to 7 hours.

- Spoon soup into 6 or 8 oven-proof bowls, top with slices of toasted bread and cover with slices of cheese. Place bowls on baking sheet under broiler; broil for 1 or 2 minutes or until cheese melts. Serve immediately. Serves 6 to 8.

Easy French Onion Soup

¼ cup (½ stick) butter	60 g
3 large onions, sliced	
3 (14 ounce) cans beef broth	3 (395 g)
1 teaspoon Worcestershire sauce	5 ml
½ cup dry white wine	125 ml
Butter, softened	
4 thick slices French bread, toasted	
½ cup grated gruyere or parmesan cheese	50 g

- Melt butter in skillet over medium heat. Stir in onions and cook for about 15 minutes or until onions are soft and very light brown. Place onions in sprayed slow cooker and add broth, Worcestershire and wine.

- Cover and cook on LOW for 4 to 4 hours 30 minutes. Spread light layer of butter on each slice of toasted bread. Ladle soup into 4 individual bowls; top with a slice of toasted bread and cheese. Serves 4.

Satin Green Pea Soup

1 (16 ounce) package frozen green peas, thawed	455 g
1 cup milk	250 ml
2 (10 ounce) cans cream of chicken soup	2 (280 g)
2 (14 ounce) cans chicken broth	2 (395 g)
1 (8 ounce) carton whipping cream	230 g
1 cup shredded Swiss cheese	115 g

- Combine peas and milk in blender and blend until mixture is smooth and place in sprayed slow cooker. Add soup and broth to cooker. Cover and cook on LOW for 3 to 4 hours.

- Stir in cream, cover and cook for additional 20 to 30 minutes or until soup is thoroughly hot. Sprinkle a little cheese over each serving. Serves 4 to 6.

Luncheon Pea Soup

1 cup instant mashed potato flakes	60 g
½ cup Italian salad dressing	125 ml
1 (16 ounce) package frozen peas and pearl onions, thawed	455 g
2 (14 ounce) cans chicken broth	2 (395 g)
1 (10 ounce) can cream of chicken soup	280 g
½ cup sour cream	120 g

- Combine potato flakes, salad dressing, peas and pearl onions, broth, soup, ½ teaspoon (2 ml) salt and 1¼ cups (310 ml) water in sprayed slow cooker. Cover and cook on LOW for 4 to 6 hours.

- Let cool for 10 to 15 minutes, transfer soup mixture to blender and blend in batches until smooth. Return to slow cooker, cover and cook for additional 20 to 30 minutes or until soup is thoroughly hot. Stir in sour cream just before serving. Serves 4 to 6.

Delicious Split Pea Soup

1 (16 ounce) package dried green split peas, soaked overnight	455 g
1 onion, finely chopped	
1 large potato, peeled, grated	
2 ribs celery, chopped	
1 cup cooked, shredded ham	140 g
2 (14 ounce) can chicken broth	2 (395 g)
1 cup shredded carrots	110 g
1 teaspoon minced garlic	5 ml

- Drain soaked peas and place in sprayed slow cooker. Add onion, grated potato, celery, ham, broth, carrots, garlic, 2 cups (500 ml) water and 1 teaspoon (5 ml) salt. Cover and cook on LOW for 6 to 8 hours. Serves 6.

Split Pea-Tortellini Soup

⅓ cup dry split peas	65 g
1 small onion, finely chopped	
1½ teaspoons dried basil	7 ml
½ cup shredded carrots	55 g
1 (10 ounce) can diced tomatoes and green chilies	280 g
1 cup cooked, cubed ham	140 g
2 (14 ounce) cans chicken broth	2 (395 g)
1 (8 ounce) package cheese-filled tortellini	230 g

- Combine split peas, onion, basil, carrots, tomatoes and green chilies, ham, 1½ cups (375 ml) water and broth in sprayed slow cooker. Cover and cook on LOW for 6 to 8 hours.

- Cook tortellini according to package directions and stir into soup. With heat still on, cover and let stand for about 15 minutes before serving. Serves 6.

Green Chile-Potato Soup

1 onion, finely chopped	
2 ribs celery, finely chopped	
3 medium potatoes, peeled, cut into small cubes	
1 (10 ounce) can cream of potato soup	280 g
1 cup shredded cheddar cheese	115 g
1 (7 ounce) can diced green chilies	200 g
2 (14 ounce) cans chicken broth	2 (395 g)
1 (1 pint) carton half-and-half cream	500 ml
5 slices bacon, fried, crumbled	

- Combine onion, celery, potatoes, potato soup, cheese, green chilies, broth and 1 teaspoon (5 ml) salt in sprayed slow cooker. Cover and cook on LOW for 5 to 7 hours.

- Stir in half-and-half cream; cover and cook for additional 15 minutes or until soup is thoroughly hot. Sprinkle crumbled bacon over each serving. Serves 6.

Cheesy Potato Soup

6 medium potatoes, peeled, cubed
1 onion, very finely chopped
2 (14 ounce) cans chicken broth   2 (395 g)
1 (8 ounce) package shredded American cheese   230 g
1 cup half-and-half cream   250 ml

- Combine potatoes, onion, chicken broth and a little pepper in sprayed slow cooker. Cover and cook on LOW for 8 to 10 hours.

- Mash potatoes in slow cooker. Stir in cheese and cream and cook for additional 1 hour. Serves 4 to 6.

Garlic-Potato Soup

1 quart milk   1 L
1 (7 ounce) package roasted-garlic instant mashed potatoes   200 g
2 (10 ounce) cans cream of celery soup   2 (280 g)
2 (14 ounce) cans chicken broth   2 (395 g)
1 (4 ounce) can chopped pimentos   115 g
1 (8 ounce) packages shredded sharp cheddar cheese, divided   230 g

- Combine milk, instant mashed potato mix, soup, broth, pimentos, 1 teaspoon (5 ml) salt and 2 cups (500 ml) water in sprayed slow cooker. Cover and cook on LOW for 4 to 6 hours.

- Stir in half cheese; cover and let stand for 10 to 15 minutes or until cheese melts. Spoon into individual soup bowls and sprinkle each serving with a little cheese. Serves 6.

Savory Potato-Cheese Soup

3 large baking potatoes, peeled, cubed
2 carrots, peeled, sliced
1 onion, chopped
1 (32 ounce) carton chicken broth   910 g
¼ teaspoon thyme   1 ml
½ teaspoon crushed rosemary   2 ml
¼ teaspoon garlic powder   1 ml
1 (8 ounce) package shredded cheddar cheese   230 g
1 (1 pint) carton half-and-half cream   500 ml

- Combine potatoes, carrots, onion, broth, thyme, rosemary, garlic, 1 cup (250 ml) water and 1 teaspoon (5 ml) each of salt and pepper in sprayed slow cooker. Cover and cook on LOW for 6 to 8 hours.

- Stir in cheese and half-and-half cream. Cover and cook for additional 45 minutes or until soup is thoroughly hot. Serves 6.

Rich Potato Soup

2 tablespoons butter	30 g
1 large onion, finely chopped	
3 (14 ounce) cans chicken broth	3 (395 g)
3 - 4 large potatoes, peeled diced	
1 (4 ounce) can chopped green chilies	115 g
¼ cup flour	30 g
1 (16 ounce) carton half-and-half cream	455 g
1 - 2 cups shredded cheddar cheese	115 - 230 g

- Melt butter in skillet over medium high heat and cook onions until they are transparent. Transfer to sprayed slow cooker and stir in broth, potatoes, green chilies, 1 cup (250 ml) water and a little salt and pepper.

- Cover and cook on LOW for 6 to 7 hours, stirring occasionally. Use potato masher to mash about half of potatoes in slow cooker.

- Whisk flour and half-and-half cream in bowl; add to slow cooker and cook for additional 30 minutes or until steaming hot; stir in cheese. Serves 6.

EZ Potato-Pepper Soup

1 (18 ounce) package frozen hash-brown potatoes with onions and peppers, thawed	510 g
2 red bell peppers, seeded, chopped	
1 (10 ounce) can cream of celery soup	280 g
1 (10 ounce) can cream of chicken soup	280 g
3 (14 ounce) cans chicken broth	3 (395 g)
1 (8 ounce) carton whipping cream	230 g
4 green onions, chopped	

- Combine hash browns, bell peppers, celery soup, chicken soup, broth, 1 teaspoon (5 ml) each of salt and pepper in sprayed slow cooker. Cover and cook on LOW for 7 to 9 hours.

- Stir in cream, cover and let stand for about 15 minutes or until soup is thoroughly hot. Sprinkle about 1 teaspoon (5 ml) chopped onions over each serving. Serves 6.

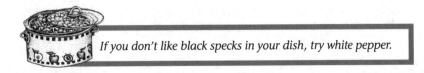

If you don't like black specks in your dish, try white pepper.

The Works Potato Soup

3½ pounds red potatoes, cubed	1.6 kg
1 onion, chopped	
1 (32 ounce) carton chicken broth	910 g
1 pint half-and-half cream	500 ml
1 (8 ounce) package shredded cheddar cheese	230 g
1 (4 ounce) package prepared bacon bits	115 g

- Place potatoes and onions in sprayed slow cooker. Combine broth and 1 teaspoon (5 ml) each of salt and pepper; add to slow cooker. Cover and cook on HIGH for 3 to 4 hours.

- Mash mixture and add half-and-half cream. Cover and cook for additional 20 minutes. Top each serving with cheese and bacon bits. Serves 6.

Yummy Potato Soup

2 tablespoons butter	30 g
½ cup chopped onion	80 g
1 tablespoons flour	15 ml
1 carrot, peeled, shredded	
3 potatoes, peeled, cut in ½-inch (1.2 cm) cubes	
3 (14 ounce) cans chicken broth	3 (395 g)
1 cup half-and-half cream	250 ml
1 - 2 cups shredded cheddar cheese	115 - 230 g

- Melt butter in skillet over medium heat and cook onion until translucent. Stir in flour until smooth and gradually add carrots and a little salt and pepper.

- Place potatoes, broth and half-and-half cream in sprayed slow cooker and pour in flour-vegetable mixture. Cover and cook on LOW for 8 hours or on HIGH for 5 hours.

- Puree about 3 cups (750 ml) soup in blender and return to slow cooker. Stir in cheese and mix well. Serves 6.

Slow cooking retains most of the moisture in food, therefore if a recipe results in too much liquid at the end of cooking time, remove cover, increase heat to high setting and cook another 45 minutes.

Choice Spinach Soup

2 (10 ounce) package frozen chopped spinach, thawed	2 (280 g)
1 onion, chopped	
2 (10 ounce) cans cream of celery soup	2 (280 g)
2 (14 ounce) cans chicken broth	2 (395 g)
1 (4 ounce) can chopped pimentos	115 g
1 (8 ounce) carton whipping cream	230 g

- Combine spinach, onion, soup, broth, pimentos, ½ teaspoon (2 ml) salt and ½ cup (125 ml) water in sprayed slow cooker. Cover and cook on LOW for 4 to 6 hours.

- Stir in cream; cover and cook for additional 15 minutes or until soup is thoroughly hot. Serves 6.

Summer Veggie Soup

1 tablespoon canola oil	15 ml
1 green bell pepper, seeded, chopped	
1 onion, chopped	
3 small yellow squash, halved lengthwise, sliced	
3 small zucchini, halved lengthwise, sliced	
1 cup fresh green peas or black-eyed peas	200 g
1 (15 ounce) can great northern beans, rinsed, drained	425 g
2 (15 ounce) cans stewed tomatoes	2 (425 g)
2 (14 ounce) cans chicken broth	395 g
1 teaspoon seasoned salt	5 ml

- Heat oil in skillet and saute bell pepper and onion for about 5 minutes, stirring often and place in sprayed slow cooker. Add squash, zucchini, green peas, beans, tomatoes and broth.

- Cover and cook on LOW for 4 to 6 hours. Stir in seasoned salt and ½ teaspoon pepper. Serves 5 to 6.

Squash Soup

¼ cup (½ stick) butter, melted	60 g
1 onion, chopped	
2 (16 ounce) packages frozen yellow squash, thawed	2 (455 g)
1 (32 ounce) carton chicken broth	910 g
1 (7 ounce) can chopped green chilies	200 g
1 (8 ounce) carton whipping cream	230 g

- Combine butter, onion, squash, broth, green chilies and 1 teaspoon (5 ml) each of salt and pepper in sprayed slow cooker. Cover and cook on LOW for 5 to 7 hours.

- Cool soup for about 15 minutes and puree soup in batches in blender until mixture is smooth.

- Return mixture to cooker, add cream, cover and cook for additional 15 minutes or just until soup is thoroughly hot. Serves 6.

Harvest Sweet Potato Soup

3 (15 ounce) cans sweet potatoes with liquid	3 (425 g)
¼ cup (½ stick) butter, melted	60 g
1 cup sliced scallions, white part only	160 g
3 (14 ounce) cans chicken broth	3 (395 g)
¼ teaspoon ground cinnamon	1 ml
1 (8 ounce) carton whipping cream	230 g

- Drain sweet potatoes, set aside liquid and place, 1 can at a time, in shallow bowl and mash with fork.

- Combine mashed sweet potatoes, liquid, butter, scallions, broth, cinnamon and ¼ teaspoon (1 ml) salt in sprayed slow cooker. Cover and cook on LOW for 5 to 7 hours.

- Stir in whipping cream, cover and let stand for about 15 minutes or until soup is thoroughly hot. Serves 4 to 6.

Easy-Fix Tomato-Bean Soup

1 (16 ounce) package frozen chopped bell peppers and onions, thawed	455 g
2 ribs celery, sliced	
2 (15 ounce) cans pork and beans with liquid	2 (425 g)
1 (15 ounce) can stewed tomatoes	425 g
1 (10 ounce) can tomato soup	280 g
2 cups cooked, chopped ham	280 g

- Combine bell peppers and onions, celery, beans, tomatoes, tomato soup, ham and ½ teaspoon (2 ml) salt in sprayed slow cooker. Cover and cook on LOW for 5 to 7 hours. Serves 6.

Creamy Tomato Soup

2 (28 ounce) cans diced tomatoes	2 (795 g)
¼ cup (½ stick) butter, melted	60 g
2 tablespoons brown sugar	30 g
2 tablespoons tomato paste	35 g
2 tablespoons flour	15 g
1 (14 ounce) can chicken broth	395 g
1 (8 ounce) carton whipping cream	230 g

- Drain tomatoes (reserving liquid) and place in blender; puree tomatoes and pour into sprayed slow cooker. Add reserved liquid, butter, brown sugar, tomato paste and ½ teaspoon (2 ml) salt.

- Mix flour with about ½ cup (125 ml) broth in bowl until mixture is smooth and stir in remaining broth. Add flour-broth mixture to cooker. Cover and cook on LOW for 6 to 8 hours.

- Stir in cream, cover and cook for additional 20 minutes or until soup is thoroughly hot. Serves 6.

Tomato-Tortilla Soup

1 (10 ounce) package frozen chopped bell peppers and onions, thawed	280 g
½ teaspoon cumin	2 ml
2 teaspoons minced garlic	
2 (15 ounce) cans diced tomatoes	2 (425 g)
1 (4 ounce) can diced green chilies	115 g
3 (14 ounce) cans chicken broth	3 (395 g)
2 - 3 tablespoons canola oil	30 - 45 ml
8 corn tortillas, cut into strips	
1 (8 ounce) package shredded Mexican 3-cheese blend	230 g

- Combine bell peppers and onions, cumin, garlic, tomatoes, green chilies and broth in sprayed slow cooker. Cover and cook on LOW for 5 to 7 hours.

- Heat oil in skillet and fry tortilla strips until crisp; drain. Place a few tortilla strips and a little shredded cheese in each bowl, pour soup into bowls and serve immediately. Serves 4 to 6.

Fiesta Vegetable Soup

1 (15 ounce) can Mexican-style stewed tomatoes	425 g
1 (15 ounce) can whole kernel corn	425 g
1 (15 ounce) can pinto beans, drained	425 g
1 green bell pepper, seeded, chopped	
2 (14 ounce) cans chicken broth	2 (395 g)
2 (10 ounce) cans fiesta nacho soup	2 (280 g
1 - 2 cups crushed tortilla chips	55 - 100 g

- Combine tomatoes, corn, beans, bell pepper, broth and soup in sprayed slow cooker. Cover and cook on LOW for 5 to 7 hours. Sprinkle crushed chips over each serving. Serves 4 to 6.

Pepe's Tortilla con Queso Soup

3 (14 ounce) cans chicken broth	3 (395 g)
1 (15 ounce) can stewed tomatoes	425 g
4 green onions, chopped	
2 (10 ounce) cans diced tomatoes and green chilies	2 (280 g)
1 teaspoon minced garlic	5 ml
1 (16 ounce) package cubed Mexican Velveeta® cheese	455 g
2 tablespoons canola oil	30 ml
6 corn tortillas	

- Combine broth, stewed tomatoes, green onion, tomatoes and green chilies, garlic, cheese and ½ teaspoon (2 ml) salt in sprayed slow cooker. Cover and cook on LOW for 3 to 4 hours.

- While soup is cooking, cut tortillas into long, narrow strips. Heat oil in skillet and fry strips until crisp; drain. Spoon soup in individual soup bowls and top with a few crisp tortilla strips. Serves 6.

Zippy Soup Mix

2 (15 ounce) cans Mexican stewed tomatoes	2 (425 g)
2 (14 ounce) cans chicken broth	2 (395 g)
2 (10 ounce) cans chicken noodle soup	2 (280 g)
1 (15 ounce) can shoe-peg corn, drained	425 g
1 (15 ounce) can cut green beans, drained	425 g
Shredded pepper-Jack cheese	

- Place all ingredients except cheese in sprayed slow cooker and mix well. Cover and cook on LOW for 2 to 3 hours. Sprinkle cheese over each serving. Serves 4 to 6.

Spicy Tomato Soup

2 (10 ounce) cans tomato soup	2 (280 g)
1 (15 ounce) can Mexican-style stewed tomatoes	425 g
1 (10 ounce) can cheddar cheese soup	280 g
½ cup sour cream	120 g
4 - 6 slices bacon, fried, crumbled	

- Place tomato soup, stewed tomatoes, cheese soup and ½ cup (125 ml) water in sprayed slow cooker; mix until blended well. Cover and cook on LOW for 2 to 3 hours.

- Stir in sour cream. Sprinkle 1 heaping teaspoon (15 ml) crumbed bacon over each serving. Serves 6.

Cream of Zucchini Soup

3 medium zucchini, grated	
1 onion, finely chopped	
3 (14 ounce) cans chicken broth	3 (395 g)
1 (10 ounce) can cream of celery soup	280 g
½ teaspoon sweet basil	2 ml
1 (1 pint) carton half-and-half cream	500 ml

- Combine zucchini, onion, broth, soup, basil and ½ teaspoon (2 ml) salt in sprayed slow cooker. Cover and cook on LOW for 4 to 6 hours.

- Stir in half-and-half cream; cover and cook for additional 20 minutes or until soup is thoroughly hot. Serves 4 to 6.

Slow cookers use far less electricity than other methods – and – they don't heat up the kitchen!

Fresh Zucchini Summertime Soup

1 small onion, very finely chopped	
3½ - 4 cups grated zucchini with peel	440 - 500 g
2 (14 ounce) cans chicken broth	2 (395 g)
1 teaspoon seasoned salt	5 ml
1 teaspoon dried dill weed	5 ml
2 tablespoons butter, melted	30 g
1 (8 ounce) carton sour cream	230 g

- Combine all ingredients except sour cream with a little pepper in sprayed small slow cooker. Cover and cook on LOW for 2 hours. Fold in sour cream, cover and cook for about 10 minutes or just until soup is hot. Serves 4.

Seasoned Zucchini Mix

½ cup (1 stick) butter, melted	115 g
3 - 4 medium zucchini, coarsely chopped	
2 ribs celery, sliced	
1½ teaspoons Italian seasoning	7 ml
1 (14 ounce) chicken broth	395 g
½ - 1 teaspoon curry powder	2 - 5 ml
1 (10 ounce) can cream of potato soup	280 g
1 (10 ounce) can French onion soup	280 g
2 cups milk	500 ml

- Combine butter, zucchini, celery, broth, curry powder, potato soup, onion soup, milk and 1 teaspoon (5 ml) salt in sprayed slow cooker. Cover and cook on LOW for 4 to 6 hours. Serves 6.

Mixed-Up Veggie Soup

2 large potatoes, peeled, diced	
1 (16 ounce) package frozen chopped bell peppers and onions, thawed	455 g
3 (14 ounce) cans chicken broth	3 (395 g)
1 (4 ounce) can sliced mushrooms, drained	115 g
1 (16 ounce) package frozen mixed vegetables, thawed	455 g
1 (10 ounce) can cream of celery soup	280 g
1 (12 ounce) package shredded Velveeta® cheese	340 g

- Combine potatoes, bell peppers and onions, broth, mushrooms, mixed vegetables, celery soup, 1 to 1 teaspoons (5 to 10 ml) salt and 2 cups (500 ml) water in sprayed slow cooker. Cover and cook on LOW for 7 to 9 hours.

- Stir in cheese; cover and let stand for 5 or 10 minutes for cheese to melt. Serves 6 to 8.

Rainbow Vegetable Soup

3 medium potatoes, peeled, chopped	
1 (15 ounce) can cut green beans, drained	425 g
1 (8 ounce) can whole kernel corn, drained	230 g
1 (15 ounce) can navy beans, drained	425 g
2 carrots, peeled, sliced	
¼ cup (½ stick) butter, melted	60 g
3 (14 ounce) cans chicken broth	3 (395 g)
2 ribs celery, sliced	
2 teaspoons ground cumin	10 ml
1 pint half-and-half cream	500 ml

- Combine potatoes, green beans, corn, navy beans, carrots and melted butter in large bowl. Stir in chicken broth, celery, cumin and a little salt and pepper; pour into sprayed slow cooker.

- Cover and cook on LOW for 8 to 9 hours or on HIGH for 4 to 5 hours.

- Stir in half-and-half cream and cook on HIGH for additional 20 to 25 minutes or until soup is piping hot. Serves 10 to 12.

Fresh Vegetable-Garden Soup

3 (14 ounce) cans chicken broth	3 (395 g)
¼ cup (½ stick) butter, melted	60 g
1 (16 ounce) package frozen mixed vegetables	455 g
1 onion, chopped	
3 ribs celery, sliced	
1 teaspoon ground cumin	5 ml
3 zucchini, coarsely chopped	
2 cups chopped, fresh broccoli	480 ml
1 cup half-and-half cream	250 ml

- Combine broth, butter, vegetables, onion, celery, cumin, 1 teaspoon (5 ml) each of salt and pepper in sprayed large slow cooker and stir well. Cover and cook on LOW for 6 to 7 hours or on HIGH for 3 to 4 hours.

- Stir in zucchini and broccoli. (If cooking on LOW, increase heat to HIGH.) Cover and cook for additional 30 minutes to 1 hour or until broccoli is tender-crisp.

- Turn off heat and stir in half-and-half cream. Let stand for 10 minutes before serving. Serves 6 to 8.

Guiltless Vegetable Cup

2 (15 ounce) cans cannellini beans, drained	2 (425 g)
1 (16 ounce) package frozen mixed vegetables	455 g
1 (14 ounce) can Italian stewed tomatoes	395 g
1 (14 ounce) can great northern beans, drained	395 g
1 (12 ounce) bottle vegetable juice cocktail	340 g
1 (14 ounce) can vegetables broth	395 g
½ cup penne pasta	40 g
1 cup crumbled corn chips	55 g

- Combine cannellini beans, mixed vegetables, stewed tomatoes, great northern beans, vegetable juice and vegetable broth in sprayed slow cooker; mix well. Cover and cook on LOW for 8 to 9 hours.

- About 20 minutes before serving, stir in penne pasta; increase heat to HIGH and cook for additional 20 minutes or until pasta is tender.

- Just before serving, sprinkle a few crumbled corn chips over each serving. Serves 6.

Southwestern Bean Soup

¼ cup (½ stick) butter, melted	60 g
1 (10 ounce) package frozen chopped bell peppers	
and onions, thawed	280 g
2 - 3 (14 ounce) cans beef broth	2 - 3 (395 g)
2 (15 ounce) cans Mexican stewed tomatoes	2 (425 g)
1 (15 ounce) can pinto beans, rinsed, drained	425 g
1 (15 ounce) can black beans, rinsed, drained	425 g
1 (15 ounce) can kidney beans, rinsed, drained	425 g
1 tablespoon chili powder	15 ml
1 (8 ounce) package shredded Velveeta® cheese	230 g
1 cup shredded Monterey Jack cheese	115 g

- Combine butter, bell peppers and onions, broth, tomatoes, beans, chili powder, cheese and 1 teaspoon (5 ml) salt in sprayed slow cooker. Cover and cook on LOW for 6 to 8 hours. Sprinkle a little Jack cheese over each serving. Serves 8.

South-of-the-Border Bean Soup

1 (15 ounce) can refried beans	425 g
2 (14 ounce) cans beef broth	2 (395 g)
2 (15 ounce) cans pinto beans with jalapenos, rinsed, drained	2 (425 g)
1 (8 ounce) can tomato sauce	230 g
1 cup hot salsa	265 g
1 (10 ounce) package frozen chopped bell peppers	
and onions, thawed	280 g

- Combine refried beans and broth in sprayed slow cooker and stir until mixture blends well. Add beans, tomato sauce, salsa, bell peppers and onions and 1 cup (250 ml) water to sprayed slow cooker. Cover and cook on LOW for 4 to 7 hours. Serves 6.

Bayou Pinto Bean Soup

4 (15 ounce) cans seasoned pinto beans with liquid	4 (425 g)
1 (10 ounce) package frozen chopped bell peppers and onions	280 g
2 cups chopped celery	200 g
2 (14 ounce) cans chicken broth	2 (395 g)
1 teaspoon Cajun seasoning	5 ml
⅛ teaspoon cayenne pepper	.5 ml

- Place all ingredients plus 1 cup (250 ml) water in sprayed slow cooker and stir well. Cover and cook on LOW 5 to 6 hours. Serves 6 to 8.

Bean Bash Soup

2 (15 ounce) cans great northern beans with liquid	2 (425 g)
2 (15 ounce) cans pinto beans with liquid	2 (425 g)
1 large onion, chopped	
1 tablespoon instant beef bouillon granules	15 ml
1 tablespoon minced garlic	15 ml
2 teaspoons Italian seasoning	10 ml
2 (15 ounce) cans Italian stewed tomatoes	2 (425 g)
1 (15 ounce) can cut green beans, drained	425 g

- Combine northern beans, pinto beans, onion, beef bouillon, garlic, Italian seasoning and 2 cups (500 ml) water in sprayed large slow cooker. Cover and cook on LOW for 6 to 8 hours.

- Turn heat to HIGH, add stewed tomatoes and green beans and stir well. Cover and cook for additional 30 minutes or until green beans are tender. Serves 6 to 8.

TIP: Serve with crispy Italian toast.

Quickie Bean and Barley Bounty

2 (15 ounce) cans pinto beans with liquid	2 (425 g)
3 (14 ounce) cans chicken broth	3 (395 g)
½ cup quick-cooking barley	100 g
1 (15 ounce) can Italian stewed tomatoes	425 g

- Combine beans, broth, barley, stewed tomatoes and ½ teaspoon (2 ml) pepper in sprayed slow cooker and stir well. Cover and cook on LOW for 4 to 5 hours. Serves 6 to 8.

Veggie Mix Special

2 (19 ounce) cans lentil home-style soup	2 (540 g)
1 (15 ounce) can stewed tomatoes	425 g
1 (14 ounce) can chicken broth	395 g
1 onion, chopped	
1 green bell pepper, chopped	
3 ribs celery, sliced	
1 carrot, halved lengthwise, sliced	
2 teaspoons minced garlic	10 ml
1 teaspoon dried marjoram leaves	5 ml

- Combine all ingredients in sprayed slow cooker and stir well. Cover and cook on LOW for 5 to 6 hours. Serves 6 to 8.

Bonzo Garbanzo Soup

1 (16 ounce) package frozen chopped bell peppers	
and onions, thawed	455 g
1 pound Italian sausage, cut up	455 g
2 (14 ounce) cans beef broth	2 (395 g)
1 (15 ounce) can Italian stewed tomatoes	425 g
2 (15 ounce) can garbanzo beans, rinsed, drained	2 (425 g)

- Combine bell peppers and onions, sausage, broth, tomatoes, beans and ½ teaspoon (2 ml) salt in sprayed slow cooker. Cover and cook on LOW for 4 to 6 hours. Serves 6.

Hot-to-Trot Bean Soup

2 (15 ounce) cans refried beans	2 (425 g)
2 (14 ounce) cans chicken broth	2 (395 g)
1 (7 ounce) can chopped green chilies	200 g
1 teaspoon minced garlic	5 ml
2 - 3 jalapeno chilies, seeded chopped	
5 sliced bacon, cut into ½-inch (1.2 cm) pieces	
1 bunch green onions, chopped, divided	
3 ribs celery, sliced	
1 green bell pepper, seeded, chopped	
1 (8 ounce) package shredded cheddar cheese	230 g

- Place refried beans and broth in sprayed slow cooker and stir until mixture blends well. Add green chilies, garlic, jalapeno chilies, bacon pieces, half chopped onions, celery and bell pepper.

- Cover and cook on LOW for 5 to 7 hours. Spoon into individual bowls and sprinkle with cheese and remaining green onions. Serves 6.

Ranch Bean Pot

1½ pounds dried pinto beans, soaked overnight	680 g
5 slices bacon, cut into ½-inch (1.2 cm) pieces	
2 onions, chopped	
1 teaspoon garlic powder	5 ml
½ teaspoon cayenne pepper	2 ml
Flour tortillas	
Jalapenos	

- Drain beans from soaking water and place in sprayed slow cooker. Add bacon pieces, onion, garlic powder, cayenne pepper and 1 teaspoon (5 ml) salt.

- Cover and cook on LOW for 8 to 10 hours. Serve with flour tortillas and jalapenos on the side. Serves 4 to 6.

Good Luck Soup

Great to serve on New Year's Day.

1 (16 ounce) package dried black-eyed peas	455 g
2 (10 ounce) can bean and bacon soup	2 (280 g)
6 carrots, peeled, grated	
1 large onion, chopped	
1 (2 pound) beef or pork roast, cut in 2-inch cubes	910 g/5 cm
1 teaspoon minced garlic	5 ml

- Sort black-eyed peas to remove any stones; then rinse and drain. Place all ingredients plus 4 cups (1 L) water in sprayed slow cooker.

- Cover and cook on LOW for 9 to 10 hours. Before serving, stir in ½ teaspoon (2 ml) salt. Serves 6.

Tango Black Bean Soup

2 (14 ounce) cans chicken broth	2 (395 g)
3 (15 ounce) cans black beans, rinsed, drained	3 (425 g)
2 (10 ounce) cans diced tomatoes and green chilies	2 (280 g)
1 onion, chopped	
1 teaspoon ground cumin	5 ml
½ teaspoon dried thyme	2 ml
½ teaspoon dried oregano	2 ml
2 - 3 cups cooked, finely diced ham	280 - 420 g

- Combine chicken broth and black beans in sprayed slow cooker and turn cooker to HIGH. Cook just long enough for ingredients to get hot. Mash about half beans in cooker.

- Reduce heat to LOW and add tomatoes and green chilies, onion, cumin, thyme, oregano, ham, and ¾ cup (175 ml) water. Cover and cook for 5 to 6 hours. Serves 6 to 8.

Tasty Black Bean Soup

1 pound hot sausage	455 g
1 onion, chopped	
2 (14 ounce) cans chicken broth	2 (395 g)
2 (15 ounce) cans Mexican stewed tomatoes	2 (425 g)
1 green bell pepper, seeded, chopped	
2 (15 ounce) cans black beans, rinsed, drained	2 (425 g)

- Break up sausage and brown with onion in large skillet. Drain off fat and place in sprayed large slow cooker.

- Add chicken broth, stewed tomatoes, bell pepper, black beans and 1 cup (250 ml) water. Cover and cook on LOW for 3 to 5 hours. Serves 4 to 6.

Seasoned Black Bean Soup

2 (14 ounce) cans chicken broth	2 (395 g)
1 (10 ounce) package frozen chopped bell peppers and onions, thawed	280 g
2 (15 ounce) cans black beans, rinsed, drained	2 (425 g)
1 teaspoon minced garlic	
2 ribs celery, sliced	
1 carrot, shredded	
1 (10 ounce) can diced tomatoes and green chilies	280 g
½ pound Polish sausage, sliced	230 g
½ teaspoon dried thyme	2 ml

- Combine broth, bell peppers and onions, beans, garlic, celery, carrot, tomatoes and green chilies, sausage, and thyme in sprayed slow cooker. Cover and cook on LOW for 5 to 6 hours or on HIGH for 3 to 4 hours. Serves 6.

Overnight Black Bean Soup

1 pound dried black beans, soaked overnight	455 g
4 slices bacon, cut into 1-inch (2.5 cm) pieces	
1 (32 ounce) carton chicken broth	910 g
1 (14 ounce) can chicken broth	395 g
1 (10 ounce) can diced tomatoes and green chilies	280 g
1 tablespoon chili powder	15 ml
1 teaspoon minced garlic	5 ml
¼ - ½ teaspoon cayenne pepper	1 - 2 ml

- Drain beans, rinse and drain again. Place beans, bacon pieces, chicken broth, tomatoes and green chilies, chili powder, garlic and cayenne pepper in sprayed slow cooker.

- Cover and cook HIGH for 4 hours. Reduce heat to LOW and cook for additional 1 hour or until beans are tender. Serves 6.

TIP: If you want a creamy version, place half the soup in blender and pulse 1 or 2 times.

At-Home Black Bean Soup

3 (15 ounce) cans black beans, rinsed, drained, divided	3 (425 g)
2 (14 ounce) cans beef broth, divided	2 (395 g)
2 onions, chopped	
2 teaspoons minced garlic	10 ml
1½ teaspoons dried cumin	7 ml
2 teaspoons chili powder	10 ml
1 cup shredded sharp cheddar cheese	115 g

- Place 1 can of beans in food processor with ½ cup (125 ml) broth and process until smooth. Combine processed-broth mixture, remaining beans, remaining broth, onions, garlic, cumin, chili powder and ½ teaspoon (2 ml) salt in sprayed slow cooker. Cover and cook on LOW for 4 to 6 hours. Stir in cheese; cover and let stand for about 10 minutes or until cheese melts. Serves 4 to 6.

Black Bean-Corn Soup

1 onion, chopped	
2 teaspoons minced garlic	10 ml
1 (28 ounce) can diced tomatoes	795 g
2 (15 ounce) cans black beans, rinsed, drained	2 (425 g)
1 (16 ounce) package frozen corn, thawed	455 g
1 red bell pepper, seeded, chopped	
1 teaspoon dried cumin	5 ml
1 tablespoon chili powder	15 ml
1 (14 ounce) can beef broth	395 g

- Combine onion, garlic, tomatoes, beans, corn, bell pepper, cumin, chili powder, broth and ½ teaspoon (2 ml) salt in sprayed slow cooker. Cover and cook on LOW for 5 to 7 hours. Serves 6.

Ranchero Black Bean Soup

1 cup dried black beans, soaked overnight	260 g
3 (14 ounce) cans beef broth	3 (395 g)
1 bunch green onions with tops, chopped	
5 ribs celery, chopped	
2 teaspoons minced garlic	10 ml
1 (10 ounce) can diced tomatoes and green chilies	280 g
½ cup (1 stick) butter, melted	115 g
¼ teaspoon cayenne pepper	1 ml
½ cup instant rice	50 g
1 cup shredded Mexican 3-cheese blend	115 g

- Drain soaked beans and place in sprayed slow cooker. Add broth, onions, celery, garlic, tomatoes and green chilies, butter, cayenne pepper and 1 teaspoon (5 ml) salt. Cover and cook on LOW for 7 to 9 hours or until beans are tender.

- Stir in rice and ½ cup (125 ml) water (or more if needed); cover and cook for additional 20 to 30 minutes or until rice is tender. Sprinkle a little cheese over each serving. Serves 6.

Convenient Bean Soup

1 (20 ounce) package dried bean soup mix, rinsed	570 g
1 (32 ounce) carton chicken broth	910 g
1 (16 ounce) package frozen chopped bell peppers and onions, thawed	455 g
3 large ribs celery, sliced	
2 tablespoons tomato paste	35 g
1½ teaspoons seasoned salt	7 ml
1 (15 ounce) can diced tomatoes	425 g
½ teaspoon hot sauce	
Green onions, optional	

- Combine beans, broth, bell peppers and onions, celery, tomato paste, seasoned salt and 1 cup (250 ml) water in sprayed slow cooker.

- Cover and cook on LOW for 9 to 10 hours or until beans are tender. About half way through cooking time, stir and check if more water is needed.

- Stir in tomatoes and hot sauce; cover and cook for about 20 minutes or until piping hot. Serve in warmed soup bowls. Garnish with sliced green onions, if you like. Serves 10.

Minestrone

2 (15 ounce) cans Italian stewed tomatoes	2 (425 g)
2 (16 ounce) packages frozen vegetables and pasta seasoned sauce	2 (455 g)
3 (14 ounce) cans beef broth	3 (395 g)
2 ribs celery, chopped	
2 potatoes, peeled, cubed	
1 teaspoon Italian herb seasoning	5 ml
2 (15 ounce) cans kidney beans, drained, rinsed	2 (425 g)
2 teaspoons minced garlic	10 ml

- Combine tomatoes, vegetables, broth, celery, potatoes, seasoning, beans, garlic and 1 cup (250 ml) water in sprayed large slow cooker and mix well. Cover and cook on LOW for 4 to 6 hours. Serves 8 to 10.

Mexican-Style Minestrone Soup

1 (16 ounce) package frozen garlic-seasoned pasta and vegetables, thawed	455 g
1 (16 ounce) jar thick-and-chunky salsa	455 g
2 (15 ounce) cans pinto beans, rinsed, drained	2 (425 g)
1 teaspoon chili powder	5 ml
1 teaspoon ground cumin	5 ml
1 (14 ounce) can beef broth	395 g
1 (8 ounce) package shredded Mexican 4-cheese blend	230 g

- Combine pasta and vegetables, salsa, beans, chili powder, cumin, broth and 1 cup (250 ml) water in sprayed slow cooker. Cover and cook on LOW for 5 to 7 hours. Sprinkle each serving with cheese. Serves 6 to 8.

Italian Minestrone

1 (16 ounce) package frozen chopped bell peppers	
and onions, thawed	455 g
3 ribs celery, chopped	
2 teaspoons minced garlic	10 ml
¼ cup (½ stick) butter, melted	60 g
2 (15 ounce) cans diced tomatoes	2 (425 g)
1 teaspoon dried oregano	5 ml
1 teaspoon dried basil	5 ml
2 (14 ounce) can beef broth	2 (395 g)
2 (15 ounce) cans kidney beans, rinsed, drained	2 (395 g)
2 medium zucchini, sliced	
1 cup elbow macaroni	105 g

- Combine bell peppers and onions, celery, garlic, butter, tomatoes, oregano, basil, broth, beans and zucchini in sprayed slow cooker. Cover and cook on LOW for 5 to 7 hours.

- Cook macaroni according to package directions and drain. Stir in cooked macaroni. Serves 6 to 8.

Tomato-Ravioli Soup

2 (15 ounce) can stewed tomatoes	2 (425 g)
2 (14 ounce) cans chicken broth	2 (395 g)
¾ teaspoon Italian seasoning	4 ml
2 small zucchini, sliced	
1 onion, chopped	
1 (9 ounce) package refrigerated cheese ravioli	255 g

- Combine tomatoes, broth, Italian seasoning, zucchini, onion and ½ cup (125 ml) water in sprayed slow cooker. Cover and cook on LOW for 3 to 4 hours.

- Stir in ravioli, cover and cook for additional 1 hour. Serves 4 to 6.

Root vegetables such as carrots, potatoes or onions cook more slowly than meats, therefore many recipes call for first placing vegetables in the bottom of the slow cooker and then the meat. Frozen and more tender vegetables can be added the last 30 to 45 minutes to retain their color and texture.

Cheese-Filled Tortellini Soup

2 (15 ounce) cans Italian stewed tomatoes	2 (425 g)
2 (14 ounce) cans chicken broth	2 (395 g)
1 (16 ounce) package frozen chopped bell peppers	
and onions, thawed	455 g
2 ribs celery, sliced	
1 carrot, peeled, shredded	
½ teaspoon dried oregano	2 ml
½ teaspoon dried basil	2 ml
2 (9 ounce) packages refrigerated cheese tortellini	2 (255 g)

- Combine tomatoes, broth, bell peppers and onions, celery, carrot, oregano and basil in sprayed slow cooker. Cover and cook on LOW for 6 to 8 hours or on HIGH for 4 to 5 hours.

- During last hour of cooking, stir in tortellini and cook for additional 50 to 60 minutes or until tortellini are tender. Serves 8.

Creamy Tortellini-Alfredo Soup

2 (16 ounce) jars alfredo pasta sauce	2 (455 g)
2 (14 ounce) cans vegetable broth	2 (395 g)
1 (10 ounce) package frozen chopped bell peppers	
and onions, thawed	280 g
2 ribs celery, sliced	
1 (4 ounce) can sliced pimentos	115 g
1 (8 ounce) package dried cheese-filled tortellini	230 g

- Combine alfredo sauce, broth, bell peppers and onions, celery and pimentos in sprayed slow cooker. Cover and cook on LOW for 5 to 6 hours or on HIGH for 2 hours 30 minutes to 3 hours.

- (If cooking on LOW, increase heat to HIGH.) Stir in tortellini, cover and cook for additional 1 hour. Serves 4 to 6.

Warm Your Soul Soup

3 (14 ounce) cans chicken broth	3 (395 g)
1 (15 ounce) can Italian stewed tomatoes	425 g
1 (10 ounce) package frozen chopped bell peppers	
and onions, thawed	280 g
3 ribs celery, sliced	
¼ cup (1/2 stick) butter, melted	55 g
½ cup elbow macaroni	55 g

- Place broth, tomatoes, bell peppers and onions, celery and butter in sprayed slow cooker.

- Cover and cook on LOW for 3 to 5 hours. Stir in macaroni, cover and cook for additional 1 hour. Serves 4.

Pasta-Veggie Soup

2 yellow squash, peeled, chopped	
2 zucchini, sliced	
1 (10 ounce) package frozen whole kernel corn, thawed	280 g
1 red bell pepper, chopped	
1 (15 ounce) can stewed tomatoes	425 g
1 teaspoon Italian seasoning	5 ml
2 teaspoons dried oregano	10 ml
2 (14 ounce) cans beef broth	2 (395 g)
¾ cup small shell pasta	80 g
Shredded mozzarella cheese	

- Combine squash, zucchini, corn, bell pepper, tomatoes, Italian seasoning, oregano, broth and 2 cups (500 ml) water in sprayed slow cooker. Cover and cook on LOW for 6 to 7 hours.

- Add pasta shells and cook for additional 30 to 45 minutes or until pasta is tender. Garnish sprinkle a little cheese on each serving. Serves 4 to 5.

Funny Corkscrews in My Soup

1 (32 ounce) carton chicken broth	910 g
2 (12 ounce) cans tomato juice	2 (375 ml)
2 carrots, peeled, sliced	
3 ribs celery, chopped	
1 onion, chopped	
1 (15 ounce) can stewed tomatoes	425 g
1 teaspoon dried basil	
1 (10 ounce) package frozen green peas, thawed	280 g
1 (8 ounce) package whole wheat rotini (corkscrew) pasta	230 g

- Combine broth, tomato juice, carrots, celery, onion, tomatoes, basil and a little salt and pepper in sprayed slow cooker. Cover and cook on LOW for 8 to 9 hours.

- Increase heat to HIGH and stir in peas and pasta. Cover and cook for additional 15 to 20 minutes or until pasta is tender. Serves 8 to 10.

Souper Fettuccini

1 (32 ounce) carton chicken broth	910 g
2 (15 ounce) cans Italian-stewed tomatoes	2 (425 g)
1 onion, chopped	
2 ribs celery, sliced	
1 (8 ounce) box fettuccini	230 g

- Combine broth, tomatoes, onion and celery in sprayed slow cooker. Cover and cook on LOW for 4 to 6 hours.

- Cook fettuccini according to package directions, drain and add to cooker. Cover and cook for additional 20 minutes for flavors to blend. Serves 4 to 6.

Pizza Soup

3 (10 ounce) cans tomato bisque soup	3 (280 g)
1 (10 ounce) can French onion soup	280 g
2 teaspoons Italian seasoning	10 ml
¾ cup tiny pasta shells	80 g
1½ cups shredded mozzarella cheese	170 g

- Combine soups, Italian seasoning and 1½ soup cans water in sprayed slow cooker. Cover and cook on HIGH for 1 hour or until mixture is hot.

- Add pasta shells, cover and cook for 1 hour 30 minutes to 2 hours or until pasta is cooked. Stir several times to keep pasta from sticking to bottom of slow cooker. Turn heat off, add mozzarella cheese and stir until cheese melts. Serves 6 to 8.

TIP: For a special way to serve this soup, sprinkle some french-fried onions on each serving.

Cream of Peanut Soup

½ cup (1 stick) butter, melted	115 g
1 onion, finely chopped	
1 red bell pepper, seeded, chopped	
3 ribs celery, thinly sliced	
2 (14 ounce) cans chicken broth	2 (395 g)
1½ cups peanut butter	435 g
1 (1 pint) carton half-and-half cream	500 ml

- Combine butter, onion, bell pepper, celery, broth and peanut butter in sprayed slow cooker. Cover and cook on LOW for 3 to 5 hours.

- Stir in half-and-half cream, cover and cook for additional 30 minutes or until mixture is thoroughly hot. Serves 4 to 6.

One-Pot Meal

1½ pounds lean ground beef	680 g
1 teaspoon seasoned salt	5 ml
1 (32 ounce) carton beef broth	910 g
2 (15 ounce) cans stewed tomatoes	2 (425 g)
1 (15 ounce) can pinto beans, rinsed, drained	425 g
2 ribs celery, sliced	
1 (8 ounce) can sliced carrots	230 g
1 cup macaroni, cooked, drained	190 g
1 cup shredded cheddar cheese	115 g

- Crumble beef into sprayed slow cooker and add seasoned salt, broth, tomatoes, beans, celery and carrots. Cover and cook on LOW for 6 to 8 hours. Increase heat to HIGH, add cooked macaroni and cook for additional 15 minutes. Sprinkle a heaping tablespoon (15 ml) cheese over each individual serving. Serves 6.

Serious Hamburger Soup

2 pounds lean ground beef	910 g
2 (15 ounce) cans Mexican-style stewed tomatoes	2 (425 g)
1 (16 ounce) package frozen stew vegetables	455 g
1 (32 ounce) carton beef broth	910 g
⅓ cup barley	70 g
1 teaspoon dried thyme	5 ml
1 tablespoon Worcestershire sauce	15 ml
Cornbread or muffins	

- Brown ground beef in non-stick skillet and stir often. Place beef, tomatoes, vegetables, broth, barley, thyme and Worcestershire in sprayed slow cooker.

- Cover and cook on HIGH for 3 to 4 hours. This soup is great served with cornbread muffins. Serves 6 to 8.

Saucy Cabbage Soup

1 pound lean ground beef	455 g
1 small head cabbage, chopped	
2 (15 ounce) cans jalapeno pinto beans with liquid	2 (425 g)
1 (15 ounce) can tomato sauce	425 g
1 (15 ounce) can Mexican stewed tomatoes	425 g
1 (14 ounce) can beef broth	395 g
2 teaspoons ground cumin	10 ml

- Brown ground beef in skillet, drain and place in sprayed slow cooker.

- Add cabbage, beans, tomato sauce, tomatoes, broth, cumin and 1 cup (250 ml) water and mix well. Cover and cook on LOW for 5 to 6 hours or until cabbage is tender. Serves 4 to 6.

Comfort Cabbage Soup

1 pound lean ground beef	455 g
1 (16 ounce) package frozen chopped bell peppers and onions, thawed	455 g
5 cups chopped (bite-size) cabbage	350 g
2 (15 ounce) cans pinto beans, drained	2 (425 g)
1 (15 ounce) can kidney beans, rinsed, drained	425 g
1 (8 ounce) can tomato sauce	230 g
2 (14 ounce) cans beef broth	2 (395 g)
1 (16 ounce) jar hot salsa	455 g

- Cook beef and bell peppers and onions in skillet over medium heat for about 10 minutes, stirring well to crumble beef. Transfer to sprayed slow cooker.

- Stir in cabbage, beans, tomato sauce, broth, salsa and a little salt. Cover and cook on LOW for 6 to 8 hours or on HIGH for 3 to 4 hours. Serves 6 to 8.

Easy-Fix Taco Soup

1 pound lean ground beef	455 g
1 onion, chopped	
2 (15 ounce) can chili beans with liquid	2 (425 g)
1 (11 ounce) can Mexicorn®	310 g
2 tablespoons tomato paste	35 g
2 (15 ounce) cans Mexican-style stewed tomatoes	2 (425 g)
1 (1 ounce) packet taco seasoning mix	30 g
1 (8 ounce) package Mexican 3-cheese blend	230 g

- Book ground beef in non-stick skillet for 5 to 10 minutes, stirring often. Drain and spoon into sprayed slow cooker.

- Stir in onion, beans, corn, tomato paste, stewed tomatoes and taco seasoning mix. Cover and cook on LOW for 8 hours. Sprinkle each serving with cheese. Serves 6 to 8.

Taco Soup

1½ pounds lean ground beef	680 g
1 (1 ounce) packet taco seasoning	30 g
2 (15 ounce) cans Mexican stewed tomatoes	2 (425 g)
2 (15 ounce) cans chili beans with liquid	2 (425g)
1 (15 ounce) can whole kernel corn, drained	425 g
Crushed tortilla chips	
Shredded cheddar cheese	

- Brown ground beef in skillet until it is no longer pink. Place in sprayed slow cooker. Add taco seasoning, tomatoes, chili beans, corn and 1 cup (250 ml) water and mix well. Cover and cook on LOW for 4 hours or on HIGH for 1 to 2 hours.

- Serve over crushed tortilla chips and sprinkle some shredded cheddar cheese over top of each serving. Serves 6 to 8.

Amigos Taco Soup Olé

2 pounds lean ground beef	910 g
2 (15 ounce) cans ranch-style beans with liquid	2 (425 g)
1 (15 ounce) can whole kernel corn, drained	425 g
2 (15 ounce) cans stewed tomatoes	2 (425 g)
1 (10 ounce) can tomatoes and green chilies	280 g
1 (.04 ounce) packet ranch dressing mix	10 g
1 (1 ounce) packet taco seasoning	30 g
Shredded cheddar cheese	

- Brown ground beef in large skillet, drain and transfer to sprayed slow cooker. Add remaining ingredients and stir well. Cover and cook on LOW for 8 to 10 hours. When serving, sprinkle cheese over each serving. Serve 6 to 8.

Beef and Black Bean Soup

1 pound lean ground beef	455 g
2 onions, chopped	
2 cups sliced celery	480 ml
2 (14 ounce) cans beef broth	2 (395 g)
1 (15 ounce) can Mexican stewed tomatoes	425 g
2 (15 ounce) cans black beans, rinsed, drained	2 (425 g)

- Brown beef in skillet until no longer pink. Place in sprayed slow cooker.

- Add onions, celery, broth, tomatoes, black beans, ¾ cup (175 ml) water plus a little salt and pepper. Cover and cook on LOW for 6 to 7 hours or on HIGH for 3 hours to 3 hours 30 minutes. Serves 6 to 8.

TIP: If you like a zestier soup, add 1 teaspoon (5 ml) chili powder.

Beef and Noodle Soup

1½ pounds lean ground beef	680 g
1 onion, chopped	
2 (15 ounce) cans mixed vegetables, drained	2 (425 g)
2 (15 ounce) cans Italian stewed tomatoes	2 (425 g)
2 (14 ounce) cans beef broth	2 (395 g)
1 teaspoon dried oregano	5 ml
1 cup medium egg noodles	75 g

- Brown and cook ground beef in skillet until no longer pink and transfer to sprayed slow cooker.

- Add onion, mixed vegetables, stewed tomatoes, beef broth and oregano. Cover and cook on LOW for 4 to 5 hours.

- Cook noodles according to package direction. Add noodles to slow cooker and cook for additional 30 minutes. Serves 4 to 6.

Beef and Barley Soup

1 pound lean ground beef	455 g
3 (14 ounce) cans beef broth	3 (395 g)
¾ cup quick-cooking barley	150 g
3 cups sliced carrots	365 g
2 cups sliced celery	200 g
2 teaspoons beef seasoning	10 ml

- Brown ground beef in skillet, drain and transfer to sprayed slow cooker.

- Add beef broth, barley, carrots, celery and beef seasoning. Cover and cook on LOW for 7 to 8 hours. Serves 4.

Tasty Cabbage and Beef Soup

1 pound lean ground beef	455 g
1 (16 ounce) package coleslaw mix	455 g
1 (15 ounce) can cut green beans	425 g
1 (15 ounce) can whole kernel corn	425 g
2 (15 ounce) cans Italian stewed tomatoes	2 (425 g)
2 (14 ounce) cans beef broth	2 (395 g)
Cornbread	

- Brown ground beef in skillet, drain and place in sprayed, large slow cooker.

- Add slaw mix, green beans, corn, tomatoes and beef broth and add a little salt and pepper. Cover and cook on LOW for 7 to 9 hours. Serve with cornbread. Serves 6 to 8.

Enchilada Soup

1 pound lean ground beef, browned, drained	455 g
1 (15 ounce) can Mexican stewed tomatoes	425 g
1 (15 ounce) can pinto beans with liquid	425 g
1 (15 ounce) can whole kernel corn with liquid	425 g
1 onion, chopped	
2 (10 ounce) cans enchilada sauce	2 (280 g)
1 (8 ounce) package shredded 4-cheese blend	230 g
Tortilla chips, optional	

- Combine beef, tomatoes, beans, corn, onion, enchilada sauce and 1 cup (250 ml) water in sprayed slow cooker and mix well. Cover and cook on LOW for 6 to 8 hours or on HIGH for 3 to 4 hours.

- Stir in shredded cheese until it melts. If desired, top each serving with a few crushed tortilla chips. Serves 6 to 8.

Hamburger Soup

2 pounds lean ground beef	910 g
2 (15 ounce) cans chili without beans	2 (425 g)
1 (16 ounce) package frozen mixed vegetables, thawed	455 g
3 (14 ounce) cans beef broth	3 (395 g)
2 (15 ounce) cans stewed tomatoes	2 (425 g)
1 teaspoon seasoned salt	5 ml

- Brown ground beef in skillet until no longer pink. Place in sprayed slow cooker.

- Add chili, vegetables, broth, tomatoes, 1 cup (250 ml) water and seasoned salt and stir well. Cover and cook on LOW for 6 to 7 hours. Serves 6 to 8.

Fresh Beefy Vegetable Soup

1 pound lean ground beef	455 g
1 onion, chopped	
1 (15 ounce) can Italian stewed tomatoes	425 g
1 (8 ounce) can whole kernel corn	230 g
1 large potato, peeled, cubed	
3 ribs celery, sliced	
1 carrot, peeled, sliced	
1 (8 ounce) can green peas or lima beans	230 g
1 teaspoon dried Italian seasoning	5 ml
¼ teaspoon hot sauce	1 ml
3 (14 ounce) cans beef broth	3 (395 g)
2 tablespoons cornstarch	15 g

- Brown ground beef in skillet, drain and combine with onion, tomatoes, corn, potato, celery, carrot, green peas (or lima beans) Italian seasoning, hot sauce and beef broth in sprayed slow cooker. Cover and cook on LOW for 6 to 8 hours.

- Mix cornstarch with 2 tablespoons (30 ml) water in bowl until smooth. Stir into soup, cover and cook for about 15 minutes or until soup thickens. Serves 6 to 8.

Down-Home Beefy Soup

1½ pounds lean ground beef	680 g
1 (16 ounce) package frozen chopped bell peppers	
and onions, thawed	455 g
2 ribs celery, sliced	
2 teaspoons minced garlic	10 ml
2 (15 ounce) cans Italian stewed tomatoes	2 (425 g)
3 teaspoons Italian seasoning	15 ml
1½ cups macaroni	160 g
Shredded cheddar cheese	

- Brown ground beef in skillet, drain and combine with bell peppers and onions, celery, garlic, tomatoes and Italian seasoning in sprayed slow cooker. Cover and cook on LOW for 6 to 8 hours.

- Cook macaroni according to package directions. Add macaroni to slow cooker. Cover and cook for additional 15 minutes. Top each serving with cheese. Serves 6 to 8.

Add ingredients in the order given. There is a method to the madness.

Cantina Taco Soup

1½ pounds lean ground beef	680 g
1 (14 ounce) can beef broth	395 g
1 (1 ounce) packet taco seasoning	30 g
2 (15 ounce) cans Mexican stewed tomatoes	2 (425 g)
1 (15 ounce) can whole kernel corn	425 g
1 - 2 cups crushed tortilla chips	55 - 110 g
1 (8 ounce) package shredded cheddar cheese	230 g

- Brown ground beef in skillet, drain and combine with broth, taco seasoning, tomatoes and corn in sprayed slow cooker. Cover and cook on LOW for 6 to 8 hours.

- Place some crushed tortilla chips in individual soup bowl, add soup and top each serving with shredded cheese. Serves 6.

Italian Vegetable Soup

1 pound lean ground beef	455 g
2 teaspoons minced garlic	10 ml
1 green bell pepper, seeded, chopped	
3 (14 ounce) cans beef broth	3 (395 g)
1 (15 ounce) can stewed tomatoes	425 g
2 (15 ounce) can cannellini beans, rinsed, drained	2 (425 g)
1 teaspoon Italian seasoning	5 ml
2 medium zucchini, sliced	
1 (10 ounce) package frozen chopped spinach, thawed	280 g

- Brown ground beef in skillet, drain and combine with garlic, bell pepper, broth, tomatoes, beans and Italian seasoning in sprayed slow cooker. Cover and cook on LOW for 5 to 7 hours.

- Stir in zucchini and chopped spinach and cook for additional 1 hour. Serves 6 to 8.

Mother's Beef-Veggie Soup

1 pound lean ground beef	455 g
1 (1 ounce) packet onion soup mix	30 g
3 (14 ounce) cans beef broth	3 (395 g)
2 (15 ounce) cans stewed tomatoes	2 (425 g)
2 (15 ounce) cans mixed vegetables with liquid	2 (425 g)
1 cup shell macaroni	105 g

- Combine crumbled beef, onion soup mix, broth, tomatoes and mixed vegetables in sprayed slow cooker. Cover and cook on LOW for 6 to 8 hours.

- Stir in macaroni, cover and cook for additional 1 hour. Serves 6 to 8.

My Hamburger Soup

1½ pounds lean ground beef	680 g
1 (15 ounce) can stewed tomatoes	425 g
3 (14 ounce) cans beef broth	3 (395 g)
1 (1 ounce) packet golden onion soup mix	30 g
2 tablespoons tomato paste	35 g
1 (15 ounce) cans mixed vegetables	425 g
½ cup elbow macaroni	55 g

- Brown ground beef in skillet, drain and combine with tomatoes, broth, onion soup mix, tomato paste and 1 cup (250 ml) water in sprayed slow cooker. Cover and cook on LOW for 5 to 6 hours.

- Stir in mixed vegetables and macaroni, cover and cook for additional 1 to 2 hours or until macaroni is tender. Serves 4 to 6.

Across-the-Border Tamale Soup

1 pound lean ground beef	455 g
1 (16 ounce) package frozen chopped bell peppers and onions, thawed	455 g
1 (10 ounce) package frozen corn, thawed	280 g
2 (14 ounce) cans beef broth	2 (395 g)
1 (15 ounce) can pinto beans with jalapenos, drained	425 g
2 tablespoons chili powder	30 ml
1 teaspoon ground cumin	5 ml
1 (28 ounce) can tamales with liquid, unwrapped, quartered	795 g

- Brown ground beef in skillet, drain and combine with bell peppers and onions, corn, broth, beans, chili powder and cumin in sprayed slow cooker. Cover and cook on LOW for 5 to 7 hours.

- Add tamale chunks; cover and cook for additional 30 minutes. Stir gently so tamales will not break up. Serves 6 to 8.

Kitchen-Sink Taco Soup

1½ pounds lean ground beef	680 g
1 onion, chopped	
1 (1 ounce) packet ranch dressing mix	30 g
2 (15 ounce) cans pinto beans with jalapenos, drained	2 (425 g)
1 (15 ounce) can whole kernel corn	425 g
1 (15 ounce) can cream-style corn	425 g
2 (15 ounce) cans stewed tomatoes	(425 g)
1 - 2 cups coarsely crushed tortilla chips	55 - 110 g
1 (8 ounce) package shredded Monterey Jack cheese	230 g

- Brown ground beef in skillet, drain and combine with onion, dressing mix, pinto beans, corn, cream-style corm and tomatoes in sprayed slow cooker. Cover and cook on LOW for 6 to 8 hours.

- Sprinkle crushed chips in individual soup bowls, spoon soup over chips and sprinkle with cheese. Serves 6 to 8.

Beefy Veggie Soup

1 pound lean ground beef	455 g
1 (46 ounce) can cocktail vegetable juice	1.3 kg
1 (1 ounce) packet onion soup mix	30 g
1 (16 ounce) package frozen mixed vegetables, thawed	455 g
1 (3 ounce) package beef-flavored ramen noodles, broken up	85 g

- Brown ground beef in skillet, drain and combine with vegetable juice, onion soup mix and vegetables in sprayed slow cooker. Cover and cook on LOW for 5 to 7 hours.

- Stir in ramen noodles, cover and cook for additional 20 minutes. Serves 6.

Speedy-Fix Vegetable Soup

1 pound lean ground beef	455 g
2 (15 ounce) cans stewed tomatoes	2 (425 g)
3 (14 ounce) cans beef broth	3 (395 g)
1 (16 ounce) package frozen mixed vegetables, thawed	455 g
1 teaspoon seasoned salt	5 ml
½ cup instant brown rice	95 g

- Brown ground beef in skillet, drain and combine with tomatoes, broth, mixed vegetables and seasoned salt in sprayed slow cooker. Cover and cook on LOW for 6 to 8 hours.

- Stir in brown rice, cover and cook for additional 20 minutes. Serves 6.

Vegetable-Beef Soup

1½ pounds lean ground beef	680 g
3 (15 ounce) cans mixed vegetables with liquid	3 (425 g)
1 (1 ounce) packet onion soup mix	30 g
1 (48 ounce) can cocktail vegetable juice	1.3 kg
1 (14 ounce) can beef broth	395 g
½ cup barley	100 g

- Brown ground beef in skillet, drain and combine with vegetables, soup mix, vegetable juice, broth and 1 cup (250 ml) water in sprayed slow cooker. Cover and cook on LOW for 6 to 8 hours.

- Stir in barley; cover and cook for additional 20 minutes. Serves 6 to 8.

Quick-Fix Enchilada Soup

1 pound lean ground beef	455 g
1 (14 ounce) can beef broth	395 g
1 (15 ounce) can stewed tomatoes	425 g
2 (15 ounce) cans pinto beans, rinsed, drained	2 (425 g)
1 (15 ounce) can whole kernel corn	425 g
1 onion, chopped	
2 (10 ounce) can enchilada sauce	2 (280 g)
1 (8 ounce) package shredded 4-cheese blend	230 g

- Brown ground beef in skillet, drain and combine with broth, tomatoes, beans, corn, onion, enchilada sauce in sprayed slow cooker. Cover and cook on LOW for 5 to 7 hours. Sprinkle each serving with cheese. Serves 6.

Southwestern Soup

1½ pounds lean ground beef	680 g
1 large onion, chopped	
2 (15 ounce) cans pinto beans, rinsed, drained	2 (425 g)
1 (15 ounce) can ranch-style beans, drained	425 g
2 (15 ounce) cans whole kernel corn	2 (425 g)
2 (15 ounce) cans Mexican-style stewed tomatoes	2 (425 g)
2 (14 ounce) cans beef broth	2 (395 g)
2 (1 ounce) packets taco seasoning	2 (30 g)

- Brown ground beef in skillet, drain and combine with onion, beans, corn, tomatoes, broth, 1½ cups (375 ml) water and taco seasoning in sprayed slow cooker. Cover and cook on LOW for 6 to 8 hours. Serves 8.

Select Beef-Potato Soup

1 pound boneless beef chuck, cut into 1-inch pieces	455 g/2.5 cm
1 (15 ounce) can green peas, drained	425 g
1 (5 ounce) box au gratin potato mix	145 g
½ teaspoon dried thyme	2 ml
1 (10 ounce) can cream of celery soup	280 g
1 cup half-and-half cream	250 ml
Grated parmesan cheese	

- Place beef pieces, peas, potato mix, thyme, celery soup and 3 cups (750 ml) water in sprayed slow cooker. Pour 3 (750 ml) cups water over beef-potato mixture. Cover and cook on LOW for 7 to 8 hours or on HIGH for 3 hours 30 minutes to 4 hours.

- (If cooking on HIGH, reduce heat to LOW.) Stir in half-and-half cream; cover and cook for additional 15 to 20 minutes. Sprinkle parmesan cheese over each serving. Serves 4 to 5.

Beef Noodle Soup

1 pound lean ground beef	455 g
1 (46 ounce) can tomato juice	1.4 L
1 (1 ounce) packet onion soup mix	30 g
1 (15 ounce) package frozen mixed vegetables, thawed	425 g
1 (3 ounce) package beef ramen noodles	85 g

- Brown ground beef in skillet, drain and combine with tomato juice, onion soup mix and mixed vegetables. Cover and cook on LOW for 5 to 7 hours.

- Stir in ramen noodles, cover and cook for additional 10 minutes. Serves 6.

Knockout Minestrone

1 (15 ounce) can cannellini beans, rinsed, drained	425 g
1 (15 ounce) can pinto beans, drained	425 g
1 (15 ounce) can kidney beans, rinsed, drained	425 g
2 (15 ounce) cans Italian stewed tomatoes with liquid	2 (425 g)
1 pound boneless beef chuck, cut in ½-inch pieces	455 g/1.2 cm
1 cup peeled, shredded carrots	110 g
1 cup dried favorite pasta	75 g
1 medium zucchini, sliced	
Parmesan cheese	

- Combine beans, stewed tomatoes, beef, carrots and a little salt and pepper in sprayed slow cooker. Cover and cook on LOW for 8 to 9 hours or on HIGH for 4 hours to 4 hours 30 minutes.

- Add pasta and zucchini and cook on HIGH heat for 30 to 45 minutes. Sprinkle each serving with a little parmesan cheese. Serves 8.

Chunky Beefy Noodle Soup

1 pound round steak, cut into 1-inch pieces	455 g (2.5 cm)
1 (10 ounce) package frozen chopped bell peppers and onions, thawed	280 g
2 ribs celery, chopped	
1 tablespoon chili powder	15 ml
½ teaspoon dried oregano	2 ml
1 (15 ounce) can stewed tomatoes	425 g
2 (14 ounce) cans beef broth	3 (395 g)
1 (3 ounce) package beef-flavored ramen noodles, broken up	85 g

- Combine steak pieces, bell peppers and onions, celery, chili powder, oregano, tomatoes, 2 cups (500 ml) water and broth in sprayed slow cooker. Cover and cook on LOW for 6 to 8 hours.

- Stir in noodles and seasoning packet; cover and cook for additional 15 minutes. Serves 6.

Quick-Fix Beefy Veggie Soup

1 pound round steak, cut into 1-inch pieces	455 g (2.5 cm)
2 (14 ounce) cans beef broth	2 (395 g)
1 (6 ounce) can tomato sauce	170 g
1 (15 ounce) can Mexican stewed tomatoes	425 g
2 (15 ounce) cans mixed vegetables with liquid	2 (425 g)
1 (8 ounce) can whole kernel corn	230 g

- Combine steak pieces, broth, tomato sauce, ½ cup (125 ml) water, tomatoes, mixed vegetables and corn in sprayed slow cooker. Cover and cook on LOW for 6 to 8 hours. Serves 6.

Almost Taco Soup

2 pounds very lean stew meat	910 g
2 (15 ounce) cans Mexican stewed tomatoes	2 (425 g)
1 (1 ounce) package taco seasoning mix	30 g
2 (15 ounce) cans pinto beans, drained	2 (425 g)
1 (8 ounce) can whole kernel corn, drained	230 g
2 (14 ounce) cans beef broth	2 (395 g)

- Combine stew meat, tomatoes, taco seasoning, beans, corn, broth and 1 cup (250 ml) water in sprayed slow cooker. Cover and cook on LOW for 8 to 10 hours. Serves 8.

Taco-Chili Soup

2 pounds very lean stew meat	910 g
2 (15 ounce) cans Mexican stewed tomatoes	2 (425 g)
1 (1 ounce) packet taco seasoning	30 g
2 (15 ounce) cans pinto beans with liquid	2 (425 g)
1 (15 ounce) can whole kernel corn with liquid	425 g
Green onions, chopped	

- Cut large pieces of stew meat in half and brown in large skillet.

- Combine stew meat, tomatoes, taco seasoning, beans, corn and ¾ cup (175 ml) water in sprayed slow cooker. (If you are not into "spicy", use original recipe stewed tomatoes instead of Mexican.)

- Cover and cook on LOW for 5 to 7 hours. Garnish each serving with chopped green onions. Serves 6 to 8.

Beefy Rice Soup

1 pound lean beef stew meat	455 g
1 (14 ounce) can beef broth	395 g
1 (7 ounce) box beef-flavored rice and vermicelli mix	200 g
1 (10 ounce) package frozen peas and carrots	280 g
2½ cups vegetable juice	625 ml

- Sprinkle stew meat with seasoned pepper, brown in non-stick skillet, drain and place in sprayed, large slow cooker.

- Add broth, rice and vermicelli mix, peas and carrots, vegetable juice and 2 cups (500 ml) water. Cover and cook on LOW for 6 to 7 hours. Serves 4 to 6.

Meatball and Macaroni Soup

1 (18 ounce) package frozen meatballs, thawed	510 g
1 (15 ounce) can Mexican-style stewed tomatoes	425 g
1 (6 ounce) can tomato sauce	170 g
1 (32 ounce) carton beef broth	910 g
⅔ cup elbow macaroni	70 g
1 (15 ounce) can black-eyed peas, rinsed, drained	425 g
1 (16 ounce) package frozen mixed vegetables	455 g

- Combine meatballs, tomatoes, tomato sauce, broth, macaroni, peas, mixed vegetables and 1 teaspoon (5 ml) each of salt and pepper in sprayed slow cooker; stir to mix well. Cover and cook on LOW for 4 to 5 hours. Serves 6.

Vegetable-Meatball Soup

1 (32 ounce) package frozen meatballs	910 g
2 (15 ounce) cans stewed tomatoes	2 (425 g)
3 large potatoes, peeled, diced	
4 carrots, peeled, sliced	
2 medium onions, chopped	
2 (14 ounce) cans beef broth	2 (395 g)
2 tablespoons cornstarch	15 g

- Combine meatballs, tomatoes, potatoes, carrots, onions, beef broth, a little salt and pepper and 1 cup (250 ml) water in sprayed slow cooker. Cover and cook on LOW for 5 to 6 hours.

- Turn heat to HIGH and combine cornstarch with ¼ cup (60 ml) water in bowl. Stir into cooker and cook for additional 10 or 15 minutes or until slightly thick. Serves 4 to 6.

Mexican Meatball Soup

3 (14 ounce) cans beef broth	3 (395 g)
1 (16 ounce) jar hot salsa	455 g
1 (16 ounce) package frozen whole kernel corn, thawed	455 g
1 (16 ounce) package frozen meatballs, thawed	455 g
1 teaspoon minced garlic	5 ml

- Combine all ingredients in sprayed, slow cooker and stir well. Cover and cook on LOW for 5 to 7 hours. Serves 6 to 8.

Italian Meatball Soup

1 (18 ounce) package frozen Italian meatballs, thawed	510 g
2 (15 ounce) can Italian stewed tomatoes	2 (425 g)
3 (14 ounce) cans beef broth	3 (395 g)
2 ribs celery, sliced	
1 cup baby carrots, halved lengthwise	135 g
2 zucchini, sliced	
1 teaspoon dried basil	5 ml
½ cup pasta	40 g
1 cup shredded mozzarella cheese	115 g

- Combine meatballs, tomatoes, broth, celery, carrots, zucchini and basil in sprayed slow cooker. Cover and cook on LOW for 5 to 6 hours.

- Cook pasta according to package directions, drain and stir into slow cooker.

- Spoon soup into individual bowls and top each with 2 heaping tablespoons (15 g) cheese. Serves 4 to 6.

Easy Meaty Minestrone

2 (26 ounce) cans minestrone soup	2 (740 g)
1 (14 ounce) can beef broth	395 g
1 (15 ounce) can pinto beans, rinsed, drained	425 g
1 (18 ounce) package frozen Italian meatballs, thawed	510 g
1 (5 ounce) package grated parmesan cheese	145 g

- Combine soup, broth, beans and meatballs in sprayed slow cooker. Cover and cook on LOW for 6 to 8 hours. Sprinkle each serving with a little parmesan cheese. Serves 6.

Meatball Soup

1 (32 ounce) package frozen Italian meatballs, thawed	910 g
2 (14 ounce) cans beef broth	2 (395 g)
1 (15 ounce) can Italian stewed tomatoes	425 g
2 (10 ounce) cans diced tomatoes and green chilies	(280 g)
2 (10 ounce) cans tomato soup	2 (280 g)
1 (16 ounce) package frozen stew vegetables, thawed	455 g

- Combine meatballs, broth, stewed tomatoes, tomatoes and green chilies, soup, and stew vegetables in sprayed slow cooker. Cover and cook on LOW for 6 to 8 hours. Serves 8.

Spaghetti Soup

1 (18 ounce) package frozen cooked meatballs, thawed	510 g
1 (14 ounce) can beef broth	395 g
1 (26 ounce) can spaghetti sauce	740 g
1 (15 ounce) can Mexican stewed tomatoes	425 g
1 (8 ounce) package thin spaghetti, broken up	230 g

- Combine meatballs, broth, spaghetti sauce and tomatoes in sprayed slow cooker. Cover and cook on LOW for 6 to 8 hours.

- Cook spaghetti according to package directions and drain. Stir into soup, cover and cook for additional 15 minutes. Serves 6 to 8.

The Mighty Meatball Soup

1 (18 ounce) package frozen cooked meatballs	510 g
1 (32 ounce) carton beef broth	910 g
2 (15 ounce) cans stewed tomatoes	2 (425 g)
1 (16 ounce) package frozen mixed vegetables	455 g
1 teaspoon Italian seasoning	5 ml

- Combine frozen meatballs (they might stick together if thawed), broth, ¾ cup (175 ml) water, and tomatoes in sprayed slow cooker. Cover and cook on LOW for 9 hours.

- Stir in frozen vegetables, Italian seasoning and ½ teaspoon (2 ml) pepper and mix well. Increase heat to HIGH, cover and cook for additional 1 hour. Serves 6.

Chili-Soup Warmer

2 (10 ounce) cans tomato bisque soup	2 (280 g)
1 (10 ounce) can french onion soup	280 g
2 (15 ounce) cans chili	2 (425 g)
1 (14 ounce) can beef broth	395 g
1 (15 ounce) cans kidney beans, rinsed, drained	425 g

- Combine soups, chili, broth, 1 cup (250 ml) water and beans in sprayed slow cooker. Cover and cook on LOW for 5 to 6 hours. Serves 6.

Chili Soup

3 (15 ounce) cans chili with beans	3 (425 g)
1 (15 ounce) can whole kernel corn	425 g
1 (14 ounce) can beef broth	395 g
2 (15 ounce) cans Mexican stewed tomatoes	2 (425 g)
2 teaspoons ground cumin	10 ml
2 teaspoons chili powder	10 ml
Flour tortillas	

• Combine chili, corn, broth, tomatoes, cumin, chili powder and 1 cup (250 ml) water in sprayed slow cooker. Cover and cook on LOW for 4 to 5 hours. Serve with warm, buttered flour tortillas. Serves 6 to 8.

Franks and Veggie Soup

2 onions, chopped	
1 red bell pepper, seeded, chopped	
2 teaspoons minced garlic	10 ml
1 (28 ounce) can baked beans with liquid	795 g
1 (16 ounce) package frozen mixed vegetables, thawed	455 g
2 (14 ounce) cans beef broth	2 (395 g)
6 beef frankfurters, cut into ½-inch (1.2 cm) pieces	
1 tablespoon Worcestershire sauce	15 ml
1 cup shredded colby cheese	115 g

• Combine onion, bell pepper, garlic, baked beans, vegetables, broth, frankfurters and Worcestershire sauce in sprayed slow cooker. Cover and cook on LOW for 5 to 7 hours.

• Ladle into individual soup bowls and sprinkle each serving with cheese. Serves 6.

No-Brainer Heidelberg Soup

2 (10 ounce) cans cream of potato soup	2 (280 g)
1 (10 ounce) can cream of celery soup	280 g
1 soup can milk	
1 (14 ounce) cans beef broth	395 g
6 - 10 slices salami, chopped	
1 bunch green onions, chopped	

• Combine soups, milk, broth and salami in sprayed slow cooker. Cover and cook on LOW for 5 to 7 hours.

• Stir in chopped green onions, cover and cook for additional 20 minutes. Serves 6.

Easy Tortilla Soup

3 boneless, skinless chicken breast halves, cooked, cubed	
1 (10 ounce) package frozen corn, thawed	280 g
1 onion, chopped	
3 (14 ounce) cans chicken broth	3 (395 g)
2 (10 ounce) cans diced tomatoes and green chilies	2 (280 g)
2 teaspoons ground cumin	10 ml
1 teaspoon chili powder	5 ml
6 corn tortillas	

- Combine chicken, corn, onion, broth, tomatoes and green chilies, cumin and chili powder in sprayed slow cooker. Cover and cook on LOW for 5 to 7 hours.

- While soup simmers, cut tortillas into 1-inch (2.5 cm) strips and place on baking sheet. Bake at 350° (175° C) for about 5 minutes or until tortillas are crisp. Serve tortilla strips with each serving. Serves 6.

Tempting Tortilla Soup

3 large boneless, skinless chicken breast halves, cubed	
1 (10 ounce) package frozen whole kernel corn, thawed	280 g
1 onion, chopped	
3 (14 ounce) cans chicken broth	3 (395 g)
1 (6 ounce) can tomato paste	170 g
2 (10 ounce) cans tomatoes and green chilies	2 (280 g)
2 teaspoons ground cumin	10 ml
1 teaspoon chili powder	5 ml
1 teaspoon minced garlic	5 ml
6 corn tortillas	

- Combine chicken cubes, corn, onion, broth, tomato paste, tomatoes and green chilies, cumin, chili powder, 1 teaspoon (5 ml) salt and garlic in sprayed large slow cooker. Cover and cook on LOW for 5 to 7 hours or on HIGH for 3 hours to 3 hours 30 minutes.

- Preheat oven to 375° (190° C).

- While soup is cooking, cut tortillas into ¼-inch (6 mm) strips and place on baking sheet. Bake for about 5 minutes or until crisp. Serve baked tortilla strips with soup. Serves 6 to 8.

Chicken-Broccoli-Rice Soup

1 (6 ounce) package chicken-wild rice mix	170 g
1 (10 ounce) package frozen chopped broccoli, thawed	280 g
2 (10 ounce cans cream of chicken soup	2 (280 g)
1 (12 ounce) can chicken breast chunks with liquid	340 g

- Combine rice mix, broccoli, soup, chicken and 5 cups (1.2 L) water in sprayed slow cooker. Cover and cook on LOW for 5 to 7 hours. Serves 6.

Tasty Chicken and Rice Soup

1 pound boneless, skinless chicken breasts	455 g
½ cup brown rice	95 g
1 (10 ounce) can cream of chicken soup	280 g
1 (10 ounce) can cream of celery soup	280 g
1 (14 ounce) can chicken broth with roasted garlic	395 g
1 (16 ounce) package frozen sliced carrots, thawed	455 g
1 cup half-and-half cream	250 ml

- Cut chicken into 1-inch pieces. Place pieces in sprayed slow cooker.

- Mix rice, soups, chicken broth and carrots in bowl and pour over chicken. Cover and cook on LOW 7 to 8 hours.

- Turn heat to HIGH, add half-and-half cream, cover and cook for additional 15 to 20 minutes. Serves 6 to 8.

A New Twist on Soup

3 (14 ounce) cans chicken broth	3 (395 g)
2 carrots, peeled, sliced	
1 onion, finely chopped	
2 large boneless, skinless chicken breast halves, cut into ½-inch (1.2 cm) pieces	
1 (10 ounce) can cream of celery soup	280 g
1¼ cups rice	120 g
Juice of 1 lime	
1 teaspoon dried thyme	5 ml

- Combine chicken broth, carrots, onion, chicken and celery soup in sprayed large slow cooker. Cover and cook on LOW for 4 to 5 hours.

- Stir in rice; cover and cook for additional 2 to 3 hours. Stir in lime juice and thyme. Keep heat on LOW for additional 5 minutes. Serves 4.

Cheddar Soup Plus

2 cups milk	500 ml
1 (7 ounce) package cheddar-broccoli soup starter	200 g
1 cup cooked, finely chopped chicken breasts	140 g
1 (10 ounce) frozen green peas, thawed	280 g
Shredded cheddar cheese	

- Place 5 cups (1.2 L) water and milk in sprayed slow cooker. Set heat on HIGH until water and milk come to a boil.

- Stir contents of soup starter into hot water and milk and stir well. Add chopped chicken, green peas and a little salt and pepper. Cover and cook on LOW for 2 to 3 hours. Sprinkle cheddar cheese over each serving. Serves 4.

Chicken, Carrots and Cheddar

2 large boneless, skinless chicken breast halves, cut into 1-inch (2.5 cm) pieces	
2 large potatoes, peeled, finely chopped	
3 (14 ounce) can chicken broth	3 (395 g)
1 (12 ounce) package baby carrots, cut in half	340 g
1 teaspoon minced garlic	5 ml
½ teaspoon dried marjoram leaves	2 ml
1 (8 ounce) package shredded cheddar cheese	230 g
Sour cream	

- Combine chicken, potatoes, broth, carrots, garlic, marjoram and a little pepper in sprayed slow cooker. Cover and cook on LOW for 6 hours to 6 hours 30 minutes or on HIGH for 3 to 4 hours.

- Stir in cheese and serve in individual soup bowls with a dollop of sour cream on each serving. Serves 4 to 5.

Tortellini Soup

1 (1 ounce) packet white sauce mix	30 g
3 boneless, skinless chicken breast halves	
1 (14 ounce) can chicken broth	395 g
1 teaspoon minced garlic	5 ml
½ teaspoon dried basil	2 ml
½ teaspoon oregano	2 ml
½ teaspoon cayenne pepper	2 ml
1 (8 ounce) package cheese tortellini	230 g
1½ cups half-and-half cream	375 ml
6 cups fresh baby spinach	180 g

- Place white sauce mix in sprayed slow cooker.   Stir in 4 cups (1 L) water and stir gradually until mixture is smooth.

- Cut chicken into 1-inch (2.5 cm) pieces. Add chicken, broth, garlic, basil, oregano, cayenne pepper and ½ teaspoon (2 ml) salt to cooker. Cover and cook on LOW for 6 to 7 hours or on HIGH for 3 hours.

- Stir in tortellini, cover and cook for additional 1 hour on HIGH. Stir in cream and fresh spinach and cook just enough for soup to get hot. Serves 4 to 6.

TIP: Sprinkle a little shredded parmesan cheese on top of each serving.

Quick-Fix Chicken-Noodle Soup

2 (14 ounce) cans chicken broth	2 (395 g)
2 boneless, skinless chicken breast halves, cubed	
1 (8 ounce) can sliced carrots, drained	230 g
2 ribs celery, sliced	
1 (3 ounce) package chicken-flavored ramen noodles	85 g

- Combine broth, chicken, carrots and celery in sprayed slow cooker. Cover and cook on LOW for 5 to 7 hours.

- Stir in noodles and seasoning packet; cover and cook for additional 15 minutes. Serves 4 to 6.

All-American Soup

3 boneless, skinless chicken breast halves, cut into strips	
1 onion, chopped	
1 (10 ounce) can diced tomatoes and green chilies	280 g
2 (14 ounce) cans chicken broth	2 (395 g)
2 large baking potatoes, peeled, cubed	
1 (10 ounce) can cream of celery soup	280 g
1 cup milk	250 ml
1 teaspoon dried basil	5 ml
1 (8 ounce) package shredded Velveeta® cheese	230 g
½ cup sour cream	120 g

- Place chicken strips, onion, tomatoes and green chilies, broth, potatoes, soup, milk, and basil in sprayed slow cooker. Cover and cook on LOW for 6 to 8 hours.

- Stir in cheese and sour cream. Cover and cook for additional 10 to 15 minutes or just until cheese melts. Serves 6 to 8.

TIP: You can leave the 2 cans of broth out and serve this chicken dish over hot cooked rice topped with about 1 cup (55 g) of lightly crushed potato chips.

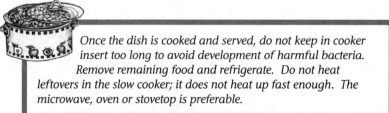

Once the dish is cooked and served, do not keep in cooker insert too long to avoid development of harmful bacteria. Remove remaining food and refrigerate. Do not heat leftovers in the slow cooker; it does not heat up fast enough. The microwave, oven or stovetop is preferable.

County's Best Chicken Soup

4 - 6 boneless, skinless chicken thighs	
3 (14 ounce) cans chicken broth	3 (395 g)
2 tablespoons butter, melted	30 g
3 medium new (red) potatoes, cut into wedges	
2 ribs celery, chopped	
1 carrot, peeled, grated	
1 (10 ounce) package frozen green peas, thawed	280 g
¼ teaspoon cayenne pepper	1 ml
¼ cup flour	30 g
1½ cups buttermilk*, divided	375 ml

- Cut chicken thighs in fourths and place in sprayed slow cooker. Add broth, butter, potatoes, celery, carrots and green peas. Cover and cook on LOW for 5 to 7 hours.

- Combine cayenne pepper, flour and about ½ cup (125 ml) buttermilk in bowl and mix until blended well; stir in remaining buttermilk. Cover and cook for additional 1 hour. Serves 6.

TIP: To make buttermilk, mix 1 cup (250 ml) milk with 1 tablespoon (15 ml) lemon juice or vinegar and let milk stand for about 10 minutes.

Seaside Soup Cancun

1 (32 ounce) carton chicken broth	910 g
1 bunch fresh cilantro, coarsely chopped	
6 boneless, skinless chicken thighs, cut in half	
1 ear fresh corn, cut into 6 rounds	
1 tablespoon ground cumin	15 ml
2 tablespoons butter, melted	30 g
2 onions, chopped	
1 red bell pepper, seeded, chopped	
2 tomatoes, chopped	
1 poblano chile, seeded, chopped	
½ teaspoon sugar	2 ml
4 corn tortillas	
Canola oil	
¼ cup lime juice	60 ml

- Combine broth, cilantro, chicken, corn, cumin, butter, onions, bell pepper, tomatoes, poblano chile and sugar in sprayed slow cooker. Cover and cook on LOW for 5 to 7 hours.

- While soup is cooking, cut tortillas into thin strips and fry in skillet with hot oil until crispy; drain.

- Stir lime juice into soup before serving. Garnish each serving with strips of fried tortillas. Serves 8.

TIP: Wear rubber gloves when handling hot peppers.

South-of-the-Border Soup

1½ pounds boneless chicken thighs, cut in ½-inch pieces	680 g/1.2 cm
2 (10 ounce) cans cream of chicken soup	2 (280 g)
1 (15 ounce) can pinto beans, drained	425 g
1 (15 ounce) can black beans, rinsed, drained	425 g
1 (15 ounce) can Mexican stewed tomatoes	425 g
1½ teaspoons ground cumin	7 ml
½ teaspoon chili powder	2 ml
Crushed tortilla chips	

- Cook chicken, half at a time in sprayed skillet until light brown. Transfer chicken to sprayed slow cooker.

- Combine soups, pinto beans, black beans, tomatoes, cumin, chili powder and 2 cups (500 ml) water and pour over chicken. Cover and cook on LOW for 4 to 6 hours or on HIGH for 2 to 3 hours. Sprinkle crushed chips over each serving. Serves 6.

La Placita Enchilada Soup

6 - 8 boneless, skinless chicken thighs, cut in half	
½ cup (1 stick) butter, melted	115 g
1 teaspoon minced garlic	5 ml
1 (14 ounce) can chicken broth	395 g
1 (10 ounce) can enchilada sauce	280 g
1 (15 ounce) can Mexican-style stewed tomatoes	425 g
1 (7 ounce) can chopped green chilies	200 g
⅓ cup flour	40 g
1 (8 ounce) carton sour cream	230 g
1 (8 ounce) package shredded cheddar cheese	230 g

- Combine chicken, butter, garlic, broth, enchilada sauce, tomatoes and green chilies in sprayed slow cooker. Cover and cook on LOW for 5 to 7 hours.

- Mix flour and sour cream in small bowl and stir into soup. Cover and cook for additional 15 minutes or until soup thickens. Sprinkle each serving with cheese. Serves 6.

Because slow cooker recipes rely on blended flavors, they are usually just as good or even better when reheated in oven or microwave or on top of the stove.

Chicken Minestrone

1 pound boneless, skinless chicken thighs, cubed	455 g
1 baking potato, peeled, diced	
1 (28 ounce) can stewed tomatoes	795 g
1 (32 ounce) carton chicken broth	910 g
½ cup chopped onion	80 g
½ cup chopped carrots	65 g
½ cup chopped celery	50 g
1 (15 ounce) can green beans, drained	425 g
1 (15 ounce) can cannellini beans, drained	425 g

- Place chicken, potato, tomatoes, broth, onion, carrots, celery, and 1 teaspoon (5 ml) each salt and pepper in slow cooker. Cover and cook on LOW 7 to 8 hours. Increase heat to HIGH, add beans and cook for additional 15 minutes. Serves 6.

Old-Time Chicken Soup

6 boneless, skinless chicken thighs, cut into 1-inch (2.5 cm) pieces	
3 (14 ounce) cans chicken broth	3 (395 g)
1 carrot, sliced	
2 ribs celery, sliced	
1 onion, chopped	
1 (15 ounce) can stewed tomatoes	425 g
1 (8 ounce) can green peas, drained	230 g
1 teaspoon dried thyme leaves	5 ml
½ cup elbow macaroni	55 g

- Combine chicken pieces, broth, carrot, celery, onion, tomatoes, peas, thyme and 1 teaspoon (5 ml) each of salt and pepper in sprayed slow cooker. Cover and cook on LOW for 6 hours 30 minutes to 7 hours.

- Increase heat to HIGH, add macaroni, cover and cook for additional 30 minutes. Serves 6.

Curly Noodle Soup

6 - 7 boneless chicken thighs	
1 (16 ounce) package baby carrots, cut in half	455 g
1 (8 ounce) can sliced bamboo shoots, drained	230 g
1 (8 ounce) can sliced water chestnuts, drained	230 g
1 (3 ounce) package Oriental-flavor ramen noodle soup mix	85 g
1 (32 ounce) carton chicken broth	910 g
2 tablespoons butter, melted	30 g
1 (10 ounce) package frozen green peas, thawed, drained	280 g

- Layer chicken thighs, carrots, bamboo shoots, water chestnuts, seasoning packet from noodles, broth and butter in sprayed slow cooker. Cover and cook on LOW for 7 to 8 hours.

- Remove chicken thighs with slotted spoon and shred with 2 forks. Return chicken to slow cooker and add peas and noodles; cover and cook for additional 10 minutes or until noodles are tender. Serves 6.

Credit This Chunky Noodle Soup

1 (16 ounce) package baby carrots, cut in half	455 g
4 ribs celery, sliced	
1 onion, chopped	
1 green bell pepper, seeded, chopped	
½ teaspoon dried thyme	2 ml
2 teaspoons seasoned salt	10 ml
2 - 2½ pounds boneless, skinless chicken thighs	910 g - 1.2 kg
1 (14 ounce) can chicken broth	395 g
1 (16 ounce) package egg noodles	455 g

- Place carrots, celery, onion, bell pepper, thyme, ½ teaspoon (2 ml) pepper, 6 cups (1.4 L) water and seasoned salt in sprayed slow cooker. Place chicken thighs on top of vegetables. Cover and cook on LOW for 8 to 9 hours or on HIGH for 4 to 5 hours.

- Remove chicken thighs with slotted spoon and cut into 4 to 5 pieces; return to slow cooker. Stir in broth and noodles and cook on HIGH for additional 20 minutes. Serves 8.

TIP: *Make this recipe a main dish by leaving out the broth. Place soup mixture in casserole dish, sprinkle french-fried onions on top and bake in 350° (175° C) oven just until it is thoroughly hot.*

Confetti Chicken Soup

1 pound boneless, skinless chicken thighs	455 g
1 (6 ounce) package chicken and herb-flavored rice	170 g
3 (14 ounce) cans chicken broth	3 (395 g)
3 carrots, sliced	
1 (10 ounce) can cream of chicken soup	280 g
1½ tablespoons chicken seasoning	22 ml
1 (10 ounce) package frozen whole kernel corn, thawed	280 g
1 (10 ounce) package frozen baby green peas, thawed	280 g

- Cut thighs in thin strips. Combine chicken, rice, chicken broth, carrots, soup, seasoning and 1 cup (250 ml) water in sprayed slow cooker. Cover and cook on LOW for 8 to 9 hours.

- Increase heat to HIGH and add corn and peas to cooker. Cover and cook for additional 30 minutes. Serves 4 to 6.

Chicken-Pasta Soup

1½ pounds boneless, skinless chicken thighs, cubed	680 g
1 onion, chopped	
3 carrots, sliced	
½ cup halved, pitted ripe olives	65 g
1 teaspoon minced garlic	5 ml
3 (14 ounce) cans chicken broth	3 (395 g)
1 (15 ounce) can Italian stewed tomatoes	425 g
1 teaspoon Italian seasoning	5 ml
½ cup small shell pasta	55 g
Parmesan cheese	

- Combine all ingredients except shell pasta and parmesan cheese in sprayed slow cooker.   Cover and cook on LOW for 8 to 9 hours.

- About 30 minutes before serving, add pasta and stir. Increase heat to HIGH and cook for additional 20 to 30 minutes. Garnish with parmesan cheese. Serves 6 to 8.

Chicken and Barley Soup

1½ - 2 pounds boneless, skinless chicken thighs	680 - 910 g
1 (16 ounce) package frozen stew vegetables	455 g
1 (1 ounce) packet dry vegetable soup mix	30 g
1¼ cups pearl barley	250 g
2 (14 ounce) cans chicken broth	2 (395 g)

- Combine all ingredients with 1 teaspoon (5 ml) each of salt and pepper and 4 cups (1 L) water in sprayed large slow cooker. Cover and cook on LOW for 5 to 6 hours or on HIGH for 3 hours. Serves 6 to 8.

Creamy Chicken-Spinach Soup

2 (14 ounce) cans chicken broth	2 (395 g)
1 (10 ounce) can cream of chicken soup	280 g
1 (12 ounce) can chicken chunks with liquid	340 g
1 (10 ounce) package frozen chopped spinach	280 g
2 cups milk	500 ml
½ teaspoon dried thyme	2 ml
1 (9 ounce) package refrigerated cheese filled tortellini, cooked	255 g

- Combine broth, soup, chicken, spinach, milk, thyme and a little pepper in sprayed slow cooker. Cover and cook on LOW for 5 to 7 hours.

- Stir in cooked tortellini. cover and cook for additional 15 minutes or until soup is thoroughly hot. Serves 6.

Terrific Tortilla Soup Treat

2 (15 ounce) cans diced tomatoes	2 (425 g)
2 (14 ounce) can chicken broth	2 (395 g)
1 (12 ounce) can chicken chunks with liquid	340 g
2 onions, finely chopped	
1 (15 ounce) can kidney beans, rinsed, drained	425 g
6 corn tortillas, cut into thin strips	
1 (8 ounce) package shredded Monterey Jack cheese	230 g

- Combine tomatoes, broth, chicken, onions and beans in sprayed slow cooker. Cover and cook on LOW for 7 to 9 hours or on HIGH for 4 to 5 hours.

- Place tortilla strips on large baking sheet and mist them with cooking spray. Broil strips for about 5 minutes or until they are crisp and golden. (Watch closely).

- Spoon soup into individual bowls and top each serving with tortilla strips and 1 to 2 heaping tablespoons (15 to 30 ml) cheese. Serves 6.

Screamin' Jalapeno Soup

3 carrots, peeled, chopped	
2 ribs celery, sliced	
1 green bell pepper, seeded, chopped	
¼ cup (½ stick) butter, melted	60 g
2 (14 ounce) can chicken broth	2 (395 g)
2 (12 ounce) cans chicken chunks with liquid	2 (340 g)
3 - 5 jalapenos, seeded, chopped	
2 teaspoons ground cumin	10 ml
¼ cup flour	30 g
1 pint whipping cream, divided	500 ml

- Combine carrots, celery, bell pepper, butter, broth, chicken, jalapenos and cumin in sprayed slow cooker. Cover and cook on LOW for 5 to 7 hours.

- Mix flour with 2 tablespoons (30 ml) cream until blended well. Stir in remaining cream; add whipping cream mixture to cooker. Cover and cook for additional 15 minutes. Serves 6 to 8.

TIP: Wear rubber gloves when handling and removing seeds from jalapenos.

Speedy-Fix Gonzalez Soup

1 (12 ounce) can chicken chunks with liquid	340 g
2 (14 ounce) cans chicken broth	2 (395 g)
1 (16 ounce) jar milk thick-and-chunky salsa	455 g
2 (15 ounce) cans ranch-style beans, rinsed, drained	2 (425 g)
1 (15 ounce) can whole kernel corn, drained	425 g

- Combine all ingredients in sprayed slow cooker. Cover and cook on LOW for 4 to 6 hours. Serves 6 to 8.

Chicken-Veggie Soup

1 (32 ounce) carton chicken broth	910 g
2 carrots, peeled, sliced	
2 ribs celery, sliced	
1 (8 ounce) can green peas, drained	230 g
1 cup cooked rice	165 g
1 (12 ounce) can chicken chunks with liquid	340 g
2 teaspoons fresh chopped tarragon	10 ml

- Combine broth, carrots, celery, peas, rice and chicken in sprayed slow cooker. Cover and cook on LOW for 5 to 7 hours. Stir in tarragon and a little salt and pepper. Serves 6.

Zesty Creamy Chicken Soup

1 (10 ounce) package frozen chopped bell peppers and onions, thawed	280 g
1 carrot, peeled, grated	
1 (10 ounce) can cream of celery soup	280 g
2 (10 ounce) cans cream of chicken soup	2 (280 g)
2 (14 ounce) cans chicken broth	2 (395 g)
2 soup cans milk	
1 tablespoon dried parsley flakes	15 ml
2 (12 ounce) cans chicken chunks with liquid	2 (340 g)
1 (16 ounce) package cubed Mexican Velveeta® cheese	455 g

- Combine bell peppers and onions, carrots, soups, broth, milk, parsley flakes and chicken in sprayed slow cooker. Cover and cook on LOW for 5 to 7 hours. Add cheese and stir until cheese melts. Serves 6 to 8.

Feel Better
Chicken-Noodle Soup

2 (14 ounce) cans chicken broth	2 (395 g)
1 (10 ounce) package frozen green peas, thawed	280 g
2 tablespoons butter, melted	30 g
1 (4 ounce) jar sliced mushrooms, drained	115 g
3 cups cooked, cubed chicken	420 g
1 (3 ounce) package chicken-flavored ramen noodles, broken	85 g

- Combine broth, peas, butter, mushrooms and chicken in sprayed slow cooker. Cover and cook on LOW for 4 to 6 hours.

- Stir in noodles and seasoning packet, cover and cook for additional 15 minutes. Serves 6.

Chicken, Chilies and Rice Soup

2 (12 ounce) cans chicken chunks with liquid	2 (340 g)
2 (14 ounce) can chicken broth	2 (395 g)
3 ribs celery, sliced	
2 - 4 large fresh green chilies, seeded, chopped	
1 cup instant rice	95 g

- Combine chicken, broth, celery and green chilies in sprayed slow cooker. Cover and cook on LOW for 5 to 7 hours.

- Stir in rice, cover and cook for additional 15 minutes. Serves 6.

Lucky Chicken Soup

3 cups cooked, cubed chicken	410 g
1 (15 ounce) can stewed tomatoes	425 g
1 (10 ounce) can enchilada sauce	280 g
1 onion, chopped	
1 teaspoon minced garlic	5 ml
1 (14 ounce) can chicken broth	395 g
1 (15 ounce) can whole kernel corn	425 g
1 teaspoon chili powder	5 ml

- Combine chicken, tomatoes, enchilada sauce, onion, garlic, broth, corn, chili powder and 2 cups (500 ml) water in sprayed slow cooker. Cover and cook on LOW for 6 to 8 hours or on HIGH for 3 to 4 hours. Serves 8.

No Fuss Tortilla Soup

1 (32 ounce) carton chicken broth	910 g
1 (15 ounce) can Mexican-style stewed tomatoes	425 g
2 - 2½ cups cooked, cubed chicken	280 - 350 g
1 (16 ounce) package frozen stir-fry vegetables	455 g
1 onion, finely chopped	
2 tablespoons cilantro	30 ml
1 (8 ounce) package cubed mozzarella cheese	230 g
2 avocados, peeled, diced	
1½ cups crushed tortilla chips	85 g

- Combine broth, stewed tomatoes, chicken, stir-fry vegetables, onion and cilantro in sprayed slow cooker until mixture blends well. Cover and cook on LOW for 6 to 7 hours or on HIGH for 3 hours to 3 hours 30 minutes.

- When ready to serve, place about ¼ cup (30 g) cheese and chopped avocados in each of 4 individual soup bowls. Spoon soup into bowls and top with crushed tortilla chips. Serve immediately. Serves 4.

Chicken and Rice Soup

1 (6 ounce) package long grain-wild rice mix	170 g
1 (1 ounce) packet chicken noodle soup mix	30 g
2 (10 ounce) cans cream of chicken soup	2 (280 g)
2 ribs celery, chopped	
1 - 2 cups cooked, cubed chicken	140 - 280 g

- Combine rice mix, noodle soup mix, chicken soup, celery, chicken and about 6 cups (1.4 L) water in sprayed slow cooker. Cover and cook on LOW for 2 to 3 hours. Serves 4 to 6.

Chicken-Veggie Surprise

3 (14 ounce) can chicken broth	3 (395 g)
1 (15 ounce) can sliced carrots, drained	425 g
1 (15 ounce) can green peas, drained	425 g
1 red bell pepper, seeded, chopped	
1 teaspoon dried tarragon	5 ml
2 cups cooked, cubed chicken	280 g
1 (16 ounce) package frozen broccoli florets	455 g
4 ounces thin egg noodles	115 g

- Combine broth, carrots, peas, bell pepper, tarragon, chicken and broccoli in sprayed slow cooker. Cover and cook on LOW for 5 to 7 hours.

- Stir in noodles, cover and cook for additional 1 hour. Serves 6 to 8.

One Easy Chicken-Noodle Soup

2 (3 ounce) packages chicken-flavored ramen noodles	2 (85 g)
3 cups cooked, cubed chicken (or turkey)	420 g
1 (16 ounce) package frozen stir-fry vegetables, thawed	455 g
1 (10 ounce) package frozen chopped bell peppers	
and onions, thawed	280 g
½ teaspoon cayenne pepper	2 ml
1 tablespoon soy sauce	15 ml

- Combine 6 cups (1.4 L) water and seasoning packets from noodles in sprayed large slow cooker; stir well. Add chicken, stir-fry vegetables and bell peppers and onions.

- Cover and cook on LOW for 5 to 6 hours or on HIGH 2 hours 30 minutes to 3 hours.

- Stir in noodles, cayenne pepper and soy sauce. (If you have been cooking on LOW, turn heat to HIGH.) Cook for additional 10 minutes or just until noodles are tender. Serves 8.

Fast-Fix Fiesta Soup

1 (15 ounce) can Mexican stewed tomatoes	425 g
1 (15 ounce) cans whole kernel corn	425 g
1 (15 ounce) can pinto beans, rinsed, drained	425 g
2 (14 ounce) cans chicken broth	2 (395 g)
2 (10 ounce) cans fiesta nacho soup	2 (280 g)
1 - 2 (12 ounce) cans chicken chunks with liquid	1 - 2 (340 g)

- Combine all ingredients in sprayed slow cooker. Cover and cook on LOW for 4 to 6 hours. Serves 6.

Turkey and Mushroom Soup

Another great way to use leftover chicken or turkey

2 cups sliced shitake mushrooms	145 g
2 ribs celery, sliced	
1 small onion, chopped	
2 tablespoons butter	30 g
1 (15 ounce) can sliced carrots	425 g
2 (14 ounce) cans chicken broth	395 g
½ cup orzo pasta	40 g
2 cups cooked, chopped turkey	280 g

- Saute mushrooms, celery and onion in butter in skillet.

- Transfer vegetables to sprayed slow cooker and add carrots, broth, orzo and turkey. (Do not use smoked turkey.) Cover and cook on LOW for 2 to 3 hours or on HIGH for 1 to 2 hours. Serves 4 to 6.

TIP: *Make a main dish by omitting 1 can of chicken broth and adding another cup of turkey. Place in a casserole dish and sprinkle with slivered almonds. Bake in 350° (175° C) oven for about 10 to 15 minutes.*

Turkey-Tortilla Soup

This is great for leftover turkey.

2 (14 ounce) cans chicken broth	2 (395 g)
2 (15 ounce) cans Mexican stewed tomatoes	2 (425 g)
1 (16 ounce) package frozen succotash, thawed	455 g
2 teaspoons chili powder	10 ml
1 teaspoon dried cilantro	5 ml
2 cups crushed tortilla chips, divided	110 g
2½ cups cooked, chopped turkey (do not use smoked turkey)	350 g

- Combine broth, tomatoes, succotash, chili powder, cilantro, ⅓ cup (19 g) crushed tortilla chips and turkey in sprayed, large slow cooker and stir well. Cover and cook on LOW for 3 to 5 hours.

- When ready to serve, sprinkle remaining chips over each serving. Serves 6 to 8.

So Easy Creamy Turkey Soup

1 (10 ounce) can cream of celery soup	280 g
1 (10 ounce) can cream of chicken soup	280 g
1 (15 ounce) can cream-style corn	425 g
1 soup can milk	
1 - 2 cups cooked, diced turkey	140 - 280 g

- Combine all ingredients in sprayed slow cooker. Cover and cook on LOW for 4 to 6 hours. Serves 4.

Smoked Turkey Sausage Soup

1 (10 ounce) package frozen chopped bell peppers	
and onions, thawed	280 g
3 (14 ounce) cans chicken broth	3 (395 g)
2 medium potatoes, peeled, cubed	
½ teaspoon dried basil	2 ml
1 pound smoked turkey kielbasa, sliced	455 g
1 (15 ounce) can green peas, drained	425 g

- Combine all ingredients in sprayed slow cooker. Cover and cook on LOW for 5 to 7 hours. Serves 4 to 6.

Fast-Fix Gobbler Soup

1 (16 ounce) package frozen chopped bell peppers	
and onions, thawed	455 g
2 (10 ounce) cans cream of chicken soup	2 (280 g)
2 cups cooked, cubed turkey	280 g
2 ribs celery, sliced	
2 (3 ounce) packages chicken-flavored ramen noodles,	
broken up	2 (85 g)

- Combine bell peppers and onions, soup, turkey, celery and 4 cups (1 L) water in sprayed slow cooker. Cover and cook on LOW for 5 to 7 hours.

- Stir in noodles and seasoning packet; cover and cook for additional 20 minutes or until soup is thoroughly hot. Serves 6.

15-Minute Fix Turkey Soup

3 (14 ounce) cans chicken broth	3 (395 g)
3 (15 ounce) cans navy beans, drained	3 (425 g)
2 (15 ounce) cans stewed tomatoes	2 (425 g)
3 cups cooked, cubed turkey	420 g
1 teaspoon minced garlic	5 ml
¼ teaspoon cayenne pepper	1 ml
1 (6 ounce) package baby spinach, stems removed	170 g

- Combine broth, beans, tomatoes, turkey, garlic and cayenne pepper in sprayed slow cooker. Cover and cook on LOW for 5 to 7 hours.

- Stir in spinach; cover and cook for additional 30 minutes. Serves 6 to 8.

Corny Turkey Soup

1 onion, chopped
1 red bell pepper, seeded, chopped
1 (15 ounce) can cream-style corn   425 g
1 (15 ounce) can whole kernel corn   425 g
2 (14 ounce) cans chicken broth   2 (395 g)
1 cup whipping cream   250 ml
2 - 3 cups cooked, cubed turkey   280 - 420 g
4 green onions, sliced

- Combine onion, bell pepper, cream-style corn, whole kernel corn, broth, cream and cubed turkey in sprayed slow cooker. Cover and cook on LOW for 5 to 7 hours. Scatter a few sliced green onions over each serving. Serves 4 to 6.

Turkey Tender Gobbler's Soup

3 ribs celery, sliced
1 onion, chopped
1 (4 ounce) can sliced mushrooms, drained   115 g
¼ cup (½ stick) butter, melted   60 g
3 (14 ounce) cans chicken broth   3 (395 g)
1½ pounds turkey tenders, sliced in half   680 g
1 (15 ounce) can stewed tomatoes   425 g

- Combine all ingredients in sprayed slow cooker. Cover and cook on LOW for 6 to 8 hours. Serves 6.

Turkey and Rice Soup

1 (10 ounce) package frozen chopped bell peppers
       and onions, thawed   280 g
¼ cup (½ stick) butter, melted   60 g
2 (14 ounce) cans turkey or chicken broth   2 (395 g)
1 (6 ounce) box roasted garlic and long grain-wild rice   170 g
2 (10 ounce) cans cream of chicken soup   2 (280 g)
2 cups cooked, diced turkey   280 g
1 cup milk   250 ml
1 (8 ounce) can green peas, drained   230 g

- Combine all ingredients in sprayed slow cooker. Cover and cook on LOW for 6 to 8 hours. Serves 6.

Tasty Turkey-Veggie Soup

3 (14 ounce) cans chicken broth	3 (395 g)
2 teaspoons minced garlic	10 ml
1 (16 ounce) package frozen corn, thawed	455 g
1 (10 ounce) package frozen cut green beans, thawed	280 g
1 (8 ounce) can sliced carrots	230 g
2 (15 ounce) cans stewed tomatoes	2 (425 g)
3 cups cooked, cubed turkey	420 g
1 cup shredded mozzarella cheese	115 g

• Combine broth, garlic, corn, green beans, carrots, tomatoes and turkey in sprayed slow cooker. Cover and cook on LOW for 5 to 7 hours. Top each serving with a little cheese. Serves 6.

Peppery Black Bean-Ham Soup

½ pound cooked, chopped ham	230 g
3 (14 ounce) cans chicken broth	3 (395 g)
3 (15 ounce) cans black beans, rinsed, drained	3 (425 g)
1 (16 ounce) package chopped frozen bell peppers and onions, thawed	455 g
2 - 3 medium jalapeno peppers, seeded, chopped	
1 (12 ounce) package shredded carrots	340 g
1 teaspoon ground cumin	5 ml

• Combine ham, broth, beans, bell peppers and onions, jalapeno peppers, carrots and cumin sprayed, large slow cooker. Cover and cook on LOW for 6 to 8 hours or on HIGH for 4 to 6 hours. Serves 6.

Winter Beans-Veggies-Ham Soup

2 (15 ounce) cans pinto beans, drained	2 (425 g)
2 (15 ounce) cans navy beans, drained	2 (425 g)
1 (15 ounce) can black beans, rinsed, drained	425 g
1 (10 ounce) package frozen chopped bell peppers and onions, thawed	280 g
2 cups chopped celery	200 g
1 (8 ounce) can sliced carrots, drained	230 g
2 cups cooked, cubed ham	280 g
3 (14 ounce) cans chicken broth	3 (395 g)
1 teaspoon Cajun seasoning	5 ml
⅛ teaspoon cayenne pepper	.5 ml

• Combine beans, bell peppers and onions, celery, carrots, ham, broth, Cajun seasoning, cayenne pepper, 1 teaspoon (5 ml) salt and 2 cups (500 ml) water in sprayed slow cooker. Cover and cook on LOW for 5 to 6 hours. Serves 8.

Good-Night Bedtime Soup

3 (15 ounce) cans navy beans with liquid	3 (425 g)
2 (14 ounce) cans chicken broth	2 (395 g)
1 - 2 cups cooked, chopped ham	140 - 280 g
1 large onion, chopped	
2 ribs celery, sliced	
½ teaspoon garlic powder	2 ml

• Combine all ingredients in sprayed slow cooker. Cover and cook on
  LOW for 5 to 7 hours. Serves 4 to 6.

Bayou Gator Bean Soup

1 (20 ounce) package Cajun-flavored, 16-bean soup mix with flavor packet	570 g
2 cups cooked, finely chopped ham	280 g
1 chopped onion	
2 (15 ounce) cans stewed tomatoes	2 (425 g)
Cornbread	

• Soak beans overnight in sprayed large slow cooker. After soaking,
  drain water and cover with 2 inches water over beans. Cover and cook
  on LOW for 5 to 6 hours or until beans are tender.

• Add ham, onion, stewed tomatoes and flavor packet in bean soup
  mix. Cover and cook on HIGH for 30 to 45 minutes. Serve with
  cornbread. Serves 4 to 6.

Palo Pinto Bean Soup

1 (12 ounce) package grated carrots	340 g
1 (16 ounce) package frozen chopped bell peppers and onions, thawed	455 g
1 (15 ounce) cans pinto beans with jalapenos, drained	425 g
1 (15 ounce) can pinto beans without jalapenos, drained	425 g
1 (10 ounce) can diced tomatoes and green chilies	280 g
2 cups cooked, diced ham	280 g
2 (14 ounce) cans chicken broth	2 (395 g)

• Combine all ingredients in sprayed slow cooker. Cover and cook on
  LOW for 5 to 7 hours. Serves 4 to 6.

Old-Fashioned Hoppin' John Soup

2 (15 ounce) cans black-eyed peas with jalapenos, with liquid   2 (425 g)
1 (14 ounce) can chicken broth   395 g
1 teaspoon minced garlic   5 ml
1 (10 ounce) package frozen chopped bell peppers
    and onions, thawed   280 g
1½ - 2 cups cooked, cubed ham   210 - 280 g
½ cup instant rice   50 g
1 (10 ounce) package frozen mustard greens, coarsely chopped   280 g

- Combine black-eyed peas, broth, garlic, bell peppers and onions and ham in sprayed slow cooker. Cover and cook on LOW for 5 to 7 hours.

- Stir in rice and mustard greens, cover and cook for additional 30 minutes. Serves 4 to 6.

Hearty Bean and Ham Soup

1 (15 ounce) can sliced carrots, drained   425 g
3 ribs celery, sliced
1 green bell pepper, seeded, chopped
2 - 3 cups cooked, cubed ham   280 - 420 g
2 (15 ounce) cans navy beans drained   2 (425 g)
2 (15 ounce) cans pinto beans with jalapenos   2 (425 g)
3 (14 ounce) cans chicken broth   3 (395 g)
2 teaspoons chili powder   10 ml

- Combine all ingredients in sprayed slow cooker. Cover and cook on LOW for 5 to 7 hours. Serves 6 to 8.

Italian Bean-o-rama Soup

1 pound hot Italian sausage   455 g
1 onion, chopped
1 (15 ounce) can Italian stewed tomatoes   425 g
2 (5 ounce) cans black beans, rinsed, drained   2 (145 g)
2 (15 ounce) cans navy beans with liquid   2 (425 g)
2 (14 ounce) cans beef broth   2 (395 g)
1 teaspoon minced garlic   5 ml
1 teaspoon dried basil   5 ml

- Cut sausage into ½-inch (1.2 cm) pieces. Brown sausage and onion in skillet, drain and transfer to sprayed slow cooker.

- Stir in tomatoes, black beans, navy beans, broth, garlic and basil and mix well. Cover and cook on LOW for 5 to 7 hours. Serves 6 to 8.

Black-Eyed Soup Kick

5 slices thick-cut bacon, diced
1 onion, chopped
1 green bell pepper, chopped
3 ribs celery, sliced
3 (15 ounce) cans jalapeno black-eyed peas with liquid   3 (425 g)
2 (15 ounce) cans stewed tomatoes with liquid   2 (425 g)
1 teaspoon chicken seasoning   5 ml

• Cook bacon pieces in skillet until crisp, drain on paper towel and
  place in sprayed slow cooker. With bacon drippings in skillet, saute
  onion and bell peppers, but do not brown.

• Add onions, bell pepper, celery, black-eyed peas, stewed tomatoes,
  1½ cups (375 ml) water and chicken seasoning to sprayed slow cooker.
  Cover and cook on LOW for 3 to 4 hours. Serves 6 to 8.

Mess Hall Navy Bean Soup

8 slices thick-cut bacon, divided
1 carrot
3 (15 ounce) cans navy beans with liquid   3 (425 g)
3 ribs celery, chopped
1 onion, chopped
2 (15 ounce) cans chicken broth   2 (425 g)
1 teaspoon Italian herb seasoning   5 ml
1 (10 ounce) can cream of chicken soup   280 g

• Cook bacon in skillet, drain and crumble. (Reserve 2 crumbled slices
  for garnish.) Cut carrot in half lengthwise and slice.

• Combine most of crumbled bacon, carrot, beans, celery, onion, broth,
  seasoning, 1 cup (250 ml) water in sprayed slow cooker and stir to
  mix. Cover and cook on LOW for 5 to 6 hours.

• Ladle 2 cups (500 ml) soup mixture into food processor or blender
  and process until smooth. Return to cooker, add cream of chicken
  soup and stir to mix. Turn heat to HIGH and cook for additional
  10 to 15 minutes. Serves 6 to 8.

Tomato and White Bean Soup

1 (10 ounce) package frozen chopped bell peppers
   and onions, thawed   280 g
1 (15 ounce) can diced tomatoes   425 g
2 (14 ounce) cans chicken broth   2 (395 g)
2 (15 ounce) cans navy beans, rinsed, drained   2 (425 g)
1½ cups cooked, diced ham   210 g
½ cup chopped fresh parsley   30 g

• Combine all ingredients in sprayed slow cooker. Cover and cook on
  LOW for 5 to 7 hours. Serves 4

Popeye's Special Spinach-Ham Soup

3 - 4 cups cooked, cubed ham	420 - 560 g
1 (16 ounce) package shredded carrots	455 g
2 ribs celery, sliced	
1 (10 ounce) can cream of onion soup	280 g
1½ teaspoons dried oregano, crushed	7 ml
1 (32 ounce) carton chicken broth	910 g
1 (6 ounce) package fresh baby spinach, stems removed	170 g

- Place ham, carrots, celery, soup, oregano and a little pepper in sprayed slow cooker. Stir in broth and 1 cup (250 ml) water. Cover and cook on LOW for 8 to 10 hours or on HIGH for 4 to 5 hours.

- Stir in spinach; cover and cook for additional 10 minutes or just until soup is thoroughly hot. Serves 4 to 5.

Veggie Potato Soup

1 (32 ounce) carton chicken broth	910 g
1 (12 ounce) package shredded carrots	340 g
3 potatoes, peeled, cubed	
1½ cups chopped cabbage	105 g
1 onion, finely chopped	
2 ribs celery, thinly sliced	
½ cup whipping cream	125 ml
½ pound bacon, cooked, crumbled	230 g
1 cup shredded cheddar cheese	115 g

- Combine broth, carrots, potatoes, cabbage, onion, celery and a little salt and pepper in sprayed slow cooker. Cover and cook on LOW for 8 to 10 hours or on HIGH for 4 to 5 hours.

- Stir in cream, bacon and cheese, cover and cook for additional 15 minutes or until soup is piping hot. Serves 6.

Supper-Ready Potato Soup

1 (18 ounce) package frozen hash-brown potatoes with onions and peppers, thawed	510 g
2 (14 ounce) cans chicken broth	2 (395 g)
3 ribs celery, thinly sliced	
2 (10 ounce) cans cream of chicken soup	2 (280 g)
2 cups milk	500 ml
2 cups cooked, shredded ham	280 g
2 teaspoons minced garlic	10 ml
1 teaspoon dried parsley flakes	5 ml

- Combine hash-brown potatoes, broth, celery, soup, milk, ham, garlic, parsley flakes, 1 teaspoon (5 ml) salt and a little pepper in sprayed slow cooker. Cover and cook on LOW for 6 to 8 hours. Serves 6.

Easy Bacon-Potato Soup

2 (14 ounce) cans chicken broth   2 (395 g)
1 (10 ounce) can cream of chicken soup   280 g
2 medium potatoes, peeled, cut into small cubes
1 onion, very finely chopped
6 sliced bacon, fried, crumbled

- Combine broth, soup, potatoes, onion, ½ teaspoon (2 ml) salt and a little pepper in sprayed slow cooker. Cover and cook on LOW for 5 to 7 hours. Sprinkle each serving with crumbled bacon. Serves 4.

Potato Soup Deluxe

5 medium potatoes, peeled, cubed
2 cups cooked, cubed ham   280 g
1 cup fresh broccoli florets, cut very, very fine   70 g
1 (10 ounce) can cheddar cheese soup   280 g
1 (10 ounce) can fiesta nacho cheese soup   280 g
1 (14 ounce) can chicken broth   395 g
2½ soup cans milk
Paprika

- Place potatoes, ham and broccoli in sprayed slow cooker. Combine soups and milk in saucepan. Heat just enough to mix until smooth. Stir into ingredients already in slow cooker.

- Cover and cook on LOW for 7 to 9 hours. Sprinkle a little paprika over each serving. Serves 6 to 8.

Ski Hut Potato-Ham Soup

1½ cups cooked, cubed ham   210 g
4 large potatoes, peeled, shredded
2 ribs celery, sliced
1 onion, chopped
1 (10 ounce) can cream of chicken soup   280 g
2 (14 ounce) cans chicken broth   2 (395 g)
1 cup milk   250 ml
1 (8 ounce) package cream cheese, cut into slices   230 g

- Combine ham, potatoes, celery, onion, soup and broth in sprayed slow cooker. Cover and cook on LOW for 6 to 8 hours or on HIGH for 4 to 6 hours.

- (If cooking on LOW, increase heat to HIGH.) Stir in milk and cream cheese. Cover and cook for additional 10 to 15 minutes. Stir until cream cheese melts and blends well. Serves 8.

If you don't like black specks in your dish, try white pepper.

Winter Potato-Leek Soup

1 (1 ounce) packet white sauce mix	30 g
1 (28 ounce) package frozen hash-brown potatoes with	
onions and peppers	795 g
3 medium leeks, sliced	
3 cups cooked, cubed ham	420 g
1 (12 ounce) can evaporated milk	375 ml
1 (8 ounce) carton sour cream	230 g

- Pour 3 cups (750 ml) water in sprayed slow cooker and stir white sauce until smooth. Add hash-brown potatoes, leeks, ham and evaporated milk.

- Cover and cook on LOW for 7 to 9 hours or on HIGH for 3 hours 30 minutes to 4 hours 30 minutes.

- (If cooking on LOW, increase heat to HIGH.) Take out about 2 cups (500 ml) hot soup and pour into separate bowl. Stir in sour cream and return to cooker. Cover and cook for additional 15 minutes or until mixture is thoroughly hot. Serves 6 to 8.

New Year's Black-Eyed Pea Soup

1 onion, chopped	
2 cups cooked, cubed ham	280 g
2 (15 ounce) cans black-eyed peas with jalapenos with liquid	2 (425 g)
2 ribs celery, sliced	
1 (14 ounce) can chicken broth	395 g
1 teaspoon minced garlic	5 ml
1 teaspoon dried sage	5 ml

- Combine all ingredients in sprayed slow cooker. Cover and cook on LOW for 5 to 7 hours. Serves 4.

Tasty Cabbage-Ham Soup

1 (16 ounce) package cabbage slaw mix	455 g
1 (10 ounce) package frozen, chopped bell peppers	
and onions, thawed	280 g
1 teaspoon minced garlic	5 ml
2 (14 ounce) cans chicken broth	2 (395 g)
1 (15 ounce) cans stewed tomatoes	425 g
2 cups cooked, cubed ham	280 g
¼ cup packed brown sugar55 g	
2 tablespoons lemon juice	30 ml

- Combine all ingredients in sprayed slow cooker. Cover and cook on LOW for 5 to 7 hours. Serves 6.

Southern Soup

1½ cups dried black-eyed peas	360 g
2 - 3 cups cooked, cubed ham	280 - 420 g
1 (15 ounce) can whole kernel corn	425 g
1 (10 ounce) package frozen cut okra, thawed	280 g
1 onion, chopped	
1 large potato, cut into small cubes	
2 teaspoons Cajun seasoning	10 ml
1 (14 ounce) can chicken broth	395 g
2 (15 ounce) cans Mexican stewed tomatoes	2 (425 g)

- Rinse peas and drain. Combine peas and 5 cups (1.2 L) water in large saucepan. Bring to a boil, reduce heat, simmer for about 10 minutes and drain.

- Combine peas, ham, corn, okra, onion, potato, seasoning, broth and 2 cups (500 ml) water in sprayed slow cooker. Cover and cook on LOW for 6 to 8 hours.

- Add tomatoes, cover and cook for additional 1 hour. Serves 6 to 8.

Ham, Bean and Pasta Soup

1 onion, finely chopped	
2 ribs celery, chopped	
2 teaspoons minced garlic	10 ml
2 (14 ounce) cans chicken broth	2 (395 g)
2 (15 ounce) cans pork and beans with liquid	2 (425 g)
3 cups cooked, cubed ham	420 g
⅓ cup pasta shells	35 g
Bacon, cooked crisp, crumbled	

- Combine onion, celery, garlic, chicken broth, beans, ham and 1 cup (250 ml) water in sprayed slow cooker. Cover and cook on LOW for 4 to 5 hours.

- Turn cooker to HIGH, add pasta and cook for additional 35 to 45 minutes or until pasta is tender. Garnish each serving with bacon. Serves 6 to 8.

Most slow cooker users suggest "tasting" before serving in order to add any needed seasonings such as salt, pepper, lemon juice, herb blends, Worcestershire sauce, etc.

Ham and Black Bean Soup

1 pound dried black beans, soaked overnight	455 g
2 cups cooked, diced ham	280 g
1 onion, chopped	
2 ribs celery, chopped	
3 jalapeno peppers, seeded, chopped	
2 (14 ounce) cans chicken broth	2 (395 g)
2 teaspoons ground cumin	10 ml
1 teaspoon dried oregano	5 ml
1 teaspoon chili powder	5 ml
½ teaspoon cayenne pepper	2 ml
1 (8 ounce) carton sour cream	230 g

- Combine black beans, ham, onion, celery, jalapeno peppers, broth, cumin, oregano, chili powder, 8 cups (1.9 L) water and 1 teaspoon (5 ml) salt in sprayed slow cooker. Cover and cook on LOW for 8 to 10 hours. Stir sour cream into soup and serve immediately. Serves 8.

TIP: *Wear rubber gloves when handling and removing seeds from jalapenos.*

Home-Style Ham and Bean Soup

2 cups cooked, cubed ham	280 g
1 (15 ounce) can chick-peas, rinsed, drained	425 g
1 (16 ounce) package baby carrots, cut in half	455 g
3 ribs celery, sliced	
1 (14 ounce) can chicken broth	395 g
2 (12 ounce) bottles of tomato juice	2 (750 ml)

- Combine ham, chick-peas, carrots and celery in sprayed slow cooker. Pour broth and tomato juice over all. Cover and cook on LOW for 7 to 9 hours. Serves 4 to 6.

Ham and Fresh Okra Soup

1 (10 ounce) package frozen butter beans or lima beans, drained, thawed	280 g
2 cups cooked, cubed ham	280 g
1 (14 ounce) can chicken broth	395 g
1 (15 ounce) can stewed tomatoes	425 g
2 large onions, chopped	
3 cups small fresh whole okra	215 g
2 cups instant rice	190 g

- Combine beans, ham, broth, tomatoes, onions and a little salt and pepper in sprayed slow cooker. Cover and cook on LOW for 5 to 7 hours.

- Stir in okra; cover and cook for additional 30 to 35` minutes. Cook rice according to package directions and place in individual soup bowls and spoon soup over rice. Serves 6.

Soup with an Attitude

1 (32 ounce) carton chicken broth	910 g
3 large potatoes, peeled, grated	
2 onions, chopped	
3 ribs celery, chopped	
1 (7 ounce) can chopped green chilies	200 g
3 cups cooked, cubed ham	420 g
1 (16 ounce) package cubed Mexican Velveeta® cheese	455 g
1 (1 pint) carton half-and-half cream	500 ml

- Combine broth, grated potatoes, onions, celery, green chilies and ham in sprayed slow cooker. Cover and cook on LOW for 6 to 8 hours.

- Add cheese and stir until cheese melts. Stir in half-and-half cream, cover and cook for additional 20 minutes or until soup is thoroughly hot. Serves 8.

Wild Rice and Ham Soup

1 (6 ounce) box long grain-wild rice	170 g
¼ cup (½ stick) butter, melted	60 g
1 (16 ounce) package frozen chopped bell peppers and onions, thawed	455 g
2 (10 ounce) cans cream of celery soup	2 (280 g)
2 (14 ounce) cans chicken broth	2 (395 g)
2 cups cooked, diced ham	280 g
2 (15 ounce) cans black-eyed peas with jalapenos with liquid	2 (425 g)
1 (8 ounce) carton sour cream	230 g

- Combine rice, butter, bell peppers and onions, soup, broth, ham black-eyed peas, 2 cups (500 ml) water and ½ teaspoon (2 ml) salt in sprayed slow cooker. Cover and cook on LOW for 5 to 7 hours.

- Stir in sour cream and let stand for about 10 minutes. Serves 6.

Soup That's Soul Food

3 (15 ounce) cans navy beans with liquid, divided	3 (425 g)
2 onions, finely chopped	
2 teaspoon minced garlic	
3 medium potatoes, peeled, cut into small cubes	
2 cups cooked, diced ham	280 g
3 (14 ounce) cans chicken broth	3 (395 g)
1 (10 ounce) package frozen chopped turnip greens	280 g

- Place 1 can beans in shallow bowl and mash with fork.

- Combine mashed beans, beans, onions, garlic, potatoes, ham, broth and a little salt and pepper in sprayed slow cooker. Cover and cook on LOW for 5 to 7 hours.

- Stir in turnip greens, cover and cook for additional 30 minutes or until potatoes and greens are tender. Serves 6.

Great Soup Florentine-Style

3 - 4 large potatoes, peeled, diced	
1 onion, finely diced	
1 (1 pound) ham hock	455 g
1 (32 ounce) carton chicken broth	910 g
1½ teaspoons seasoned salt	7 ml
½ teaspoon dry mustard	2 ml
1 (10 ounce) package frozen chopped spinach,	
thawed, well drained*	280 g
1 cup shredded cheddar or Swiss cheese	115 g

- Combine potatoes, onion, ham hock (or 2 cups/280 g diced ham), broth, seasoned salt, a little pepper and mustard in sprayed slow cooker. Cover and cook on LOW for 7 to 8 hours.

- Remove ham hock, chop meat and discard bone; return meat to slow cooker. Increase heat to HIGH, add spinach; cover and cook for additional 20 minutes. Add cheese, stirring until cheese melts. Serves 4 to 6.

*TIP: Squeeze spinach between paper towels to completely remove excess moisture.

Sausage-Tortellini Soup

1 pound Italian sausage	455 g
1 onion, chopped	
3 ribs celery, sliced	
2 (14 ounce) cans chicken broth	2 (395 g)
½ teaspoon dried basil	2 ml
1 (15 ounce) can sliced carrots	425 g
1 medium zucchini, halved, sliced	
1 (15 ounce) can Italian stewed tomatoes	425 g
1 (9 ounce) package refrigerated meat-filled tortellini	255 g
1 cup shredded mozzarella cheese	115 g

- Combine crumbled sausage, onion, celery, broth, basil, carrots, zucchini, tomatoes and 1 cup (250 ml) water in sprayed slow cooker. Cover and cook on LOW for 5 to 7 hours.

- Stir in tortellini, cover and cook for additional 1 hour. Sprinkle cheese over each serving. Serves 6.

Sausage-Vegetable Soup

1 pound bulk Italian sausage	455 g
2 onion, chopped	
2 teaspoons minced garlic	10 ml
1 (1 ounce) packet beefy soup mix	30 g
1 (15 ounce) can sliced carrots	425 g
2 (15 ounce) cans Italian stewed tomatoes	2 (425 g)
2 (15 ounce) cans garbanzo beans, rinsed, drained	2 (425 g)
1 cup elbow macaroni	105 g

• Combine crumbled sausage, onion, garlic, soup mix, carrots. tomatoes, beans and a little salt and pepper in sprayed slow cooker. Cover and cook on LOW for 5 to 7 hours.

• Cook macaroni according to package directions, drain and stir in soup. Cover and cook for additional 30 minutes for flavors to blend. Serves 6.

Supper Sausage Soup

1 pound bulk Italian sausage	455 g
1 (16 ounce) package frozen chopped bell peppers and onions, thawed	455 g
2 (15 ounce) cans stewed tomatoes	2 (425 g)
1 (4 ounce) can sliced mushrooms, drained	115 g
2 (14 ounce) cans chicken broth	2 (395 g)
¾ cup hot thick-and-chunky salsa	200 g
1 teaspoon dried basil	5 ml
1 teaspoon sugar	5 ml
1 (8 ounce) package shredded mozzarella cheese	230 g

• Combine crumbled sausage, bell peppers and onions, tomatoes, mushrooms, broth, salsa, basil, sugar and a little salt and pepper in sprayed slow cooker. Cover and cook on LOW for 5 to 7 hours. Sprinkle a little cheese over each serving. Serves 6.

Potato-Sausage Soup

1 pound Polish sausage, cut into ½-inch pieces	455 g/1.2 cm
3 ribs celery, sliced	
1 (10 ounce) package frozen, chopped bell peppers and onions, thawed	280 g
2 (10 ounce) cans cream of potato soup	2 (280 g)
1 (10 ounce) can cream of celery soup	280 g
½ cup milk	125 ml
1 (14 ounce) can chicken broth	395 g

• Combine all ingredients in sprayed slow cooker. Cover and cook on LOW for 5 to 7 hours. Serves 4 to 6.

Cowboy Sausage-Bean Soup

1 pound pork sausage	455 g
2 (15 ounce) cans pinto beans, rinsed, drained	2 (425 g)
1 (10 ounce) package frozen chopped bell peppers	
and onions, thawed	280 g
¼ teaspoon garlic powder	1 ml
½ teaspoon thyme	1 ml
1 tablespoon chili powder	15 ml
¼ teaspoon dried coriander	1 ml
1 large potato, peeled, grated	
1 (8 ounce) package cubed Velveeta® cheese	230 g
¾ cup shredded Monterey Jack cheese	85 g

- Combine crumbled sausage, beans, bell peppers and onions, garlic powder, thyme, chili powder, coriander, potato and Velveeta® cheese in sprayed slow cooker. Cover and cook on LOW for 5 to 7 hours. Sprinkle each serving with Monterey Jack cheese. Serves 6.

Sausage Pizza Soup

1 (16 ounce) package Italian link sausage, thinly sliced	455 g
1 onion, chopped	
2 (4 ounce) cans sliced mushrooms	2 (115 g)
1 small green bell pepper, cored, seeded, julienned	
1 (15 ounce) can Italian stewed tomatoes	425 g
1 (14 ounce) can beef broth	395 g
1 (8 ounce) can pizza sauce	230 g
Shredded mozzarella cheese	

- Combine all ingredients except cheese in sprayed slow cooker and stir well. Cover and cook on LOW for 4 to 5 hours. Sprinkle mozzarella cheese over each serving. Serves 4 to 6.

Minestrone Extra

1 pound Italian sausage	455 g
1 medium onion, chopped	
2 (19 ounce) cans minestrone soup	2 (540 g)
1 (15 ounce) can navy beans, drained	425 g
1 (15 ounce) can pinto beans, drained	425 g
1 (10 ounce) can beef broth	280 g
½ cup shredded parmesan cheese	50 g

- Place sausage and onion in skillet and cook on medium-high heat until mixture is brown. Drain.

- Place sausage, onion, soup, beans, broth and 1 cup (250 ml) water in sprayed slow cooker. Cover and cook on LOW for 7 to 8 hours or on HIGH for 3 hours 30 minutes to 4 hours. Top each serving with parmesan cheese. Serves 6.

Winter Minestrone

1 pound Italian sausage links	455 g
2 medium potatoes, peeled	
2 medium fennel bulbs, trimmed	
2½ cups butternut or acorn squash	285 g
1 onion, chopped	
1 (15 ounce) can kidney beans, rinsed, drained	425 g
2 teaspoons minced garlic	10 ml
1 teaspoon Italian seasoning	5 ml
2 (14 ounce) cans chicken broth	2 (395 g)
1 cup dry white wine	250 ml
3 - 4 cups fresh spinach	90 - 120 g

- Cut sausage, potatoes and fennel into ½-inch (1.2 cm) slices. Cook sausage in skillet until brown and drain.

- Combine squash, potatoes, fennel, onion, beans, garlic and Italian seasoning in sprayed, large slow cooker. Top with sausage and pour chicken broth and wine over all. Cover and cook on LOW for 7 to 9 hours.

- Stir in spinach, cover and cook for additional 10 minutes. Serves 6 to 8.

Continental Sausage Soup

1 pound Italian pork sausage	455 g
3 carrots, peeled, sliced	
1 (15 ounce) can whole new potatoes, drained	425 g
2 (15 ounce) cans Italian stewed tomatoes	2 (425 g)
2 (14 ounce) cans beef broth	2 (395 g)
1 (15 ounce) can garbanzo beans, drained	425 g
1 teaspoon minced garlic	
3 small zucchini, cut in 1-inch (2.5 cm) slices	

- Cook sausage in non-stick skillet, stirring often. Drain and place in sprayed slow cooker. Add carrots, potatoes, tomatoes, broth, beans, garlic and 1 cup (250 ml) water. Cover and cook on LOW for 7 to 9 hours.

- Gently stir in zucchini, cover and cook for additional 30 minutes. Serves 6 to 7.

With only minutes of preparation time in the morning, you can come home to the warmth and enticing aroma of a delicious and hearty meal.

Spicy Sausage Soup

1 pound mild bulk sausage	455 g
1 pound hot bulk sausage	455 g
2 (15 ounce) cans Mexican stewed tomatoes	2 (425 g)
3 cups chopped celery	305 g
1 cup sliced carrots	120 g
1 (15 ounce) can cut green beans, drained	425 g
1 (14 ounce) can chicken broth	395 g
1 teaspoon seasoned salt	5 ml

- Combine mild and hot sausage, shape into small balls and place in non-stick skillet. Brown thoroughly, drain and place in sprayed large slow cooker.

- Add remaining ingredients plus 1 cup (250 ml) water and stir gently so meatballs will not break-up. Cover and cook on LOW 6 to 7 hours. Serves 6 to 8.

Pork and Hominy Soup

2 pounds pork shoulder	910 g
1 onion, chopped	
2 ribs celery, sliced	
2 (15 ounce) cans yellow hominy with liquid	2 (425 g)
2 (15 ounce) cans stewed tomatoes	2 (425 g)
2 (14 ounce) cans chicken broth	2 (395 g)
1½ teaspoons ground cumin	7 ml
Flour tortillas	
Shredded cheese	
Green onions, chopped	

- Cut pork into ½-inch (1.2 cm) cubes. Sprinkle pork cubes with a little salt and pepper and brown in skillet. Place in sprayed slow cooker.

- Combine onion, celery, hominy, stewed tomatoes, cumin and 1 cup (250 ml) water in bowl. Pour over pork cubes. Cover and cook on HIGH for 6 to 7 hours.

- Serve with warmed, buttered tortillas and top each serving with some shredded cheese and chopped green onions. Serves 6 to 8.

The slow cooker is best suited to tougher, less expensive cuts of meat. Premium cuts of meat such as prime rib or leg of lamb may be better if cooked in the oven.

Carolina She-Crab Soup

4 cups milk	1 L
¼ teaspoon mace	1 ml
1 teaspoon grated lemon peel	5 ml
1 pound fresh crabmeat, flaked	455 g
1 (1 pint) carton whipping cream	500 ml
¼ cup (½ stick) butter, melted	60 g
½ cup finely crushed cracker crumbs	30 g
2 tablespoons sherry	30 ml

- Combine milk, mace, lemon peel, crabmeat, whipping cream, butter and a little salt and pepper in sprayed slow cooker. Cover and cook on LOW for 3 hours to 3 hours 30 minutes.

- Stir in cracker crumbs a little at a time to get consistency desired, cover and cook for additional 15 minutes. Just before serving, stir in sherry. Serves 6.

Spiked Crab Soup

1 (1 ounce) packet onion soup mix	30 g
2 (6 ounce) cans crabmeat, flaked	2 (170 g)
3 ribs celery, thinly sliced	
1 (8 ounce) can whole kernel corn, drained	230 g
2 tablespoons cornstarch	15 g
1 (1 pint) carton whipping cream, divided	500 ml
½ cup white wine	125 ml

- Combine soup mix, crabmeat, celery, corn and 2 cups (500 ml) water in sprayed slow cooker. Cover and cook on LOW for 2 hours 30 minutes to 3 hours.

- Combine cornstarch with about 2 tablespoons (30 ml) cream in bowl and mix until smooth; stir in remaining cream. Stir cream mixture into cooker, cover and cook for additional 30 minutes or until soup thickens. Stir in wine just before serving. Serves 4 to 6.

Slow cookers blend flavors deliciously, but colors can fade over long cooking times, therefore you can "dress up" your dish with colorful garnishes such as fresh parsley or chives, salsa, extra shredded cheese, a sprinkle of paprika or a dollop of sour cream.

Oyster Soup

2 (14 ounce) cans chicken broth	2 (395 g)
1 large onion, chopped	
3 ribs celery, sliced	
1 red bell pepper seeded, chopped	
2 teaspoons minced garlic	10 ml
½ cup (1 stick) butter, melted	115 g
1 tablespoon dried parsley	15 ml
2 (1 pint) cartons fresh oysters, rinsed, drained	2 (455 g)
¼ cup flour	30 g
2 cups milk, divided	500 ml

- Combine broth, onion, celery, bell pepper, garlic, butter and parsley in sprayed slow cooker. Cover and cook on LOW for 5 to 6 hours.

- Boil oysters in 2 cups (500 ml) water in saucepan for 2 minutes, stirring often or until edges of oysters begin to curl. Remove oysters with slotted spoon and coarsely chop half oysters.

- Mix flour and about 2 tablespoons (30 ml) milk in bowl until mixture is smooth; stir in remaining milk. Stir milk mixture, chopped oysters, and a little salt and pepper into cooker. Cover and cook for additional 30 minutes or until soup thickens. Stir in remaining whole oysters. Serves 6.

Creole Soup

¼ cup (½ stick) butter, melted	60 g
1 (16 ounce) package frozen chopped bell peppers and onions, thawed	455 g
2 ribs celery, sliced	
1 teaspoon minced garlic	5 ml
1 (6 ounce) package garlic-butter flavored rice	170 g
2 (15 ounce) cans stewed tomatoes	2 (425 g)
1 teaspoon Creole seasoning	5 ml
1 (16 ounce) package frozen salad shrimp, thawed, drained	455 g

- Combine butter, bell peppers and onions, celery, garlic, rice, tomatoes, Creole seasoning and 1 cup (250 ml) water in sprayed slow cooker. Cover and cook on LOW for 5 to 7 hours.

- Stir in shrimp, cover and cook for additional 15 minutes. Serves 6.

Superior Beef Stew

2 - 2½ pounds beef stew meat	910 g - 1.4 kg
2 (15 ounce) cans whole potatoes, quartered, drained	2 (425 g)
1 (16 ounce) package baby carrots, halved	455 g
3 ribs celery, sliced	
2 (15 ounce) cans stewed tomatoes	2 (425 g)
1 (1 ounce) package onion soup mix	30 g
1 (4 ounce) can chopped green chilies	115 g

- Combine stew meat, potatoes, carrots, celery, tomatoes, soup mix, green chilies and ½ cup (125 ml) water in sprayed slow cooker; stir to blend well. Cover and cook on LOW for 8 to 9 hours or on HIGH for 4 hours to 4 hours 30 minutes. Serves 6 to 8.

Simple Simon Super Stew

1½ pounds beef stew meat	680 g
2 onions, finely chopped	
2 ribs celery, sliced	
2 carrots, sliced	
2 potatoes, peeled, diced	
1 (15 ounce) can Mexican stewed tomatoes	425 g
½ cup pearl barley	100 g
2 (14 ounce) cans beef broth	2 (395 g)
½ cup flour	60 g
1 (15 ounce) can cut green beans, drained	425 g

- Brown stew meat in skillet on medium heat for about 10 minutes; transfer to sprayed, large slow cooker. Stir in onions, celery, carrots, potatoes, tomatoes and barley.

- Combine beef broth and flour in bowl and add to slow cooker; stir to mix well. Cover and cook on LOW 6 to 9 hours. Stir in green beans, cover and cook for 1 additional hour. Serves 8.

Quick-Fix Comfort Stew

1½ pounds select stew meat	680 g
2 (10 ounce) cans French onion soup	2 (280 g)
1 (10 ounce) can cream of onion soup	280 g
1 (10 ounce) can cream of celery soup	280 g
1 (14 ounce) can beef broth	395 g
2 (16 ounce) packages frozen stew vegetables, thawed	2 (455 g)

- Combine stew meat, soups, broth and vegetables in sprayed slow cooker. Cover and cook on LOW for 8 to 10 hours. Serves 8.

Comfort Stew

1½ pounds select stew meat	680 g
2 (10 ounce) cans French onion soup	2 (280 g)
1 (10 ounce) can cream of onion soup	280 g
1 (10 ounce) can cream of celery soup	280 g
1 (16 ounce) package frozen stew vegetables, thawed	455 g

- Place stew meat in sprayed slow cooker. Add soups as listed and spread evenly over meat. DO NOT STIR. Cook on HIGH just long enough for ingredients to get hot.

- Reduce heat to LOW, cover and cook for 6 to 7 hours. Add vegetables and cook for additional 1 hour. Serves 4 to 6.

Beneficial Beef and Barley Stew

1 pound beef stew meat, fat removed	455 g
1 (10 ounce) package frozen green beans	280 g
1 carrot, shredded	
2 ribs celery, sliced	
½ cup regular pearl barley	100 g
1 (12 ounce) jar mushroom gravy	340 g
2 (14 ounce) cans beef broth	2 (395 g)
½ teaspoon dried thyme leaves	2 ml

- Combine stew meat, green beans, carrots, celery, barley, gravy, beef broth, thyme leaves and a little salt and pepper in sprayed slow cooker. Cover and cook on LOW for 10 to 12 hours. Serves 5 to 6.

Independent Bean Stew

1 (16 ounce) package dried bean soup mix (with seasoning packet)	455 g
2 onions, finely chopped	
2 pounds well-trimmed beef stew meat	910 g
1 (14 ounce) can beef broth	395 g
2 teaspoons minced garlic	10 ml
1 (10 ounce) can diced tomatoes and green chilies	280 g
1 teaspoon Italian seasoning	5 ml
1 (8 ounce) package shredded mozzarella cheese	230 g

- Cover beans with water and soak overnight; drain and rinse. Place beans, seasoning packet, onions, stew meat, beef broth, 1½ cups (375 ml) water, garlic, and tomatoes and green chilies in sprayed slow cooker. Cover and cook on LOW for 8 to 9 hours or until beans are soft and beef is tender.

- Stir in Italian seasoning. Spoon into individual soup bowls and top with cheese. Serves 6 to 8.

Meat and Potato Stew

2 pound beef stew meat	910 g
3 medium potatoes, peeled, sliced	
1 (16 ounce) package baby carrots	455 g
1 (14 ounce) can beef broth	395 g
2 (10 ounce) cans French onion soup	2 (280 g)

- Combine stew meat, potatoes, carrots, broth, 1 cup (250 ml) water and soup in sprayed slow cooker. Cover and cook on LOW for 7 to 9 hours. Serves 6 to 8.

Vegetable-Beef Stew

1 pound stew meat	455 g
1 (14 ounce) can beef broth	395 g
1 (28 ounce) can stewed tomatoes	795 g
2 (15 ounce) cans mixed vegetables with liquid	2 (425 g)
½ cup barley	100 g

- Combine stew meat, broth, tomatoes, mixed vegetables and barley in sprayed slow cooker. Cover and cook on LOW for 7 to 9 hours. Serves 6.

Stroganoff Stew

1 (1 ounce) packet onion soup mix	30 g
2 (10 ounce) cans golden mushroom soup	2 (280 g)
2 pounds stew meat	910 g
1 onion, chopped	
1 (4 ounce) can sliced mushrooms	115 g
1 (8 ounce) carton sour cream	230 g
1 (8 ounce) package wide noodles	230 g

- Combine soup mix, soup, 2 soup cans water, stew meat, onion and mushrooms in sprayed slow cooker. Cover and cook on LOW for 7 to 9 hours.

- Cook noodles according to package directions and place on serving platter. Stir sour cream into stew and spoon stew over noodles. Serves 6 to 8.

Simple Pinto Bean Stew

1 pound dried pinto beans, soaked overnight	455 g
2 (14 ounce) cans beef broth	2 (395 g)
1 pound beef stew meat	455 g
1 onion, chopped	
1 (6 ounce) can tomato paste	170 g
¼ cup packed brown sugar	55 g
½ teaspoon dry mustard	2 ml
1 (1 ounce) packet taco seasoning	30 g

- Drain beans and combine with broth, stew meat, onion, tomato paste, brown sugar, dry mustard, taco seasoning and 4 cups (1 L) water in sprayed slow cooker. Cover and cook on LOW for 6 to 8 hours. Serves 6.

Cattle Drive Chili Stew

3 pounds stew meat	1.4 kg
1 onion, chopped	
3 ribs celery, sliced	
2 (15 ounce) cans Mexican-style stewed tomatoes	2 (425 g)
2 (14 ounce) cans beef broth	2 (395 g)
1 (10 ounce) package frozen corn, thawed	280 g
1 cup diced fresh green chilies	240 g

- Combine stew meat, onion, celery, tomatoes, broth, corn, green chilies and 1 teaspoon (5 ml) salt and a little pepper in sprayed slow cooker. Cover and cook on LOW for 7 to 9 hours. Serves 6 to 8.

Our Choice Beef Stew

6 medium potatoes, peeled, cut in 1-inch (2.5 cm) cubes	
4 carrots, peeled, cut into ½-inch (1.2 cm) pieces	
1 green bell pepper, seeded, chopped	
2 onions, coarsely chopped	
1½ pounds beef stew meat, cut into 1-inch cubes	680 g/2.5 cm
1 (10 ounce) can cream of golden mushroom soup	280 g
1 (1 ounce) packet beefy onion soup mix	30 g

- Place potatoes, carrots, bell pepper, onions and stew meat in sprayed slow cooker.
- Heat soup, onion soup mix and ⅔ cup (150 ml) water in saucepan and mix until they blend well. Pour over meat and vegetables. Cover and cook on LOW for 8 to 9 hours. Serves 5.

Summer Stew

1½ - 2 pounds beef stew meat	680 - 910 g
1 teaspoon seasoned salt	5 ml
5 small zucchini, cut into 1-inch (2.5 cm) slices	
1 onion, chopped	
3 fresh tomatoes, each cut into 8 wedges	
2 cups fresh (off the cob) corn or 1 (15 ounce) can corn	330 g/425 g
1 (10 ounce) can beef broth	280 g
2 tablespoons steak sauce	30 ml
1 tablespoon marinade for chicken	15 ml
3 tablespoons cornstarch	20 g

• Place stew meat in sprayed slow cooker and sprinkle with seasoned salt. Top with all vegetables, broth, steak sauce and marinade for chicken. Cover and cook on LOW for 7 to 9 hours.

• Increase heat to HIGH and mix cornstarch with 2 tablespoons (30 ml) water in bowl; stir into stew. Continue cooking while stirring for additional 15 minutes or until mixture thickens. Serves 6.

A Different Stew

2 pounds premium lean beef stew meat	910 g
1 (16 ounce) package frozen Oriental stir-fry vegetables, thawed	455 g
1 (10 ounce) can beefy mushroom soup	280 g
1 (10 ounce) can beef broth	280 g
⅔ cup sweet-and-sour sauce	150 ml
1 tablespoon beef seasoning	15 ml

• Brown stew meat sprinkled with ½ teaspoon (2 ml) pepper in skillet and place in sprayed slow cooker.

• Combine vegetables, soup, broth, sweet-and-sour sauce, beef seasoning and 1 cup (250 ml) water in bowl. Pour over stew meat and stir well. Cover and cook on LOW for 5 to 7 hours. Serves 4 to 6.

Minute-Fix Stew

1 pound lean ground beef	455 g
1 (14 ounce) can beef broth	395 g
3 ribs celery, sliced	
1 (15 ounce) can stewed tomatoes	425 g
1 (8 ounce) can whole kernel corn	230 g
2 (15 ounce) cans stew vegetables	2 (425 g)

• Brown beef in skillet, drain and combine with broth, celery, tomatoes, corn and stew vegetables in sprayed slow cooker. Cover and cook on LOW for 5 to 7 hours. Serves 6.

Hearty Ranch Bean Stew

1 pound lean beef stew meat	455 g
1 pound pork loin, cubed	455 g
1 (14 ounce) can beef broth	395 g
2 (15 ounce) cans chili beans, drained	2 (425 g)
2 (15 ounce) cans Mexican stewed tomatoes	2 (425 g)
1 (10 ounce) package frozen chopped bell peppers	
and onions, thawed	280 g
1 (11 ounce) can Mexicorn®	310 g
1 (0.4 ounce) packet ranch dressing mix	10 g
1 teaspoon ground cumin	5 ml
1 ancho chile	
2 cups crushed tortilla chips	110 g

- Combine stew meat, pork, broth, beans, tomatoes, bell peppers and onions, corn, dressing mix, cumin, chile, ½ cup (125 ml) water and 1 teaspoon (5 ml) salt in sprayed slow cooker. Cover and cook on LOW for 8 to 10 hours.

- Sprinkle crushed chips over each serving. Serves 6 to 8.

Hearty Stew Filled with Cheese

2 pounds lean ground beef	910 g
2 (14 ounce) cans beef broth	2 (395 g)
1 green bell pepper, seeded, chopped	
1 (11 ounce) can Mexicorn®	310 g
2 (15 ounce) cans pinto beans, drained	2 (425 g)
1 (15 ounce) can stewed tomatoes	425 g
½ teaspoon cayenne pepper	2 ml
1 (16 ounce) package shredded Velveeta® cheese	455 g

- Cook ground beef in large skillet over medium heat, stirring often for about 10 minutes. Drain and place in sprayed slow cooker.

- Add broth, bell pepper, corn, beans, tomatoes and cayenne pepper. Cover and cook on LOW for 7 to 9 hours.

- Stir in cheese; cover and cook for about 15 minutes or until cheese melts. Serves 8.

TIP: Cornbread is a "must" to serve with this stew.

Olé! for Stew

1½ - 2 pounds lean beef stew meat	680 - 910 g
2 (15 ounce) cans pinto beans with liquid	2 (425 g)
1 onion, chopped	
3 carrots, sliced	
2 medium potatoes, cubed	
1 (1 ounce) packet taco seasoning	30 g
2 (15 ounce) cans Mexican stewed tomatoes	2 (425 g)
Flour tortillas, optional	

- Brown stew meat in non-stick skillet. Combine meat, pinto beans, onion, carrots, potatoes, taco seasoning and 2 cups (500 ml) water in sprayed large slow cooker. Cover and cook on LOW for 6 to 7 hours. Add stewed tomatoes, cover and cook for additional 1 hour. Serves 4 to 6.

TIP: This is great served with warmed, buttered, flour tortillas.

Santa Fe Stew

A hearty, filling stew.

1½ pounds lean ground beef	680 g
1 (14 ounce) can beef broth	395 g
1 (15 ounce) can whole kernel corn with liquid	425 g
2 (15 ounce) cans pinto beans with liquid	2 (425 g)
2 (15 ounce) cans Mexican stewed tomatoes	2 (425 g)
1 teaspoon beef seasoning	5 ml
1 (16 ounce) package cubed Velveeta® cheese	455 g

- Brown beef in skillet until no longer pink. Place in sprayed slow cooker and add broth, corn, beans, tomatoes and beef seasoning. Cover and cook on LOW for 5 to 6 hours. Fold in cheese and stir until cheese melts. Serves 6 to 8.

TIP: Cornbread is a "must" to serve with this stew.

Hearty Bean Stew

1½ pounds lean ground beef	680 g
6 slices bacon, chopped	
1 (15 ounce) can navy beans, drained	425 g
1 (15 ounce) can kidney beans, rinsed, drained	425 g
1 (15 ounce) can pinto beans with jalapenos, drained	425 g
1 (15 ounce) can butter beans, rinsed, drained	425 g
1 (10 ounce) can diced tomatoes and green chilies	280 g
2 (15 ounce) cans sloppy Joe sauce	2 (425 g)

- Cook beef and bacon in skillet until meat is no longer pink. Drain. Place beef-bacon mixture in sprayed slow cooker and stir in beans, tomatoes and green chilies, sloppy Joe sauce and 2 cups (500 ml) water. Cover and cook on LOW for 4 to 6 hours or on HIGH for 2 to 3 hours. Serves 8.

Blue Norther Stew

1½ pounds lean ground beef	680 g
1 onion, chopped	
1 (1 ounce) packet taco seasoning	30 g
1 (1 ounce) packet ranch dressing mix	30 g
1 (15 ounce) can whole kernel corn	425 g
1 (15 ounce) can kidney beans, rinsed, drained	425 g
2 (15 ounce) can pinto beans, rinsed, drained	2 (425 g)
2 (15 ounce) cans Mexican stewed tomatoes	2 (425 g)
1 (10 ounce) can diced tomatoes and green chilies	280 g

- Brown beef in skillet, drain and combine with onion, taco seasoning, ranch dressing mix, corn, kidney beans, pinto beans, 1 cup (250 ml) water and tomatoes and green chilies in sprayed slow cooker. Cover and cook on LOW for 7 to 9 hours. Serves 8.

Pirate Stew for the Crew

3 pound beef chuck roast, cut into cubes	1.4 kg
2 (15 ounce) cans diced tomatoes	2 (425 g)
1 (32 ounce) can cocktail vegetable juice	945 ml
2 (14 ounce) cans beef broth	2 (395 g)
2 (15 ounce) cans cut green beans, drained	2 (425 g)
2 (15 ounce) cans field peas with snaps, drained	2 (425 g)
1 (12 ounce) package shredded carrots	340 g
2 (15 ounce) cans lima beans, drained	2 (425 g)
2 (16 ounce) package frozen corn, thawed	2 (455 g)
3 onions, chopped	
2 medium potatoes, peeled, cubed	

- Combine beef cubes, tomatoes, vegetable juice, broth, green beans, field peas, carrots, lima beans, corn, onions, 2 cups (500 ml) water and potatoes in sprayed slow cooker. Cover and cook on LOW for 8 to 10 hours. Serves 12 to 14.

TIP: Serve half the stew and freeze remainder for another supper.

Easy Beef and Bean Stew

2 pound beef chuck roast, cut in ¾-inch pieces	910 g/1.8 cm
1 (15 ounce) can pinto beans, drained	425 g
1 (15 ounce) can navy beans, drained	425 g
1 (8 ounce) can sliced carrots, drained	230 g
2 (15 ounce) cans stewed tomatoes with liquid	2 (425 g)

- Sprinkle beef pieces with a little salt and pepper and place in sprayed slow cooker. Add pinto beans, navy beans, carrots and tomatoes. Cover and cook on LOW for 8 to 9 hours. Serves 8 to10.

Blue Ribbon Beef Stew

1 (2½ - 3 pound) beef chuck roast, cubed	1.1 - 1.4 kg
2 (14 ounce) cans beef broth	2 (395 g)
1 teaspoon dried thyme	5 ml
2 teaspoons minced garlic	10 ml
1 pound new (red) potatoes, quartered	455 g
2 carrots, peeled, sliced	
3 ribs celery, sliced	
1 (1 ounce) packet onion soup mix	30 g
1 (16 ounce) package frozen green peas, thawed, drained	455 g

• Combine cubed beef, broth, ¾ cup (175 ml) water, thyme, garlic, potatoes, carrots, celery and onion soup mix in sprayed slow cooker. Cover and cook on LOW for 7 to 9 hours.

• Stir in green peas, cover and let stand for about 10 minutes. Serves 6 to 8.

South-of-the-Border Beef Stew

1½ - 2 pounds boneless, beef chuck roast	680 - 910 g
1 green bell pepper, cut into ½-inch (1.2 cm) slices	
2 onions, coarsely chopped	
2 (15 ounce) cans pinto beans with liquid	2 (425 g)
½ cup rice	95 g
1 (14 ounce) can beef broth	395 g
2 (15 ounce) cans Mexican stewed tomatoes	2 (425 g)
1 cup mild or medium green salsa	265 g
2 teaspoons ground cumin	10 ml
Flour tortillas	

• Trim fat from beef and cut into 1-inch (2.5 cm) cubes. Brown beef in large skillet and place in sprayed, large slow cooker.

• Add remaining ingredients plus 1½ cups (375 ml) water and a little salt. Cover and cook on LOW for 7 to 8 hours. Serve with warm flour tortillas. Serves 6 to 8.

Roast and Vegetable Stew

3 cups leftover roast beef, cubed	420 g
2 (15 ounce) cans stewed tomatoes	2 (425 g)
1 (16 ounce) package frozen mixed vegetables, thawed	455 g
2 (14 ounce) cans beef broth	2 (395 g)
1 cup cauliflower florets	100 g
1 cup broccoli florets	70 g

• Combine all ingredients except cauliflower and broccoli in sprayed slow cooker. Add a little salt and pepper. Cover and cook on LOW for 3 to 4 hours. Stir in cauliflower and broccoli, cover and cook for additional 2 hours until tender. Serves 6 to 8.

Italian Stew

1 (18 ounce) package frozen Italian meatballs, thawed	510 g
1 (16 ounce) package frozen chopped bell peppers and onions, thawed	455 g
2 (15 ounce) cans Italian stewed tomatoes	2 (425 g)
1 (8 ounce) can sliced carrots, drained	230 g
¼ cup tomato paste	65 g
2 tablespoons cornstarch	15 g
1 (10 ounce) package frozen green peas, thawed	280 g
½ cup grated parmesan cheese	50 g

- Combine meatballs, bell peppers and onions, stewed tomatoes, carrots, tomato paste and ½ teaspoon (2 ml) salt in sprayed slow cooker. Cover and cook on LOW for 6 to 8 hours.

- About 30 minutes before serving, combine cornstarch and 2 tablespoons (30 ml) water in bowl, mixing well. Add cornstarch and green peas to slow cooker, stirring to mix well.

- Increase heat to HIGH and cook for additional 15 to 20 minutes or until stew thickens. Sprinkle 1 spoonful of cheese over each serving. Serves 4 to 5.

Meatball Stew

1 (18 ounce) package frozen prepared Italian meatballs, thawed	510 g
1 (14 ounce) can beef broth	395 g
1 (15 ounce) can cut green beans	425 g
1 (16 ounce) package baby carrots	455 g
2 (15 ounce) cans stewed tomatoes	2 (425 g)
1 tablespoon Worcestershire sauce	15 ml
½ teaspoon ground allspice	2 ml

- Combine all ingredients in sprayed slow cooker. Cover and cook on LOW for 3 to 5 hours. Serves 4 to 6.

Easy Meatball-Veggie Stew

1 (18 ounce) package frozen cooked meatballs, thawed	510 g
1 (16 ounce) package frozen mixed vegetables	455 g
1 (15 ounce) can stewed tomatoes	425 g
1 (12 ounce) jar beef gravy	340 g
2 teaspoons crushed dried basil	10 ml

- Place meatballs and mixed vegetables in sprayed slow cooker.

- Combine stewed tomatoes, gravy, basil, ½ teaspoon (2 ml) black pepper and ½ cup (125 ml) water in bowl. Pour over meatballs and vegetables. Cover and cook on LOW for 6 to 7 hours. Serves 4 to 6.

Blue Ribbon Meatball Stew

1 (28 ounce) package frozen meatballs, thawed	795 g
2 (15 ounce) cans Italian stewed tomatoes	2 (425 g)
2 (14 ounce) cans beef broth	2 (395 g)
2 (15 ounce) cans new potatoes	2 (425 g)
1 (16 ounce) package baby carrots	455 g
1 tablespoon Step 1 beef seasoning	15 ml

- Place meatballs, stewed tomatoes, beef broth, potatoes, carrots and beef seasoning in sprayed slow cooker. Cover and cook on LOW for 6 to 7 hours. Serves 6 to 8.

Italian Meatball Stew

1 (18 ounce) package frozen Italian meatballs, thawed	510 g
1 (15 ounce) can Italian stewed tomatoes	425 g
1 (14 ounce) can beef broth	395 g
⅓ cup barley	70 g
3 ribs celery, sliced	
1 (15 ounce) can great northern beans, rinsed, drained	425 g
2 teaspoons Italian seasoning	10 ml
1 (16 ounce) package frozen Italian-style mixed vegetables, thawed	455 g

- Combine meatballs, stewed tomatoes, broth, barley, celery, beans, Italian seasoning and ¼ teaspoon (1 ml) pepper in sprayed slow cooker. Cover and cook on LOW for 4 hours 30 minutes to 5 hours.

- Stir in mixed vegetables; increase heat to HIGH and cook for additional 15 to 20 minutes. Serves 6.

Major Meatball Stew

1 (18 ounce) package frozen meatballs, thawed	510 g
2 (15 ounce) cans Italian-style stewed tomatoes	2 (425 g)
1 (15 ounce) can cannelloni beans, rinsed, drained	425 g
1 (15 ounce) can pinto beans, drained	425 g
2 carrots, peeled, sliced	
1 (4 ounce) can diced green chilies	115 g
1 teaspoon Italian seasoning	5 ml
1 cup shredded mozzarella cheese	115 g

- Combine meatballs, tomatoes, beans, carrots, green chilies and seasoning in sprayed, large slow cooker and stir to blend well. Cover and cook on LOW for 5 to 7 hours or on HIGH for 2 hours 30 minutes to 3 hours 30 minutes. Top each serving with 1 heaping tablespoon (15 ml) cheese. Serves 6.

Bronco Stew

2 pounds ground round steak, cut into 1-inch pieces	910 g (2.5 cm)
1 (16 ounce) package frozen chopped bell peppers and onions, thawed	455 g
1 (14 ounce) can beef broth	395 g
1 (1 ounce) packet taco seasoning	30 g
2 (15 ounce) cans Mexican stewed tomatoes	2 (425 g)
2 (15 ounce) cans pinto beans, rinsed, drained	2 (425 g)
1 (16 ounce) package shredded Mexican-style Velveeta® cheese	455 g
1 (13 ounce) package tortilla chips, crushed	370 g

- Combine ground round steak, bell peppers and onions, broth, taco seasoning, tomatoes and beans in sprayed slow cooker. Cover and cook on LOW for 7 to 9 hours.

- Add cheese and stir until cheese melts. Place about ¾ cup (40 g) crushed chips in individual soup bowls, spoon stew over chips and serve immediately. Serves 8.

Steakhouse Stew

1 pound beef round steak, cut into 1-inch pieces	455 g (2.5 cm)
1 (15 ounce) can stewed tomatoes	425 g
1 (14 ounce) can beef broth	395 g
2 (10 ounce) cans French onion soup	2 (280 g)
1 (10 ounce) can tomato soup	280 g
1 (16 ounce) package frozen stew vegetables, thawed	455 g

- Combine steak pieces, tomatoes, broth, onion soup, tomato soup, 1 cup (250 ml) water and stew vegetables in sprayed slow cooker. Cover and cook on LOW for 7 to 9 hours. Serves 6 to 8.

Green Chile Stew Pot (Caldillo)

2 pounds round steak, cut into cubes	910 g
1 (14 ounce) can beef broth	395 g
2 large onions, chopped	
2 large potatoes, peeled, cubed	
2 teaspoons minced garlic	10 ml
6 - 8 fresh green chilies, roasted, peeled, seeded, diced	

- Combine steak cubes, broth, onions, potatoes, garlic, chilies, 1 teaspoon (5 ml) salt and a little pepper in sprayed slow cooker. Cover and cook on LOW for 7 to 9 hours. Serves 6.

Border-Crossing Stew

1½ pounds round steak, cut into 1-inch pieces	680 g (2.5 cm)
2 onions, chopped	
1 (14 ounce) can beef broth	395 g
1 (15 ounce) can Mexican-style stewed tomatoes	425 g
1 (7 ounce) can chopped green chilies	200 g
3 medium potatoes, peeled, sliced	
2 teaspoons minced garlic	10 ml
2 teaspoons ground cumin	10 ml

- Combine steak pieces, onions, broth, stewed tomatoes, green chilies, potatoes, garlic, cumin and 1cup (250 ml) water in sprayed slow cooker. Cover and cook on LOW for 7 to 9 hours. Serves 6.

Hungarian Stew

2 pounds boneless short ribs	910 g
1 cup pearl barley	200 g
1 small onion, chopped	
1 green bell pepper, cored, seeded, chopped	
1 teaspoon minced garlic	5 ml
2 (15 ounce) cans kidney beans, drained	2 (425 g)
2 (14 ounce) cans beef broth	2 (395 g)
1 tablespoon paprika	15 ml

- Combine all ingredients plus 1 cup (250 ml) water in sprayed slow cooker. Cover and cook on LOW for 8 to 9 hours or on HIGH for 4 hours 30 minutes to 5 hours. Serves 4 to 6.

Sausage and Shrimp Stew

1 (15 ounce) can stewed tomatoes	425 g
1 potato, peeled, cut into ½-inch (1.2 cm) cubes	
1 (12 ounce) package fresh baby carrots	340 g
1 (15 ounce) can whole baby corn, drained	425 g
½ pound cooked, smoked beef sausage, cut in ½-inch slices	230 g/1.2 cm
1 teaspoon seasoned salt	5 ml
1 (8 ounce) package refrigerated salad shrimp, drained	230 g

- Combine tomatoes, potato, carrots, corn, sausage and seasoned salt in sprayed slow cooker. Cover and cook on LOW for 7 to 9 hours.

- Stir in shrimp, cover and cook for 1 additional hour. Serves 6.

Chicken Stew

4 large boneless, skinless chicken breast halves, cubed
3 medium potatoes, peeled, cubed
1 (26 ounce) jar meatless spaghetti sauce   740 g
1 (15 ounce) can cut green beans, drained   425 g
1 (15 ounce) can whole kernel corn   425 g
1 tablespoon chicken seasoning   15 ml

- Combine chicken, potatoes, spaghetti sauce, green beans, corn, chicken seasoning and ¾ cup (175 ml) water in sprayed slow cooker. Cover and cook on LOW for 6 to 7 hours. Serves 4 to 6.

Chicken Chili Stew

1 pound boneless, skinless chicken breast, cut
    into ½-inch cubes   455g/1.2 cm
1 yellow onion, chopped
1 (10 ounce) package frozen corn, thawed   280 g
2 jalapeno peppers, seeded, chopped
1 (14 ounce) can chicken broth   395 g
2 (15 ounce) cans stewed tomatoes   2 (425 g)
2 tablespoons chili powder   30 ml

- Layer chicken, onion, corn and jalapeno peppers in spayed slow cooker.

- Combine chicken broth, tomatoes and chili powder in large bowl and mix well. Pour broth mixture over chicken-corn mixture. Cover and cook on LOW for 8 hours. Serves 4 to 6.

Favorite Chicken-Tomato Stew

1 pound boneless, skinless chicken breast halves, cut into strips   455 g
1 (10 ounce) package frozen chopped bell peppers
    and onions, thawed   280 g
1 (14 ounce) can chicken broth   395 g
2 (15 ounce) cans Mexican stewed tomatoes   2 (425 g)
2 (15 ounce) cans navy beans, drained   2 (425 g)
1 cup salsa   265 g
2 teaspoons ground cumin   10 ml
1½ cups crushed tortilla chips   85 g

- Combine chicken, bell peppers and onions, broth, tomatoes, beans, salsa and cumin in sprayed slow cooker. Cover and cook on LOW for 5 to 7 hours. Sprinkle crushed tortilla chips on top of each serving. Serves 6 to 8.

Chunky Chicken Stew

2 pounds boneless, skinless chicken thighs, cut	
into 1-inch cubes	910 g/2.5 cm
2 carrots, cut into 1-inch (2.5 cm) chunks	
2 onions, quartered	
3 medium potatoes, peeled, cut into 1-inch (2.5 cm) cubes	
1 (15 ounce) can whole kernel corn, drained	425 g
3 ribs celery, sliced in 1-inch (2.5 cm) pieces	
2 (14 ounce) cans chicken broth	2 (395 g)
1 teaspoon dried thyme leaves	5 ml

- Combine chicken, carrots, onions, potatoes, corn celery, broth, thyme and 1 teaspoon (5 ml) each of salt and pepper in sprayed slow cooker. Cover and cook on LOW for 7 to 9 hours or on HIGH for 4 to 6 hours. Serves 8.

Zesty Chicken Stew

8 boneless, skinless chicken thighs, cut into fourths	
¾ teaspoon dried oregano	4 ml
¾ teaspoon dried basil	4 ml
1 onion, chopped	
1 cup cooking wine	250 ml
1 (14 ounce) can chicken broth	395 g
3 medium new (red) potatoes, cubed	
1 (15 ounce) can diced tomatoes, drained	425 g
1 (8 ounce) can sliced carrots, drained	230 g
3 tablespoons chopped fresh cilantro	5 g
2 cups instant brown rice	370 g

- Combine chicken, oregano, basil, onion, wine, broth, potatoes, tomatoes, carrots and cilantro in sprayed slow cooker. Cover and cook on LOW for 5 to 7 hours.

- Cook brown rice according to package directions and place in individual soup bowls. Spoon stew over rice. Serves 6.

Chicken-Tortellini Stew

1 (9 ounce) package refrigerated cheese-filled tortellini	255 g
2 medium yellow squash, halved, sliced	
1 red bell pepper, seeded, coarsely chopped	
1 onion, chopped	
2 (14 ounce) cans chicken broth	2 (395 g)
1 teaspoon dried rosemary	5 ml
½ teaspoon dried basil	2 ml
2 cups cooked, chopped chicken	280 g

- Place tortellini, squash, bell pepper and onion in sprayed slow cooker. Stir in broth, rosemary, basil and chicken. Cover and cook on LOW for 2 to 4 hours or until tortellini and vegetables are tender. Serves 4.

Chicken Stew over Biscuits

2 (1 ounce) packets chicken gravy mix	2 (30 g)
2 cups sliced celery	200 g
1 (10 ounce) package frozen sliced carrots	280 g
1 (10 ounce) package frozen green peas, thawed	280 g
1 teaspoon dried basil	5 ml
3 cups cooked, cubed chicken	280 g
Buttermilk biscuits	

- Combine gravy mix, 2 cups (500 ml) water, celery, carrots, peas, basil, ¾ teaspoon (4 ml) each of salt and pepper and chicken in sprayed slow cooker. Cover and cook on LOW for 6 to 7 hours. Serve over baked refrigerated buttermilk biscuits. Serves 4 to 6.

TIP: If you like thick stew, mix 2 tablespoons (15 g) cornstarch with ¼ cup (60 ml) water and stir into chicken mixture. Cook for additional 30 minutes to thicken.

Chicken-Sausage Stew

1 (16 ounce) package frozen stew vegetables, thawed	455 g
2 (12 ounce) cans chicken chunks with liquid	2 (340 g)
½ pound Italian sausage, sliced	230 g
2 (15 ounce) cans Italian stewed tomatoes	2 (425 g)
1 (14 ounce) can chicken broth	395 g
¼ teaspoon cayenne pepper	1 ml
1 cup cooked rice	165 g

- Combine vegetables, chicken, sausage, tomatoes, broth, cayenne pepper and ½ teaspoon salt in sprayed slow cooker. Cover and cook on LOW for 5 to 7 hours.

- Stir in cooked rice, cover and cook for additional 15 minutes or until stew is thoroughly hot. Serves 6 to 8.

Chicken and Rice Stew

2 (12 ounce) can chicken chunks with liquid	2 (340 g)
2 (14 ounce) cans chicken broth	2 (395 g)
1 (15 ounce) cans stewed tomatoes	425 g
½ cup hot salsa	130 g
1 (15 ounce) can whole kernel corn	425 g
1 (15 ounce) cans cut green beans, drained	425 g
½ teaspoon ground cumin	2 ml
½ teaspoon chili powder	2 ml
2 cups instant brown rice	370 g

- Combine chicken, broth, tomatoes, salsa, corn, green beans, cumin and chili powder in sprayed slow cooker. Cover and cook on LOW for 4 to 6 hours.

- Stir in instant brown rice; cover and cook for additional 15 minutes or until rice is tender. Serves 6 to 8.

Chicken and Lima Bean Stew

1½ pound boneless, skinless chicken thighs, cubed	680 g
1 (28 ounce) can diced tomatoes	795 g
1 (15 ounce) can baby lima beans, drained	425 g
1 (15 ounce) can whole kernel corn, drained	425 g
1 tablespoon chopped garlic	15 ml
1 tablespoon ground cumin	15 ml
1 tablespoon dried oregano	15 ml
3 tablespoons Worcestershire sauce	45 ml
¼ cup tomato paste	65 g

- Place all ingredients in slow cooker and mix well. Cover and cook on LOW 5 to 6 hours. Serves 6.

Turkey Tango

3 cups cooked, cubed turkey	420 g
3 (14 ounce) cans chicken broth	3 (395 g)
2 (10 ounce) cans diced tomatoes and green chilies	2 (280 g)
1 (15 ounce) can whole kernel corn, drained	425 g
1 onion, chopped	
1 (10 ounce) can tomato soup	280 g
1 teaspoon minced garlic	5 ml
1 teaspoon dried oregano	5 ml
3 tablespoons cornstarch	45 ml

- Combine turkey, broth, tomatoes and green chilies, corn, onion, soup, garlic and oregano in sprayed slow cooker. Cover and cook on LOW for 5 to 7 hours.

- Combine cornstarch with 2 tablespoons (30 ml) water in bowl and stir until smooth. Stir into stew; cover and cook for additional 30 minutes. Stir before serving. Serves 6.

Southern Turnip Greens Stew

2 (16 ounce) packages frozen chopped turnip greens	2 (455 g)
1 (16 ounce) package frozen chopped bell peppers and onions, thawed	455 g
1 (10 ounce) can diced tomatoes and green chilies	280 g
2 cups cooked, diced ham	280 g
2 (14 ounce) cans chicken broth	2 (395 g)

- Combine all ingredients in sprayed slow cooker. Cover and cook on LOW for 5 to 7 hours. Serves 4 to 6.

Corny Turnip Greens Stew

2 cups cooked, chopped ham	280 g
2 (14 ounce) cans chicken broth	2 (395 g)
2 (16 ounce) packages frozen chopped turnip greens	2 (455 g)
1 (16 ounce) package frozen chopped bell peppers	
and onions, thawed	455 g
1 (10 ounce) package frozen corn, thawed	280 g
1 teaspoon sugar	5 ml

- Combine, ham, broth, turnip greens, bell peppers and onions, corn, sugar and a little salt and pepper. Cover and cook on LOW for 5 to 7 hours. Serves 4 to 6.

Ham and Lentil Stew

1 (1 ounce) packet onion-mushroom soup mix	30 g
1 (14 ounce) can chicken broth	395 g
1 cup lentils, rinsed, drained	190 g
2 onions, chopped	
3 ribs celery, thinly sliced	
2 (15 ounce) cans diced tomatoes	2 (425 g)
1 (15 ounce) can sliced carrots, drained	425 g
2 cups cooked, cubed ham	280 g
1 tablespoon apple cider vinegar	15 ml
1 cup instant brown rice	185 g

- Combine soup mix, broth, lentils, onions, celery, tomatoes, carrots, ham, 2 cups (500 ml) water and vinegar in sprayed slow cooker. Cover and cook on LOW for 5 to 7 hours.

- Stir in brown rice, cover and cook for additional 20 minutes. Serves 6.

Ham and Sausage Stew

3 cups cooked, diced ham	420 g
1 pound Polish sausage, sliced	455 g
3 (14 ounce) cans chicken broth	3 (395 g)
2 (15 ounce) cans Mexican stewed tomatoes	2 (425 g)
1 tablespoon ground cumin	15 ml
2 (15 ounce) cans navy or pinto beans, drained	2 (425 g)
2 (15 ounce) cans whole kernel corn, drained	2 (425 g)
Flour tortillas	

- Combine ham, sausage, broth, tomatoes, cumin, beans, corn and 1 teaspoon (5 ml) each of salt and pepper in sprayed slow cooker. Cover and cook on LOW for 5 to 7 hours. Serve with warm, buttered flour tortillas. Serves 8.

Southern Ham Stew

This is great served with cornbread.

2 cups dried black-eyed peas	480 g
3 cups cooked, cubed ham	420 g
1 large onion, chopped	
2 cups sliced celery	200 g
1 (15 ounce) can yellow hominy, drained	425 g
2 (15 ounce) cans stewed tomatoes	2 (425 g)
1 (10 ounce) can chicken broth	280 g
2 teaspoons seasoned salt	10 ml
2 tablespoons cornstarch	15 g

- Rinse and drain dried black-eyed peas in saucepan. Cover peas with water, bring to a boil and drain again.

- Place peas in sprayed large slow cooker and add 5 cups (1.2 L) water, ham, onion, celery, hominy, tomatoes, broth and seasoned salt. Cover and cook on LOW for 7 to 9 hours.

- Mix cornstarch with ⅓ cup (75 ml) water in bowl, turn cooker to HIGH heat, pour in cornstarch mixture and stir well. Cook for about 10 minutes or until stew thickens. Serves 6 to 8.

TIP: If you would like a little spice in the stew, substitute one of the cans of stewed tomatoes with Mexican stewed tomatoes.

Pancho Villa Stew

3 cups cooked, diced ham	420 g
1 pound smoked sausage	455 g
3 (14 ounce) cans chicken broth	3 (395 g)
1 (15 ounce) can diced tomatoes	425 g
1 (7 ounce) can chopped green chilies	200 g
1 onion, chopped	
2 (15 ounce) cans pinto beans with liquid	2 (425 g)
1 (15 ounce) can whole kernel corn	425 g
1 teaspoon garlic powder	5 ml
2 teaspoons ground cumin	10 ml
2 teaspoons cocoa	10 ml
1 teaspoon dried oregano	5 ml
Flour tortillas	

- Cut sausage into ½-inch (1.2 cm) pieces.

- Combine all ingredients except tortillas in sprayed slow cooker and stir well. Cover and cook on LOW for 5 to 7 hours. Serve with buttered flour tortillas. Serves 6 to 8.

Ham and Cabbage Stew

2 (15 ounce) can Italian stewed tomatoes	2 (425 g)
3 cups shredded cabbage	210 g
1 onion, chopped	
1 red bell pepper, seeded, chopped	
2 tablespoons butter, sliced	30 g
1 (14 ounce) can chicken broth	395 g
¾ teaspoon seasoned salt	4 ml
3 cups cooked, diced ham	420 g
Cornbread	

- Combine all ingredients with ¾ teaspoon (4 ml) pepper and 1 cup (250 ml) water in sprayed large slow cooker and stir to mix well. Cover and cook on LOW for 5 to 7 hours. Serve with cornbread. Serves 4 to 6.

Pecos Pork Stew

2 pounds boneless pork shoulder, cubed	910 g
1 (16 ounce) package frozen chopped bell peppers and onions, thawed	455 g
1 teaspoon minced garlic	5 ml
¼ cup chopped fresh cilantro	5 g
3 tablespoons chili powder	45 ml
2 (14 ounce) cans chicken broth	2 (395 g)
2 medium potatoes, peeled, cubed	
1 (16 ounce) package frozen corn, thawed	455 g

- Combine all ingredients in sprayed slow cooker. Cover and cook on LOW for 8 to 10 hours. Serves 6

Posole

A delicious traditional stew in Mexico and the Southwest.

1 pound boneless pork shoulder, cubed	455 g
1 teaspoon minced garlic	5 ml
1 onion, chopped	
1 (15 ounce) can pinto beans, rinsed, drained	425 g
1 (7 ounce) can chopped green chilies	200 g
2 teaspoons chopped fresh cilantro	10 ml
½ teaspoon cayenne pepper	2 ml
2 (14 ounce) cans chicken broth	2 (395 g)
1 (15 ounce) can hominy, drained	425 g

- Combine all ingredients in sprayed slow cooker. Cover and cook on LOW for 7 to 9 hours. Serves 4 to 6.

Pork Stew with a Kick

1 large onion, chopped	
2 teaspoons minced garlic	10 ml
2 pounds boneless pork shoulder, cut into 1-inch pieces	910 g/2.5 cm
¼ cup cornmeal	40 g
1 tablespoon ground cumin	15 ml
½ teaspoon dried oregano leaves	2 ml
2 (15 ounce) cans chili beans with liquid	2 (425 g)
2 (10 ounce) cans diced tomatoes and green chilies	2 (280 g)
1 (10 ounce) can chicken broth	280 g
¼ teaspoon cayenne pepper	1 ml
1 (16 ounce) package frozen corn, thawed	455 g

- Place onion and garlic in sprayed slow cooker and top with pork pieces.

- Combine cornmeal, cumin, oregano and ½ teaspoon (2 ml) salt in bowl; sprinkle over pork and mix well. Stir in beans, tomatoes and green chilies, broth and cayenne pepper. Cover and cook on LOW for 8 to 10 hours.

- Stir in corn and cook for additional 30 minutes or until corn is tender. Serves 6.

Supper-Ready Stew

2 pounds pork shoulder, cut into 1-inch cubes	910 g/2.5 cm
1 large onion, chopped	
2 (15 ounce) cans pinto beans, rinsed, drained	2 (425 g)
1 (12 ounce) package baby carrots, cut in half	340 g
2 ribs celery, sliced	
1 (14 ounce) can chicken broth	395 g
3 tablespoons tomato paste	50 g
1 teaspoon dried thyme	5 ml
1 (10 ounce) can diced tomatoes and green chilies	280 g
1 (3 ounce) package real bacon bits	85 g

- Combine pork cubes, onion, beans, carrots, celery, broth, tomato paste, thyme and a little salt and pepper in sprayed slow cooker. Cover and cook on LOW for 8 to 10 hours or on HIGH for 4 hours.

- Stir in tomatoes and green chilies and cook for additional 15 minutes. Sprinkle about 1 tablespoon (15 ml) bacon bits on each serving. Serves 6 to 7.

Couldn't Be Easier Pork Stew

3 pounds boneless pork shoulder, cubed	1.4 kg
2 baking potatoes, chopped	
1 onion, chopped	
1 (14 ounce) can chicken broth	395 g
1 (18 ounce) bottle barbecue sauce	510 g
1 (15 ounce) can baby lima beans, drained	425 g
1 (15 ounce) can whole kernel corn, drained	425 g
1 (28 ounce) can stewed tomatoes	795 g
½ cup packed brown sugar	110 g

- Combine all ingredients in slow cooker. Cover and cook on LOW 8 to 10 hours, or until potatoes are tender. Serves 8.

Polish Vegetable Stew

1 (10 ounce) package frozen chopped bell peppers and onions, thawed	280 g
2 carrots, peeled chopped	
2 (15 ounce) cans stewed tomatoes	2 (425 g)
2 (15 ounce) cans new potatoes, drained, quartered	2 (425 g)
1 pound Polish sausage, sliced	455 g
1 teaspoon seasoned salt	5 ml
1 (10 ounce) package coleslaw mix	280 g

- Combine bell peppers and onions, carrots, tomatoes, potatoes, sausage and seasoned salt in sprayed slow cooker. Cover and cook on LOW for 5 to 7 hours.

- Stir in coleslaw mix, cover and cook for additional 35 to 40 minutes. Serves 6.

Red Potato-Sausage Stew

1 pound cooked Polish sausage, sliced	455 g
1 pound red potatoes, diced	455 g
1 (14 ounce) can beef broth	395 g
1 onion, cut in wedges	
2 ribs celery, cut in 1-inch (2.5 cm) slices	
1 (10 ounce) package frozen green peas, thawed	280 g
1 (8 ounce) can sliced carrots, drained	230 g
1 teaspoon seasoned salt	5 ml

- Combine sausage, potatoes, broth, onion, celery and a little pepper in sprayed slow cooker. Cover and cook on LOW for 5 to 7 hours or on HIGH for 3 to 5 hours.

- Stir in green peas, carrots and seasoned salt and cook for additional 10 to 15 minutes. Serves 5.

Black Bean Stew Supper

1 pound pork sausage links, thinly sliced	455 g
2 onions, chopped	
1 green bell pepper, seeded, chopped	
3 ribs celery, sliced	
3 (15 ounce) cans black beans, rinsed, drained	3 (425 g)
2 (10 ounce) cans diced tomatoes and green chilies	2 (280 g)
2 (14 ounce) can chicken broth	2 (395 g)

- Combine all ingredients in sprayed slow cooker. Cover and cook on LOW for 5 to 7 hours. Serves 6.

Italian-Style Sausage Stew

1 pound Italian sausage	455 g
2 (15 ounce) cans cannellini beans, rinsed, drained	425 g
1 (15 ounce) cans Italian stewed tomatoes	425 g
3 ribs celery, sliced	
2 (14 ounce) cans chicken broth	2 (395 g)
½ teaspoon Italian seasoning	2 ml
1 (9 ounce) package refrigerated cheese-filled tortellini	455 g

- Brown Italian sausage in non-stick skillet, stirring often, drain and place in sprayed slow cooker. Add beans, tomatoes, celery, broth and seasoning. Cover and cook on LOW for 5 to 6 hours.

- Stir in tortellini, cover and cook for additional 30 minutes. Serves 6.

Serious Bean Stew

1 (16 ounce) package smoked sausage links	455 g
1 (28 ounce) can baked beans with liquid	795 g
1 (15 ounce) can great northern beans with liquid	425 g
1 (15 ounce) can pinto beans with liquid	425 g
1 (15 ounce) can lentil soup	425 g
1 onion, chopped	
1 teaspoon Cajun seasoning	5 ml
2 (15 ounce) cans stewed tomatoes	2 (425 g)
Corn muffins	

- Peel skin from sausage links and slice. Place in sprayed slow cooker, add remaining ingredients and stir to mix. Cover and cook on LOW for 3 to 4 hours. Serve with corn muffins. Serves 6 to 8.

Italian Vegetable Stew

1½ - 2 pounds Italian sausage	680 - 910 g
2 (16 ounce) packages frozen vegetables	2 (455 g)
2 (15 ounce) cans Italian stewed tomatoes	2 (425 g)
1 (14 ounce) can beef broth	395 g
1 teaspoon Italian seasoning	5 ml
½ cup pasta shells	55 g

- Brown sausage and cook in skillet for about 5 minutes and drain.

- Combine sausage, vegetables, stewed tomatoes, broth, Italian seasoning and shells in sprayed slow cooker and mix well. Cover and cook on LOW for 3 to 5 hours. Serves 4 to 6.

Pork-Vegetable Stew

1 (2 pound) pork tenderloin	910 g
1 onion, coarsely chopped	
1 red bell pepper, julienned	
1 (16 ounce) package frozen mixed vegetables, thawed	455 g
2 tablespoons flour	15 g
½ teaspoon dried rosemary leaves	2 ml
½ teaspoon oregano leaves	2 ml
1 (10 ounce) can chicken broth	280 g
1 (6 ounce) package long grain-wild rice	170 g

- Cut tenderloin into 1-inch (2.5 cm) cubes. Brown tenderloin cubes in non-stick skillet and place in sprayed large slow cooker. Add onion, bell pepper and mixed vegetables.

- Combine flour, rosemary and oregano with chicken broth in bowl and pour over vegetables. Cover and cook on LOW for 4 hours to 4 hours 30 minutes.

- When ready to serve, cook rice according to package directions. Serve pork and vegetables over rice. Serves 4 to 6.

Easy-Fix Pork Tenderloin Stew

2 - 3 pounds cooked, cubed pork tenderloin or roast	910 g - 1.4 kg
1 (12 ounce) jar pork gravy	340 g
2 ribs celery, sliced	
1 red bell pepper, seeded, chopped	
1 cup salsa	265 g
1 teaspoon seasoned salt	5 ml
1(16 ounce) package frozen stew vegetables, thawed	455 g

- Combine pork, gravy, ½ cup (125 ml) water, celery, bell pepper, salsa, seasoned salt and stew vegetables in sprayed slow cooker. Cover and cook on LOW for 5 to 7 hours. Serves 4 to 6.

Praised Pork Stew

2 (14 ounce) cans chicken broth, divided	2 (395 g)
1 - 2 pound pork tenderloin, cut into 1-inch (2.5 cm) pieces	
3 ribs celery, sliced	
1 (16 ounce) package frozen cut green beans, thawed	455 g
1 (8 ounce) package frozen pearl onions, thawed	230 g
1 (12 ounce) package grated carrots	340 g
2 medium potatoes, peeled, cubed	
1 teaspoon dried thyme	5 ml
¼ cup cornstarch	30 g

- Set aside ½ cup (125 ml) chicken broth.

- Place remaining broth, pork pieces, celery, green beans, onions, carrots, potatoes, thyme and ¾ teaspoon (4 ml) salt in sprayed slow cooker. Cover and cook on LOW for 8 to 10 hours or on HIGH for 4 to 5 hours.

- Combine ½ cup (125 ml) chicken broth with cornstarch in bowl; mix well. (If cooking on LOW, increase heat to HIGH.) Stir broth-cornstarch mixture into stew, cover and cook for additional 30 minutes for stew to thicken. Serves 6 to 8.

Southwest Pork Stew

1 (16 ounce) package frozen chopped bell peppers and onions, thawed	455 g
3 teaspoons minced garlic	15 ml
2 pounds pork tenderloin, cubed	910 g
2 (14 ounce) cans chicken broth	2 (395 g
2 baking potatoes, peeled, cubed	
2 (15 ounce) cans Mexican stewed tomatoes	2 (425 g)
1 (15 ounce) can hominy, drained	425 g
2 teaspoons chili powder	10 ml
1 teaspoon ground cumin	5 ml

- Combine all ingredients and ½ teaspoon (2 ml) salt in sprayed slow cooker. Cover and cook on LOW for 6 to 8 hours. Serves 6.

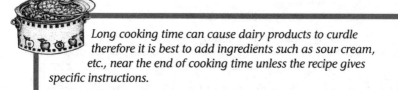

Long cooking time can cause dairy products to curdle therefore it is best to add ingredients such as sour cream, etc., near the end of cooking time unless the recipe gives specific instructions.

Pork, Potatoes, Peas in a Bowl

2 (14 ounce) cans chicken broth, divided	2 (395 g)
1 - 1½ pound boneless pork loin, cut	
into ½-inch (1.2 cm) cubes	455 - 680 g
3 medium potatoes, peeled, cubed	
1 onion, chopped	
1 red bell pepper, seeded, chopped	
½ teaspoon dried thyme	2 ml
¼ cup cornstarch	30 g
1 (16 ounce) package frozen green peas, thawed	455 g

- Set aside ½ can broth.

- Sprinkle pork loin cubes with a little salt and pepper and place in sprayed slow cooker. Add remaining broth, potatoes, onion, bell pepper and thyme. Cover and cook on LOW for 8 to 9 hours or on HIGH for 4 to 5 hours.

- Mix cornstarch with ½ can broth in bowl. (If cooking on LOW, increase heat to HIGH.) Stir green peas and cornstarch-broth mixture into stew. Cover and cook for additional 30 to 45 minutes or until mixture is thick. Serves 6 to 8.

Easy Oyster Stew

4 green onions, finely chopped	
½ cup (1 stick) butter, melted	115 g
1 teaspoon Worcestershire sauce	5 ml
2 (12 ounce) containers fresh oysters with liquid	2 (340 g)
1 (8 ounce) carton whipping cream	230 g
3 cups milk	750 ml
Dash of cayenne pepper	

- Combine onions, butter and Worcestershire in sprayed slow cooker. Cover and cook on LOW for 2 hours or until mixture is hot.

- Stir in oysters with liquid, cream, milk, cayenne pepper and a little salt. Cover and cook for about 30 minutes or until oyster edges begin to curl and stew is thoroughly hot. Serves 6.

Spicy Vegetable Chili

2 (15 ounce) cans stewed tomatoes	2 (425 g)
2 (15 ounce) cans kidney beans, rinsed, drained	2 (425 g)
1 (15 ounce) can tomato sauce	425 g
1 onion, chopped	
2 ribs celery, thinly sliced	
1 (1 ounce) packet chili seasoning mix	30 g

- Combine tomatoes, beans, tomato sauce, onion celery, chili seasoning and 1 cup (250 ml) water in sprayed slow cooker. Cover and cook on LOW for 6 to 7 hours or on HIGH for 3 hours to 3 hours 30 minutes. Serves 5 to 6.

Bean and Corn Chili

2 (15 ounce) cans pinto beans, drained	2 (425 g)
2 (11 ounce) cans Mexicorn®, drained	2 (310 g)
1 (28 ounce) cans stewed tomatoes	795 g
1 (10 ounce) package frozen chopped bell peppers	
and onions, thawed	280 g
2 teaspoons minced garlic	10 ml
2½ tablespoons chili powder	35 ml
1 tablespoon ground cumin	15 ml
1 teaspoon dried oregano	5 ml
½ teaspoon hot sauce	2 ml

- Combine beans, corn, tomatoes, bell peppers and onions, garlic, chili powder, cumin, oregano and 1 teaspoon (5 ml) salt in sprayed slow cooker. Cover and cook on LOW for 5 to 6 hours or on HIGH for 3 to 4 hours. Stir in hot sauce. Serves 6 to 8.

Chunky Veggie Chili

1 (15 ounce) can lima beans, rinsed, drained	425 g
1 (15 ounce) can kidney beans, rinsed, drained	425 g
1 (12 ounce) package baby carrots, cut in halves	340 g
1 (11 ounce) can Mexicorn®, drained	310 g
2 ribs celery, cut in 1-inch (2.5 cm) pieces	
2 onions, coarsely chopped	
1 (8 ounce) can tomato paste	230 g
1 (4 ounce) can diced green chilies	115 g
1 tablespoon chili powder	15 ml
2 teaspoons ground cumin	10 ml
1 (10 ounce) can vegetable broth	280 g

- Combine beans, carrots, Mexicorn®, celery, onion, tomato paste, green chilies, chili powder and cumin in sprayed slow cooker. Add broth, stirring until vegetables are well mixed.

- Cover and cook on LOW for 5 hours 30 minutes to 6 hours 30 minutes. Stir in 1 teaspoon salt before serving. Serves 6.

Supper-Ready Vegetable Chili

1 (28 ounce) can diced tomatoes	795 g
1 (16 ounce) jar thick-and-chunky salsa	455 g
1 (15 ounce) can black beans (or kidney beans), rinsed, drained	425 g
1 (15 ounce) can pinto beans, drained	425 g
1 (8 ounce) can whole kernel corn	230 g
1 tablespoon chili powder	15 ml
1 (8 ounce) package shredded cheddar cheese	230 g

- Combine tomatoes, salsa, black beans, pinto beans, corn, chili powder and 1 teaspoon (5 ml) salt in sprayed slow cooker. Cover and cook on LOW for 5 to 7 hours. Sprinkle cheese over top of each serving. Serves 6.

First Class Vegetarian Chili

1 tablespoon canola oil	15 ml
1 (16 ounce) package frozen chopped bell peppers and onions, thawed	455 g
1 teaspoon minced garlic	5 ml
2 (15 ounce) cans stewed tomatoes	2 (425 g)
1 (15 ounce) can navy beans, rinsed, drained	425 g
1 (15 ounce) can kidney beans, rinsed, drained	425 g
1 (8 ounce) can whole kernel corn, drained	230 g
¼ cup tomato paste	65 g
2 teaspoons ground cumin	10 ml
1 tablespoon chili powder	15 ml

- Heat oil in skillet on medium-high heat and cook bell peppers and onions, and garlic for about 5 minutes, stirring often. Place mixture in sprayed slow cooker.

- Add tomatoes, beans, corn, tomato paste, cumin, chili powder and a little salt and pepper; mix well. Cover and cook on LOW for 4 to 5 hours. Serves 6.

Favorite Veggie-Lovers' Chili

2 onions, coarsely chopped	
2 (15 ounce) cans diced tomatoes	2 (425 g)
1 cup medium-hot salsa	265 g
2 teaspoons ground cumin	10 ml
½ teaspoon dried oregano	2 ml
2 (15 ounce) cans pinto beans with jalapenos, drained	2 (425 g)
1 (15 ounce) can kidney beans, rinsed, drained	425 g
1 green and 1 red bell pepper, seeded, chopped	
1 cup grated carrots	110 g
2 cup instant rice	190 g
1 (8 ounce) package shredded cheddar cheese	230 g

- Combine onions, tomatoes, salsa, cumin, oregano, beans, bell peppers, carrots and 1 teaspoon (5 ml) salt in sprayed slow cooker. Cover and cook on LOW for 5 to 7 hours.

- Cook rice according to package directions, spoon rice into individual soup bowls and ladle chili over rice. Sprinkle generous amount of cheese on top of each serving. Serves 6.

Vegetables You'll Remember

2 (15 ounce) cans mixed vegetables, drained	2 (425 g)
2 ribs celery, sliced	
1 onion, chopped	
1 (8 ounce) can sliced water chestnuts, drained	230 g
1 (8 ounce) package shredded Velveeta® cheese	230 g
½ cup mayonnaise	110 g
6 tablespoons (¾ stick) butter	90 g
1½ cups crushed round buttery crackers	90 g

- Combine mixed vegetables, celery, onion, water chestnuts, cheese and mayonnaise in sprayed slow cooker. Cover and cook on LOW for 5 to 6 hours.

- Just before serving, melt butter in skillet on medium heat, add cracker crumbs and stir constantly until crumbs are light brown and warm. Sprinkle over vegetables before serving. Serves 8 to 10.

Garden Casserole

1 pound yellow squash, sliced	455 g
1 pound zucchini, sliced	455 g
1 green bell pepper, seeded, chopped	
1 red bell pepper, seeded, chopped	
3 ribs celery, sliced	
2 (10 ounce) cans cream of chicken soup	2 (280 g)
½ cup (1 stick) butter plus 3 tablespoons	160 g
1 (6 ounce) box herb-stuffing mix	170 g

- Combine squash, zucchini, bell peppers, celery and soup in large bowl; gently mix until soup is well mixed with vegetables.

- Melt ½ cup (115 g) butter in skillet and add stuffing mix; mix well and set aside 1 cup for topping. Stir into vegetable-soup mixture and spoon into sprayed slow cooker. Cover and cook on LOW for 3 to 5 hours.

- Reheat the set aside stuffing in same skillet and sprinkle over top of vegetables and drizzle with 3 tablespoons (45 g) melted butter; serve immediately. Serves 8 to 10.

Winter Vegetables

1 (16 ounce) package baby carrots	455 g
8 - 10 small new (red) potatoes, cut in half	
1 (16 ounce) package frozen pearl onions, thawed	455 g
1 (10 ounce) can cream of broccoli soup	280 g
1 (10 ounce) can cheddar cheese soup	280 g
3 ribs celery, cut in 1-inch (2.5 cm) lengths	
1 (10 ounce) package frozen cut green beans, thawed, drained	280 g
1 teaspoon seasoned salt	5 ml

- Combine carrots, potatoes, pearl onions, soups, celery and green beans in sprayed slow cooker. Stir as you sprinkle with seasoned salt and pepper. Cover and cook on LOW for 6 to 7 hours. Serves 10 to 12.

Creamed Vegetable Bake

2 (16 ounce) packages frozen broccoli, cauliflower,	
carrots, thawed	2 (455 g)
1 (10 ounce) package frozen green peas, thawed	280 g
1 (10 ounce) package frozen corn, thawed	280 g
3 ribs celery, cut into 1-inch (2.5 cm) slices	
½ cup milk	125 ml
1 (8 ounce) package cream cheese, softened	230 g
1 (10 ounce) can cream of mushroom soup	280 g
1 (10 ounce) can cheddar cheese soup	280 g
2 cups seasoned croutons	80 g

- Combine broccoli, cauliflower, carrots, peas, corn and celery in sprayed slow cooker.

- Combine milk, cream cheese and mushroom soup in saucepan on medium-low heat. Cook, stirring constantly until cream cheese melts; stir in cheese soup, mix well and pour over vegetables. Cover and cook on LOW for 6 to 8 hours.

- Sprinkle croutons over vegetables just before serving. Serves 10 to 12.

Cajun Beans and Rice

1 pound dry black or kidney beans	455 g
2 onions, chopped	
2 teaspoons minced garlic	10 ml
1 tablespoon ground cumin	15 ml
1 (14 ounce) can chicken broth	400 g
1 cup instant brown rice	190 g

- Place beans in saucepan, cover with water and soak overnight. Drain.

- Combine beans, onion, garlic, cumin, chicken broth, 2 teaspoons (10 ml) salt and 2 cups (500 ml) water in sprayed slow cooker. Cover and cook on LOW for 4 to 6 hours.

- Stir in instant rice, cover and cook for additional 20 minutes. Serves 4 to 6.

TIP: If soaking beans overnight is not an option, place beans in saucepan and add enough water to cover by 2 inches (5 cm). Bring to a boil, reduce heat and simmer for 10 minutes. Let stand for 1 hour, drain and rinse beans.

Better Butter Beans

2 cups sliced celery	200 g
2 onions, chopped	
1 green bell pepper, julienned	
1 (15 ounce) can stewed tomatoes	425 g
¼ cup (½ stick) butter, melted	60 g
1 tablespoon chicken seasoning	15 ml
3 (15 ounce) cans butter beans, drained	3 (425 g)

- Combine all ingredients in sprayed slow cooker and mix well. Cover and cook on LOW for 3 to 4 hours. Serves 6 to 8.

TIP: To make this a one-dish dinner, add 2 to 3 cups (280 to 420 g) cooked, cubed ham.

Italian Beans

2 (15 ounce) cans garbanzo beans, drained	2 (425 g)
1 (15 ounce) can red kidney beans, drained	425 g
1 (15 ounce) can cannellini beans, drained	425 g
2 (15 ounce) cans great northern beans, drained	2 (425 g)
1 teaspoon Italian seasoning	5 ml
1 (1 ounce) packet onion soup mix	30 g
1 teaspoon minced garlic	5 ml
½ cup beef broth	125 ml

- Combine all ingredients in sprayed slow cooker and stir well. Cover and cook on LOW for 5 to 6 hours or on HIGH for 2 hours 30 minutes to 3 hours. Serves 6 to 8.

Creamy Limas

2 (16 ounce) packages frozen baby lima beans, thawed	2 (455 g)
1 (10 ounce) can cream of celery	280 g
1 (10 ounce) can cream of onion soup	280 g
1 red bell pepper, seeded, julienned	
1 (4 ounce) jar sliced mushrooms, drained	115 g
¼ cup milk	60 ml
1 cup shredded cheddar-colby cheese	115 g

- Combine lima beans, soups, bell pepper, mushrooms and ½ teaspoon (2 ml) salt in saucepan and heat just enough to mix well. Pour into sprayed slow cooker. Stir well. Cover and cook on LOW for 8 to 9 hours.

- Just before serving, stir in milk. Spoon limas in serving bowl and sprinkle cheese over top. Serves 6 to 8.

Beans and More Beans

4 thick slices bacon, cooked crisp, crumbled	
1 (15 ounce) can kidney beans, drained	425 g
1 (15 ounce) can lima beans with liquid	425 g
1 (15 ounce) can pinto beans with liquid	425 g
1 (15 ounce) can navy beans with liquid	425 g
1 (15 ounce) can pork and beans with liquid	425 g
1 onion, chopped	
¾ cup chili sauce	205 g
1 cup packed brown sugar	220 g
1 tablespoon Worcestershire sauce	15 ml

- Combine all ingredients in sprayed slow cooker and mix well. Cover and cook on LOW for 5 to 6 hours. Serves 6 to 8.

A Different Bean

3 (15 ounce) cans black beans, rinsed, drained	3 (425 g)
3 (15 ounce) cans great northern beans, rinsed, drained	3 (425 g)
1 (16 ounce) jar hot thick-and-chunky salsa	455 g
½ cup packed brown sugar	110 g

- Combine beans, salsa and brown sugar in sprayed slow cooker. Cover and cook on LOW for 3 to 4 hours. Serves 6 to 8.

TIP: To include pinto beans in this dish, use 2 cans black beans and 1 can pinto beans.

Italian-Style Beans and Rice

1 (16 ounce) package frozen chopped bell peppers and onions, thawed	455 g
2 (15 ounce) cans Italian stewed tomatoes	2 (425 g)
1 (4 ounce) can diced green chilies	115 g
2 (15 ounce) cans great northern beans, rinsed, drained	2 (425 g)
1 teaspoon Italian seasoning	5 ml
1 (14 ounce) can chicken broth	395 g
¼ teaspoon cayenne pepper	1 ml
2 cups instant rice	190 g

- Combine bell peppers and onions, stewed tomatoes, green chilies, beans, Italian seasoning, broth and ½ cup (125 ml) water in sprayed slow cooker. Cover and cook on LOW for 5 to 7 hours.

- Stir in cayenne pepper and rice, cover and cook for 30 minutes or until rice is tender. Serves 8.

Hoppin' John

3 (15 ounce) cans black-eyed peas with liquid	3 (425 g)
1 onion, chopped	
1 (6 ounce) package parmesan-butter rice	170 g
2 cups cooked, chopped ham	280 g
2 tablespoons butter, melted	30 g

- Combine peas, onion, rice mix, ham, butter and 1¾ cups (425 ml) water in sprayed slow cooker and mix well. Cover and cook on LOW for 2 to 4 hours. Serves 6 to 8.

Southerner's Red Beans

1 (10 ounce) package frozen chopped bell peppers and onions, thawed	280 g
2 (15 ounce) cans kidney beans, rinsed, drained	2 (425 g)
1 (4 ounce) can diced green chilies	115 g
4 slices bacon, cut into ½-inch pieces	4 (1.2 cm)
1 (8 ounce) can tomato sauce	230 g
1 teaspoon minced garlic	5 ml
1 teaspoon dried thyme	5 ml

- Place bell peppers and onions in sprayed slow cooker. Layer beans, green chilies, bacon, tomato sauce, garlic and thyme. Cover and cook on LOW for 4 to 6 hours. Stir before serving. Serves 8.

TIP: Southerners serve beans with a bottle of pepper sauce.

Saucy Seasoned Red Beans

1 large ham hock	
1 (1 pound) package dried pinto beans, rinsed	455 g
1 large onion, chopped	
8 strips bacon, cooked, chopped	
1 (15 ounce) can stewed tomatoes with liquid	455 g
1 (7 ounce) can diced green chilies	200 g
1 teaspoon dried cilantro	

- Place ham hock, beans and onion in sprayed slow cooker. Add 10 to 11 cups (2.4 to 2.6 L) water and cook on LOW for 8 to 10 hours or overnight.

- Remove ham hock and cut off small pieces of ham. Stir in pieces of ham, 1 teaspoon salt (5 ml), bacon, tomatoes, green chilies and cilantro; cover and cook for additional 30 minutes. Serves 10 to 12.

TIP: If beans are cooked overnight, refrigerate until serving time. The flavor will improve when beans are reheated.

Record-Breaking Beans

1 pound dried pinto beans	455 g
2 onions, finely chopped	
1 green bell pepper, seeded, chopped	
1 (18 ounce) bottle barbecue sauce	510 g
½ cup molasses	125 ml

- Sort beans; rinse twice and drain twice. Place beans, onions, bell pepper, barbecue sauce, molasses, ½ teaspoon (2 ml) pepper and 3½ cups (875 ml) water in sprayed slow cooker. Stir to mix well. Cover and cook on LOW for 8 to 9 hours or until beans are tender. Before serving, stir in 1 teaspoon (5 ml) salt. Serves 6 to 8.

Protein-Packed Beans and Corn

1 (15 ounce) can pinto beans, drained	425 g
1 (15 ounce) can black beans, rinsed, drained	425 g
1 (10 ounce) package frozen corn	280 g
1 (15 ounce) can tomato sauce	425 g
1 (1 ounce) packet chili seasoning	30 g
2 (15 ounce) cans Mexican stewed tomatoes with liquid	2 (425 g)

- Combine pinto beans, black beans, corn, tomato sauce, chili seasoning, tomatoes and 1 cup (250 ml) water in sprayed slow cooker, mix well. Cover and cook on LOW for 6 to 7 hours. Serves 6.

Barbecued Beans

2 (15 ounce) cans pinto beans, rinsed, drained	2 (425 g)
2 (15 ounce) cans navy beans, rinsed, drained	2 (425 g)
1 teaspoon minced garlic	5 ml
1 onion, finely chopped	
¾ cup ketchup	205 g
½ cup packed brown sugar	110 g
¼ cup barbecue sauce	70 g
1 tablespoon Worcestershire sauce	15 ml
1 tablespoon chili powder	15 ml
Dash of red pepper sauce, optional	
1 (3 ounce) package precooked crumbled bacon	85 g

- Place beans, garlic, onion, ketchup, brown sugar, barbecue sauce, Worcestershire and chili powder in sprayed slow cooker. Gently stir and sprinkle crumbled bacon on top. Cover and cook on LOW for 4 to 6 hours. Serves 10.

TIP: *If taking these beans for potluck, secure the lid on cooker and plug in when you arrive. Beans will keep on LOW for 2 hours.*

Beans to the Rescue

1 pound dried pinto beans	455 g
⅓ cup brown rice	60 g
1 (32 ounce) carton chicken broth	910 g
1 (8 ounce) package small smoked cocktail sausage links	230 g
1 (10 ounce) package frozen chopped bell peppers	
and onions, thawed	280 g
1 teaspoon minced garlic	5 ml
½ teaspoon extra spicy salt-free seasoning	2 ml
1 (11 ounce) can Mexicorn®, drained	310 g

- Rinse and drain dried beans. Place beans, rice, broth, sausage, bell peppers and onions, garlic, and spicy seasoning in sprayed slow cooker. Cover and cook on LOW for 7 to 9 hours.

- Stir in corn, cover and cook for additional 30 minutes. Serves 6.

Bountiful Bean Bake

2 (15 ounce) cans navy beans, rinsed, drained	2 (425 g)
1 (15 ounce) can butter beans, rinsed, drained	425 g
1 (12 ounce) package grated carrots	340 g
1 (10 ounce) package frozen chopped bell peppers	
and onions, thawed	280 g
2 ribs celery, sliced	
1 teaspoon dried marjoram	5 ml
½ - 1 pound cooked smoked sausage, cut	
into ½-inch (1.2 cm) slices	230 - 455 g
½ cup chicken broth	125 ml

- Combine beans, carrots, bell peppers and onions, celery, marjoram, sausage, broth and ½ teaspoon salt in sprayed slow cooker. Cover and cook on LOW for 6 to 8 hours. Stir before serving. Serves 6.

Great Beans and Tomatoes

1 pound dried navy beans, sorted, rinsed	455 g
1½ cups cooked, cubed ham	210 g
1 (10 ounce) package frozen chopped bell peppers	
and onions, thawed	280 g
1 (14 ounce) can chicken broth	395 g
1 teaspoon dried basil	5 ml
¾ cup oil-packed sun-dried tomatoes, finely chopped	40 g

- Combine beans, ham, bell pepper and onions, broth, basil and 4 cups (1 L) water in sprayed slow cooker. Cover and cook on LOW for 5 to 7 hours or until beans are tender.

- About half way through cooking time, stir and check if more water is needed. Stir in sun-dried tomatoes before serving. Serves 6.

Maple Baked Beans

2 cups dried navy beans, sorted, rinsed	525 g
1 (10 ounce) package frozen chopped bell peppers	
and onions, thawed	280 g
1½ cups cooked, chopped ham	210 g
¾ cup maple syrup	175 ml
¼ cup packed brown sugar	55 g
1 teaspoon dry mustard	5 ml
½ teaspoon ground ginger	2 ml
Dash of hot sauce	

- Place beans in large saucepan with about 10 cups (2.4 L) water; heat to boiling. Reduce heat, cover and simmer for 2 hours, drain.

- Spoon beans into sprayed slow cooker; add ¾ cup (175 ml) water, bell peppers and onions, ham, syrup, brown sugar, mustard, ginger, and 1 teaspoon salt. Cover and cook on LOW for 8 to 10 hours or until most liquid has been absorbed.

- Stir in the dash of hot sauce. Serves 8.

Best Bean Bake

2 (15 ounce) cans baked beans	2 (425 g)
5 slices bacon, fried, crumbled	
1 (10 ounce) package frozen chopped bell peppers	
and onions, thawed	280 g
2 teaspoons chili powder	10 ml
1 teaspoon mustard	5 ml
1 cup chunky hot (or mild) salsa	265 g
⅓ cup packed brown sugar	75 g

- Drain 1 can of beans and place in sprayed slow cooker. Add second can beans with liquid. Stir in crumbled bacon, bell peppers and onions, chili powder, mustard, salsa, and brown sugar. Cover and cook on LOW for 8 to 10 hours or on HIGH for 3 to 4 hours. Serves 6 to 8.

TIP: These beans are great served with ham.

As with any recipe, read the entire recipe before you begin preparing food for the slow cooker.

Black-Eyes for Luck

1 (16 ounce) package frozen black-eyed peas, thawed	455 g
⅓ cup rice	30 g
1 cup cooked, chopped ham	140 g
1 (10 ounce) can diced tomatoes and green chilies	280 g
1 (10 ounce) package frozen chopped bell peppers	
and onions, thawed	280 g
1 teaspoon dried oregano	5 ml
1 (10 ounce) can chicken broth	280 g

- Place black-eyed peas, rice, ham, tomatoes and green chilies, bell peppers and onions, oregano, broth, and ½ teaspoon (2 ml) salt in sprayed slow cooker. Cover and cook on LOW for 5 to 6 hours. Serves 6.

Another Rice and Beans

2 (15 ounce) cans navy beans, rinsed, drained	2 (425 g)
1 (6 ounce) box long grain-wild rice	170 g
1 (14 ounce) can chicken broth	395 g
¼ cup (½ stick) butter, melted	55 g
3 ribs celery, sliced	
1 small onion, chopped	
¾ cup pesto sauce	190 g
⅓ cup grated parmesan cheese	35 g

- Combine beans, rice, contents of seasoning packet, broth, melted butter, celery and ½ cup (125 ml) water in sprayed slow cooker. Cover and cook on LOW for 3 to 3 hours 30 minutes or until rice is tender.

- Remove crockery insert to heatproof surface and stir in pesto sauce and cheese. Cover and let stand for about 5 minutes or until cheese melts. Serve immediately. Serves 6 to 8.

Spicy Spanish Rice

1½ cups white rice	280 g
1 (10 ounce) can diced tomatoes and green chilies	280 g
1 (15 ounce) can stewed tomatoes	425 g
1 (1 ounce) packet taco seasoning	30 g
1 large onion, chopped	

- Combine all ingredients plus 2 cups (500 ml) water in sprayed slow cooker and stir well. Cover and cook on LOW for 5 to 7 hours. (The flavor will go through the rice better if you stir 2 or 3 times during cooking time.) Serves 4.

TIP: Make this "a main dish" by slicing 1 pound (455 g) Polish sausage slices to rice mixture.

Delicious Risotto Rice

1½ cups Italian risotto rice	280 g
3 (14 ounce) cans chicken broth	3 (395 g)
3 tablespoons butter, melted	40 g
1½ cups sliced, fresh mushrooms	110 g
1 cup sliced celery	100 g

- Combine rice, broth, butter, mushrooms and celery in sprayed slow cooker. Cover and cook on LOW for 2 to 3 hours or until rice is tender. Serves 4 to 6.

Creamy Rice Casserole

2 (6 ounce) boxes long grain-wild rice mix	2 (170 g)
1 (10 ounce) can cream of chicken soup	280 g
½ cup (1 stick) butter, melted	115 g
1 (10 ounce) package frozen chopped bell peppers and onions, thawed	280 g
3 ribs celery, thinly sliced	
1 (4 ounce) can diced pimentos	115 g
1 (8 ounce) package shredded Velveeta® cheese	230 g

- Place rice mix, contents of seasoning packet, 2½ cups (625 g) water, soup, butter, bell peppers and onions, celery, pimentos, and cheese in sprayed slow cooker. Cover and cook on LOW for 6 to 10 hours or on HIGH for 2 to 3 hours 30 minutes. Serves 6 to 8.

Flavors of Autumn

1 cup brown rice	185 g
1½ cups orange juice	375 ml
1 apple, peeled, cored, chopped	
⅓ cup Craisins®	40 g
⅓ cup chopped pecans	40 g
2 tablespoons brown sugar	30 g
½ teaspoon ground cinnamon	2 ml

- Place rice, orange juice, apple, Craisins®, pecans, brown sugar, cinnamon and ½ teaspoon (2 ml) salt in sprayed slow cooker. Cover and cook on LOW for 4 to 5 hours. Serves 4.

Golden Rice

2 cups cooked rice	315 g
1 (16 ounce) package grated carrots	455 g
2 ribs celery, finely chopped	
1 teaspoon seasoned salt	5 ml
½ cup milk	125 ml
2 large eggs, slightly beaten	
1 (8 ounce) package shredded cheddar cheese	230 g
3 slices bacon, fried, crumbled	

- Combine rice, carrots, celery, seasoned salt, milk, eggs and cheese in large bowl and mix well. Spoon into sprayed slow cooker. Cover and cook on LOW for 7 to 9 hours or on HIGH for 2 hours 30 minutes to 3 hours.

- Sprinkle about 1 teaspoon (5 ml) crumbled bacon over each serving. Serves 4 to 6.

Thai Rice and Veggies

1 (14 ounce) can chicken broth	395 g
1 cup rice	185 g
1 tablespoon soy sauce	15 ml
1 (8 ounce) can sliced water chestnuts, rinsed, drained	230 g
2 teaspoons Thai seasoning	10 ml
1 teaspoon minced garlic	5 ml
1 bunch fresh broccoli, cut into florets	

- Combine broth, rice, soy sauce, water chestnuts, Thai seasoning and garlic in sprayed slow cooker. Cover and cook on LOW for 3 to 4 hours.

- Stir in broccoli florets, cover and cook for additional 20 minutes. Serves 6.

Good Fortune Rice and Veggies

1 (16 ounce) package frozen cauliflower, broccoli and carrots	455 g
1 (15 ounce) can pinto beans with jalapenos, drained	425 g
1 (15 ounce) can navy beans, drained	425 g
1 (10 ounce) can cream of onion soup	280 g
2 ribs celery, sliced	
1 cup instant rice	95 g
1 (8 ounce) package shredded Velveeta® cheese	230 g

- Place frozen vegetables and beans in sprayed slow cooker.

- Combine onion soup, celery, rice, cheese and 1 cup (250 ml) water in bowl and pour over vegetable mixture. Cover and cook on LOW for 3 hours 30 minutes to 4 hours 30 minutes or until rice is thoroughly cooked. Stir well before serving. Serves 4 to 5.

Crunchy Couscous

When rice is boring, try couscous.

1 (10 ounce) box original plain couscous	280 g
2 cups sliced celery	200 g
1 red bell pepper, seeded, chopped	
1 yellow bell pepper, seeded, chopped	
1 (16 ounce) jar creamy alfredo sauce	455 g

- Combine couscous, celery, bell peppers, alfredo sauce and 1½ cups (375 ml) water in sprayed slow cooker and mix well. Cover and cook on LOW for 2 hours, stir once or twice.

- Check to make sure celery and peppers are cooked, but still crunchy. Serves 4 to 6.

Carnival Couscous

1 (5.7 ounce) box herbed-chicken couscous	155 g
1 red bell pepper, seeded, julienned	
1 green bell pepper, seeded, julienned	
2 small yellow squash, sliced	
1 (16 ounce) package frozen mixed vegetables, thawed	455 g
1 (10 ounce) can French onion soup	280 g
¼ cup (½ stick) butter, melted	60 g
½ teaspoon seasoned salt	2 ml

- Combine all ingredients with 1½ cups (375 ml) water in sprayed slow cooker and mix well. Cover and cook on LOW for 2 to 4 hours. Serves 4.

Sweet Peppers and Pasta

2 yellow bell peppers, seeded, julienned	
2 green bell peppers, seeded, julienned	
2 (15 ounce) can Mexican stewed tomatoes with liquid	2 (425 g)
1 (15 ounce) can tomato sauce	425 g
2 ribs celery, sliced	
1 (9 ounce) package refrigerated cheese-filled tortellini	255 g
Shredded cheddar cheese	

- Combine bell peppers, tomatoes, tomato sauce and celery in sprayed slow cooker. Cover and cook on LOW for 6 to 8 hours or on HIGH for 3 to 4 hours.

- (If cooking on LOW, increase heat to HIGH.) Stir in tortellini; cover and cook for additional 30 minutes. Serves 10.

Cheese, Spaghetti and Spinach

1 (7 ounce) box ready-cut spaghetti	200 g
2 tablespoons butter	30 g
1 (8 ounce) carton sour cream	230 g
1 cup shredded cheddar cheese	115 g
1 (8 ounce) package Monterey Jack cheese, divided	230 g
1 (12 ounce) package frozen, chopped spinach, thawed, well drained*	340 g
1 (6 ounce) can cheddar french-fried onions, divided	170 g

- Cook spaghetti according to package directions, drain and stir in butter until it melts.

- Combine sour cream, cheddar cheese, half Monterey Jack cheese, spinach and half can onions in large bowl. Fold into spaghetti and spoon into sprayed slow cooker. Cover and cook on LOW for 2 to 4 hours.

- When ready to serve, sprinkle remaining Jack cheese and fried onions over top. Serves 4.

*TIP: Squeeze spinach between paper towels to completely remove excess moisture.

St. Pat's Noodles

1 (12 ounce) package medium noodles	340 g
1 cup half-and-half cream	250 ml
1 (10 ounce) package frozen chopped spinach, thawed	280 g
6 tablespoons (¾ stick) butter, melted	85 g
2 teaspoons seasoned salt	10 ml
1½ cups shredded cheddar-Monterey Jack cheese	170 g

- Cook noodles according to package directions and drain. Place in sprayed slow cooker. Add half-and-half cream, spinach, butter and seasoned salt and stir until they blend well. Cover and cook on LOW for 2 to 3 hours. When ready to serve, fold in cheese. Serves 4.

Healthy Macaroni and Cheese

3 cups milk	750 ml
1 large egg, beaten	
3½ cups shredded cheddar cheese	400 g
1 (8 ounce) package whole wheat macaroni	230 g

- Combine milk, egg and cheddar cheese in bowl, mix well and place in sprayed slow cooker. Cover and cook on HIGH for 1 hour.

- Cook macaroni according to package directions, drain and add to slow cooker and mix well. Reduce heat to LOW, cover and cook for additional 4 hours. Serves 7 to 8.

Credit This
Macaroni and Cheese

1 (8 ounce) package elbow macaroni	230 g
1 (12 ounce) package shredded sharp cheddar cheese	340 g
1 (12 ounce) can evaporated milk	375 g
1¼ cups milk	310 g
2 eggs, beaten	

- Cook macaroni according to package directions and drain. Place macaroni, cheese, evaporated milk, milk, eggs, and a little salt and pepper in sprayed slow cooker. Cover and cook on LOW for 5 to 6 hours or until macaroni and cheese is firm.

- Serve immediately without stirring macaroni and cheese either before or after the cooking process. Serves 6.

Serious Stuffing

¾ cup (1½ sticks) butter	170 g
2 medium onions, finely chopped	
3 ribs celery, sliced	
12 cups day-old bread cubes	710 g
2 teaspoons dried sage	10 ml
1 teaspoon poultry seasoning	5 ml
1 (32 ounce) carton chicken broth	910 g
2 eggs, beaten	

- Melt butter in skillet and cook onion and celery, stirring often, for about 10 minutes. Place in large bowl and add bread cubes, sage and poultry seasoning.

- Stir in enough broth to moisten (you may not need all the broth but it may require all of the 32 ounces – it depends how dry the bread is). Stir in beaten eggs and spoon into sprayed slow cooker. Cover and cook on HIGH for 45 minutes; reduce heat to LOW and cook for 4 to 6 hours. Serves 12.

Main Dishes

Beef • Chicken

Pork • Seafood

Nostalgic Shepherd's Pie

2 pounds lean ground beef	910 g
1 onion, chopped	
1 teaspoon seasoned salt	5 ml
1 (16 ounce) package frozen mixed vegetables	455 g
1 (10 ounce) can tomato soup	280 g
1 (15 ounce) can chili with beans	425 g
1 (16 ounce) container refrigerated mashed potatoes	455 g
Shredded cheddar cheese	

- Cook and slightly brown beef, onion and seasoned salt in large skillet; drain.

- Combine beef mixture, mixed vegetables, soup and chili in sprayed slow cooker. Cover and cook on LOW for 6 to 8 hours or HIGH for 3 to 4 hours.

- Heat mashed potatoes according to package directions. Serve pie with large tablespoon of mashed potatoes on each serving. Sprinkle with cheese. Serves 8.

Supper over Noodles

2 pounds lean ground beef	910 g
¾ cup sweet-and-sour sauce (from 10 ounce bottle)	175
ml/280 g	
1 (10 ounce) package frozen, chopped bell peppers	
and onions, thawed	280 g
2 (14 ounce) packages frozen stir-fry vegetables, thawed	2 (395 g)
2 (3 ounce) packages Oriental-flavor ramen noodles, broken up	2 (85 g)
1 (6 ounce) package chow mein noodles	170 g

- Cook beef in skillet on medium-high heat for about 10 minutes or until beef is no longer pink; stir often. Drain and place in sprayed slow cooker.

- Stir in sweet-and-sour sauce, bell peppers and onions, stir-fry vegetables, 3 cups (750 ml) water and seasoning packet with ramen noodles. Cover and cook on LOW for 6 to 8 hours.

- Stir in ramen noodles; cover and cook for additional 20 to 30 minutes. Place chow mein noodles on individual plates and spoon beef-vegetable mixture over noodles. Serves 8 to 10.

TIP: When ingredients are cooked, taste mixture; you may want a little more flavor by adding remaining sweet-and-sour sauce.

Stuffed Cabbage

10 - 12 large cabbage leaves	
1½ pounds lean ground beef	680 g
½ cup brown rice	95 g
1 egg, beaten	
¼ teaspoon ground cinnamon	1 ml
1 (15 ounce) can tomato sauce	425 g

- Wash cabbage leaves, place in saucepan of boiling water and turn off heat. Soak for about 5 minutes. Remove leaves, drain and cool.

- Combine beef, rice, egg, 1 teaspoon (5 ml) salt, ½ teaspoon (2 ml) pepper and cinnamon in bowl and mix well. Place 2 tablespoons (30 ml) beef mixture on each cabbage leaf and roll tightly. (If you can't get 10 to 12 large leaves, put 2 together to make 1 large leaf.)

- Stack rolls in sprayed, oval slow cooker and pour tomato sauce over rolls. Cover and cook on HIGH for 1 hour, reduce heat to LOW and cook for additional 6 to 7 hours. Serves 4 to 6.

Superior Stuffed Cabbage

⅓ cup rice	60 g
1 large egg, beaten	
½ teaspoon ground allspice	2 ml
¾ teaspoon seasoned salt	4 ml
1½ pounds lean ground beef	680 g
12 outer cabbage leaves	
1 (16 ounce) can whole cranberry sauce	455 g
1 (15 ounce) can stewed tomatoes	425 g
⅓ cup packed brown sugar	75 g
¼ cup lemon juice	60 ml
1 teaspoon Worcestershire sauce	5 ml

- Combine rice, egg, allspice, seasoned salt, beef and about ¾ teaspoon (4 ml) pepper in bowl.

- Spoon rounded ¼ cup (60 ml) rice-beef mixture in center of each cabbage leaf; turn in sides and roll. (Cabbage leaves can be made easier to fold if you will freeze for 24 hours before you are ready to use). Stack cabbage rolls in sprayed slow cooker, seam-side down.

- Combine cranberry sauce, stewed tomatoes, brown sugar, lemon juice and Worcestershire sauce in large saucepan; heat just until mixture blends well. Pour over cabbage rolls. Cover and cook on LOW for 7 hours. Serves 6.

Kid's Favorite Supper

5 slices bacon, fried, crumbled	
1 pound lean ground beef	455 g
1 (10 ounce) package frozen chopped bell peppers	
and onions, thawed	280 g
2 (15 ounce) cans baked beans	2 (425 g)
⅓ cup ketchup	90 g
¼ cup molasses	60 ml
½ teaspoon dry mustard	2 ml

- Set bacon aside for garnish. In same skillet in which bacon was fried, cook beef for 5 to 10 minutes, stirring often; drain and place in sprayed slow cooker.

- Combine bell peppers and onions, beans, ketchup, molasses and mustard in bowl and mix thoroughly. Add mixture to slow cooker. Cover and cook on HIGH for 1 to 1 hour 30 minutes. Garnish with crumbled bacon. Serves 6.

My Man's Meat and Potatoes

1½ pounds lean ground beef	680 g
1 (3 ounce) can french-fried onions, divided	85 g
1 (10 ounce) cream of celery soup	280 g
½ cup milk	125 ml
1 (10 ounce) package frozen chopped bell peppers	
and onions, thawed	280 g
1 red bell pepper, seeded, chopped	
1 (18 ounce) package frozen hash-brown potatoes, thawed	510 g
1 (16 ounce) package frozen cut green beans, thawed	455 g
½ cup crushed potato chips	30 g

- Cook ground beef in skillet on medium heat for about 10 minutes, stirring often or until meat is no longer pink in color; drain. Stir in half fried onions, soup, milk, bell peppers and onions, red bell pepper, and a little salt and pepper; mix well.

- Spread layer of hash browns and then layer of green beans in sprayed slow cooker. Top with layer of beef mixture and spread evenly. Cover and cook on LOW for 6 to 7 hours.

- Combine remaining fried onions and potato chips in bowl and sprinkle over top of casserole. Serves 4 to 6.

Chili Mac for Supper

2 pounds lean ground beef	910 g
1 (15 ounce) can Mexican-style stewed tomatoes	425 g
1 (10 ounce) package frozen chopped bell peppers	
and onions, thawed	280 g
2 tablespoons chili powder	30 ml
1 teaspoon ground cumin	5 ml
2 cups elbow macaroni	210 g

- Cook beef in non-stick skillet, stirring often for about 10 minutes, drain and spoon into sprayed slow cooker.

- Combine tomatoes, bell peppers and onions, chili powder, cumin, and 1 teaspoon (5 ml) salt in bowl. Pour mixture over beef in slow cooker. Cover and cook on LOW for 4 hours.

- Cook macaroni according to package directions, drain and stir into slow cooker. Cover and cook for additional 1 hour. Serves 4 to 5.

Easy Family Supper

1 (15 ounce) can great northern beans, drained	425 g
1 (15 ounce) can red kidney beans, rinsed, drained	425 g
1 (15 ounce) can pinto beans, drained	425 g
1 (15 ounce) can pork and beans	425 g
1 large onion, chopped	
1½ pounds lean ground beef	680 g
6 - 8 slices bacon, cut in 1-inch (2.5 cm) pieces	
1 cup hot and spicy ketchup	270 g
1 cup packed brown sugar	220 g
2 teaspoons mustard	10 ml

- Place beans, onion, beef, bacon, ketchup, brown sugar and mustard in sprayed slow cooker; mix until they blend well. Cover and cook on LOW for 6 hours. Serves 8.

Hash Browns to the Rescue

1 (28 ounce) package frozen shredded hash browns, thawed	795 g
1 pound ground beef	455 g
1 small onion, chopped	
1 (16 ounce) package frozen California-blend vegetables	455 g
1 (10 ounce) can cream of chicken soup	280 g
1 cup milk	250 ml
1 (16 ounce) box Velveeta® cheese, cubed	455 g
1 (3 ounce) can french-fried onions	85 g

- Add hash browns and 1 teaspoon (5 ml) each of salt and pepper to sprayed slow cooker. Brown beef and onion in skillet. Add meat and then vegetables to potatoes. Combine soup and milk and pour into cooker. Cover and cook on LOW for 4 hours.

- Add Velveeta®, cover and cook 30 additional minutes or until cheese melts. Top servings with french-fried onions. Serves 6 to 8.

Hamburger Solution

1½ pounds lean ground beef	680 g
4 medium potatoes, peeled, sliced	
1 (15 ounce) can green beans, drained	425 g
3 carrots, peeled, sliced	
1 (15 ounce) can whole kernel corn, drained	425 g
2 ribs celery, sliced	
2 onions, chopped	
2 (10 ounce) cans tomato soup	280 g

- Brown ground beef in skillet and crumble. Layer potatoes, green beans, carrots, corn, celery, onions and ground beef in sprayed slow cooker. Season with a little salt and pepper as you layer the vegetables.

- Place tomato soup and 1 cup (250 ml) water in saucepan on medium-high heat. Stir and mix, heating just until mixture blends well. Pour mixture over vegetables and beef. Cover and cook on LOW for 6 to 8 hours or on HIGH for 2 to 4 hours. Serves 6 to 8.

It's Time to Eat

1½ pounds lean ground beef	680 g
1 (10 ounce) package frozen, chopped bell peppers and onions, thawed	280 g
5 tablespoons steak sauce	75 ml
2 (15 ounce) cans baked beans with liquid	2 (425 g)
2 (11 ounce) cans Mexicorn®, drained	2 (310 g)
2 cups crushed garlic-flavored croutons	80 g

- Cook beef in skillet on medium-high heat for about 10 minutes or until beef is no longer pink; stir often. Drain and place in sprayed slow cooker and add bell peppers and onions, steak sauce, baked beans, corn and a little salt and pepper. Cover and cook on LOW for 5 to 7 hours.

- Sprinkle with croutons and serve immediately. Serves 8.

TIP: You can make this with turkey, too! Just replace the beef with 1½ pounds (680 g) ground turkey. Replace steak sauce with 2 tablespoons (30 ml) marinade for chicken. Replace baked beans with 2 cans great northern beans. Cook as directed and sprinkle with crushed croutons.

Pop's Beef and Potato Supper

2 pounds lean ground beef	910 g
1 (10 ounce) package frozen, chopped bell peppers and onions, thawed	280 g
3 ribs celery, sliced	
1 (18 ounce) package frozen tater tots, thawed	510 g
1 (8 ounce) package shredded Velveeta® cheese	230 g
2 (10 ounce) cans cream of mushroom soup	2 (280 g)
1 soup can milk	
1 (8 ounce) package shredded cheddar cheese	230 g

- Cook ground beef in skillet over medium-high heat and cook for about 10 minutes or until beef is no longer pink; stir often. Place in sprayed slow cooker.

- Combine bell peppers and onions, celery, tater tots, Velveeta® cheese, soup, and milk; stir until well mixed. Add to cooker. Cover and cook on LOW for 6 to 8 hours.

- Sprinkle with cheese. Serves 8 to 10.

Jack's Meat Loaf

2 pounds lean ground beef	910 g
2 eggs	
½ cup chili sauce	135 g
1¼ cups seasoned breadcrumbs	150 g
1 (8 ounce) package shredded Monterey Jack cheese, divided	230 g

- Make foil handles for slow cooker (see TIP below).

- Combine beef, eggs, chili sauce and breadcrumbs in bowl and mix well. Shape half beef mixture into flat loaf and place in sprayed slow cooker. Sprinkle half cheese over meat loaf and press into meat. Form remaining meat mixture in same shape as first layer, place over cheese and seal seams. Cover and cook on LOW for 6 to 7 hours.

- When ready to serve, sprinkle remaining cheese over loaf and leave in cooker until cheese melts. Carefully remove loaf with foil handles and place on serving plate. Serves 4 to 6.

TIP: *To easily remove loaf from slow cooker, make foil "handles" by cutting 3 (3 x 18 inch/8 x 45 cm) strips of heavy foil; place in bottom of slow cooker in crisscross strips (resembles spokes on wheel) up and over sides. Place loaf on foil. Fold extended foil strips over loaf. When finished cooking, lift loaf out by "handles".*

Meat Loaf Magic

1½ pounds lean ground beef	680 g
⅔ cup cracker crumbs	40 g
2 eggs, beaten	
2 tablespoon plus ½ cup ketchup	170 g
¼ cup finely minced onion	40 g
1 teaspoon seasoned salt	5 ml
1 teaspoon black pepper	5 ml
¼ cup packed brown sugar	55 g
1 teaspoon mustard	5 ml
½ teaspoon ground nutmeg	2 ml

- Make foil handles for meat loaf (see TIP on page 213).

- Combine beef, cracker crumbs, eggs, 2 tablespoons (35 g) ketchup, onion, seasoned salt and black pepper in large bowl. Shape into log or loaf shape and place in sprayed slow cooker. Cover and cook on LOW for 5 to 6 hours.

- A few minutes before serving, combine remaining ketchup, brown sugar, mustard and nutmeg in bowl and spoon over meatloaf. Cover and cook on HIGH for about 15 additional minutes. Serves 6.

Big Family Meat Loaf

1 egg, beaten	
⅓ cup milk	75 ml
1 teaspoon dried thyme	5 ml
2 pounds lean ground beef	910 g
1 pound ground pork	455 g
1 teaspoon minced garlic	5 ml
1⅓ cups Italian breadcrumbs	160 g
1 teaspoon dried parsley	5 ml
1 (12 ounce) jar beef gravy	340 g

- Make foil handles for meat loaf (see TIP on page 213).

- Combine egg, milk, thyme and 1 teaspoon (5 ml) pepper in bowl. Mix well and set aside.

- In separate bowl, combine ground beef, ground pork, garlic, breadcrumbs and parsley in large bowl and mix with spoon until thoroughly blended. Gradually drizzle egg-milk mixture into meat mixture and mix until liquid is absorbed.

- On large piece of wax paper, mold mixture into oblong shape loaf. Place in sprayed large slow cooker for this large meatloaf. Top loaf with beef gravy. Cover and cook on LOW for 6 to 8 hours or on HIGH for 4 to 5 hours. Serves 10 to 12 (or 8 with enough leftover for meatloaf sandwiches the next day).

Mac Cheese Supper

1½ pounds lean ground beef	680 g
2 (7 ounce) packages macaroni and cheese dinners	2 (200 g)
1 (15 ounce) can whole kernel corn, drained	425 g
1½ cups shredded Monterey Jack cheese	170 g

- Sprinkle ground beef with 1 teaspoon (5 ml) salt, brown in skillet until no longer pink and drain. Prepare macaroni and cheese according to package directions.

- Spoon beef, macaroni and corn in sprayed slow cooker and mix well. Cover and cook on LOW for 4 to 5 hours.

- When ready to serve, sprinkle cheese over top and leave in cooker until cheese melts. Serves 4 to 6.

Meat on the Table

1½ - 2 pounds lean ground beef	680 - 910 g
1 (1 ounce) packet beefy onion soup mix	30 g
⅔ cup quick-cooking oats	55 g
2 eggs	
1 (12 ounce) bottle chili sauce, divided	340 g

- Make foil handles for meat loaf (see TIP on page 213).

- Combine beef, onion soup mix, oats, eggs, ¾ cup (204 g) chili sauce and 1 teaspoon (5 ml) pepper in bowl and mix well. Shape meat mixture into round ball, place in sprayed slow cooker and pat down into loaf shape. Cover and cook on LOW for 3 to 4 hours.

- Spread remaining chili sauce over top of loaf, cover and cook for additional 30 minutes. Serves 4 to 6.

Cheeseburger Supper

1 (5 ounce) box bacon and cheddar scalloped potatoes	145 g
⅓ cup milk	75 ml
¼ cup (½ stick) butter, melted	60 g
1½ pounds lean ground beef	680 g
1 onion, coarsely chopped	
Canola oil	
1 (15 ounce) can whole kernel corn with liquid	425 g
1 (8 ounce) package shredded cheddar cheese	230 g

- Place scalloped potatoes in sprayed slow cooker. Pour 2¼ cups (560 ml) boiling water, milk and butter over potatoes.

- Brown ground beef and onion in little oil in skillet, drain and spoon over potatoes. Top with corn. Cover and cook on LOW for 6 to 7 hours. When ready to serve, sprinkle cheese over top. Serves 4 to 6.

Hash Brown Dinner

1½ pounds lean ground chuck, browned	680 g
1 (1 ounce) packet brown gravy mix	30 g
1 (15 ounce) can cream-style corn	425 g
1 (15 ounce) can whole kernel corn	425 g
1 (8 ounce) package shredded cheddar cheese, divided	230 g
1 (18 ounce) package frozen hash browns, partially thawed	510 g
1 (10 ounce) can golden mushroom soup	280 g
1 (5 ounce) can evaporated milk	150 ml

- Place browned beef in sprayed slow cooker and toss with dry brown gravy mix. Add cream-style corn and whole kernel corn and cover with half cheddar cheese. Top with hash browns and remaining cheese.

- Combine mushroom soup and evaporated milk in bowl. Mix well and pour over hash browns and cheese. Cover and cook on LOW for 6 to 8 hours. Serves 4 to 6.

TIP: *For a little change, use ground turkey instead of ground chuck and a packet of alfredo sauce mix instead of the brown gravy mix. Omit the mushroom soup and use 1 can cream of celery soup. Cook as recipe directs.*

Colorful Peppers with Stuffing

6 medium size red bell peppers	
1 pound lean ground beef	455 g
½ cup finely chopped onion	55 g
¾ cup instant rice	70 g
1 (15 ounce) can black beans, rinsed, drained	425 g
⅓ cup seasoned breadcrumbs	40 g
1 (8 ounce) package shredded Monterey Jack cheese, divided	230 g
1 (16 ounce) jar hot chunky salsa, divided	455 g

- Cut tops of bell peppers off and scoop out membranes and seeds. Set aside.

- Cook and brown ground beef in large skillet, stirring to crumble. Drain and stir in onion, rice, beans, breadcrumbs, half cheese and half salsa, mix well. Spoon filling into bell peppers and mound tops on each.

- Place ¾ cup (175 ml) water and remaining salsa in sprayed slow cooker. Arrange stuffed peppers, filling side up in cooker. Cover and cook on LOW for 6 to 7 hours or on HIGH for 3 hours to 3 hours 30 minutes.

- Transfer stuffed peppers to serving plate and sprinkle remaining cheese over tops. Serves 6.

TIP: *These peppers can be served over hot cooked rice with sauce from slow cooker poured over the rice.*

Special Stuffed Peppers

4 large red or yellow bell peppers
1 (8 ounce) can tomato sauce, divided   230 g
1 pound lean ground beef   455 g
1 (15 ounce) can Spanish rice   425 g
1 onion, finely chopped
1 cup seasoned breadcrumbs   120 g
2 tablespoons chopped walnuts   15 g

- Cut tops off bell peppers and scoop out seeds and core. Pour half can tomato sauce into sprayed slow cooker.

- Combine beef, rice, onion, breadcrumbs and ½ teaspoon each of salt and pepper. Stuff mixture into bell peppers and place each in slow cooker. Pour remaining tomato sauce over bell peppers. Cover and cook on HIGH for 4 hours. Serves 4.

Beef and Macaroni Supper

1 (10 ounce) package macaroni, cooked, drained   280 g
3 tablespoons canola oil   45 ml
1½ pounds lean ground beef, browned, drained   680 g
1 onion, chopped
3 ribs celery, chopped
2 (10 ounce) cans tomato soup   2 (280 g)
1 (6 ounce) can tomato paste   170 g
1 teaspoon beef bouillon granules   5 ml
1 (8 ounce) package cubed Velveeta® cheese   230 g

- Toss cooked macaroni with oil to make sure macaroni does not stick together. Place in sprayed slow cooker.

- Add beef, onion, celery, tomato soup, tomato paste, beef bouillon and ⅔ cup (150 ml) water and stir to mix well. Cover and cook on LOW for 3 to 5 hours.

- Stir in cubed cheese, cover and cook for 1 additional hour. Serves 4 to 6.

Purchase a slow cooker that has a removable ceramic insert; it is easier to clean. Allow it to cool completely before washing or soaking. With most models, the removable bowl can be used as a ready-to-go serving dish.

Beef and Bean Medley

1 pound lean ground beef	455 g
1 onion, chopped	
6 slices bacon, cooked, crumbled	
2 (15 ounce) cans pork and beans	2 (425 g)
1 (15 ounce) can butter beans, rinsed, drained	425 g
1 (15 ounce) can kidney beans, rinsed, drained	425 g
¼ cup ketchup	70 g
¼ cup packed brown sugar	70 g
3 tablespoons vinegar	45 ml
1 (13 ounce) bag original corn chips	370 g
1 (8 ounce) package shredded cheddar cheese	230 g

- Brown ground beef and onion in skillet, drain and transfer to sprayed slow cooker. Add bacon and beans.

- Combine ketchup, brown sugar and vinegar in bowl. Add to cooker and stir. Cover and cook on LOW for 4 to 6 hours.

- When ready to serve, spoon over corn chips and sprinkle cheese over top. Serves 4 to 6.

Beef and Noodles al Grande

1½ pounds lean ground beef	680 g
1 (16 ounce) package frozen onions and bell peppers, thawed	455 g
1 (16 ounce) box Velveeta® cheese, cubed	455 g
2 (15 ounce) cans Mexican stewed tomatoes with liquid	425 g
2 (15 ounce) cans whole kernel corn, drained	2 (425 g)
1 (8 ounce) package medium egg noodles	230 g
1 cup shredded cheddar cheese	115 g
Fresh parsley or green onions	

- Brown ground beef in skillet and drain fat. Place beef in sprayed slow cooker, add onions and peppers, cheese, tomatoes, corn, and about 1 teaspoon (5 ml) salt and mix well. Cover and cook on LOW for 4 to 5 hours.

- Cook noodles according to package direction, drain and fold into beef-tomato mixture. Cook for additional 30 minutes to heat thoroughly.

- When ready to serve, top with cheddar cheese, several sprinkles of chopped fresh parsley or chopped fresh green onions. Serves 4 to 6.

Meat and Potatoes

4 medium potatoes, peeled, sliced
1¼ pounds lean ground beef, browned   570 g
1 onion, sliced
1 (10 ounce) can cream of mushroom soup   280 g
1 (10 ounce) can vegetable beef soup   280 g

- Layer all ingredients with a little salt and pepper in sprayed large slow cooker. Cover and cook on LOW for 5 to 6 hours. Serves 4 to 6.

TIP: *For a change, use sliced pork tenderloin instead of beef and 2 cans of fiesta nacho cheese soup instead of the soups in this recipe.*

Beef-Potato Casserole

1 (20 ounce) package frozen hash-brown potatoes, thawed   570 g
1½ pounds lean ground beef, cooked, crumbled   680 g
1 onion, chopped
1 (15 ounce) can sloppy Joe sauce   425 g
1 (10 ounce) can beef broth   280 g
1 (8 ounce) package shredded cheddar cheese   230 g

- Place hash-brown potatoes in sprayed slow cooker.

- Combine crumbled beef, onion, sloppy Joe sauce and broth in bowl. Mix well and spoon over potatoes. Cover and cook on LOW for 6 to 8 hours. Serves 8.

Cowboy Feed

1½ pounds lean ground beef   680 g
2 onions, coarsely chopped
5 medium potatoes, peeled, sliced
1 (15 ounce) can kidney beans, rinsed, drained   425 g
1 (15 ounce) can pinto beans, drained   425 g
1 (15 ounce) can Mexican stewed tomatoes   425 g
1 (10 ounce) can tomato soup   280 g
½ teaspoon basil   2 ml
½ teaspoon oregano   2 ml
2 teaspoons minced garlic   10 ml

- Sprinkle beef with some salt and pepper, brown in skillet and drain.

- Place onions in sprayed slow cooker and spoon beef over onions. On top of beef, layer potatoes, kidney and pinto beans. Pour stewed tomatoes and tomato soup over beans and potatoes and sprinkle with basil, oregano and garlic. Cover and cook on LOW for 7 to 8 hours. Serves 4 to 6.

Fiesta Beef and Rice

1½ pounds lean ground beef	680 g
1 (15 ounce) can Mexican stewed tomatoes	425 g
1 (7 ounce) box beef-flavored rice mix	200 g
1 (11 ounce) can Mexicorn®, drained	310 g
Salsa	

- Sprinkle salt and pepper over ground beef and shape into small patties. Place in sprayed oval slow cooker.

- Combine stewed tomatoes, rice, corn and 2 cups (500 ml) water in bowl and mix well. Spoon over beef patties. Cover and cook on LOW for 4 to 5 hours.

- When ready to serve, place large spoonful of salsa on each serving. Serves 4 to 6.

Green Chili-Beef Bake

1½ pounds lean ground beef	680 g
1 (10 ounce) package frozen chopped bell peppers and onions, thawed	280 g
1 (1 ounce) packet taco seasoning mix	30 g
2 (7 ounce) cans whole green chilies	2 (200 g)
1 (15 ounce) can refried beans	425 g
1 (16 ounce) jar thick-and-chunky salsa	455 g
8 - 10 cups just slightly crushed tortilla chips	450 - 560 g
1 (12 ounce) package shredded Mexican 4-cheese blend	340 g

- Cook and stir beef and, bell peppers and onions in skillet over medium heat for about 10 minutes. Stir in taco seasoning and ¼ cup (60 ml) water.

- Cut chilies in half, remove seeds and arrange evenly in sprayed slow cooker. Spoon over beef mixture. Spoon refried beans as evenly as you can over beef and top with remaining chilies (halved and seeded). Pour salsa over all. Do not stir. Cover and cook on LOW for 8 to 10 hours.

- Place about ¾ cup (40 g) crushed tortilla chips on individual plates, spoon beef mixture over chips and top with about ¼ cup (30 g) cheese. Serves 8 to 10.

Pipin' Hot Enchilada Supper

1½ pounds lean ground beef	680 g
1 (10 ounce) package frozen chopped bell peppers	
and onions, thawed	280 g
1 teaspoon minced garlic	5 ml
1 (10 ounce) can fiesta nacho cheese soup	280 g
1 (10 ounce) can diced tomatoes and green chilies	280 g
1 (10 ounce) can enchilada sauce, divided	280 g
10 corn tortillas, each cut in 4 strips, divided	
1 (12 ounce) package Velveeta® cheese, divided	340 g
3 fresh green onions, sliced	

- Cook ground beef, bell peppers and onions, and garlic in large skillet on medium heat until brown, stirring often; drain. Stir in soup and tomatoes and green chilies.

- Spread about ¼ cup (60 ml) enchilada sauce in sprayed slow cooker. Place strips from 4 tortillas over sauce to make even layer. Top with one-third beef mixture, spread evenly. Drizzle with ¼ cup (60 ml) enchilada sauce and sprinkle 1 cup (115 g) cheese.

- Repeat layering twice using strips from only 3 tortillas each time, half remaining beef mixture, half remaining enchilada sauce and half remaining cheese on each layer.

- Cover and cook on LOW for 4 hours 30 minutes to 5 hours 30 minutes. Let stand for 10 minutes before serving. Garnish with green onions. Serves 6 to 8.

Cowboy-Pleasing Beef and Beans

1 pound lean beef chuck, cut into 1-inch pieces	455 g/2.5 cm
1 pound dried pinto beans	455 g
3 slices bacon, cut into ½-inch (1.2 cm) pieces	
1 (32 ounce) carton beef broth	910 g
1 (10 ounce) can diced tomatoes and green chilies	280 g
1 teaspoon minced garlic	5 ml
1 tablespoon chili powder	15 ml
1 teaspoon ground cumin	5 ml

- Combine beef, beans, bacon, broth, tomatoes and green chilies, garlic, chili powder, cumin, and 1 teaspoon (5 ml) salt in sprayed slow cooker. Cover and cook on LOW for 11 to 12 hours. Serves 6.

Hallelujah!
Enchiladas Tonight

1 pound lean ground beef	455 g
1 teaspoon minced garlic	5 ml
1 onion, finely chopped	
1 (10 ounce) can fiesta nacho cheese soup	280 g
1 (4 ounce) can diced green chilies	115 g
1 (10 ounce) can enchilada sauce	280 g
10 corn tortillas, each cut into 3 sections	
1 (12 ounce) package shredded Mexican Velveeta® cheese	340 g

- Brown beef, garlic and onion in large non-stick skillet, stirring often. Stir in soup and green chilies.

- Spread ¼ cup (60 ml) enchilada sauce in sprayed slow cooker. Place 4 cut-up tortillas on top with one-third beef-green chilies mixture, spreading evenly. Drizzle with ¼ cup (60 ml) enchilada sauce and sprinkle with 1 cup (115 g) cheese.

- Repeat layering twice, using only 3 cut-up tortillas and half remaining beef mixture, half remaining enchilada sauce and half remaining cheese on each layer. Cover and cook on LOW for 4 hours 30 minutes to 5 hours 30 minutes. Let stand for 10 minutes before serving. Serves 6.

TIP: Try using 2 cups (280 g) cooked shredded turkey instead of the beef. Instead of the enchilada sauce, use a 10 ounce (280 g) can of cream of chicken soup.

Southern Taco Pie

1 pound lean ground beef	455 g
1 (10 ounce) package frozen chopped bell peppers	
and onions, thawed	280 g
2 jalapeno peppers, seeded, chopped	
1 (15 ounce) can Mexican stewed tomatoes	425 g
1 tablespoon chili powder	15 ml
1 (8 ounce) package shredded Velveeta® cheese	230 g
1 (8 ounce) box corn muffin mix	230 g
1 egg	
¼ cup milk	60 ml

- Brown beef, drain, and combine with bell peppers and onions, jalapeno peppers, stewed tomatoes, chili powder, and cheese in bowl; mix well and spoon into sprayed slow cooker. Cover and cook on HIGH for 2 hours.

- Combine muffin mix, egg and milk in bowl; mix well and spoon over beef mixture. Reduce heat to LOW, cover and cook for additional 3 to 4 hours. Serves 6.

Chili Frijoles

2 cups dry pinto beans	525 g
2 onions, finely chopped	
2 tablespoons chili powder	30 ml
1 teaspoon minced garlic	5 ml
1 (15 ounce) can tomato sauce	425 g
1½ pounds lean ground beef	680 g

- Soak beans overnight in water. Drain and transfer beans to sprayed large slow cooker. Add onion, chili powder, garlic, tomato sauce and 8 cups (1.9 L) water.

- Brown ground beef in skillet, drain and transfer to cooker. Cover and cook on LOW for 8 to 9 hours or until beans are tender; stir occasionally.

- Stir in 1 teaspoon (5 ml) salt just before serving. Serves 6 to 8.

TIP: If you forget to soak beans overnight, here's Plan B. Place beans in large saucepan and cover with water. Bring to a boil, turn off heat and let stand for 1 hour.

Twenty-Minute Fix for Lasagna

1 pound lean ground beef	455 g
1 small onion, chopped	
1 (26 ounce) jar spaghetti sauce, divided	740 g
1 (8 ounce) can tomato sauce	230 g
½ teaspoon garlic powder	2 ml
8 no-boil lasagna noodles (from 9 ounce package)	8 (255 g)
1 (16 ounce) jar alfredo pasta sauce	455 g
1 (12 ounce) package shredded mozzarella cheese, divided	340 g
⅓ cup grated parmesan cheese	35 g

- Brown beef and onion in large skillet over medium-high heat, using back of large spoon to break up beef; drain.

- Spread ¾ cup (190 g) spaghetti sauce in sprayed slow cooker. Stir remaining spaghetti sauce, tomato sauce and garlic powder into ground beef.

- Layer 3 lasagna noodles over sauce (breaking noodles if necessary to fit). Top with one-third alfredo sauce, spreading evenly. Top with one-third mozzarella cheese and one-third beef mixture, spreading evenly.

- Repeat layering twice, using only 2 lasagna noodles in last layer. Sprinkle parmesan cheese over top.

- Cover and cook on LOW for 3 hours 30 minutes to 4 hours 30 minutes. Cut into wedges to serve. Serves 8.

Make-Believe Lasagna

1 pound lean ground beef	455 g
1 onion, chopped	
½ teaspoon garlic powder	2 ml
1 (18 ounce) can spaghetti sauce	510 g
½ teaspoon ground oregano	2 ml
6 - 8 lasagna noodles, divided	
1 (12 ounce) carton cottage cheese, divided	340 g
½ cup grated parmesan cheese, divided	50 g
1 (12 ounce) package shredded mozzarella cheese, divided	340 g

- Brown ground beef and onion in large skillet. Add garlic powder, spaghetti sauce and oregano. Cook just until thoroughly warm.

- Spoon layer of meat sauce in sprayed oval slow cooker. Add layer lasagna noodles (break to fit slow cooker).

- Top with layer of half remaining meat sauce, half cottage cheese, half parmesan cheese and half mozzarella cheese. Repeat layer, starting with lasagna noodles. Cover and cook on LOW for 6 to 8 hours. Serves 4 to 6.

Slow Cooker Ziti

1 pound ground beef	455 g
1 tablespoon Italian seasoning	15 ml
2 (26 ounce) cans spaghetti sauce	2 (735 g)
2 (8 ounce) packages shredded mozzarella cheese, divided	2 (230 g)
1 (15 ounce) carton ricotta cheese	425 g
1 cup grated parmesan cheese	100 g
1 (16 ounce) box ziti noodles	455 g

- Brown ground beef in skillet. Add Italian seasoning, 1 teaspoon (5 ml) each salt and pepper, and sauce to meat. Combine 1 package mozzarella, ricotta and parmesan in separate bowl.

- In slow cooker, layer 2 cups (500 ml) meat mixture, half ziti and half cheese mixture. Repeat. Cover with remaining meat mixture. Cover and cook on LOW for 5 to 6 hours.

- Top with remaining mozzarella and serve when cheese is melted. Serves 6 to 8.

If there is too much liquid in the slow cooker at the end of the cooking time, just remove the food and pour the liquid into a saucepan and simmer to reduce. Add seasonings after the liquid is reduced.

Abundant Stuffed Shells

20 - 22 jumbo pasta shells	
1 pound lean ground beef, browned, drained	455 g
½ cup finely chopped onion	80 g
1 cup shredded cheddar cheese	115 g
½ cup seasoned breadcrumbs	60 g
1 teaspoon minced garlic	5 ml
½ teaspoon Italian seasoning	2 ml
2 eggs, beaten	
2 (26 ounce) jars spaghetti sauce, divided	2 (740 g)
½ cup shredded mozzarella cheese	60 g

- Cook pasta shells about 7 minutes in boiling water (they need to be only partially cooked), drain and place on sheet of wax paper.

- Combine beef, onion, cheddar cheese, breadcrumbs, garlic, Italian seasoning and egg in bowl. Carefully stuff pasta shells with spoonful of meat mixture.

- Pour 1 jar spaghetti sauce in sprayed slow cooker. Place stuffed shells on top of sauce. Pour remaining sauce evenly over pasta. Sprinkle with mozzarella cheese. Cover and cook on LOW for 4 to 5 hours. Do not overcook. Serves 4 to 6.

Requested Ragu over Rigatoni

1 onion, chopped	
2 ribs celery, sliced	
2 carrots, peeled, chopped	
2 teaspoons minced garlic	10 ml
2 pounds lean ground beef, browned, drained	910 g
1 (28 ounce) can diced tomatoes	795 g
1 (14 ounce) can beef broth	395 g
1 (6 ounce) can tomato sauce	170 g
2 teaspoons sugar	10 ml
1 (15 ounce) can great northern beans, drained	425 g
2 teaspoons Italian seasoning, divided	10 ml
½ teaspoon cayenne pepper	2 ml
1 (16 ounce) package rigatoni, cooked	455 g
Grated parmesan cheese	

- Place onion, celery, carrots and garlic in food processor and pulse until finely diced. Combine with beef, tomatoes, broth, tomato sauce, sugar and beans in large bowl and mix until they blend well. Stir in 1 teaspoon (5 ml) Italian seasoning and spoon into sprayed large slow cooker. Cook on LOW for 8 hours or on HIGH for 5 hours 30 minutes.

- Stir in remaining Italian seasoning, cayenne pepper and 1 teaspoon (5 ml) salt and cook for additional 30 minutes. For a little more spice, add additional ½ teaspoon (2 ml) cayenne pepper.

- Toss half of meat sauce with rigatoni and serve with parmesan cheese. Reserve remaining sauce, which can be frozen, for another meal. Serves 8.

Italy's Best

2 pounds lean ground beef	910 g
1 (10 ounce) package frozen chopped bell peppers	
and onions, thawed	280 g
1 teaspoon minced garlic	5 ml
1 (8 ounce) can tomato sauce	230 g
1 (15 ounce) can Italian stewed tomatoes	425 g
2 teaspoons Italian seasoning	10 ml
1 (16 ounce) package penne pasta	455 g
1 (10 ounce) package frozen, chopped spinach, thawed	280 g
1 (12 ounce) package shredded mozzarella cheese	340 g

• Brown and cook ground beef, bell peppers and onions, and garlic in large skillet for about 15 minutes. Drain and place mixture in sprayed slow cooker.

• Stir in tomato sauce, stewed tomatoes, Italian seasoning and a little salt and pepper. Cover and cook on LOW for 6 to 7 hours or on HIGH for 3 hours 30 minutes.

• Cook pasta according to package directions and drain. (If cooking on LOW, increase heat to HIGH.) Stir in pasta, spinach and cheese, cover and cook for additional 30 minutes. Serves 6 to 8.

Italian Tortellini

½ pound ground round steak	230 g
1 (1 pound) package bulk Italian sausage	455 g
1 (15 ounce) carton refrigerated marinara sauce	425 g
1 (15 ounce) can Italian stewed tomatoes with liquid	425 g
1½ cups sliced fresh mushrooms	110 g
1 (9 ounce) package refrigerated cheese tortellini	255g
1½ cups shredded mozzarella cheese	170 g

• Brown and cook ground beef and sausage in large skillet for about 10 minutes on medium-low heat and drain.

• Combine meat mixture, marinara sauce, tomatoes and mushrooms in sprayed slow cooker.   Cover and cook on LOW 6 to 8 hours.

• Stir in tortellini and sprinkle with mozzarella cheese. Turn cooker to HIGH, cover and cook for additional 10 to 15 minutes or until tortellini is tender. Serves 4 to 6.

Easy-Fix Lasagna

1 pound lean ground beef	455 g
½ pound ground pork	230 g
1 small onion, finely chopped	
1 (26 ounce) jar spaghetti sauce, divided	740 g
1 (8 ounce) can tomato sauce	230 g
8 no-boil lasagna noodles (from 9 ounce package)	255 g
1 (16 ounce) bottle alfredo sauce	455 g
1 (12 ounce) package shredded Italian cheese blend	340 g

- Place ground beef, pork and onion in skillet on medium to high heat and cook, stirring often for about 10 minutes. Drain.

- Spread ¾ cup (190 g) spaghetti sauce in sprayed slow cooker. Add remaining spaghetti sauce and tomato sauce into meat mixture and mix well.

- Layer 3 lasagna noodles over sauce in cooker, breaking noodles if necessary. Spread evenly with one-third alfredo sauce and sprinkle with one-third cheese. Top with one-third meat mixture.

- Repeat layering twice, using only 2 lasagna noodles in last layer. Cover and cook on LOW for 3 hours 30 minutes to 4 hours 30 minutes. Lasagna can be cut into wedges to serve. Serves 8.

Southwest Spaghetti

1½ pounds lean ground beef	680 g
2½ teaspoons chili powder	12 ml
1 (15 ounce) can tomato sauce	425 g
1 (7 ounce) package spaghetti	200 g
1 heaping tablespoon beef seasoning	15 ml
Shredded cheddar-Jack cheese	

- Brown ground beef in skillet until no longer pink. Place in sprayed slow cooker.

- Add chili powder, tomato sauce, spaghetti, 2⅓ cups (575 ml) water and beef seasoning and mix well. Cover and cook on LOW for 6 to 7 hours.

- When ready to serve, cover with lots of cheese. Serves 4 to 6.

Beef Roulades

1½ pounds beef flank steak	680 g
5 slices bacon	
¾ cup finely chopped onion	120 g
1 (4 ounce) can mushrooms pieces	115 g
1 tablespoon Worcestershire sauce	15 ml
⅓ cup Italian-seasoned breadcrumbs	40 g
1 (12 ounce) jar beef gravy	340 g
Mashed potatoes	

- Cut steak into 4 to 6 serving-size pieces. Cut bacon into small pieces and combine with onion, mushrooms, Worcestershire and breadcrumbs in bowl.

- Place about ½ cup (125 ml) onion mixture on each piece of steak. Roll meat and secure ends with toothpicks. Dry beef rolls with paper towels. In skillet, brown steak rolls and transfer to sprayed slow cooker.

- Pour gravy evenly over steaks to thoroughly moisten. Cover and cook on LOW for 7 to 9 hours. Serve with mashed potatoes. Serves 4 to 6.

TIP: *This is really good served with mashed potatoes. Have you tried instant mashed potatoes as a time-saver?*

Teriyaki Steak

1½ - 2 pounds flank steak	680 - 910 g
1 (15 ounce) can sliced pineapple with juice	425 g
1 tablespoon marinade for chicken	15 ml
⅓ cup packed brown sugar	75 g
3 tablespoons soy sauce	45 ml
½ teaspoon ground ginger	2 ml
1 (14 ounce) can chicken broth	400 g
1 cup long grain rice	200 g

- Roll flank steak, tie in place and cut into 7 to 8 individual steaks.

- Combine ½ cup (125 ml) pineapple juice, marinade for chicken, brown sugar, soy sauce and ginger in bowl large enough for marinade to cover individual steaks. Add steak rolls and marinate for 1 hour in sauce. Discard marinade.

- Pour chicken broth into sprayed slow cooker. Add rice and ¾ cup (175 ml) water. Place steaks over rice and broth. Cover and cook on LOW for 8 to 10 hours. Serves 4 to 6.

Saucy Steak

Great sauce with mashed potatoes	
1 ½ pounds lean round steak	680 g
1 onion, halved, sliced	
2 (10 ounce) cans golden mushroom soup	2 (280 g)
1 ½ cups hot, thick-and-chunky salsa	360 ml

- Trim fat from steak and cut into serving-size pieces. Sprinkle with 1 teaspoon (5 ml) pepper and place in sprayed large slow cooker.

- Place onion slices over steak. Combine mushroom soup and salsa in bowl and mix well. Spoon over steak and onions. Cover and cook on LOW for 7 to 8 hours. Serves 4 to 6.

Pepper Steak

1 ½ pounds round steak	680 g
Canola oil	
¼ cup soy sauce	60 ml
1 onion, sliced	
1 teaspoon minced garlic	5 ml
1 teaspoon sugar	5 ml
¼ teaspoon ground ginger	1 ml
1 (15 ounce) can stewed tomatoes	425 g
2 green bell peppers, seeded, julienned	
1 teaspoon beef bouillon granules	5 ml
1 tablespoon cornstarch	15 ml
Rice or noodles, cooked	

- Slice beef in strips, brown in skillet with a little oil and place in sprayed oval slow cooker.

- Combine soy sauce, onion, garlic, sugar and ginger in bowl and pour over beef. Cover and cook on LOW for 5 to 6 hours.

- Add tomatoes, bell peppers and bouillon and cook for additional 1 hour.

- Combine cornstarch and ¼ cup water (60 ml) in cup and stir into cooker. Continue cooking until liquid thickens. Serve over rice or noodles. Serves 4 to 6.

While reheating leftovers in a slow cooker is not recommended, the ceramic insert is usually ovenproof as well as microwaveable. Check the manufacturer's directions.

Crowd-Pleasing Pepper Steak

¼ cup flour	30 g
1½ pounds beef round steak	680 g
2 tablespoons canola oil	30 ml
1 onion, chopped	
2 large green bell peppers, seeded, julienned, divided	
1 (15 ounce) can Italian stewed tomatoes	425 g
½ cup beef broth	125 ml
1 tablespoon Worcestershire sauce	15 ml
1 cup instant rice	95 g

- Combine flour, 1 teaspoon (5 ml) each of salt and pepper in shallow bowl. Cut steak into strips and toss with flour mixture to coat thoroughly. Heat oil in skillet and cook steak strips until slightly brown, turning often.

- Place steak, onion, 1 julienned bell pepper, tomatoes, broth and Worcestershire in sprayed slow cooker. Cover and cook on LOW for 7 to 9 hours.

- Add remaining julienned pepper to slow cooker, cover and cook for 1 additional hour.

- Cook rice according to package directions and place on serving platter and top with pepper steak. Serves 4.

Pepper Steak Treat

1½ - 2 pound round steak, cut into 2-inch strips	680 - 910 g/5 cm
1 teaspoon Italian seasoning	5 ml
3 tablespoons canola oil	45 ml
1 (10 ounce) can beef broth	280 g
2 tablespoons cornstarch	15 g
1 small onion, finely chopped	
2 bell peppers, seeded, chopped	
2 tablespoons soy sauce	30 ml
1 (12 ounce) package egg noodles, cooked, drained	340 g

- Sprinkle steak strips with Italian seasoning. Brown steak strips in oil in large skillet over medium-high heat. Transfer to a sprayed slow cooker.

- Combine broth and cornstarch in bowl, stirring until cornstarch dissolves. Pour into slow cooker and add onion, bell peppers and soy sauce. Cover and cook on HIGH for 3 to 4 hours or on LOW for 6 to 8 hours. Serve over noodles. Serves 6.

Amazing Asian Pepper Steak

2 pounds (¾ inch thick) beef round steak	910 g (1.8 cm)
3 bell peppers, 1 red, 1 green, 1 yellow, seeded, julienned	
2 onions, halved and cut into ½-inch (1.2 cm) slices	
1 (15 ounce) can stewed tomatoes, drained	425 g
2 teaspoons minced garlic	10 ml
1 (10 ounce) can beef broth	280 g
¼ cup light soy sauce	60 ml
2 tablespoons rice wine vinegar	30 ml
2½ tablespoons cornstarch	25 g
1 teaspoon sugar	5 ml
1 (8 ounce) can bamboo shoots, drained	230 g
1½ cups instant rice, cooked	150 g

- Cut round steak into serving size pieces and place in sprayed large slow cooker. Top with bell peppers, onions, tomatoes and garlic.

- Whisk beef broth, soy sauce, vinegar, cornstarch and sugar in bowl and pour over steak and vegetables. Sprinkle bamboo shoots over the top. Cover and cook on HIGH for 4 hours or on LOW for 7 hours. Serve over rice. Serves 8.

Swiss Steak

1 - 1½ pounds boneless, round steak	455 - 680 g
½ teaspoon seasoned salt	2 ml
½ teaspoon seasoned pepper	2 ml
8 - 10 medium new (red) potatoes with peels, halved	
1 cup baby carrots	135 g
1 onion, sliced	
1 (15 ounce) can stewed tomatoes	425 g
1 (12 ounce) jar beef gravy	340 g

- Cut steak in 6 to 8 serving-size pieces, season with seasoned salt and pepper and brown in non-stick skillet. Layer steak pieces, potatoes, carrots and onion in sprayed slow cooker.

- Combine tomatoes and beef gravy in bowl and spoon over vegetables. Cover and cook on LOW for 7 to 8 hours. Serves 4 to 6.

Spicy Swiss Steak

1½ pounds boneless, beef round steak	680 g
4 ounces spicy bratwurst	115 g
2 small onions	
2 tablespoons quick-cooking tapioca	35 g
1 teaspoon dried thyme	5 ml
2 (15 ounce) cans Mexican stewed tomatoes	2 (425 g)
Noodles, cooked	

- Trim fat from steak and cut into 4 serving-size pieces. Brown steak and bratwurst in skillet. Drain and place in sprayed slow cooker.

- Slice onions and separate into rings. Cover meat with onions and sprinkle with tapioca, thyme, and a little salt and pepper. Pour stewed tomatoes over onion and seasonings. Cover and cook on LOW for 5 to 8 hours. Serve over noodles. Serves 4 to 6.

Stroganoff

2 pounds beef round steak	910 g
¾ cup flour, divided	90 g
½ teaspoon mustard	2 ml
2 onions, thinly sliced	
½ pound fresh mushrooms, sliced	230 g
1 (10 ounce) can beef broth	280 g
¼ cup dry white wine or cooking wine	60 ml
1 (8 ounce) carton sour cream	230 g
Noodles, cooked	

- Trim excess fat from steak and cut into 3-inch (8 cm) strips about ½-inch (1.2 cm) wide.

- Combine ½ cup (60 ml) flour, mustard and a little salt and pepper in bowl and toss with steak strips. Place strips in sprayed oval slow cooker.

- Cover with onions and mushrooms. Add beef broth and wine. Cover and cook on LOW for 8 to 10 hours.

- Just before serving, combine sour cream and ¼ cup (60 ml) flour in bowl. Stir into cooker and cook for additional 10 to 15 minutes or until stroganoff thickens slightly. Serve over cooked noodles. Serves 4 to 6.

Mushroom Smothered Steak

2 - 2½ pound round steak	910 g - 1.2 kg
2 tablespoons Worcestershire sauce	30 ml
1 tablespoon canola oil	15 ml
1 teaspoon garlic powder	5 ml
2 onions, thinly sliced	
1 red bell pepper, seeded, julienned	
1 (8 ounce) carton fresh mushrooms, sliced	230 g

- Score steak about ⅛-inch (6 mm) deep in diamond pattern on top side. Rub in Worcestershire sauce and oil. Season with garlic powder and a little salt and pepper.

- Place onion slices, bell peppers and mushrooms in sprayed slow cooker. Roll steak to fit easily in slow cooker and place on top of onion-mushroom mixture. Cover and cook on LOW for 8 to 9 hours or on HIGH for 4 hours 30 minutes.

- Remove steak to platter and cut into thin diagonal slices and serve with bell pepper and mushrooms; spoon liquid over all. Serves 6.

Italian Steak

1 pound round steak, cubed	455 g
2 cups fresh mushroom halves	145 g
1 (15 ounce) can Italian stewed tomatoes	425 g
1 (10 ounce) can beef broth	280 g
½ cup red wine	125 ml
2 teaspoons Italian seasoning	10 ml
3 tablespoons quick-cooking tapioca	50 g
Linguine, cooked	

- Place beef in sprayed slow cooker. Combine mushrooms, tomatoes, beef broth, wine, Italian seasoning, tapioca and a little salt and pepper in bowl. Pour over steak. Cover and cook on LOW for 8 to 10 hours. Serve over linguine. Serves 4.

Mushroom Round Steak

1½ - 2 pounds round steak	680 - 910 g
1 (1 ounce) packet onion soup mix	30 g
½ cup dry red wine	125 ml
1 (8 ounce) carton fresh mushrooms, sliced	230 g
1 (10 ounce) can French onion soup	280 g

- Cut round steak in serving-size pieces and place in sprayed oval slow cooker. Combine soup mix, red wine, mushrooms, French onion soup and ½ cup (125 ml) water in bowl, spoon over steak pieces. Cover and cook on LOW for 7 to 8 hours. Serves 4 to 6.

Beefy Onion Supper

1 - 1½ pounds round steak	455 - 680 g
1 onion, sliced and separated into rings	
2 cups fresh sliced mushrooms	145 g
1 (10 ounce) can French onion soup	280 g
1 (6 ounce) package herb stuffing mix	170 g
½ cup (1 stick) butter, melted	115 g

- Cut beef into 5 to 6 serving-size pieces. Place steak pieces in sprayed oval slow cooker and top with onions and mushrooms.

- Pour soup over ingredients in cooker. Cover and cook on LOW for 7 to 9 hours.

- Just before serving, combine stuffing mix with butter and ½ cup (125 ml) liquid from cooker and toss to mix. Place stuffing mixture on top of steak and increase heat to HIGH. Cover and cook for additional 15 minutes or until stuffing is fluffy. Serves 4 to 6.

Beef and Gravy

2 pounds sirloin steak or thick round steak	910 g
Canola oil	
1 (1 ounce) packet onion soup mix	30 g
1 (10 ounce) can golden mushroom soup	280 g
1 (4 ounce) can sliced mushrooms, drained	115 g
Noodles, cooked	

- Cut steak in ½-inch (1.2 cm) pieces. Brown beef in skillet in a little oil and place in sprayed large slow cooker.

- Combine onion soup mix, mushroom soup, mushrooms and ½ cup (125 ml) water in bowl and mix well. Spoon over beef. Cover and cook on LOW for 7 to 8 hours. Serve over noodles. Serves 4 to 6.

Tender Steak and Potatoes

8 - 10 small new (red) potatoes	
2 onions, sliced	
1½ - 2 pound boneless round steak	680 - 910 g
1 (1 ounce) packet ranch onion soup mix	30 g
1 (10 ounce) can golden mushroom soup	280 g

- Layer potatoes and onions in sprayed slow cooker. Cut round steak into serving size pieces and place on top of potatoes and onions.

- Combine onion soup mix, soup and ⅔ cup (150 ml) water in bowl; mix well and pour over steak. Cover and cook on LOW for 7 to 9 hours. Serves 6.

Spectacular Beef and Broccoli

1 - 1½ pounds boneless round steak, cut into 1-inch (2.5 cm) cubes	455 - 680 g
1 (10 ounce) package frozen chopped bell peppers and onions, thawed	280 g
2 ribs celery, cut in 1-inch (2.5 cm) slices	
1 (10 ounce) can beef broth	280 g
3 tablespoons teriyaki baste and glaze	45 ml
2 cups instant rice	190 g
2 tablespoons cornstarch	15 g
1 (16 ounce) package frozen broccoli florets, thawed	455 g
Rice, cooked	

- Place steak cubes, bell peppers and onions, celery, broth, teriyaki baste and glaze, and ½ teaspoon (2 ml) pepper in sprayed slow cooker. Cover and cook on LOW for 8 to 10 hours.

- Mix cornstarch into 2 to 3 tablespoons (30 to 45 ml) water in small bowl. Stir cornstarch mixture and broccoli florets into slow cooker, cover and cook for additional 25 to 30 minutes. Serve over rice. Serves 4 to 6.

Simple Steak and Gravy

2 tablespoons canola oil	30 ml
4 - 6 cube steaks	
1 (8 ounce) package frozen pearl onions, thawed	230 g
2 (10 ounce) cans cream of celery soup	2 (280 g)
1 cup milk	250 ml
1 (1 ounce) packet ranch soup and dip mix	30 g
1 (20 ounce) package frozen mashed potatoes	570 g

- Sprinkle a little salt and pepper over steaks. Heat oil in skillet and brown cube steaks. Place pearl onions in sprayed slow cooker and top with browned steaks.

- Combine soup, milk, ranch soup mix and 1 cup (250 ml) water in bowl; mix well. Pour soup mixture over steaks. Cover and cook on LOW for 4 to 6 hours.

- Heat mashed potatoes according to package directions and serve with steak and gravy. Serves 4 to 6.

Smothered Steak

1 (10 ounce) can cream of mushroom soup	280 g
1 - 1½ pounds beef round steak, cut	
into 5 to 6 serving-size pieces	455 - 680 g
1 tablespoon brown sugar	15 ml
1 teaspoon minced garlic	5 ml
¾ cup chipotle chunky salsa (from 16 ounce jar)	200 g/455 g
Rice, cooked	

- Spoon soup into sprayed slow cooker and top with steak pieces.

- Combine brown sugar, garlic and salsa in bowl; mix well and pour over steak. Cover and cook on LOW for 8 to 9 hours. Serve with over rice. Serves 5 to 6.

Home Run Steak and Gravy

1½ pound boneless beef round steak, cut ¾-inch thick	680 g/1.8 cm
3 onions, sliced	
1 green bell pepper, seeded, sliced	
1 (4 ounce) can chopped green chilies	115 g
1 (8 ounce) container whole mushrooms	230 g
1 (12 ounce) jar beef gravy	340 g
⅓ cup red cooking wine	75 ml
1 (22 ounce) container prepared mashed potatoes	625 g

- Cut any fat from round steak and cut into 6 serving-size pieces. Place onions, bell pepper and green chilies in sprayed slow cooker. Top with mushrooms and steak pieces.

- Combine gravy and wine in small bowl and pour over steak. Cover and cook on LOW for 8 to 10 hours or on HIGH for 4 to 5 hours. Serve steak-onion mixture over warmed mashed potatoes. Serves 6.

Cheaper cuts of meats are well-suited to cooking in a slow cooker. The moisture and the long cooking time result in a very tender product. The less-expensive cuts are not only easier on the pocketbook, they actually turn out better than more expensive meats.

Seriously Good Steak

1½ - 2 pounds round steak	680 - 910 g
⅓ cup teriyaki baste and glaze (from 12 ounce bottle)	75 ml/340 g
2 tablespoons canola oil	30 ml
1 teaspoon minced garlic	5 ml
1 (20 ounce) can pineapple chunks, drained, set	
aside ¼ cup juice	570 g/60 ml
3 tablespoons cornstarch	25 g
Rice, cooked	

- Cut steak into ¼-inch (6 mm) strips and place in bowl with teriyaki baste and glaze, oil, garlic and ¼ cup (60 ml) pineapple juice; stir and toss to coat well. Refrigerate for 15 minutes.

- Place steak slices in sprayed slow cooker. Cover and cook on LOW for 6 to 7 hours.

- Increase heat to HIGH and add pineapple chunks. Stir cornstarch into ¼ cup (60 ml) water in bowl and add to cooker. Cook and stir until slightly thickened. Serve over rice. Serves 6.

Savory Steak and Onions

1½ pounds boneless beef round steak	680 g
3 tablespoons flour	20 g
½ teaspoon seasoned salt	2 ml
1 teaspoon garlic powder	5 ml
2 tablespoons canola oil	30 ml
1 (16 ounce) package frozen pearl onions, thawed	455 g
1 yellow bell pepper, seeded, julienned	
1 (10 ounce) can diced tomatoes and green chilies	280 g
½ cup chunky salsa	130 g

- Cut steak into 6 pieces. Combine flour, seasoned salt and garlic powder in shallow bowl. Coat beef with flour mixture.

- Heat oil in skillet on medium heat and cook beef for about 15 minutes, turning once, until slightly brown. Place steak in sprayed slow cooker. Top with onions, bell pepper, tomatoes and green chilies and salsa. Cover and cook on LOW for 7 to 9 hours. Serves 6.

Roll Up the Steak

1½ pounds beef round steak, cut into 4 serving pieces	680 g
4 slices bacon, each slice cut in half	
1 rib celery, diced	
½ onion, finely chopped	
⅓ cup seasoned breadcrumbs	40 g
1 (12 ounce) can beef gravy	340 g
Mashed potatoes or rice, cooked	

- Sprinkle round steak with a little salt and pepper and place 2 half pieces bacon on each serving of round steak.

- Combine celery, onion, breadcrumbs and about 1 to 2 tablespoons (15 to 30 ml) water in bowl and mix well. Place about ¼ cup (60 ml) crumb mixture on each piece of steak. Roll up steak; secure with toothpicks and place in sprayed slow cooker.

- Pour beef gravy over steak; cover and cook on LOW for 8 to 10 hours. Serve over mashed potatoes or rice. Serves 4.

TIP: *If you want a lot of gravy, use 2 cans of the beef gravy.*

Confetti Beef and Beans

1½ pounds beef round steak	680 g
1 teaspoon garlic powder	5 ml
1½ teaspoons chili powder	7 ml
1 onion, chopped	
1 (16 ounce) jar salsa	455 g
1 (15 ounce) can kidney beans, rinsed, drained	425 g
1 (15 ounce) can great northern beans, rinsed, drained	425 g
4 slices bacon, cooked, crumbled	

- Trim any fat from steak. Combine garlic powder, chili powder and ½ teaspoon salt in bowl. Coat steak with dry mixture; then cut steak into ½-inch strips. Place in sprayed slow cooker and stir in onion and salsa. Cover and cook on LOW for 7 hours 30 minutes to 8 hours.

- Increase heat to HIGH, stir in beans and crumbled bacon, cover and cook for additional 30 minutes. Serves 6.

If you are using a slow cooker at high altitude, you may find you need to add 30 minutes for each hour of cooking time to allow for the effects of the altitude. Beans and other legumes definitely will need longer cooking time, sometimes twice as much as at lower altitude.

Beef Tips and Mushrooms Supreme

2 (10 ounce) cans golden mushroom soup	2 (280 g)
1 (14 ounce) can beef broth	395 g
1 tablespoon beef seasoning	15 ml
2 (4 ounce) cans sliced mushrooms, drained	2 (115 g)
2 pounds round steak, cut in slices	910 g
Noodles	
1 (8 ounce) carton sour cream	230 g

- Combine soup, beef broth, beef seasoning and sliced mushrooms in bowl. Place in sprayed slow cooker. Add slices of beef and stir well. Cover and cook on LOW for 4 to 5 hours.

- When ready to serve, cook noodles, drain, add salt and a little butter.

- Stir sour cream into sauce in slow cooker. Spoon sauce and beef over noodles. Serves 4 to 6.

Beef Tips over Noodles

½ cup plus 3 tablespoons flour, divided	80 g
3 pounds beef tips	1.4 kg
1 (8 ounce) carton fresh mushrooms, sliced	230 g
1 bunch fresh green onions, chopped	
1 small red bell pepper, seeded, chopped	
¼ cup ketchup	70 g
1 (14 ounce) can beef broth	395 g
1 tablespoon Worcestershire sauce	15 ml
Noodles, cooked	

- Coat beef tips with ½ cup (60 g) flour in bowl and transfer to sprayed slow cooker.

- Add mushrooms, onion, bell pepper, ketchup, broth, Worcestershire sauce and a little salt and pepper. Cover and cook on LOW for 7 to 8 hours.

- Turn heat to HIGH and cook for 1 additional hour. Combine remaining flour with ¼ cup (60 ml) water in small bowl, stir into cooker and cook until liquid thickens. Serve over noodles. Serves 6 to 8.

Pasta with Seasoned Beef Tips

2 - 2½ pounds lean beef stew meat	910 g
2 cups frozen, small whole onions, thawed	320 g
1 green bell pepper, seeded	
1 (6 ounce) jar pitted Greek olives or ripe olives	170 g
½ cup sun-dried tomatoes in oil, drained, chopped	30 g
1 (28 ounce) jar marinara sauce	795 g
1 (8 ounce) package pasta twirls, cooked	230 g

- Place beef and onions in sprayed slow cooker. Cut bell pepper in 1-inch (2.5 cm) cubes and add to slow cooker.

- Add olives and tomatoes and pour marinara sauce over top. Cover and cook on LOW for 8 to 10 hours. Serve over pasta twirls. Serves 4 to 6.

Mushroom Beef

1 (10 ounce) can beefy mushroom soup	280 g
1 (10 ounce) can golden mushroom soup	280 g
1 (10 ounce) can French onion soup	280 g
⅓ cup seasoned breadcrumbs	40 g
2½ pounds lean beef stew meat	1.1 kg
Noodles, cooked	

- Combine soups, ½ teaspoon (2 ml) pepper, breadcrumbs and ¾ cup (175 ml) water in sprayed large slow cooker. Stir in beef cubes and mix well. Cover and cook on LOW for 8 to 9 hours. Serve over noodles. Serves 6 to 8.

Oriental Beef Supper

2 pounds beef stew meat	680 g
1 (16 ounce) package frozen broccoli, cauliflower and carrots, thawed	455 g
1 (12 ounce) bottle sesame-ginger stir-fry sauce	355 ml
1 (10 ounce) can beef broth	280 g
¼ teaspoon cayenne pepper	1 ml
1 (8 ounce) can sliced water chestnuts, drained	230 g
1 (3 ounce) package beef-flavored ramen noodles, broken	85 g

- Trim fat off stew meat. Place vegetables in sprayed slow cooker and top with stew meat.

- Combine stir-fry sauce, beef broth and cayenne pepper in bowl and pour over beef and vegetables. Cover and cook on LOW for 9 to 10 hours or on HIGH for 4 hours 30 minutes to 5 hours.

- Stir in water chestnuts and ramen noodles, cover and cook for additional 20 minutes. Serves 6.

Easy Stroganoff

2 pounds beef stew meat	910 g
1 (10 ounce) can beef broth	280 g
2 (10 ounce) cans cream of mushroom soup	2 (280 g)
1 (4 ounce) can sliced mushrooms	115 g
2 ribs celery, sliced	
1 (1 ounce) packet onion soup mix	30 g
1 - 2 cups instant rice	95 - 190 g

- Combine stew meat, broth, mushroom soup, mushrooms, celery and soup mix in sprayed slow cooker. Cover and cook on LOW for 7 hours to 8 hours 30 minutes.

- Cook rice according to package directions and place on serving platter. Spoon meat mixture over rice. Serves 4 to 6.

Cola Roast

1 (4 pound) chuck roast	1.8 kg
1 (12 ounce) bottle chili sauce	340 g
1 onion, chopped	
1 (12 ounce) can cola	355 ml
1 tablespoon Worcestershire sauce	15 ml

- Score roast in several places and fill each slit with a little salt and pepper. Sear roast in skillet on all sides. Place in sprayed slow cooker.

- Combine chili sauce, onion, cola and Worcestershire in bowl and mix well. Pour over roast. Cover and cook on LOW for 8 to 9 hours. Serves 6 to 8.

Classic Beef Roast

1 (3 - 4 pound) beef chuck roast	1.4 - 1.8 kg
1 (1 ounce) packet onion soup mix	30 g
2 (10 ounce) cans golden mushroom soup	2 (280 g)
3 - 4 medium potatoes, quartered	

- Place roast in sprayed, large slow cooker. Sprinkle soup mix on roast and spoon on soup. Place potatoes around roast. Cover and cook on LOW for 7 to 8 hours or on HIGH for 4 hours. Serves 6 to 8.

Pot Roast and Veggies

1 (2 pound) chuck roast	910 g
4 - 5 medium potatoes, peeled, quartered	
4 large carrots, quartered	
1 onion, quartered	
1 (14 ounce) can beef broth, divided	395 g
2 tablespoons cornstarch	15 g

- Trim fat from pieces of roast. Cut roast into 2 equal pieces. Brown pieces of roast in skillet. (Coat pieces with flour, salt and pepper if you'd like a little "breading" on the outside.)

- Place potatoes, carrots and onion in sprayed slow cooker and mix well. Place browned beef over vegetables. Pour 1½ cups (375 ml) broth over beef and vegetables. Set aside remaining broth and refrigerate.

- Cover and cook on LOW for 8 to 9 hours. About 5 minutes before serving, remove beef and vegetables with slotted spoon and place on serving platter. Cover to keep warm.

- Pour liquid from slow cooker into medium saucepan. Blend remaining broth and cornstarch in bowl until smooth and add to liquid in saucepan. Boil for 1 minute and stir constantly.

- Serve gravy with roast and veggies and season with a little salt and pepper, if desired. Serves 4 to 6.

Sweet-and-Sour Beef

1 (2 pound) boneless chuck roast	910 g
½ cup flour	60 g
Canola oil	
1 onion, sliced	
½ cup chili sauce	135 g
¾ cup packed brown sugar	165 g
¼ cup red wine vinegar	60 ml
1 tablespoon Worcestershire sauce	15 ml
1 (16 ounce) package baby carrots	455 g

- Cut beef into 1-inch (2.5 cm) cubes and dredge in flour and a little salt and pepper. Brown beef in a little oil in skillet and place in sprayed slow cooker.

- Add remaining ingredients, except carrots, and 1 cup (250 ml) water. Cover and cook on LOW for 7 to 8 hours.

- Add carrots and cook for additional 1 hour 30 minutes. Serves 4 to 6.

TIP: *This recipe will work well using a 2 to 3 pound (910 g to 1.4 kg) pork roast. Increase brown sugar to 1 cup (220 g) and use marinade for chicken instead of Worcestershire sauce.*

Ready Roast, Potatoes and Gravy

1 (3 pound) boneless beef chuck roast	1.4 kg
1 (1 ounce) packet beefy-onion soup mix	30 g
1 (10 ounce) can golden mushroom soup	280 g
1 (5 ounce) box mashed potato mix	145 g
½ cup milk	125 ml
2 tablespoons butter	30 g

- Place roast in sprayed slow cooker. Add onion soup mix in one side of cooker and stir in mushroom soup. Cover and cook on LOW for 6 to 8 hours or until roast is tender.

- Prepare (timed to be ready when roast is cooked) mashed potatoes according to package directions with milk and butter.

- Remove roast, slice and serve on platter. The delicious gravy will be ready when the roast is done. Serves 6 to 8.

TIP: There will be 2 packets of soup mix in the box, but you need only one.

Wined and Dined Beef Roast

1 (8 ounce) carton fresh mushrooms	230 g
3 pounds boneless beef chuck roast, cubed	1.4 kg
1 large carrot, sliced	
1 onion, sliced	
1 (1 ounce) packet brown gravy mix	30 g
1 (14 ounce) can beef broth	395 g
1½ cups red wine	375 ml
Cooked rice	

- Cut mushrooms in half. Place roast, mushrooms, carrot and onion in sprayed slow cooker. Combine gravy mix, beef broth and red wine; pour over roast and vegetables. Cover and cook on HIGH for 6 hours. Serve over rice. Serves 5 to 6.

Fork-Tender Roast

2 - 2½ pound chuck beef roast	910 g - 1.1 kg
1 (14 ounce) can beef broth	395 g
1 (10 ounce) can diced tomatoes and green chilies	280 g
1 teaspoon seasoned salt	5 ml
1 cup baby carrots	135 g
3 medium potatoes, peeled, quartered	
2 onions, thickly sliced, separated into rings	
1 (4 ounce) package mushroom caps	115 g
½ teaspoon liquid smoke	2 ml

- Trim fat off roast. Pour broth and tomatoes and green chilies in sprayed slow cooker. Add roast and season with seasoned salt and ½ teaspoon (2 ml) pepper. Arrange carrots, potatoes, onions and mushrooms around roast. Cover and cook on LOW for 8 to 10 hours or until roast is fork-tender.

- Remove beef and vegetables to serving platter and spoon liquid smoke over roast. Skim fat from reserved cooking liquid and serve cooking liquid with sliced roast and vegetables. Serves 6.

Popular Demand for This Beef

1 (2 pound) boneless beef chuck roast, cut into ¾-inch pieces	910 g/1.8 cm
1 (16 ounce) package frozen green beans, thawed	455 g
1 (10 ounce) package frozen corn, thawed	280 g
1 (5 ounce) box au gratin potato mix	145 g
½ teaspoon dried thyme, crushed	2 ml
1½ cups half-and-half cream	375 ml
1 (8 ounce) package shredded 4-cheese blend	230 g

- Trim off any fat on beef. Combine beef, green beans, corn, potato mix and thyme in sprayed large slow cooker. Pour 3 cups (750 ml) warm water over mixture. Cover and cook on LOW for 7 to 8 hours or on HIGH for 3 hours 30 minutes to 4 hours.

- (If cooking on HIGH, reduce heat to LOW.) Stir in half-and-half cream. Cover and cook for additional 20 minutes. Sprinkle with cheese before serving. Serves 6.

Serious Spaghetti with Roast Beef

1 (2 - 3 pound) beef chuck roast	910 g - 1.4 kg
2 (14 ounce) cans Italian stewed tomatoes	395 g
1 (1 ounce) packet spaghetti seasoning mix	30 g
1 (12 ounce) package thin spaghetti	340 g
1 (8 ounce) package shredded Italian blend cheese	230 g

- Season roast with a little salt and pepper and place in sprayed slow cooker.

- Combine stewed tomatoes and spaghetti seasoning mix in bowl and pour over roast. Cover and cook on LOW for 5 to 7 hours.

- Cook spaghetti according to package directions, drain and place on serving platter. Serve sliced roast over spaghetti with sauce from slow cooker. Sprinkle with cheese. Serves 6 to 8.

Topnotch Barbecue

1 (3 - 4 pound) boneless chuck roast	1.4 - 1.8 kg
1 teaspoon garlic powder	5 ml
1 teaspoon onion powder	5 ml
1 teaspoon chili powder	5 ml
1 (18 ounce) bottle barbecue sauce	510 g

- Trim roast of any fat and place in sprayed slow cooker. Sprinkle with garlic powder, onion powder, chili powder and 1 teaspoon (5 ml) salt. Pour barbecue sauce over roast. Cover and cook on LOW for 6 to 8 hours.

- Remove roast from slow cooker and shred. Return meat to slow cooker, cover and cook for additional 1 hour. This shredded roast is great for barbecue sandwiches. Serves 8.

Because the lid forms a seal with the slow cooker, there is very little evaporation of the cooking liquid. If a stovetop recipe is converted to the slow cooker method, the amount of liquid used (water, broth, etc.) should be reduced. Liquid can be added later if needed.

Appreciate the Pot Roast

1 (10 ounce) can beef broth	280 g
1 (15 ounce) can diced tomatoes with liquid	425 g
1 (1.8 ounce) box leek soup mix	45 g
¾ cup red wine	175 ml
2 teaspoons minced garlic	10 ml
1 teaspoon dried thyme	5 ml
1 teaspoon marjoram	5 ml
1 (4 pound) lean boneless chuck pot roast	1.8 kg
1 (16 ounce) package baby carrots	455 g
3 onions, quartered	
3 tablespoons flour	20 g

- Pour broth into sprayed slow cooker and stir in tomatoes, leek soup mix, wine, garlic, thyme, marjoram and mix well. Place roast in cooker and spoon tomato-wine mixture over roast, coating well. Arrange carrots and onions around roast. Cover and cook on LOW for 9 to 11 hours or until fork tender.

- Remove roast to serving platter and cover with foil to keep warm. Whisk flour with ¼ cup (60 ml) water in bowl and add to liquid in cooker. Change heat setting to HIGH and stir several times until gravy is thick. Remove vegetables with slotted spoon and place around sliced roast and serve gravy in gravy boat. Serves 8.

Juicy and Tender Pot Roast

1 (3 pound) beef chuck roast	1.4 kg
1 (15 ounce) can new potatoes, drained, halved	425 g
1 (8 ounce) can sliced carrots, drained	230 g
2 onions, quartered	
1 (16 ounce) package frozen stew vegetables	455 g
1 (12 ounce) can cola, not diet	355 ml
1 (1 ounce) packet onion soup mix	30 g
2 tablespoons quick-cooking tapioca	35 g

- Brown roast on all sides in sprayed skillet. Place in sprayed slow cooker and top with potatoes, carrots, onions and stew vegetables.

- Combine cola, soup mix and tapioca in small bowl; mix well. Pour mixture over roast and vegetables. Cover and cook on LOW for 7 to 8 hours or on HIGH for 3 hours 30 minutes to 4 hours. Serves 6 to 8.

Family Roast and Veggies

1 (3 - 4 pound) beef rump roast	1.4 - 1.8 kg
1 garlic clove, slivered	
1 (1 ounce) package brown gravy mix, divided	30 g
1 (16 ounce) package baby carrots, cut in half	455 g
8 small red (new) potatoes, scrubbed, quartered	
2 onions, quartered	
2 tablespoons cornstarch	15 g

- Make cuts in top to roast and insert garlic slivers. Spread roast with ½ teaspoon (2 ml) gravy mix and place roast in sprayed slow cooker. Arrange carrots around roast and top with potatoes and onion.

- Combine ½ cup (125 ml) water, remaining gravy mix and a little salt and pepper in small bowl; mix until they blend well. Pour mixture over vegetables. Cover and cook on LOW for 8 to 9 hours.

- When ready to serve, place roast and vegetables on serving platter; cover and keep warm.

- Combine cornstarch and ¼ cup (60 ml) water in medium saucepan and mix well. Pour juices from slow cooker into cornstarch mixture and mix well. Bring to a boil over medium-high heat, stirring constantly; cook until mixture thickens.

- Slice roast and serve with vegetables and gravy. Serves 8 to 10.

Prominent Pot Roast

1 (4 - 5 pound) rump roast	1.8 - 2.3 kg
1 tablespoon canola oil	15 ml
1 (14 ounce) can beef broth	395 g
2 cups ketchup	545 g
⅔ cup cider vinegar	150 ml
2 teaspoons minced garlic	10 ml
½ cup packed brown sugar	110 g
3 onions, quartered	
1 (16 ounce) package baby carrots	455 g
5 ribs celery, cut in 2-inch (5 cm) pieces	
2 red bell peppers, seeded, julienned	

- Rub roast with oil and place in large skillet on high heat; brown on all sides.

- Combine broth, ketchup, vinegar, garlic and brown sugar in bowl, mix well and place in slow cooker. Add roast, onions, carrots, celery and bell peppers. Cover and cook on LOW for 8 hours or until roast is tender.

- Remove roast from cooker and let stand for about 15 minutes. Slice roast and serve with vegetables and sauce from cooker. Serves 10.

Roast at Its Best

1 teaspoon dried oregano	5 ml
1 teaspoon dries basil	5 ml
2 teaspoons garlic powder	10 ml
1 (1 ounce) packet Italian-style salad dressing mix	30 g
1 (4 pound) rump roast	1.8 kg

- Combine oregano, basil, garlic powder, 1 teaspoon (5 ml) pepper and salad dressing mix in large saucepan. Stir in 2 cups (500 ml) water and bring to a boil.

- Place roast in slow cooker and pour seasoning mixture over roast. Cover and cook on LOW for 10 to 11 hours or on HIGH for 4 to 5 hours.

- Place roast on serving platter. Roast will be so tender you can shred it for sandwiches or place on platter and slice, ready to serve for dinner. Serves 8.

Old-Time Pot Roast

1 (2 - 2½) pound boneless rump roast	910 g - 1.1 kg
5 medium potatoes, peeled, quartered	
1 (16 ounce) package peeled baby carrots	455 g
2 medium onions, quartered	
1 (10 ounce) can golden mushroom soup	280 g
½ teaspoon dried basil	2 ml
½ teaspoon seasoned salt	2 ml

- Brown roast on all sides in large, non-stick skillet.

- Place potatoes, carrots and onions in sprayed slow cooker. Place browned roast on top of vegetables.

- Combine soup, basil and seasoned salt in bowl and pour mixture over meat and vegetables. Cover and cook on LOW for 9 to 11 hours. Serves 4 to 6.

TIP: To serve, transfer roast and vegetables to serving plate. Stir juices remaining in slow cooker and spoon over roast and vegetables.

Removing the lid of a slow cooker will cause heat to escape. It will take approximately 20 minutes for the cooker to bring the heat back to the level it was before the lid was lifted.

Mom's Roast and Vegetables

1 (3 pound) rump roast	1.4 kg
Garlic powder	
2 tablespoons canola oil	30 ml
2 (10 ounce) cans cream of celery soup	2 (280 g)
1 (1 ounce) package onion soup mix	30 g
1 (16 ounce) package baby carrots	455 g
6 medium potatoes, peeled, halved	

- Season roast with lots of pepper and garlic powder and brown in oil in skillet over medium heat.

- Combine celery soup and onion soup mix in bowl; mix well. Pour into sprayed slow cooker and place roast on top of soup mixture. Arrange carrots and potatoes around roast. Cover and cook on LOW for 7 to 9 hours, stirring occasionally. Serves 6.

The Authentic Southwest Pot Roast

4 large potatoes, peeled, quartered	
1 (3 pound) boneless beef arm roast	1.4 kg
2 - 3 tablespoons flour	15 - 20 g
1 (16 ounce) package baby carrots	455 g
1 (16 ounce) jar thick-and-chunky hot salsa	455 g

- Place potatoes in sprayed slow cooker. Coat roast well with flour and place over potatoes. Arrange carrots around side of roast. Pour salsa over roast and vegetables. Cover and cook on LOW for 8 to 10 hours.

- Roast will be so tender that it will be hard to slice so pull beef into serving pieces, using 2 forks. Spoon sauce over beef and vegetables. Serves 8.

Herb-Crusted Beef Roast

1 (2 - 3 pound) beef rump roast	910 g - 1.4 kg
¼ cup chopped fresh parsley	15 g
¼ cup chopped fresh oregano leaves	15 g
½ teaspoon dried rosemary leaves	2 ml
1 teaspoon minced garlic	5 ml
1 tablespoon oil	15 ml
6 slices thick-cut bacon	

- Rub roast with a little salt and pepper. Combine parsley, oregano, rosemary, garlic and oil in small bowl and press mixture on top and sides of roast. Place roast in sprayed slow cooker. Place bacon over top of beef and tuck ends under bottom. Cover and cook on LOW for 6 to 8 hours. Serves 4 to 6.

Basic Beef Roast

1 (4 pound) boneless rump roast	1.8 kg
½ cup flour, divided	60 g
1 (1 ounce) packet brown gravy mix	30 g
1 (1 ounce) packet beefy onion soup mix	30 g

- Cut roast in half (if needed to fit into cooker). Place roast in sprayed large slow cooker and rub half of flour over roast.

- Combine remaining flour, gravy mix and soup mix in small bowl, gradually add 2 cups (500 ml) water and stir until they mix well. Pour over roast. Cover and cook on LOW for 7 to 8 hours or until roast is tender. Serves 6 to 8.

TIP: This is a great gravy to serve over mashed potatoes. Use instant mashed potatoes. They will never know the difference and will love the meal!

A Royal Roasted Dinner

1½ pounds red (new) potatoes	680 g
2 teaspoons minced garlic	10 ml
3 - 4 pound boneless beef bottom round roast	1.4 - 1.8 kg
1 (1 ounce) packet garlic-herb soup mix	
(from 2.4 ounce package)	30 g
1 (10 ounce) can beefy mushroom soup	280 g
1 (16 ounce) package frozen green beans, thawed	455 g

- Cut potatoes in halves or quarters if they are rather large. Place potatoes and garlic in sprayed slow cooker and place roast on top. Sprinkle soup mix over roast and spoon mushroom soup over all. Cover and cook on LOW for 8 to 9 hours.

- Remove beef from cooker and place on cutting board. Slice beef and place on serving platter with potatoes on the side; cover and keep warm.

- Increase heat to HIGH and add green beans to remaining sauce. Cover and cook for about 15 minutes and serve with roast and potatoes. Serves 8 to 9.

O'Brian's Hash

3 cups cooked, cubed beef roast	420 g
1 (28 ounce) package frozen hash browns with	
onions and peppers, thawed	795 g
Canola oil	
1 (16 ounce) jar salsa	455 g
1 tablespoon beef seasoning	15 ml
1 cup shredded cheddar-Jack cheese	116 g

- Place beef in sprayed, large slow cooker.

- Brown potatoes in a little oil in large skillet. Stir in salsa and beef seasoning and transfer to slow cooker. Cover and cook on HIGH for 4 to 5 hours. When ready to serve, sprinkle cheese over top. Serves 4.

The Best Ever Brisket

3 onions, sliced	
1 (8 ounce) package fresh mushrooms, halved	230 g
1 (3 - 4) pound trimmed brisket	1.4 - 1.8 kg
1 teaspoon seasoned salt	5 ml
1 (12 ounce) can beer (not light)	355 ml
1 cup chili sauce	270 g

- Layer onions and mushrooms in sprayed large oval slow cooker and sprinkle with seasoned salt. Trim brisket to fit into slow cooker and place on top of onions and mushrooms.

- Combine beer and chili sauce in medium bowl and mix well. Pour mixture over brisket. Cover and cook on LOW for 10 to 12 hours or on HIGH for 5 to 6 hours.

- Remove brisket from slow cooker; let stand for about 10 minutes, then slice meat across the grain. Place brisket on serving platter and place onions and mushrooms around brisket. Serves 8 to 10.

Easy Brisket

1 (1 ounce) packet onion soup mix	30 g
1 (10 ounce) can French onion soup	280 g
1 (3 - 5 pound) trimmed brisket	1.4 - 2.3 kg

- Combine onion soup mix and onion soup in bowl and mix well.

- Place brisket in sprayed oval slow cooker, cutting to fit if necessary. Spoon onion mixture over brisket. Cover and cook on LOW for 10 to 14 hours. Let brisket stand for 10 to 15 minutes before slicing into thin slices. Serves 8 to 10.

Brisket Dinner

4 medium potatoes, peeled, cut into fourths	
1 (16 ounce) package baby carrots	455 g
1 (3 - 4 pound) trimmed beef brisket	1.4 - 1.8 kg
1 teaspoon minced garlic	5 ml
1 (14 ounce) can beef broth	395 g

- Place potatoes and carrots in sprayed slow cooker with brisket placed on top.

- Combine garlic, broth and 1 to 2 cups (250 to 500 ml) water (or enough water, plus broth to cover brisket) in bowl and pour over brisket. Cover and cook on LOW for 6 to 8 hours. Serves 4 to 6.

Sweet and Savory Brisket

1 (3 - 4 pound) trimmed beef brisket, halved	1.4 - 1.8 kg
⅓ cup grape or plum jelly	110 g
1 cup ketchup	270 g
1 (1 ounce) packet onion soup mix	30 g

- Place half of brisket in sprayed slow cooker.

- Combine jelly, ketchup, onion soup mix and ¾ teaspoon (4 ml) pepper in saucepan and heat just enough to mix well. Spread half over brisket.

- Top with remaining brisket and jelly-soup mixture. Cover and cook on LOW for 8 to 9 hours. Slice brisket and serve with cooking juices. Serves 6 to 8.

Smoked Brisket

1 (4 - 6 pound) trimmed brisket	1.8 - 2.7 kg
1 (4 ounce) bottle liquid smoke	115 g
Garlic salt	
Celery salt	
Worcestershire sauce	
1 onion, chopped	
1 (6 ounce) bottle barbecue sauce	170 g

- Place brisket in large shallow dish and pour liquid smoke over top. Sprinkle with garlic salt and celery salt. Cover and refrigerate overnight.

- Before cooking, drain liquid smoke and douse brisket with Worcestershire sauce. Place chopped onion in slow cooker and place brisket on top of onion. Cover and cook on LOW for 6 to 8 hours.

- Pour barbecue sauce over brisket and cook for additional 1 hour. Serves 6 to 8.

Sweet & Spicy Brisket

½ cup packed brown sugar	110 g
1 tablespoon Cajun seasoning	15 ml
2 teaspoons lemon pepper	10 ml
1 tablespoon Worcestershire sauce	15 ml
1 (3 - 4 pound) trimmed beef brisket	1.4 - 1.8 kg

- Combine brown sugar, Cajun seasoning, lemon pepper and Worcestershire in small bowl and spread on brisket. Place brisket in sprayed oval slow cooker. Cover and cook on LOW for 6 to 8 hours. Serves 6 to 8.

Brisket and Gravy

1 (3 - 4 pound) trimmed beef brisket	1.4 - 1.8 kg
¼ cup chili sauce	70 g
1 (1 ounce) packet herb-garlic soup mix	30 g
2 tablespoons Worcestershire sauce	30 ml
3 tablespoons cornstarch	25 g
Mashed potatoes	

- Place beef brisket in sprayed large slow cooker. Cut to fit if necessary.

- Combine chili sauce, soup mix, Worcestershire and 1½ cups (375 ml) water in bowl and pour over brisket. Cover and cook on LOW for 9 to 11 hours.

- Remove brisket and keep warm. Pour juices into 2-cup (500 ml) glass measuring cup and skim fat.

- Combine cornstarch and ¼ cup (60 ml) water in saucepan. Add 1½ cups (375 ml) juices and cook, stirring constantly, until gravy thickens. Slice beef thinly across grain and serve with mashed potatoes and gravy. Serves 6 to 8.

A Saturday Night Reuben

2 tablespoons butter	30 g
2 large sweet onions, chopped	
½ - ¾ pound deli corned beef, sliced	230 - 340 g
1 (15 ounce) jar sauerkraut, drained, divided	425 g
6 slices Swiss cheese, divided	
1 (16 ounce) bottle thousand island salad dressing, divided	455 g

- Place butter in skillet and saute onions on medium-high heat just until onions are translucent.

- Place half corned beef in sprayed slow cooker and top with half onions and half sauerkraut. Top with 3 cheese slices and pour half salad dressing over cheese. Repeat layers. Cover and cook on LOW for 6 to 8 hours. Serves 6.

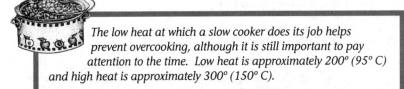

The low heat at which a slow cooker does its job helps prevent overcooking, although it is still important to pay attention to the time. Low heat is approximately 200° (95° C) and high heat is approximately 300° (150° C).

Corned Beef Supper

2 - 3 pounds corned eye of round beef	910 g - 1.4 kg
9 peppercorns	
¼ cup red wine vinegar	60 ml
1 (12 ounce) package baby carrots	340 g
6 medium potatoes, peeled, halved	
1 medium head cabbage, coarsely sliced in 6 wedges	

- Place beef, peppercorns, vinegar and 7 cups (1.7 L) water in sprayed slow cooker. Arrange carrots and potatoes around beef. Cover and cook on LOW for 8 to 10 hours.

- Place cabbage wedges around sides of slow cooker and cook for additional 15 to 20 minutes. Discard liquid in slow cooker. Serves 6.

TIP: In order to keep cabbage pieces together during cooking, leave a bit of the core with each wedge.

A Different Corned Beef

2 onions, sliced	
Lemon pepper	
1 (3 - 4 pound) seasoned corned beef	1.4 - 1.8 kg

- Place sliced onions in sprayed large slow cooker. Add 1 cup (250 ml) water. Sprinkle lemon pepper liberally over corned beef and place on top on onions. Cover and cook on LOW for 7 to 9 hours.

- Remove corned beef from slow cooker and place in ovenproof pan.

Glaze:

¼ cup honey	85 g
¼ cup frozen orange juice concentrate, thawed	60 ml
1 tablespoon mustard	15 ml

- Preheat oven to 375 (190° C).

- Combining all ingredients in bowl and spoon over corned beef. Bake for 30 minutes and baste occasionally with glaze. Serves 6 to 8.

No Hassle Short Ribs

4 - 5 pounds beef short ribs	1.8 - 2.3 kg
1 (1 ounce) packet brown gravy mix	30 g
½ cup beef broth	125 ml
1 tablespoon Worcestershire sauce	15 ml
1 (10 ounce) can golden mushroom soup	280 g

- Place ribs in sprayed slow cooker and sprinkle with a little salt and pepper. Top with gravy mix, broth, Worcestershire and soup. Cover and cook on LOW for 8 to 10 hours. Serves 4 to 6.

Justice with Short Ribs

Flour for coating ribs	
3 pounds beef short ribs	1.4 kg
3 tablespoons olive oil	45 ml
1 onion, thinly sliced	
½ cup chili sauce	135 g
¼ cup packed brown sugar	55 g
3 tablespoons vinegar	45 ml
2 tablespoons flour	15 g

- Coat ribs with lots of salt and pepper; then dredge in flour, coating well. Brown short ribs in oil in large skillet on medium-high heat until light brown.

- Place onion, chili sauce, brown sugar and vinegar in sprayed slow cooker; mix thoroughly. Add browned ribs. Cover and cook on LOW for 6 to 8 hours.

- Remove ribs to serving platter and turn slow cooker to HIGH heat. Combine 2 tablespoons (15 g) flour with ½ cup (125 ml) water in bowl and stir into sauce in slow cooker. Cook for 10 minutes or until mixture thickens. Spoon sauce over ribs. Serves 6.

Beef Ribs and Gravy

4 pounds beef short ribs	1.8 kg
1 onion, sliced	
1 (12 ounce) jar beef gravy	340 g
1 (1 ounce) packet beef gravy mix	30 g
Mashed potatoes	

- Place beef ribs in sprayed large slow cooker. Cover with onion and sprinkle with 1 teaspoon (5 ml) pepper.

- Combine beef gravy and dry gravy mix in small bowl and pour over ribs and onion. Cover and cook on LOW for 9 to 11 hours. (The ribs must cook this long on LOW to tenderize.) Serve with hot mashed potatoes and gravy. Serves 4 to 6.

Ravioli Ready to Eat

1 tablespoon olive oil	15 ml
1 medium onion, chopped	
1 green bell pepper, seeded, chopped	
1 teaspoon minced garlic	5 ml
1 (26 ounce) can four-cheese flavored spaghetti sauce	740 g
1 (10 ounce) can diced tomatoes and green chilies	280 g
1 (8 ounce) can tomato sauce	230 g
1 teaspoon dried Italian seasoning	5 ml
1 (25 ounce) package frozen beef-filled ravioli, thawed	710 g
1 (8 ounce) package shredded mozzarella cheese	230 g
2 fresh green onions, sliced	

- Heat oil in skillet and cook onion, bell pepper and garlic on medium heat for about 5 minutes, stirring often. These should be cooked but not brown. Stir in spaghetti sauce, tomatoes and green chilies, tomato sauce and Italian seasoning.

- Place 1 cup (250 ml) sauce mixture in sprayed slow cooker. Layer beef-filled ravioli and top with half cheese. Pour remaining sauce over top. Cover and cook on LOW for 5 hours 30 minutes to 6 hours 30 minutes. Sprinkle with remaining cheese and green onions. Serves 6.

Meatballs over Noodles

1 (10 ounce) can cream of mushroom soup	280 g
1 (10 ounce) can golden mushroom soup	280 g
1 (10 ounce) can beef broth	280 g
1 (10 ounce) jar brown beef gravy	280 g
1 (18 ounce) package frozen cooked meatballs, thawed	510 g
1 (12 ounce) package wide noodles	340 g

- Combine soups, beef broth and beef gravy in sprayed slow cooker and mix well. Add meatballs; cover and cook on LOW for 6 hours or on HIGH for 3 hours.

- Cook noodles according to package directions, drain and place on serving platter. Spoon meatballs and gravy over noodles or spoon gravy into gravy boat. Serves 4 to 6.

TIP: There will be plenty of gravy if you would like to add more than an 18 ounce (510 g) package of meatballs.

Sauce for Fancy Meatballs

1 (16 ounce) can whole cranberry sauce	455 g
1 cup ketchup	270 g
⅔ cup packed brown sugar	150 g
½ cup beef broth	125 ml
1 (18 ounce) package frozen meatballs, thawed	510 g

- Combine cranberry sauce, ketchup, brown sugar and broth in sprayed large slow cooker. Turn heat to HIGH and let mixture come to a boil, about 30 minutes to 1 hour.

- Place package of thawed meatballs in sauce. Cover and cook on LOW for 2 hours.

- Remove meatballs to serving dish with slotted spoon. Insert toothpicks for easy pick up. Serve as an appetizer, for supper or buffet. Serves 4 to 6.

Chili Supper

2 (15 ounce) cans chili with beans	2 (425 g)
2 (15 ounce) cans kidney beans, rinsed, drained	2 (425 g)
2 - 3 (15 ounce) cans beef tamales, unwrapped	2 - 3 (425 g)
1 (16 ounce) jar hot thick-and-chunky salsa	455 g
1 (8 ounce) package shredded Mexican 4-cheese blend	230 g
2 cups crushed ranch-flavored tortilla chips	110 g

- Spread chili evenly in sprayed slow cooker; cover with beans and then with tamales.

- Combine salsa and cheese in bowl and spread evenly over tamales. Cover and cook on LOW for 5 to 7 hours. When ready to serve, sprinkle crushed tortilla chips over top. Serves 4 to 6.

Special Hot Dog Supper

1 pound beef wieners	455 g
2 (15 ounce) cans chili without beans	2 (425 g)
1 onion, finely chopped	
1 (10 ounce) can cheddar cheese soup	280 g
1 (10 ounce) can fiesta nacho cheese soup	280 g
1 (7 ounce) can diced green chilies, drained	200 g
Corn chips or tortilla chips	

- Cut wieners in ½-inch (1.2 cm) pieces and place in sprayed slow cooker.

- Combine chili, onion, soups, and green chilies in saucepan. (Omit green chilies if serving to kids.) Heat just enough to mix ingredients well. Spoon over wieners. Cover and cook on LOW for 1 hour 30 minutes to 2 hours.

- Serve over bowl of small corn chips or crisp tortilla chips slightly crushed. Serves 4 to 6.

Home Again Beans and Franks

2 (15 ounce) cans pork and beans with liquid	2 (425 g)
1 (15 ounce) can pinto beans, drained	425 g
1 (15 ounce) can kidney beans, rinsed, drained	425 g
1 (10 ounce) can diced tomatoes and green chilies with liquid	280 g
1 small onion, finely chopped	
1 (1 pound) package beef frankfurters, cut into 1-inch pieces	455 g/2.5 cm
⅔ cup barbecue sauce	175 g
1 (6 ounce) package corn muffin mix	170 g
1 egg	
⅓ cup milk	75 ml

- Combine beans, tomatoes and green chilies, onion, frankfurters, and barbecue sauce in sprayed slow cooker. Cover and cook on LOW for 5 to 6 hours or on HIGH for 2 hours 30 minutes to 3 hours.

- About 25 to 30 minutes before serving, combine corn muffin mix, egg and milk in bowl and mix well. Pour in sprayed baking pan and bake at 400° (205° C) for 15 to 20 minutes.

- Cut cornbread into 6 portions and place in individual shallow bowls and spoon bean-frankfurter mixture over cornbread. Serve immediately. Serves 6.

Back Yard Supper

1 (8 count) package beef wieners	
1 onion, finely chopped	
2 (15 ounce) can chili with beans	2 (425 g)
1 (10 ounce) can diced tomatoes and green chilies	280 g
1 teaspoon ground cumin	5 ml
1 (8 ounce) package shredded Velveeta® cheese	230 g
Hot dog buns	

- Combine wieners, onion, chili, tomatoes and green chilies, and cumin in sprayed slow cooker. Cover and cook on LOW for 5 to 7 hours or on HIGH for 2 hours 30 minutes.

- Stir in cheese just before serving and allow cheese to melt. Serve each wiener on hot dog bun and spoon sauce over top. Serves 8.

Southwestern Chicken Pot

6 boneless, skinless chicken breast halves	
1 teaspoon ground cumin	5 ml
1 teaspoon chili powder	5 ml
1 (10 ounce) can cream of chicken soup	280 g
1 (10 ounce) can fiesta nacho cheese soup	280 g
1 cup salsa	265 g
Rice, cooked	
Flour tortillas	

- Sprinkle chicken breasts with cumin, chili powder, and a little salt and pepper and place in sprayed oval slow cooker.

- Combine soups and salsa in saucepan. Heat just enough to mix and pour over chicken breasts. Cover and cook on LOW for 6 to 7 hours. Serve over rice with warmed, flour tortillas spread with butter. Serves 4 to 6.

Senorita's Chicken

4 boneless, skinless chicken breast halves, cut into 1-inch (2.5 cm) pieces	
1 (16 ounce) package smoked sausage, cut into 1-inch (2.5 cm) pieces	455 g
1 (10 ounce) package frozen chopped bell peppers and onions, thawed	280 g
1 teaspoon minced garlic	5 ml
1 teaspoon dried oregano	5 ml
1 (28 ounce) can diced tomatoes	795 g
1 (8 ounce) can black beans, rinsed, drained	230 g
½ teaspoon cayenne pepper	2 ml
2 cups instant rice	190 g

- Combine chicken, sausage, bell peppers and onions, garlic, oregano, tomatoes, beans, and cayenne pepper in sprayed slow cooker; mix well. Cover and cook on LOW for 6 to 8 hours.

- Cook rice according to package directions and place on serving platter. Spoon chicken-sausage mixture over rice. Serves 6.

Creamy Salsa Chicken

4 - 5 boneless, skinless chicken breast halves	
1 (1 ounce) packet taco seasoning mix	30 g
1 cup salsa	265 g
½ cup sour cream	120 g

- Place chicken breasts in sprayed large slow cooker and add ¼ cup (60 ml) water. Sprinkle taco seasoning mix over chicken and top with salsa. Cover and cook on LOW for 5 to 6 hours.

- When ready to serve, remove chicken breasts and place on platter. Stir sour cream into salsa sauce and spoon over chicken breasts. Serves 4 to 5.

Serious Salsa Chicken

6 boneless, skinless chicken breast halves	
1 (16 ounce) jar medium salsa	455 g
1 teaspoon ground cumin	5 ml
¼ teaspoon chili powder	1 ml
3 tablespoons lime juice	45 ml
½ cup chicken broth	125 ml
1 (12 ounce) package thin spaghetti	340 g

- Place chicken breasts in sprayed large oval slow cooker. Pour salsa over chicken. Cover and cook on HIGH for 3 hours to 3 hours 30 minutes or until chicken is thoroughly cooked.

- Stir in cumin, chili powder, lime juice, broth and ½ teaspoon (2 ml) salt; cover and cook for additional 20 minutes.

- Cook spaghetti according to package directions and place on serving platter. Top with chicken breasts and sauce. Serves 6.

Mexicali Chicken

4 boneless, skinless chicken breast halves	
1 onion, chopped	
1 (10 ounce) can cream of chicken soup	280 g
1 (10 ounce) can diced tomatoes and green chilies	280 g
1 (10 ounce) can chicken broth	280 g
1 (8 ounce) package thin spaghetti	230 g
1 (8 ounce) package shredded Mexican 3-cheese blend	230 g

- Layer chicken breasts, onion, soup, tomatoes and green chilies, and ½ teaspoon (2 ml) salt and place in sprayed slow cooker. Pour chicken broth over all. Cover and cook on LOW for 6 to 8 hours.

- Serve chicken breast as is or cut chicken into smaller pieces and mix with other ingredients. Cook spaghetti according to package directions, drain and place on serving platter. Spoon chicken mixture over spaghetti and sprinkle with cheese. Serves 4.

Picante Chicken

4 boneless, skinless chicken breast halves	
1 green bell pepper, seeded, cut in rings	
1 (16 ounce) jar picante sauce	455 g
⅓ cup packed brown sugar	75 g
1 tablespoon mustard	15 ml

- Place chicken breasts in sprayed slow cooker with bell pepper rings over top of chicken. Combine picante, brown sugar and mustard in bowl and spoon over top of chicken. Cover and cook on LOW for 4 to 5 hours. Serves 4.

Chicken Fajitas

2 pounds boneless, skinless chicken breast halves	910 g
1 onion, thinly sliced	
1 red bell pepper, seeded, julienned	
1 teaspoon ground cumin	5 ml
1½ teaspoons chili powder	7 ml
1 tablespoon lime juice	15 ml
½ cup chicken broth	125 ml
8 - 10 warm flour tortillas	
Guacamole	
Sour cream	
Lettuce and tomatoes	

- Cut chicken into diagonal strips and place in sprayed slow cooker. Top with onion and bell pepper.

- Combine cumin, chili powder, lime juice and chicken broth in bowl and pour over chicken and vegetables. Cover and cook on LOW for 5 to 7 hours. Serve several slices of chicken mixture with sauce into center of each warm tortilla and fold. Serve with guacamole, sour cream, lettuce and/or tomatoes or plain. Serves 4 to 6.

Chicken Olé

6 boneless, skinless chicken breast halves	
1 (8 ounce) package cream cheese, softened	230 g
1 (16 ounce) jar salsa	455 g
2 teaspoons cumin	10 ml
1 bunch fresh green onions with tops, chopped	

- Pound chicken breasts to flatten. Beat cream cheese in bowl until smooth, add salsa, cumin and onions and mix gently.

- Place heaping spoonfuls of cream cheese mixture on each chicken breast and roll. (There will be leftover cream cheese mixture.) Place chicken breasts seam-side down in sprayed slow cooker. Spoon remaining cream cheese mixture over each chicken roll. Cover and cook on LOW for 5 to 6 hours. Serves 4 to 6.

Taco Chicken

3 cups cooked, chopped chicken	420 g
1 (1 ounce) packet taco seasoning	30 g
1 cup rice	200 g
2 cups chopped celery	200 g
1 green bell pepper, seeded, chopped	
2 (15 ounce) cans Mexican stewed tomatoes	2 (425 g)

- Combine chicken, taco seasoning, rice, celery, bell pepper and stewed tomatoes in bowl and mix well. Pour into sprayed slow cooker. Cover and cook on LOW for 4 to 5 hours. Serves 4 to 6.

TIP: This is a great recipe for leftover chicken or cooked chopped pork roast.

Sassy Chicken with Tex-Mex Corn

2 teaspoons garlic powder	10 ml
1 teaspoon ground cumin	5 ml
⅓ cup flour	40 g
5 - 6 boneless, skinless chicken breast halves	
1 (10 ounce) can chicken broth	280 g
1 (16 ounce) jar hot salsa	455 g
2 (11 ounce) cans Mexicorn®, drained	2 (310 g)

- Combine garlic powder, cumin, flour and ½ teaspoon (2 ml) salt in shallow bowl and coat each side of chicken with flour mixture. Place chicken in sprayed slow cooker.

- Combine broth, salsa and corn in bowl; mix well and spoon over chicken breasts. Cover and cook on LOW for 6 to 8 hours.

- Place chicken on platter and spoon corn mixture over each chicken breast. Serves 5 to 6.

Lush Pizza-Parmesan Chicken

1 large egg, beaten	
1 cup seasoned breadcrumbs	120 g
2 tablespoons canola oil	30 ml
6 boneless, skinless chicken breast halves	
1 (10 ounce) jar pizza sauce	280 g
⅔ cup grated parmesan cheese	70 g
6 slices mozzarella cheese	

- Place egg in shallow bowl. In separate shallow bowl, place breadcrumbs. Dip chicken breasts into egg and then into breadcrumbs, using spoon to coat chicken with crumbs on all sides. Heat oil in large skillet and saute chicken.

- Arrange one layer of chicken in sprayed slow cooker and pour half pizza sauce on top. Add second layer of chicken and pour remaining sauce over top. Cover and cook on LOW for 6 to 8 hours or just until chicken is tender but not dry.

- Sprinkle with parmesan cheese and add mozzarella slices on top; cover and cook for additional 15 minutes. Serves 6.

Capital Cacciatore, Italian Style

6 boneless, skinless chicken breast halves
1 (16 ounce) package frozen chopped bell peppers
    and onions thawed   455 g
1 (8 ounce) carton whole mushrooms, sliced   230 g
1 tablespoon minced garlic   15 ml
1 (28 ounce) bottle spaghetti sauce   795 g
1 (12 ounce) package thin spaghetti   340 g

- Place chicken in sprayed slow cooker and sprinkle with a little salt and pepper. Top with bell peppers and onions, mushrooms, and garlic and spread spaghetti sauce over all. Cover and cook on LOW for 7 to 9 hours.

- Cook spaghetti according to package directions, drain and place on serving plate. Place chicken breasts; add sauce and serve. Serves 6.

Rolled Chicken Florentine

6 boneless, skinless chicken breast halves
6 thin slices ham
6 slices Swiss cheese
1 (10 ounce) package frozen chopped spinach,
    thawed, well drained*   280 g
1 (16 ounce) package baby carrots   455 g
2 (10 ounce) cans cream of chicken soup   2 (280 g)
1 (10 ounce) box chicken-flavored rice   280 g

- With flat side of meat mallet, pound chicken to ¼-inch (6 mm) thickness. Place ham slice, cheese slice and ¼ cup (10 g) spinach on each chicken piece and roll chicken from short end, jellyroll-style.

- Place carrots in sprayed slow cooker and top with chicken rolls. Spoon soup over rolls; cover and cook on LOW for 6 to 8 hours.

- Cook rice according to package directions and serve carrots, chicken rolls and sauce over rice. Serves 6.

*TIP: Squeeze spinach between paper towels to completely remove excess moisture.

Chicken Linguine

1 (26 ounce) jar garlic-onion spaghetti sauce	735 g
2 (16 ounce) packages frozen broccoli, carrots and cauliflower, thawed	2 (455 g)
1 (10 ounce) package frozen chopped bell peppers and onions, thawed	280 g
⅓ cup grated parmesan cheese	35 g
1 pound boneless, skinless chicken breast halves, cut into strips	455 g
1 (12 ounce) package dry linguine	340 g

- Pour spaghetti sauce in sprayed slow cooker and add vegetables, sprinkle with parmesan cheese. Place chicken strips on top of vegetable mixture. Cover and cook on LOW for 5 to 7 hours.

- Cook linguine according to package directions, drain and place on serving platter. Top with chicken strips and vegetables. Serves 8.

TIP: Break linguine into thirds before cooking to make serving a little easier. Cooked, sliced ham also works well in this recipe if you change the parmesan cheese to ⅔ cup (75 g) shredded Italian cheese blend.

Easy Citrus Chicken

6 boneless, skinless chicken breast halves	
Canola oil	
1 (1 ounce) packet dry onion soup mix	30 g
1 (6 ounce) can frozen orange juice concentrate, thawed	175 ml

- Brown chicken breasts in a little oil in skillet and place in sprayed large slow cooker.

- Combine onion soup mix, orange juice concentrate and ½ cup (125 ml) water in bowl and pour over chicken. Cover and cook on LOW for 3 to 5 hours. Serves 4 to 6.

Once food has been cooked and served, it is best to remove the food from the ceramic insert to refrigerate. The liners of slow cookers are made of very heavy material and do not cool quickly. This can enable the growth of harmful bacteria if food is left in the ceeramic insert.

Asian Chicken

4 boneless, skinless chicken breast halves	
2 - 3 cups sliced celery	200 - 300 g
1 onion, coarsely chopped	
⅓ cup soy sauce	75 ml
¼ teaspoon cayenne pepper	1 ml
1 (14 ounce) can chicken broth	395 g
1 (15 ounce) can bean sprouts, drained	425 g
1 (8 ounce) can water chestnuts, drained	230 g
1 (6 ounce) can bamboo shoots	170 g
¼ cup flour	30 g
Chow mein noodles	

- Combine chicken, celery, onion, soy sauce, cayenne pepper and chicken broth in sprayed slow cooker. Cover and cook on LOW for 3 to 4 hours.

- Add bean sprouts, water chestnuts and bamboo shoots to chicken. Mix flour and ¼ cup (60 ml) water in bowl and stir into chicken and vegetables. Cook for additional 1 hour. Serve over chow mein noodles. Serves 4.

Chicken Chow Mein

2 (15 ounce) cans chop suey vegetables	2 (425 g)
1 (8 ounce) can sliced water chestnuts, drained	230 g
¾ cup chopped cashews	100 g
1 (10 ounce) package frozen chopped bell peppers	
and onions, thawed	280 g
3 ribs celery, sliced	
3 - 4 cups cooked, diced chicken breasts	420 - 560 g
¼ teaspoon hot sauce	1 ml
2 (10 ounce) cans cream of chicken soup	2 (280 g)
1 (5 ounce) can chow mein noodles	145 g

- Combine chop suey vegetables, water chestnuts, cashews, bell peppers and onions, celery, and chicken in sprayed slow cooker. Stir hot sauce into soup and spoon over ingredients in slow cooker. Cover and cook on LOW for 5 to 7 hours.

- Place about ¾ cup (40 g) chow mein noodles on individual plates and spoon chicken over noodles. Serves 8.

TIP: This recipe also works well with cooked, diced ham instead of chicken.

Cashew Chicken and Veggies

2 (16 ounce) packages frozen broccoli florets, thawed	2 (455 g)
1 (16 ounce) baby carrots, cut in half	455 g
1 red bell pepper, seeded, julienned	
6 boneless, skinless chicken breast halves	
1 (1 ounce) packet herb-garlic soup mix	30 g
1 (10 ounce) can cream of celery soup	280 g
2 tablespoons cornstarch	15 g
1 tablespoon soy sauce	15 ml
1 teaspoon fresh grated ginger	5 ml
1 (6 ounce) package chicken and herb-flavored rice, cooked	170 g
¾ - 1 cup whole roasted cashews	105 - 140 g

- Combine broccoli, carrots and bell pepper strips in sprayed slow cooker and top with chicken breasts.

- Combine soup mix, soup, cornstarch, soy sauce, ½ cup (125 ml) water and ginger in bowl and mix well. Spoon over chicken and vegetables. Cover and cook on LOW for 6 to 8 hours.

- Cook rice according to package directions, place on serving platter and top with chicken breasts. Sprinkle cashews over chicken. Serves 6.

Hot-n-Sour Chicky Casserole

2 (16 ounce) packages frozen broccoli, cauliflower and carrots, thawed	2 (455 g)
3 ribs celery, sliced	
3 - 4 boneless, skinless chicken breast halves, cooked, cut into strips	
1 (10 ounce) jar sweet-and-sour sauce	280 g
1 (3 ounce) package chicken-flavored instant ramen noodles	85 g

- Place broccoli, cauliflower and carrots and celery in sprayed slow cooker. Place chicken strips over top of vegetables and pour sweet-and-sour sauce on top. Cover and cook on LOW for 5 to 7 hours.

- Stir in ramen noodles, seasoning packet and 1½ cups (375 ml) boiling water. Cover and cook for additional 20 to 30 minutes. Serves 8.

It is recommended that dried beans be boiled for 10 minutes, then simmered for 1 hour to 1 hour 30 minutes before draining and adding to a slow cooker for best results. This is, of course, not necessary for canned beans.

Sweet-and-Sour Chicken

4 - 5 boneless skinless chicken breast halves	
1 (10 ounce) package frozen chopped bell peppers	
and onions, thawed	280 g
1 (10 ounce) can chicken broth	280 g
1 tablespoon hoisin sauce	15 ml
¼ cup vinegar	60 ml
½ cup apricot preserves	160 g
⅓ cup cornstarch	45 g
Rice, cooked	

- Place chicken and bell peppers and onions in sprayed slow cooker.

- Combine broth, hoisin sauce, vinegar, preserves and 1½ teaspoons (7 ml) salt and mix well. Pour mixture over chicken. Cover and cook on LOW for 5 hours.

- Increase heat to HIGH; mix cornstarch with 2 tablespoons (30 ml) water in bowl and stir into slow cooker. Cook for additional 20 minutes. Serves 4 to 5.

Colorful Chicken with Cashews

5 boneless, skinless chicken breast halves, cut	
into 1-inch (2.5 cm) strips	
2 ribs celery, sliced	
¼ cup soy sauce	60 ml
¼ teaspoon ginger	1 ml
½ cup chicken broth	125 ml
1 (8 ounce) can sliced bamboo shoots, drained	230 g
½ cup Chinese pea pods	100 g
½ cup cashews, toasted	65 g
2 tablespoons cornstarch	15 g
Rice, cooked	

- Place chicken strips and celery in sprayed slow cooker. Add soy sauce, ginger, broth and a little salt and pepper. Cover and cook on LOW for 4 to 4 hours to 30 minutes.

- Increase heat to HIGH and add bamboo shoots, pea pods and cashews. Dissolve cornstarch in 2 tablespoons (30 ml) water in bowl and stir into slow cooker. Cover and cook for about 25 minutes or until thickened, stirring once. Serve over rice. Serves 6.

Chop-Chop Suey

3 boneless, skinless chicken breast halves	
3 ribs celery, sliced	
1 onion, chopped	
½ teaspoon dried ginger	2 ml
1 (10 ounce) can chicken broth	280 g
¼ cup soy sauce	60 ml
1 (8 ounce) package fresh mushrooms	230 g
1 cup fresh bean sprouts	35 g
1 (15 ounce) can mixed Chinese vegetables	425 g
3 tablespoon cornstarch	20 g

- Cut chicken into 1½-inch (3 cm) slices and place in sprayed slow cooker. Stir in celery, onion and ginger. Combine broth and soy sauce in bowl and pour over chicken mixture. Cover and cook on LOW for 5 to 6 hours.

- Increase heat to HIGH and add mushrooms, bean sprouts and Chinese vegetables and cook for additional 10 minutes.

- Mix cornstarch with 2 tablespoons (30 ml) water in bowl and stir into chicken mixture, mixing well. Cook and stir for additional 10 minutes or until mixture thickens. Serves 6

Bacon-Wrapped Chicken

1 (2.5 ounce) jar dried beef	70 g
6 boneless, skinless chicken breast halves	
6 slices bacon	
2 (10 ounce) cans golden mushroom soup	2 (280 g)
1 (6 ounce) package parmesan-butter rice, cooked	170 g

- Place sliced dried beef in sprayed slow cooker. Roll each chicken breast half in slice of bacon and place over dried beef.

- Heat soup and ⅓ cup (75 ml) water in saucepan just enough to mix well and pour over chicken. Cover and cook on LOW for 7 to 8 hours. Serve over rice. Serves 4 to 6.

Fix It Chicken

1 (10 ounce) can cream of chicken soup	280 g
1 (4 ounce) can sliced mushrooms	115 g
1 small onion, finely chopped	
1 teaspoon Italian seasoning	5 ml
1½ pounds boneless, skinless chicken breast, cut in strips	680 g
Rice, cooked	

- Combine soup, mushrooms, onion and seasoning in sprayed slow cooker. Place chicken strips in slow cooker. Cover and cook on HIGH for 3 hours. This chicken is delicious served over rice. Serves 4.

TIP: Try using 1½ pounds (680 g) cooked, diced ham instead of chicken and add 2 ribs sliced celery.

Slow Cooker Cordon Bleu

4 boneless, skinless chicken breast halves
4 slices cooked ham
4 slices Swiss cheese, softened
1 (10 ounce) can cream of chicken soup   280 g
¼ cup milk   60 ml
Noodles, cooked

- Place chicken breasts on cutting board and pound until breast halves
  are thin. Place ham and cheese slices on chicken breasts, roll and
  secure with toothpick. Arrange chicken rolls in sprayed slow cooker.

- Pour chicken soup with milk into saucepan, heat just enough to
  mix well and pour over chicken rolls. Cover and cook on LOW
  for 4 to 5 hours. Serve over noodles and cover with sauce from
  cooker. Serves 4.

Chicken Breasts Supreme

1 (8 ounce) can sliced water chestnuts, drained   230 g
1 (8 ounce) carton whole mushrooms   230 g
2 green bell peppers, seeded, chopped
3 ribs celery, sliced
5 boneless, skinless chicken breast halves, cut
        in half lengthwise
¼ cup (½ stick) butter, melted   60 g
1 (10 ounce) can cream of chicken soup   280 g
1 (10 ounce) can chicken broth   280 g
2 cups instant rice   190 g

- Place water chestnuts, mushrooms, bell peppers and celery in sprayed
  slow cooker. Sprinkle chicken breasts with a little salt and pepper and
  place over vegetables.

- Combine melted butter, soup and chicken broth in bowl and pour over
  chicken breasts. Cover and cook on LOW for 6 to 8 hours.

- Cook rice according to package directions and place on serving plate
  and top with chicken and sauce. Serves 5.

Supper-Ready Limeade Chicken

6 boneless, skinless chicken breast halves	
1 (6 ounce) can frozen limeade concentrate, thawed	170 g
3 tablespoons brown sugar	45 g
¾ cup chili sauce	205 g
1 teaspoon dijon-style mustard	5 ml
2 cups instant rice	190 g

- Dry chicken breasts with paper towels and place in sprayed large slow cooker

- Combine limeade concentrate, brown sugar, chili sauce and mustard in saucepan over medium heat; stirring until mixture blends well. Pour over chicken breasts. Cover and cook on LOW for 6 to 8 hours.

- Cook rice according to package directions and place on large serving plate and top with chicken breasts and sauce. Serves 6.

Sweet Pepper Chicken

6 - 8 boneless, skinless chicken breast halves	
1 (20 ounce) can pineapple chunks with liquid	570 g
⅔ cup sugar	135 g
⅔ cup packed brown sugar	150 g
1 teaspoon chicken bouillon granules	5 ml
1 cup orange juice	250 ml
½ cup vinegar	125 ml
¼ cup ketchup	70 g
1 tablespoon soy sauce	15 ml
⅓ cup cornstarch	45 g
1 green bell pepper, seeded, sliced	
1 red bell pepper, seeded, sliced	
Rice, cooked	

- Dry chicken breasts with paper towels and place in sprayed large slow cooker.

- Drain pineapple and set pineapple aside. Combine pineapple juice, sugar, brown sugar, bouillon, orange juice, vinegar, ketchup, soy sauce and cornstarch in large bowl. Pour over chicken. Cover and cook on LOW for 7 to 9 hours.

- Place pineapple chunks and bell pepper slices over chicken. Serve over rice. Serves 6 to 8.

Everything Good Chicken Supper

1 cup chopped celery	100 g
3 medium zucchini, sliced 1-inch (2.5 cm) thick	
1 (16 ounce) package baby carrots	455 g
1 onion, chopped	
1 green bell pepper, seeded, sliced	
5 boneless, skinless chicken breast halves, cut in half lengthwise	
½ teaspoon dill weed	2 ml
1 teaspoon dried basil	5 ml
1 (10 ounce) can cream of chicken soup	280 g
1 (10 ounce) can fiesta nacho cheese soup	280 g
¼ cup milk	60 ml
1½ cups cracker crumbs	90 g
½ cup chopped walnuts	65 g

- Combine celery, zucchini, carrots, onion and bell pepper in sprayed slow cooker.

- Dry chicken strips with paper towels and place on top of vegetables. Sprinkle with dill weed, basil, and 1 teaspoon (5 ml) each of salt and pepper.

- Combine chicken soup, cheese soup and milk in bowl and pour over chicken and veggies. Cover and cook on LOW for 7 to 9 hours.

- About 15 minutes before serving, place crumbs and walnuts in baking pan and heat at 325° (160° C) oven for 15 minutes. Sprinkle over chicken-veggie mixture. Serves 5.

Classy Chicken Dinner

1 (6 ounce) box long grain-wild rice	170 g
1 (16 ounce) jar roasted garlic-parmesan cheesy sauce	455 g
12 - 15 frozen chicken breast tenderloins, thawed	
1 cup frozen petite green peas, thawed	145 g

- Pour 2½ cups (625 ml) water, rice and seasoning packet in sprayed slow cooker and stir well.

- Spoon in cheesy sauce and mix well. Place chicken tenderloins in slow cooker and cover with green peas. Cover and cook on LOW for 4 to 5 hours. Serves 4.

Creamy Chicken and Potatoes

4 boneless, skinless chicken breast halves	
2 teaspoons chicken seasoning	10 ml
8 - 10 small new (red) potatoes with peels	
1 (10 ounce) can cream of chicken soup	280 g
1 (8 ounce) carton sour cream	230 g

- Sprinkle chicken breast halves with chicken seasoning and place in sprayed slow cooker. Arrange new potatoes around chicken.

- Combine soup, sour cream and a good amount of pepper in bowl. Spoon over chicken breasts. Cover and cook on LOW for 4 to 6 hours. Serves 4.

Creamed Chicken

4 large boneless, skinless chicken breast halves	
Lemon juice	
1 red bell pepper, seeded, chopped	
2 ribs celery, sliced diagonally	
1 (10 ounce) can cream of chicken soup	280 g
1 (10 ounce) can cream of celery soup	280 g
⅓ cup dry white wine	75 ml
1 (4 ounce) package grated parmesan cheese	115 g
Rice, cooked	

- Wash chicken and pat dry with paper towels. Rub a little lemon juice over chicken and sprinkle with a little salt and pepper. Place in sprayed slow cooker and top with celery.

- Combine soups and wine in saucepan and heat just enough to mix thoroughly. Pour over chicken breasts and sprinkle with parmesan cheese. Cover and cook on LOW for 6 to 7 hours. Serve over rice. Serves 4.

TIP: For a change of pace, use 4 boneless pork chops instead of chicken and replace the cream of celery soup with cream of onion soup.

The slow cooker has found new popularity with the busy lifestyle of today's cook. Not only is the slow cooker a time-saver, it saves energy because it uses very little electricity. When cooking on the low setting, the slow cooker will use less energy than most light bulbs.

Chicken and Vegetables with Gravy

4 large boneless, skinless chicken breast halves
1 (10 ounce) can cream of chicken soup   280 g
1 (16 ounce) package frozen peas and carrots, thawed 455 g
1 (12 ounce) jar chicken gravy   340 g
Buttermilk biscuits or Texas toast

- Cut chicken in thin slices.

- Pour soup and ½ cup (125 ml) water into sprayed large slow cooker, mix and add chicken slices. Sprinkle a little salt and lots of pepper over chicken and soup. Cover and cook on LOW for 4 to 5 hours.

- Add peas and carrots, chicken gravy and ½ cup (125 ml) water. Increase heat to HIGH and cook for about 1 hour or until peas and carrots are tender. Serve over large, refrigerated buttermilk biscuits or over Texas toast (thick slices of bread). Serves 4.

Delightfully Creamy Chicken and Veggies

4 - 5 boneless, skinless chicken breast halves
1 (15 ounce) can whole kernel corn, drained   425 g
1 (10 ounce) box frozen green peas, thawed   280 g
1 (16 ounce) jar alfredo sauce   455 g
1 teaspoon chicken seasoning   5 ml
1 teaspoon minced garlic   5 ml
Pasta, cooked

- Brown chicken breasts in skillet and place in sprayed oval slow cooker.

- Combine corn, peas, alfredo sauce, ¼ cup (60 ml) water, chicken seasoning and minced garlic in bowl and spoon mixture over chicken breasts. Cover and cook on LOW for 4 to 5 hours. Serve over pasta. Serves 4 to 5.

Farmhouse Supper

1 (8 ounce) package medium noodles	230 g
4 - 5 boneless, skinless chicken breast halves	
Canola oil	
1 (14 ounce) can chicken broth	395 g
2 cups sliced celery	200 g
2 onions, chopped	
1 green bell pepper, seeded, chopped	
1 red bell pepper, seeded, chopped	
1 (10 ounce) can cream of chicken soup	280 g
1 (10 ounce) can cream of mushroom soup	280 g
1 cup shredded 4-cheese blend	115 g

- Cook noodles in boiling water until barely tender and drain well.

- Cut chicken into thin slices and brown lightly in skillet with a little oil. Mix noodles, chicken and broth in sprayed, large slow cooker. Make sure noodles separate and coat with broth. Stir in remaining ingredients. Cover and cook on LOW for 4 to 6 hours. Serves 4 to 5.

Golden Chicken Dinner

5 boneless, skinless chicken breast halves	
6 medium red potatoes with peels, cubed	
6 medium carrots, chopped	
1 tablespoon dried parsley flakes	15 ml
1 teaspoon seasoned salt	5 ml
1 (10 ounce) can golden mushroom soup	280 g
1 (10 ounce) can cream of chicken soup	280 g
¼ cup dried mashed potato flakes	15 g
Water or milk	

- Cut chicken into ½-inch (1.2 cm) pieces. Place potatoes and carrots in sprayed slow cooker and top with chicken breasts.

- Sprinkle parsley flakes, seasoned salt and ½ teaspoon (2 ml) pepper over chicken. Combine soups in bowl and spread over chicken. Cover and cook on LOW for 6 to 7 hours.

- Stir in potato flakes and a little water or milk if necessary to make gravy and cook for additional 30 minutes. Serves 4 to 6.

TIP: Omit the chicken and use 5 thick lean pork chops.

Hawaiian Chicken

6 boneless, skinless chicken breast halves
1 (15 ounce) can pineapple slices with juice   425 g
⅓ cup packed brown sugar   75 g
2 tablespoons lemon juice   30 ml
¼ teaspoon ground ginger   1 ml
¼ cup cornstarch   30 g
Rice, cooked

- Place chicken breasts in sprayed oval slow cooker and sprinkle with a little salt. Place pineapple slices over chicken.

- Combine pineapple juice, brown sugar, lemon juice, ginger and cornstarch in small bowl and stir until cornstarch mixes with liquids. Pour over chicken breasts. Cover and cook on LOW for 4 to 5 hours or on HIGH for 2 hours 30 minutes to 3 hours. Serve over rice. Serves 4 to 6.

Never-Fail Chicken Spaghetti

6 boneless, skinless chicken breast halves, cooked, cubed
2 (10 ounce) cans cream of chicken soup   2 (280 g)
½ cup milk   125 ml
1 (4 ounce) can sliced mushrooms, drained   115 g
¼ cup (½ stick) butter, melted   60 g
1 (12 ounce) package thin spaghetti   340 g
1 (5 ounce) package grated parmesan cheese   145 g

- Combine chicken, soup, milk, mushrooms and butter in sprayed slow cooker; stir until blended well. Cover and cook on LOW for 6 to 8 hours.

- Cook spaghetti according to package instructions and place on serving platter. Spoon chicken mixture and sauce over spaghetti and top with cheese. Serves 6 to 8.

Imperial Chicken

1 (6 ounce) box long grain-wild rice   170 g
1 (16 ounce) jar roasted garlic-parmesan cheesy sauce   455 g
6 boneless, skinless chicken breast halves
1 (16 ounce) box frozen French-style green beans, thawed 455 g
½ cup slivered almonds, toasted   85 g

- Combine 2½ cups (625 ml) water, rice and seasoning packet in sprayed oval slow cooker and stir well.

- Spoon in cheesy sauce and mix well. Place chicken breasts in slow cooker and cover with green beans. Cover and cook on LOW for 3 to 5 hours. When ready to serve, sprinkle with slivered almonds. Serves 4 to 6.

Here's the Stuff

5 boneless, skinless chicken breast halves
2 (10 ounce) cans cream of chicken soup   2 (280 g)
1 (6 ounce) box chicken stuffing mix   170 g
1 (16 ounce) package frozen green peas, thawed   455 g

- Place chicken breasts in sprayed large slow cooker and spoon soups over chicken.

- Combine stuffing mix with ingredients on package directions in bowl and spoon over chicken and soup. Cover and cook on LOW for 5 to 6 hours.

- Sprinkle drained green peas over top of stuffing. Cover and cook for additional 45 to 50 minutes. Serves 4 to 5.

TIP: For a nice variation, substitute 1 (10 ounce/280 g) can fiesta nacho cheese soup for 1 can of cream of chicken soup.

Mushroom Chicken

4 boneless, skinless chicken breasts halves
1 (15 ounce) can tomato sauce   425 g
2 (4 ounce) cans sliced mushrooms, drained   2 (115 g)
1 (10 ounce) package frozen chopped onions and bell peppers   280 g
2 teaspoons Italian seasoning   10 ml
1 teaspoon minced garlic   5 ml

- Brown chicken breasts in skillet and place in sprayed oval slow cooker.

- Combine tomato sauce, mushrooms, onions and peppers, Italian seasoning, garlic, and ¼ cup (60 ml) water in bowl and spoon over chicken breasts. Cover and cook on LOW for 4 to 5 hours. Serves 4.

Quick-Fix Chicken

4 - 6 boneless, skinless chicken breast halves
1 (8 ounce) carton sour cream   230 g
¼ cup soy sauce   60 ml
2 (10 ounce) cans French onion soup   2 (280 g)
Rice or mashed potatoes, cooked

- Wash chicken, dry with paper towels and place in sprayed oval slow cooker.

- Combine sour cream, soy sauce and soup in bowl, stir and mix well. Add to slow cooker. Cover and cook on LOW for 5 to 6 hours if chicken breasts are large, 3 to 4 hours if breasts are medium-size. Serve with rice or mashed potatoes. Serves 4 to 6.

Orange Chicken

6 boneless, skinless chicken breast halves
1 (12 ounce) jar orange marmalade   340 g
1 (8 ounce) bottle Russian salad dressing   250 ml
1 (1 ounce) packet onion soup mix   30 g

- Place chicken breasts in sprayed oval slow cooker. Combine orange marmalade, dressing, soup mix and ¾ cup (175 ml) water in bowl and stir well. Spoon mixture over chicken breasts. Cover and cook on LOW for 4 to 6 hours. Serves 4 to 6.

Oregano Chicken

½ cup (1 stick) butter, melted   115 g
1 (1 ounce) packet Italian salad dressing   30 g
1 tablespoon lemon juice   15 ml
4 - 5 boneless, skinless chicken breast halves
2 tablespoons dried oregano   30 ml

- Combine butter, dressing and lemon juice in bowl and mix well.

- Place chicken breasts in sprayed large slow cooker. Spoon butter-lemon juice mixture over chicken. Cover and cook on LOW for 4 to 5 hours.

- Baste chicken with pan juices, sprinkle oregano over chicken and cook 1 additional hour. Serves 4 to 6.

TIP: This recipe works well with boneless pork chops instead of chicken. For a complete meal, add a 10 ounce (280 g) can French onion soup and serve over thin spaghetti.

Encore Chicken

2 green bell peppers, seeded, cut into strips
6 boneless, skinless chicken breast halves
1 tablespoon canola oil   15 ml
1 (16 ounce) jar hot thick-and-chunky salsa   455 g
1½ cups packed brown sugar   330 g
1 tablespoon dijon-style mustard   15 ml
2 cups instant brown rice   375 g

- Place bell pepper strips in sprayed slow cooker.

- Heat oil in skillet on medium-high heat and cook chicken just until slightly brown and place on top of bell peppers.

- Combine salsa, brown sugar, mustard and ½ teaspoon (2 ml) salt in small bowl and pour over chicken. Cover and cook on LOW for 6 to 8 hours.

- Cook rice according to package directions; place on serving platter and top with chicken and sauce. Serves 6.

Chicken a la Orange

5 - 6 boneless, skinless chicken breast halves	
1 - 2 tablespoons salt-free garlic and herb seasoning	15 - 30 ml
2 (11 ounce) cans mandarin oranges, drained	2 (310 g)
1 (6 ounce) can frozen orange juice concentrate	175 ml
1 tablespoon lemon juice	15 ml
1 (10 ounce) can chicken broth	280 g
2 tablespoons cornstarch	15 g
2 - 3 cups cooked rice	315 - 475 g

- Place chicken breasts in sprayed slow cooker and sprinkle with garlic-herb seasoning.

- Combine oranges, orange juice concentrate, lemon juice, broth, cornstarch and ⅓ cup (75 ml) water in bowl, mix well. Pour mixture into slow cooker. Cover and cook on LOW for 6 to 8 hours.

- Place cooked rice on serving platter and top with chicken and sauce. Serves 5 to 6.

Chicken and Artichokes

¼ cup (½ stick) plus 2 tablespoons butter, divided	85 g
6 boneless, skinless chicken breast halves	
1 (14 ounce) jar water-packed artichoke hearts, drained	395 g
1 (8 ounce) can sliced water chestnuts, drained	230 g
1 red bell pepper, seeded, cut into strips	
1 green bell pepper, seeded, cut into strips	
⅛ teaspoon ground nutmeg	.5 ml
1 teaspoon dried thyme	5 ml
1 (14 ounce) can chicken broth	395 g
1 (10 ounce) can cream of celery soup	280 g
1 (8 ounce) package shredded Velveeta® cheese	230 g
1½ cups seasoned breadcrumbs	180 g

- Melt ¼ cup (55 g) butter in large skillet on medium heat, lightly brown chicken and place in sprayed slow cooker.

- Cut each artichoke heart in half and place artichokes, water chestnuts and bell peppers around chicken.

- Combine nutmeg, thyme, broth, celery soup and cheese in bowl, mix well and pour over chicken-artichoke mixture. Cover and cook on LOW for 7 to 9 hours.

- Ten minutes before serving, place breadcrumbs and 2 tablespoons (30 g) melted butter in pan and stir until crumbs are well coated with butter. Heat in 325° (160° C) oven for about 10 minutes. Sprinkle over dish. Serves 6.

Chicken for the Gods

1¾ cups flour	180 g
Scant 2 tablespoons dry mustard	30 ml
6 boneless, skinless chicken breast halves	
2 tablespoons canola oil	30 ml
1 (10 ounce) can chicken-rice soup	280 g

- Combine flour and mustard in shallow bowl and dredge chicken to coat all sides. Brown chicken breasts in oil in skillet. Place breasts in sprayed oval slow cooker.

- Pour soup over chicken and add ¼ cup (60 ml) water. Cover and cook on LOW for 6 to 7 hours. Serves 4 to 6.

Apricot Chicken

6 boneless, skinless chicken breasts halves	
1 (12 ounce) jar apricot preserves	340 g
1 (8 ounce) bottle Catalina dressing	250 ml
1 (1 ounce) packet onion soup mix	30 g

- Place chicken in sprayed large slow cooker.

- Combine apricot preserves, Catalina dressing, onion soup mix and ¼ cup (60 ml) water in bowl and stir well. Cover chicken breasts with sauce mixture. Cover and cook on LOW for 5 to 6 hours. Serves 4 to 6.

Artichoke-Chicken Pasta

1½ pounds boneless, skinless chicken breast tenders	680 g
1 (15 ounce) can artichoke hearts, quartered	425 g
¾ cup chopped roasted red peppers	110 g
1 (8 ounce) package shredded American cheese	230 g
1 tablespoon marinade for chicken	15 ml
1 (10 ounce) can cream of chicken soup	280 g
1 (8 ounce) package shredded cheddar cheese	230 g
2 cups bow-tie pasta	150 g

- Combine chicken tenders, artichoke, roasted peppers, American cheese, marinade for chicken and soup in sprayed slow cooker and mix well. Cover and cook on LOW for 6 to 8 hours.

- Cook pasta according to package directions and drain.

- Fold in cheddar cheese, hot pasta, and a little salt and pepper; cover and cook for additional 20 minutes. Serves 4.

Broccoli-Rice Chicken

1¼ cups rice	230 g
2 pounds boneless, skinless chicken breast halves	910 g
Dried parsley	
1 (2 ounce) packet cream of broccoli soup mix	60 g
1 (14 ounce) can chicken broth	395 g

- Place rice in sprayed slow cooker. Cut chicken into slices and place over rice. Sprinkle with parsley and a little pepper.

- Combine soup mix, chicken broth and 1 cup (250 ml) water in saucepan. Heat just enough to mix well. Pour over chicken and rice. Cover and cook on LOW for 6 to 8 hours. Serves 4 to 6.

Broccoli-Cheese Chicken

4 boneless, skinless chicken breast halves	
2 tablespoons butter, melted	30 g
1 (10 ounce) can broccoli-cheese soup	280 g
¼ cup milk	60 ml
1 (10 ounce) package frozen broccoli spears	280 g
Rice, cooked	

- Dry chicken breasts with paper towels and place in sprayed oval slow cooker.

- Combine melted butter, soup and milk in bowl and spoon over chicken. Cover and cook on LOW for 4 to 6 hours.

- Place broccoli over chicken. Cover and cook for additional 1 hour. Serve over rice. Serves 4.

Cream Cheese Chicken

4 boneless, skinless chicken breast halves	
2 tablespoons butter, melted	30 g
1 (10 ounce) can cream of mushroom soup	280 g
2 tablespoons dry Italian salad dressing mix	30 ml
½ cup sherry	125 ml
1 (8 ounce) package cream cheese, cubed	230 g
Noodles, cooked	

- Wash chicken breasts, dry with paper towels and brush melted butter over chicken. Place in sprayed oval slow cooker and add remaining ingredients. Cover and cook on LOW for 6 to 7 hours. Serve over noodles. Serves 4.

Chicken and Noodles

2 pounds boneless, skinless chicken breast halves	910 g
¼ cup cornstarch	30 g
⅓ cup soy sauce	75 ml
2 onions, chopped	
3 ribs celery, sliced diagonally	
1 red bell pepper, seeded, julienned	
2 (14 ounce) cans mixed Chinese vegetables, drained	2 (395 g)
¼ cup molasses	60 ml
2 cups chow mein noodles	110 g

- Place chicken breasts and 2 cups (500 ml) water in sprayed slow cooker. Cover and cook on LOW for 3 to 4 hours. Remove chicken and cut into bite-size pieces; return chicken to slow cooker.

- Combine cornstarch and soy sauce in bowl and mix well. Stir into slow cooker. Add onions, celery, bell pepper, mixed vegetables and molasses. Cover and cook on HIGH heat for 1 to 2 hours.

- Serve over chow mein noodles. Serves 4 to 6.

Chicken and Pasta

1 (16 ounce) package frozen whole green beans, thawed	455 g
1 onion, chopped	
1 cup fresh mushroom halves	70 g
3 boneless, skinless chicken breast halves	
1 (15 ounce) can Italian stewed tomatoes	425 g
1 teaspoon chicken bouillon granules	5 ml
1 teaspoon minced garlic	5 ml
1 teaspoon Italian seasoning	5 ml
1 (8 ounce) package fettuccini	230 g
1 (4 ounce) package grated parmesan cheese	115 g

- Place green beans, onion and mushrooms in sprayed slow cooker. Cut chicken into 1-inch (2.5 cm) pieces and place over vegetables.

- Combine stewed tomatoes, chicken bouillon, garlic and Italian seasoning in small bowl. Pour over chicken. Cover and cook on LOW for 5 to 6 hours.

- Cook fettuccini according to package directions and drain. Serve chicken over fettuccini and sprinkle with parmesan cheese. Serves 4.

TIP: Add ¼ cup (60 g) butter for a richer taste.

282   1001 Slow Cooker Recipes

Chicken Curry over Rice

3 large boneless, skinless chicken breast halves	
½ cup chicken broth	125 ml
1 (10 ounce) can cream of chicken soup	280 g
1 onion, coarsely chopped	
1 red bell pepper, seeded, julienned	
¼ cup golden raisins	40 g
1½ teaspoons curry powder	7 ml
¼ teaspoon ground ginger	1 ml
Rice, cooked	

- Cut chicken into thin strips and place in sprayed large slow cooker.

- Combine broth, soup, onion, bell pepper, raisins, curry powder and ginger in bowl and mix well. Pour over chicken. Cover and cook on LOW for 3 to 4 hours. Serve over rice. Serves 4.

Cheesy Chicken and Vegetables

4 - 5 boneless, skinless chicken breast halves	
2 teaspoons seasoned salt	10 ml
1 (16 ounce) package frozen broccoli, cauliflower	
and carrots, thawed	455 g
1 (10 ounce) can cream of celery soup	280 g
1 (8 ounce) package shredded cheddar-Jack cheese, divided	230 g

- Cut chicken into strips, sprinkle with seasoned salt and place in sprayed slow cooker.

- Combine vegetables, celery soup and half cheese in large bowl and mix well. Spoon over chicken breasts. Cover and cook on LOW for 4 to 5 hours.

- About 10 minutes before serving, sprinkle remaining cheese on top. Serves 4 to 6.

Chicken Delicious

5 - 6 boneless skinless chicken breast halves	
1 (16 ounce) package frozen broccoli florets, thawed	455 g
1 red bell pepper, seeded, julienned	
1 (16 ounce) jar parmesan-mozzarella cheesy sauce	455 g
3 tablespoons sherry	45 ml
Noodles, cooked	

- Brown chicken breasts in skillet and place in sprayed oval slow cooker.

- Remove stems from broccoli florets and discard stems. Combine broccoli florets, bell pepper, cheesy sauce and sherry in bowl and mix well. Spoon over chicken breasts. Cover and cook on LOW for 4 to 5 hours. Serve over noodles. Serves 4 to 6.

Chicken Delight

¾ cup rice	150 g
1 (14 ounce) can chicken broth	395 g
1 (1 ounce) packet onion soup mix	30 g
1 red bell pepper, seeded, chopped	
2 (10 ounce) cans cream of celery soup	2 (280 g)
¾ cup white cooking wine	175 ml
4 - 6 boneless skinless chicken breast halves	
1 (3 ounce) package grated fresh parmesan cheese	85 g

- Combine rice, broth, soup mix, bell pepper, celery soup, ¾ cup (175 ml) water, wine and several sprinkles of black pepper in bowl and mix well. (Make sure to mix soup well with liquids.) Place chicken breasts in sprayed oval slow cooker. Pour rice-soup mixture over chicken breasts. Cover and cook on LOW for 4 to 5 hours.

- Sprinkle parmesan cheese over chicken, cover and cook for 1 additional hour. Serves 4 to 6.

Chicken Dinner

1 cup rice	200 g
1 tablespoon chicken seasoning	15 ml
1 (1 ounce) packet dry onion soup mix	30 g
1 green bell pepper, seeded, chopped	
1 (4 ounce) jar diced pimentos, drained	115 g
¾ teaspoon dried basil	4 ml
1 (14 ounce) can chicken broth	395 g
1 (10 ounce) can cream of chicken soup	280 g
5 - 6 boneless, skinless chicken breast halves	

- Combine rice, chicken seasoning, onion soup mix, bell pepper, pimentos, basil, broth, ½ cup (125 ml) water and chicken soup in bowl and mix well. Place chicken breasts in sprayed, oval slow cooker and cover with rice mixture. Cover and cook on LOW for 6 to 7 hours. Serves 4 to 6.

Chicken for Supper

5 - 6 boneless, skinless chicken breast halves	
6 carrots, peeled, cut in 1-inch length	6 (2.5 cm)
1 (15 ounce) can cut green beans, drained	425 g
1 (15 ounce) can whole new potatoes, drained	425 g
2 (10 ounce) cans cream of mushroom soup	2 (280 g)
Shredded cheddar cheese	

- Wash chicken breasts, dry with paper towels and place in sprayed oval slow cooker.

- Combine, carrots, green beans, potatoes and mushroom soup in bowl and pour over chicken. Cover and cook on LOW for 8 to 10 hours. When ready to serve, sprinkle cheese over top. Serves 4 to 6.

Easy Green Bean Chicken

1 (6 ounce) package stuffing mix	170 g
3 cups cooked, chopped chicken breasts	420 g
1 (16 ounce) package frozen whole green beans, thawed	455 g
2 (12 ounce) jars chicken gravy	2 (340 g)

- Prepare stuffing mix according to package directions and place in sprayed oval slow cooker.

- Layer chicken over stuffing and place green beans over chicken. Pour chicken gravy over green beans. Cover and cook on LOW for 3 hours 30 minutes to 4 hours. Serves 4 to 6.

Chicken Marseilles

4 - 5 boneless, skinless chicken breast halves	
2 tablespoons butter	30 g
1 (2 ounce) packet leek soup and dip mix	60 g
½ teaspoon dill weed	2 ml
1 cup milk	250 ml
Brown rice, cooked	
¾ cup sour cream	180 g

- Place chicken breasts in sprayed large slow cooker.

- Combine butter, leek soup mix, dill weed, milk and ½ cup (125 ml) water in saucepan and heat just enough for butter to melt and ingredients to mix well. Pour over chicken. Cover and cook on LOW for 3 to 5 hours.

- When ready to serve, remove chicken breasts to platter with hot, cooked brown rice and cover to keep warm.

- Add sour cream to cooker liquid and stir well. Pour sauce over chicken and rice. Serves 4 to 5.

Velvety Chicken Pasta

5 boneless, skinless chicken breast halves	
1 (16 ounce) jar alfredo sauce	455 g
1 (16 ounce) package frozen green peas, thawed	455 g
1½ cups shredded mozzarella cheese	170 g
Noodles, cooked	

- Cut chicken into strips and place in sprayed slow cooker.

- Combine alfredo sauce, peas and cheese in bowl and mix well. Spoon over chicken strips. Cover and cook on LOW for 5 to 6 hours. Serve over noodles. Serves 4 to 5.

Chicken Breast Deluxe

4 slices bacon	
5 - 6 boneless, skinless chicken breast halves	
1 cup sliced celery	100 g
1 cup sliced red bell pepper	90 g
1 (10 ounce) can cream of chicken soup	280 g
2 tablespoons white wine or cooking wine	30 ml
5 - 6 slices Swiss cheese	
2 tablespoons dried parsley	30 ml

- Cook bacon in large skillet, drain, crumble and set aside. Place chicken in skillet with bacon drippings and lightly brown on both sides. Transfer chicken to sprayed oval slow cooker and place celery and bell pepper over chicken.

- In same skillet, combine soup and wine, stir and spoon over vegetables and chicken. Cover and cook on LOW for 3 to 4 hours. Place slices of cheese over each chicken breast and sprinkle with parsley. Cook for additional 10 minutes.

- Serve with sauce and sprinkle with crumbled bacon. Serves 4 to 6.

Potato-Chicken Dinner

4 - 5 carrots	
6 medium red potatoes with peels, quartered	
4 - 5 boneless, skinless chicken breast halves	
1 tablespoon chicken seasoning	15 ml
2 (10 ounce) cans cream of chicken soup	2 (280 g)
⅓ cup white wine or cooking wine	75 ml

- Cut carrots into ½-inch (1.2 cm) pieces. Place potatoes and carrots in sprayed slow cooker. Sprinkle chicken breasts with chicken seasoning and place over vegetables.

- Heat soups, wine and ¼ cup (60 ml) water in saucepan just to mix and pour over chicken and vegetables. Cover and cook on LOW for 5 to 6 hours. Serves 4 to 5.

TIP: Use 1 (10 ounce/280 g) can mushroom soup instead of 1 can of cream of chicken soup for a tasty change.

Three-Hour Chicken

1 (10 ounce) can cream of chicken soup	280 g
1 (4 ounce) can sliced mushrooms	115 g
1 small onion, finely chopped	
1 teaspoon Italian seasoning	5 ml
1½ pounds boneless, skinless chicken breasts, cut into strips	680 g
Rice, cooked	

- Combine soup, mushrooms, onion and seasonings in sprayed slow cooker. Add chicken strips. Cover and cook on LOW for 2 hours 30 minutes to 3 hours. Serve over rice. Serves 4.

Say Yes to This Chicken

5 - 6 boneless, skinless chicken breast halves	
1 (8 ounce) bottle Italian salad dressing	230 g
1 (10 ounce) can chicken broth	280 g
1 (11 ounce) can Mexicorn®, drained	310 g
1 (8 ounce) package shredded Velveeta® cheese	230 g
¾ teaspoon dried basil	4 ml
1 (12 ounce) package your favorite pasta	340 g

- Place chicken breasts in sprayed oval slow cooker. Pour salad dressing over chicken. Cover and cook on LOW for 6 to 8 hours.

- Drain juices from slow cooker and stir in broth, corn, cheese, basil and a little salt and pepper. Cover and cook for additional 1 hour.

- Cook your favorite pasta according to package directions, drain and place on serving platter. Place chicken over pasta and spoon corn-cheese mixture over chicken breasts. Serves 5 or 6.

Cheesy Chicken and Noodles

1 (8 ounce) package wide noodles	239 g
1 (10 ounce) can cream of chicken soup	280 g
4 cups cooked, chopped chicken breast	560 g
1 (15 ounce) carton ricotta cheese, softened, cut in cubes	425 g
1 (8 ounce) package shredded mozzarella cheese	230 g
1 (10 ounce) package frozen chopped bell peppers and onions, thawed	280 g
2 ribs celery, sliced	
1 (10 ounce) can chicken broth	280 g

- Cook noodles according to package directions and drain.

- Place noodles, soup, chicken, ricotta cheese, mozzarella cheese, bell peppers and onions, celery and broth in sprayed slow cooker; stir until ingredients blend well. Sprinkle pepper over top. Cover and cook on LOW for 7 to 9 hours or on HIGH for 3 hours 30 minutes. Serves 6.

Scrumptious Chicken Breasts

There is a lot of delicious sauce.

5 - 6 boneless, skinless chicken breast halves	
1 teaspoon chicken seasoning	5 ml
1 (10 ounce) can cream of chicken soup	280 g
1 (10 ounce) can broccoli-cheese soup	280 g
½ cup white cooking wine	125 ml
Noodles, cooked	

- Sprinkled chicken with pepper and chicken seasoning and place in sprayed oval slow cooker.

- Combine soups and wine in saucepan and heat enough to mix well. Pour over chicken. Cover and cook on LOW for 5 to 6 hours. Serve chicken and sauce over noodles. Serves 4 to 6.

TIP: This is great served with roasted garlic, oven-baked Italian toast.

TIP: If chicken breasts are very large, cut in half lengthwise.

Smothered Chicken Breasts

4 boneless, skinless chicken breast halves	
1 (10 ounce) can French onion soup	280 g
2 teaspoons chicken seasoning	10 ml
1 (4 ounce) jar sliced mushrooms, drained	115 g
1 cup shredded mozzarella cheese	115 g
Chopped green onions	

- Brown each chicken breast in skillet and place in sprayed oval slow cooker.

- Pour onion soup over chicken and sprinkle black pepper and chicken seasoning over chicken breasts. Place mushrooms and cheese over chicken breasts. Cover and cook on LOW for 4 to 5 hours. Sprinkle chopped green onions over each serving. Serves 4.

TIP: This recipe works well using boneless pork chops instead of chicken. If you want to serve this recipe over rice or noodles, use 2 cans of French onion soup instead of only one.

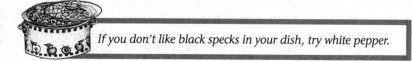

If you don't like black specks in your dish, try white pepper.

Sunday Chicken

4 large boneless, skinless chicken breast halves
Chicken seasoning
4 slices American cheese
1 (10 ounce) can cream of celery soup   280 g
½ cup sour cream   120 g
1 (6 ounce) box chicken stuffing mix   170 g
½ cup (1 stick) butter, melted   115 g

- Wash chicken breasts, dry with paper towels and place in sprayed oval slow cooker. Sprinkle each breast with chicken seasoning. Place slice of cheese over each chicken breast.

- Combine celery soup and sour cream in bowl, mix well and spoon over chicken and cheese. Sprinkle chicken stuffing mix over top. Drizzle melted butter over stuffing mix. Cover and cook on LOW for 5 to 6 hours. Serves 4.

Tasty Chicken, Rice and Veggies

4 boneless, skinless chicken breast halves
2 (10 ounce) jars sweet-and-sour sauce   2 (280 g)
1 (16 ounce) package frozen broccoli, cauliflower
     and carrots, thawed   455 g
1 (10 ounce) package frozen green peas, thawed   280 g
2 cups sliced celery   200 g
1 (6 ounce) package parmesan-butter rice mix   170 g
⅓ cup toasted, slivered almonds   55 g
Rice, cooked

- Cut chicken in 1-inch (2.5 cm) strips. Combine chicken, sweet-and-sour sauce and all vegetables in sprayed large slow cooker. Cover and cook on LOW for 4 to 6 hours.

- Cook parmesan-butter rice according to package direction and fold in almonds. Serve chicken and vegetables over rice-almond mixture. Serves 4.

So Good Chicken

4 - 5 boneless, skinless chicken breast halves
1 (10 ounce) can golden mushroom soup   280 g
1 cup white cooking wine   250 ml
1 (8 ounce) carton sour cream   230 g

- Wash chicken breasts and dry with paper towels. Add to sprayed slow cooker and sprinkle a little salt and pepper over each. Combine mushroom soup, wine and sour cream in bowl and mix well. Spoon over chicken breasts. Cover and cook on LOW for 5 to 7 hours. Serves 4 to 6.

Perfect Chicken Breasts

1 (2.5 ounce) jar dried beef	70 g
6 small boneless, skinless chicken breast halves	
6 slices bacon	
2 (10 ounce) cans golden mushroom soup	2 (280 g)

- Place slices of dried beef in sprayed oval slow cooker and overlap some.

- Roll each chicken breast with slice of bacon and secure with toothpick. Place in slow cooker, overlapping as little as possible.

- Combine mushroom soup and ½ cup (125 ml) water or milk in bowl and spoon over chicken breasts. Cover and cook on LOW for 6 to 8 hours. Serves 4 to 6.

TIP: When cooked, you will have a great sauce that is wonderful over noodles or rice.

A Honey of a Dinner

1 (16 ounce) package baby carrots	455 g
4 - 6 boneless, skinless chicken breast halves	
1 teaspoon seasoned salt	5 ml
2 cups honey	680 g
½ cup ketchup	135 g
½ cup soy sauce	125 ml
¼ cup canola oil	60 ml
Dry-roasted sunflower seeds	

- Place carrots in sprayed large slow cooker and top with chicken breasts. Sprinkle seasoned salt and a little pepper over chicken.

- Combine honey, ketchup, soy sauce and oil in medium bowl, mix well. Pour sauce over chicken breasts. Cover and cook on LOW for 6 to 8 hours or on HIGH for 3 to 4 hours. Sprinkle about 1 tablespoon (15 ml) sunflower seeds over each serving. Serves 4 to 6.

Aloha Chicken

3 pounds boneless skinless chicken breast halves	1.4 kg
1 (8 ounce) can crushed pineapple	230 g
1 tablespoon soy sauce	15 ml
2 tablespoons mustard	30 ml
1 cup packed brown sugar	220 g
½ cup (1 stick) butter, melted	115 g
½ cup lemon juice	125 ml
½ cup honey	170 g

- Place all ingredients in sprayed slow cooker. Cover and cook on LOW for 4 to 5 hours, or until chicken is thoroughly cooked. Serves 8.

An Extra Zing with This Chicken

2 (15 ounce) cans whole kernel corn, drained | 2 (425 g)
1 (15 ounce) can black beans, rinsed, drained | 425 g
1 (15 ounce) can navy beans, drained | 425 g
2 ribs celery sliced
1 teaspoon chili powder | 5 ml
1 (16 ounce) jar hot chunky salsa, divided | 455 g
4 - 6 boneless, skinless chicken breast halves, cut in half
1 cup shredded cheddar cheese 115 g

- Combine corn, beans, celery, chili powder and ½ cup (130 g) salsa in sprayed slow cooker. Top with chicken pieces and pour remaining salsa over chicken. Cover and cook on LOW for 7 to 8 hours. Spoon mixture into large serving bowl and top with cheese. Serves 6.

Asparagus and Cheesy Chicken

1 (16 ounce) package frozen cut asparagus, thawed | 455 g
1 (10 ounce) package frozen green peas, thawed | 280 g
1 red bell pepper, seeded, cut in strips
4 large boneless, skinless chicken breast halves,
    each cut into 4 strips
2 (10 ounce) cans cheddar cheese soup | 2 (280 g)
½ cup milk | 125 ml
½ cup slivered almonds, toasted | 85 g
1 (3 ounce) can fried onions | 85 g

- Place asparagus, green peas and bell pepper in sprayed slow cooker and sprinkle a little salt and pepper over vegetables. Top with chicken strips.

- Combine soups and milk in bowl and mix well. Spoon over chicken strips. Cover and cook on LOW for 7 to 9 hours.

- Place almonds and fried onions in small baking pan and heat in oven at 325° (160° C) for about 15 minutes. When ready to serve, sprinkle almonds and onions over chicken and vegetables. Serves 6.

For best results, a slow cooker should be filled from one-half to two-thirds full. Smaller amount may be cooked, but will take less cooking time.

Chicken and Dressing for a Crowd

2 (8 ounce) packages cornbread muffin mix	280 g
6 eggs, divided	
⅔ cup milk	150 ml
4 - 5 boneless, skinless chicken breast halves	
8 slices day-old bread, torn into small pieces	
3 ribs celery, thinly sliced	
1 onion, finely chopped	
1 tablespoon dried sage	15 ml
2 (10 ounce) cans cream of chicken soup	2 (280 g)
2 (14 ounce) cans chicken broth	2 (395 g)

- Preheat oven to 375° (190° C).

- Prepare cornbread muffin mix with 2 eggs and milk as directed on box. Pour into sprayed 7 x 11-inch (18 x 28 cm) baking pan. Bake for about 15 minutes. Cool and crumble.

- Place chicken breasts in saucepan, cover with water and bring to a boil. Cook for about 20 minutes. Cool and cut into bite-size pieces.

- Place crumbled cornbread, chicken, bread pieces, celery, onion, sage, soup and broth in sprayed slow cooker. Stir until mixture blends well. Cover and cook on LOW for 3 to 4 hours.

- Remove lid and fluff with fork and let stand for about 10 minutes before serving. Serves 12 to 14.

Chicken and Stuffing

6 boneless, skinless chicken breast halves	
6 slices Swiss cheese	
1 (10 ounce) can cream of golden mushroom soup	280 g
¼ cup milk	60 ml
1 (4 ounce) can sliced mushrooms	115 g
2 cups herbed stuffing mix	70 g
½ cup chicken broth	125 ml

- Place chicken breasts in sprayed oval slow cooker and top with cheese slices, layering if necessary.

- Combine soup and milk in bowl and mix well. Spread mixture over cheese layer and top with mushrooms and stuffing mix. Drizzle broth over stuffing. Cover and cook on LOW for 8 to 10 hours or on HIGH for 4 to 6 hours. Remove each chicken breast separately with stuffing on top. Serves 6.

Simple Chicken and Stuffing

1 (10 ounce) can cream of chicken soup	280 g
¼ cup (½ stick) butter, melted	60 g
1 (16 ounce) package frozen broccoli, cauliflower and carrots	455 g
1 red bell pepper, seeded, cut into strips	
2 ribs celery, cut in 1-inch (2.5 cm) strips	
2½ - 3 cups cooked, cubed chicken	350 - 420 g
1 (8 ounce) package cornbread stuffing mix	230 g

- Combine soup, butter and ¼ cup (60 ml) water in large bowl. Stir in broccoli-cauliflower mixture, bell pepper, celery, chicken and cornbread stuffing mix. Spoon into sprayed slow cooker. Cover and cook on LOW for 5 to 6 hours or on HIGH for 2 hours 30 minutes to 3 hours. Serves 6.

TIP: *This is a very good way to use up leftover chicken or turkey.*

Chicken with Mushroom Sauce

4 - 6 boneless, skinless chicken breast halves	
1 (10 ounce) can cream of mushroom soup	280 g
1 (8 ounce) carton mushrooms, sliced	230 g
1 green bell pepper, seeded, chopped	
½ cup dry white wine (or cooking wine)	125 ml
1 (8 ounce) carton sour cream	230 g
¼ cup flour	30 g
1 - 2 cups instant rice	95 - 190 g
Paprika	

- Sprinkle chicken lightly with salt and pepper and place in sprayed slow cooker.

- Combine soup, mushrooms, bell pepper and wine in medium to large bowl. In separate bowl, combine sour cream and flour and add to soup-wine mixture. Spoon mixture over chicken breasts. Cover and cook on LOW for 6 to 8 hours.

- Cook rice according to package directions and place on serving platter; top with chicken, sauce and sprinkles of paprika (or serve sauce in a separate bowl). Serve 4 to 6.

TIP: *If your family likes lots of gravy (sauce), use 2 cans mushroom soup rather than one.*

Chicken with Peanut Power

3 ribs celery, cut in 1-inch (2.5 cm) lengths
2 green bell peppers, seeded, cut in 1-inch (2.5 cm) strips
3½ - 4 pounds boneless, skinless chicken breast halves   1.6 - 1.8 kg
⅓ cup peanut butter95 g
2 tablespoons soy sauce   30 ml
½ cup orange juice   125 ml
Noodles or rice, cooked

- Place celery and bell peppers in sprayed large slow cooker and top
  with chicken breasts.

- Combine peanut butter, soy sauce, orange juice and ½ teaspoon
  (2 ml) pepper in small bowl. Spoon over chicken and vegetables.
  Cover and cook on LOW for 6 to 8 hours. Serve over noodles or rice.
  Serves 6 to 8.

Company Chicken Roll-Ups

6 boneless, skinless chicken breast halves
6 slices prosciutto
6 slices American cheese
½ teaspoon dried sage   2 ml
¾ cup chicken broth   175 ml
2 ribs celery, thinly sliced
1 green bell pepper, seeded, chopped
3 tablespoons cornstarch   20 g
½ cup half-and-half cream   125 ml
Rice, cooked

- Place chicken between 2 sheets of wax paper and pound with meat
  mallet to ½-inch (1.2 cm) thick.

- Place each slice of prosciutto on wax paper, top with chicken breast
  and slice of cheese. Sprinkle with sage and a little salt and pepper;
  roll jellyroll-style and secure with toothpicks. Place in sprayed slow
  cooker. Add chicken broth; cover and cook on LOW for 5 to 6 hours.

- Add celery and bell pepper. Dissolve cornstarch in half-and-half
  cream in bowl and stir into slow cooker. Increase heat to HIGH and
  cook for additional 20 minutes or until mixture has thickened. Serve
  over rice and top roll-ups with sauce. Serves 6.

Choice Chicken and Veggies

8 small - medium red potatoes
1 (16 ounce) package peeled baby carrots   455 g
1 green bell pepper, seeded, cut into 1-inch (2.5 cm) strips
4 large or 6 small boneless, skinless chicken breast halves
¾ cup zesty Italian salad dressing   175 ml
1 teaspoon garlic powder   5 ml

- Place potatoes, carrots and bell peppers in sprayed slow cooker and top with chicken breasts. Pour salad dressing and garlic powder over chicken. Cover and cook on LOW for 6 to 8 hours. Serves 4 to 6.

Celebrate Chicken, Carrots and Celery

1 (16 ounce) packet baby carrots   455 g
3 ribs celery, cut into 1-inch (2.5 cm) pieces
5 - 6 boneless, skinless chicken breast halves
2 (10 ounce) cans cream of chicken soup   2 (280 g)
½ cup milk   125 ml
½ cup sour cream   120 g
2 cups cooked instant rice   330 g

- Place carrots and celery in sprayed slow cooker and top with chicken breasts. Combine soups and milk in bowl and pour over chicken, make sure chicken is well coated. Cover and cook on LOW for 7 to 8 hours.

- Stir in sour cream, cover and cook for additional 30 minutes. Serve over rice. Serves 5 to 6.

Dressed-Up Beans and Rice

1 green bell pepper, seeded, cut into strips
1 red bell pepper, seeded, cut into strips
1 yellow bell pepper, seeded, cut into strips
4 large boneless, skinless chicken breast halves, cut in strips
3 ribs celery, cut in 1-inch (2.5 cm) slices
1 (12 ounce) jar chicken gravy   340 g
1 cup medium or hot salsa   265 g
1 (4 ounce) can diced green chilies   115 g
1 (7 ounce) package red beans and rice mix   200 g

- Layer bell peppers, chicken strips, celery, gravy, salsa and green chilies in sprayed slow cooker. Cover and cook on LOW for 4 to 5 hours or on HIGH for 2 hours to 2 hours 30 minutes.

- Cook beans and rice according to package directions. Place beans-rice mixture on serving platter and spoon chicken and vegetables on top. If you prefer, you could place beans and rice on 4 or 5 individual plates and top with chicken and vegetables. Serves 4 to 5.

Mom's Chicken and Dumplings

1 (16 ounce) package frozen mixed vegetables	455 g
1 green bell pepper, seeded, chopped	
1 pound boneless chicken breasts, cut in 1-inch cubes	455g/2.5 cm
2 (14 ounce) cans chicken broth, divided	2 (395 g)
1½ cups buttermilk biscuit mix	180 g

- Combine mixed vegetables, bell pepper, chicken and chicken broth (set aside ½ cup (125 ml) for later use) in sprayed slow cooker. Cover and cook on HIGH for 2 hours.

- Combine biscuit mix with set aside ½ cup (125 ml) broth in medium bowl, until moistened. Drop large tablespoons of dough onto stew pieces rather than directly into liquid. Cover and cook for additional 20 minutes. Serves 6.

Everybody's Favorite Dumplings

4 large boneless, skinless chicken breast halves	
¼ cup (½ stick) butter, melted	60 g
2 (10 ounce) cans cream of chicken soup	2 (280 g)
1 small onion, finely chopped	
2 ribs celery, sliced	
2 (10 ounce) packages refrigerated biscuits	280 g

- Place chicken breasts, butter, soup, onion and celery in sprayed large slow cooker. Fill with enough water to cover. Cover and cook on HIGH for 5 to 6 hours.

- About 30 minutes before serving, remove chicken breasts with slotted spoon and cut chicken into small pieces, return to slow cooker. Tear each biscuit into several pieces and gradually drop pieces into slow cooker. Cook until dough is no longer raw in center.

- Remove liner bowl from slow cooker and serve right from the bowl. Serves 8.

Mealtime Favorite Chicken

1 large red bell pepper, seeded, julienned	
3 ribs celery, sliced	
4 - 5 boneless, skinless chicken breast halves	
1 (10 ounce) can cream of chicken soup	280 g
½ cup milk	125 ml
¼ cup (½ stick) butter, melted	60 g
1 (10 ounce) package frozen green peas, thawed	280 g
2 cups instant rice	190 g

- Place bell pepper and celery in sprayed slow cooker and top with chicken breasts.

- Combine soup, milk and butter in bowl; stir gently to mix and spread evenly over chicken. Cover and cook on LOW for 4 hours 30 minutes to 6 hours.

- Stir in peas and rice, cover and cook for additional 20 minutes or until rice is tender. Serves 4 to 5.

Grandma's Short-Cut Chicken and Dressing

2 ribs celery, sliced	
1 small onion, chopped	
4 - 5 boneless skinless chicken breast halves	
4 - 5 slices Swiss cheese	
1 (14 ounce) can chicken broth	395 g
1 (10 ounce) can cream of celery soup	280 g
1 (10 ounce) can cream of chicken soup	280 g
3 cups seasoned stuffing mix	360 g
½ cup (1 stick) butter, melted	115 g

- Place celery and onion in sprayed slow cooker. Top with chicken breasts sprinkled with a little salt and pepper. Place 1 slice of cheese over each chicken breast.

- Pour broth over chicken. Spoon celery and chicken soup over chicken. Sprinkle stuffing mix over soups and drizzle melted butter over stuffing. Cover and cook on LOW for 6 to 8 hours or on HIGH for 3 to 4 hours. Serves 4 to 5.

No Ordinary Mozzarella Chicken

1 tablespoon canola oil	15 ml
4 - 5 boneless, chicken breast halves	
1 (15 ounce) can stewed tomatoes, drained	425 g
1 onion, cut into 4 to 5 slices	
1 (4 ounce) can diced green chilies	115 g
1 teaspoon minced garlic	5 ml
1 teaspoon sugar	5 ml
2 tablespoons red cooking wine	30 ml
1 cup shredded mozzarella cheese	115 g

- Heat oil in skillet over medium-high heat and saute chicken breasts, turning once, until chicken is light brown.

- Place tomatoes in food processor and pulse just enough to break up tomatoes. Place chicken breasts in sprayed slow cooker and top with onion slices, tomatoes, green chilies, garlic, sugar, wine and ½ teaspoon (2 ml) salt. Cover and cook on LOW for 6 to 8 hours.

- Sprinkle cheese over each chicken breast, cover and cook for additional 10 minutes or just until cheese begins to melt. Serve immediately. Serves 4 to 5.

Simple Chicken and Rice

3 (10 ounce) can cream of chicken soup	3 (280 g)
2 cups instant rice	190 g
3 ribs celery, sliced	
4 - 5 boneless, skinless chicken breast halves	
4 slices bacon, cooked, crumbled	

- Place soup, rice, celery and 1 cup (250 ml) water in sprayed slow cooker.

- Top with chicken breasts and sprinkle a little salt and pepper over each. Cover and cook on HIGH for 3 to 4 hours or on LOW for 6 to 8 hours. Sprinkle crumbled bacon over each chicken breast. Serves 4 to 5.

Be careful not to place a hot ceramic insert (bowl) on a cold surface. Cracking may result.

Six for a Chicken Dinner

1 (2 ounce) jar sliced dried beef	60 g
6 boneless, skinless chicken breast halves	
6 slices bacon	
1 (10 ounce) can cream of chicken soup	280 g
1 (10 ounce) can cream of celery soup	280 g
⅓ cup milk or cream	75 ml
¼ cup sour cream	60 g
2 tablespoons flour	15 g
1 (12 ounce) package wide egg noodles	340 g

- Place dried beef in sprayed slow cooker. Wrap each piece of chicken with strip of bacon and secure with toothpick. Place chicken over dried beef.

- Combine soups with milk in bowl and pour over chicken. Cover and cook on LOW for 7 to 9 hours or on HIGH for 3 to 4 hours.

- Cook noodles according to package directions, drain, place in serving bowl and top with chicken and sauce. Serves 6.

Supreme Sun-Dried Chicken

3 pounds boneless, skinless chicken breast halves	1.4 kg
1 tablespoon canola oil	15 ml
1 teaspoon minced garlic	5 ml
½ cup white wine (can use cooking wine)	125 ml
1 (14 ounce) can chicken broth	395 g
1 teaspoon dried basil	5 ml
¾ cup chopped sun-dried tomatoes	40 g
1 (10 ounce) box couscous	280 g

- Cut chicken into 8 to 9 serving pieces. Heat oil in large skillet and brown several pieces at a time, making sure pieces brown evenly. Place each browned piece of chicken in sprayed large slow cooker.

- Add garlic, wine, broth and basil to skillet and bring to a boil. Pour over chicken and scatter tomatoes on top. Cover and cook on LOW for 4 to 6 hours.

- Cook couscous according to package directions and place on serving platter. Place chicken pieces on top of couscous. Serve sauce on the side. Serves 8.

Stuffing Topped Chicken

½ cup flour	60 g
1 teaspoon seasoned salt	5 ml
4 - 5 boneless, skinless chicken breast halves	
¼ cup (½ stick) butter	60 g
1 (10 ounce) can cream of chicken soup	280 g
1 (10 ounce) can cream of celery soup	280 g
1 (6 ounce) box cornbread stuffing mix	170 g

- Combine flour, seasoned salt and about ½ teaspoon (2 ml) pepper in shallow bowl and dredge chicken in flour mixture. Melt butter in skillet on medium-high heat and brown chicken on both sides; place in sprayed slow cooker.

- Spread soups over chicken breasts. Mix stuffing mix with ¾ cup (175 ml) boiling water in bowl and let stand for about 5 minutes, then spoon over chicken breasts. Cover and cook on HIGH for 3 to 4 hours. Serves 4 to 5.

Stupendous Rice and Chicken

2 (10 ounce) cans cream of chicken soup	2 (280 g)
2 (6 ounce) boxes long grain-wild rice with seasoning packet	2 (170 g)
1 red and 1 green bell pepper, seeded, cut into strips	
1 (4 ounce) can sliced mushrooms	115 g
4 - 5 boneless, skinless chicken breast halves	

- Combine chicken soup, rice, seasoning packets and 2 cups (500 ml) water in large bowl. Pour half mixture into sprayed slow cooker.

- Layer bell pepper strips, mushrooms and chicken breasts on top and pour remaining soup-rice mixture over chicken. Cover and cook on LOW for 6 to 7 hours or on HIGH for 3 to 4 hours. Do not cook any longer because rice will become mushy if overcooked. Serves 4 to 5.

Swiss Chicken and Stuffing

6 (medium size) boneless, skinless chicken breast halves	
6 slices Swiss cheese	
1 red bell pepper, seeded, cut in strips	
1 (4 ounce) can sliced mushrooms, drained	115 g
1 (10 ounce) can cream of celery soup	280 g
1 (5 ounce) can evaporated milk	75 ml
2 cups stuffing mix	70 g
½ cup (1 stick) butter, melted	30 g

- Place chicken breasts in sprayed large oval slow cooker, stacking if necessary. Place 1 slice of cheese of top of each breast. Spread bell pepper strips and mushrooms on top of cheese.

- Combine soup and milk in bowl; mix well and spoon over vegetables. Sprinkle stuffing mix on top and drizzle with melted butter. Cover and cook on LOW for 8 to 9 hours or on HIGH for 4 to 5 hours. Serves 6.

The Captain's Chicken Alfredo

1½ pounds boneless, skinless chicken breast halves, cut into ¾-inch (1.8 cm) pieces	
2 ribs celery, sliced	
1 (4 ounce) jar sliced mushrooms, drained	115 g
½ cup roasted red bell pepper strips	70 g
1 (16 ounce) jar alfredo sauce	455 g
1 (16 ounce) package frozen broccoli florets, thawed	455 g
1 (10 ounce) package fettuccini	280 g
¼ cup grated parmesan cheese	25 g

- Layer chicken, celery, mushrooms and roasted bell peppers in sprayed slow cooker. Pour alfredo sauce over top. Cover and cook on LOW for 5 to 6 hours.

- Place broccoli florets over chicken mixture. Increase heat to HIGH, cover and cook for additional 20 minutes

- Cook fettuccini according to package directions. Drain and gently stir into chicken mixture and sprinkle with parmesan cheese. Serves 6.

Hearty Chicken Casserole

1 tablespoon canola oil	15 ml
4 boneless, skinless chicken breast halves, cut in 1-inch (2.5 cm) cubes	
1 (28 ounce) can stewed tomatoes	795 g
2 ribs celery, sliced	
1 green bell pepper, seeded, chopped	
1 (4 ounce) can sliced mushrooms, drained	115 g
1 tablespoon dried minced onions	15 ml
¼ teaspoon hot sauce	1 ml
1 (8 ounce) package whole wheat rotini pasta	230 g
½ cup shredded parmesan cheese	50 g

- Heat oil in skillet and cook chicken cubes on medium-high heat for 6 to 8 minutes or until chicken is light brown. Place chicken, tomatoes, celery, bell pepper, mushrooms, onion, hot sauce and ½ teaspoon (2 ml) salt in sprayed slow cooker. Cover and cook on LOW for 6 to 8 hours.

- Cook pasta according to package directions and drain. Place pasta on serving platter and spoon chicken mixture over pasta. Top with parmesan cheese. Serves 6.

Curried Chicken

1 tablespoon canola oil	15 ml
3 - 4 boneless, skinless chicken breast halves, cut	
into 1- inch (2.5 cm) cubes	
2 onions, halved lengthwise, thinly sliced	
2 ribs celery, sliced	
1 carrot, peeled, sliced	
1 teaspoon minced garlic	5 ml
1 teaspoon curry powder	5 ml
1 teaspoon chili powder	5 ml
1 teaspoon turmeric	5 ml
2 cups instant rice	190 g

- Heat oil in skillet and cook chicken cubes on medium heat for 6 to 8 minutes or until chicken is slightly brown.

- Combine chicken, onion, celery, carrot, garlic, curry powder, chili powder and turmeric in sprayed slow cooker. Cover and cook on LOW for 7 to 9 hours.

- Cook rice according to package directions and place on serving platter. Spoon chicken mixture over rice. Serves 4.

Winter Dinner

1 pound chicken tenderloins	455 g
Canola oil	
1 pound Polish sausage, cut in 1-inch pieces	455 g/2.5 cm
2 onions, chopped	
1 (28 ounce) can pork and beans with liquid	795 g
1 (15 ounce) can ranch-style beans, drained	425 g
1 (15 ounce) can great northern beans	425 g
1 (15 ounce) can butter beans, drained	425 g
1 cup ketchup	270 g
1 cup packed brown sugar	220 g
1 tablespoon vinegar	15 ml
6 slices bacon, cooked, crumbled	

- Brown chicken in a little oil in skillet and place in sprayed large slow cooker. Add sausage, onions, beans, ketchup, brown sugar and vinegar and stir gently. Cover and cook on LOW for 7 to 8 hours or on HIGH for 3 hours 30 minutes to 4 hours. When ready to serve, sprinkle crumbled bacon over top. Serves 4 to 6.

Savory Chicken Fettuccini

2 pounds boneless, skinless chicken thighs, cubed	910 g
½ teaspoon garlic powder	2 ml
1 red bell pepper, seeded, chopped	
2 ribs celery, chopped	
1 (10 ounce) can cream of celery soup	280 g
1 (10 ounce) can cream of chicken soup	280 g
1 (8 ounce) package cubed Velveeta® cheese	230 g
1 (4 ounce) jar diced pimentos	115 g
1 (16 ounce) package spinach fettuccini	455 g

- Place chicken in sprayed slow cooker. Sprinkle with garlic powder, ½ teaspoon (2 ml) pepper, bell pepper and celery. Top with soups. Cover and cook on HIGH for 4 to 6 hours or until chicken juices are clear.

- Stir in cheese and pimentos. Cover and cook until cheese melts.

- Cook fettuccini according to package directions and drain. Place fettuccini in serving bowl and spoon chicken over fettuccini. Serves 4 to 6.

Nice 'n Easy Chicken and Couscous

2 pounds boneless, skinless chicken tenderloins, cut into strips	
2 (15 ounce) cans Italian stewed tomatoes	2 (425 g)
2 ribs celery, sliced	
2 (6 ounce) boxes couscous with toasted pine nuts	2 (170 g)
⅔ cup pitted kalamata olives, chopped	85 g
1 (8 ounce) carton crumbled feta cheese	230 g

- Place chicken strips in sprayed slow cooker and pour stewed tomatoes, celery and 1½ cups (375 ml) water over chicken. Cover and cook on LOW for 5 to 6 hours or on HIGH for 2 hours 30 minutes to 3 hours.

- Stir in couscous; cover and let stand for 5 minutes. Fluff couscous-chicken mixture with fork. Top with olives and feta cheese. Serves 8.

TIP: *Another way to serve would be to use 8 individual serving plates, spoon couscous mixture on each plate and sprinkle with olives and feta cheese.*

Fish is seldom recommended for a slow cooker because it cooks rapidly. Vegetables and sauce for a fish recipe can be prepared in the slow cooker and the fish added in the last 20 to 30 minutes of cooking.

Spicy Mexican Chicken and Beans

1 - 2 pounds chicken tenderloins, each sliced in strips	455 - 910 g
2 (15 ounce) cans pinto beans, rinsed, drained	2 (425 g)
1 (15 ounce) can kidney beans, rinsed, drained	2 (425 g)
1 (15 ounce) can Mexican-style stewed tomatoes	2 (425 g)
1 (8 ounce) package frozen baby onions, thawed	230 g
1 (10 ounce) can chicken broth	280 g
2 teaspoons minced garlic	10 ml
1 teaspoon oregano	5 ml
1 teaspoon cocoa	5 ml
3 tablespoons chili powder	45 ml
Sour cream	

- Place chicken strips in sprayed skillet and cook on medium-high heat, stirring often, until chicken is slightly brown. Transfer to sprayed slow cooker.

- Stir in beans, stewed tomatoes, onions, broth, garlic, oregano, cocoa, chili powder and 1 teaspoon (5 ml) salt. Cover and cook on LOW for 5 to 7 hours.

- Divide among 6 plates and top each serving with 1 heaping tablespoon (15 ml) sour cream. Serves 6.

Alfredo Chicken Dinner

2 pounds chicken tenderloins, cut into 1-inch strips	910 g/2.5 cm
1 (16 ounce) package frozen stir-fry vegetables	455 g
3 ribs celery, sliced	
1 green bell pepper, seeded, sliced	
1 red bell pepper, seeded, sliced	
2 teaspoons Italian seasoning	10 ml
1 (16 ounce) jar alfredo sauce	455 g
1 (12 ounce) package thin spaghetti, broken into thirds	340 g
1 cup shredded mozzarella cheese	115 g

- Combine chicken strips, stir-fry vegetables, celery, bell peppers, Italian seasoning and alfredo sauce in sprayed slow cooker; stir to mix well. Cover and cook on LOW for 4 to 5 hours or on HIGH for 2 hours to 2 hours 30 minutes.

- Cook spaghetti according to package directions and drain. Stir spaghetti into slow cooker. Spoon mixture into individual bowls (or into a large serving bowl) and sprinkle with cheese. Serves 8.

Sunset Chicken over Rice

2 tablespoons canola oil	30 ml
1½ pounds chicken tenderloins, cut into 1-inch (2.5 cm) pieces	680 g
½ cup chicken broth	125 ml
1 large onion, chopped	
2 ribs celery, cut into 1-inch pieces	
1 (15 ounce) can Mexican-style stewed tomatoes	425 g
1 tablespoon chili powder	15 ml
2 tablespoons lime juice	30 ml
2 cups brown rice	390 g

- Heat oil in skillet on medium heat. Cook and stir chicken for about 5 minutes and transfer to sprayed slow cooker.

- Add broth, onion, celery, stewed tomatoes, chili powder, lime juice and ½ teaspoon (2 ml) salt. Cover and cook on LOW for 4 to 6 hours.

- Cook rice according to package directions, place on serving platter and spoon chicken over rice. Serves 6.

Spicy Orange Chicken over Noodles

1 (16 ounce) package frozen stir-fry vegetables, thawed	455 g
1½ pounds boneless, skinless chicken tenders, cut in half	680 g
2 tablespoons soy sauce	30 ml
2 tablespoons canola oil	30 ml
⅔ cup orange marmalade	215 g
2 teaspoons lime juice	10 ml
¼ teaspoon cayenne pepper	1 ml
1 (6 ounce) package chow mein noodles	170 g

- Place stir-fry vegetables in sprayed slow cooker and top with chicken tenders.

- Combine soy sauce, oil, marmalade, lime juice and cayenne pepper in bowl; mix well and pour over chicken. Cover and cook on LOW for 6 to 8 hours.

- Spread chow mein noodles on serving platter and spoon chicken and vegetables over noodles. Serves 6 to 8.

Delicious Chicken Pasta

1 pound chicken tenders	455 g
Lemon-herb chicken seasoning	
3 tablespoons butter	40 g
1 onion, coarsely chopped	
1 (15 ounce) can diced tomatoes	425 g
1 (10 ounce) can golden mushroom soup	280 g
1 (8 ounce) box angel hair pasta	230 g

- Pat chicken tenders dry with paper towels and sprinkle with ample amount of chicken seasoning. Melt butter in large skillet, brown chicken and place in sprayed oval slow cooker. Pour remaining butter and seasonings over chicken and cover with onion.

- Combine tomatoes and soup in bowl and pour over chicken and onion. Cover and cook on LOW for 4 to 5 hours.

- Cook pasta according to package directions. Serve chicken and sauce over pasta. Serves 4.

Chicken-Veggie Bowl

8 - 10 boneless, skinless chicken thighs	
2 (14 ounce) cans chicken broth	2 (395 g)
8 small new (red) potatoes	
1 (12 ounce) package baby carrots	340 g
2 onions, quartered	
1 (10 ounce) package frozen cut green beans, thawed	280 g
5 slices bacon, cooked, crumbled	
1 teaspoon seasoned salt	5 ml
2 tablespoons cornstarch	15 g

- Place chicken thighs in sprayed slow cooker. Add broth, potatoes, carrots, onions, green beans, crumbled bacon, seasoned salt and pepper. Cover and cook on LOW for 8 to 10 hours.

- Combine cornstarch and 2 tablespoons (30 ml) water in bowl and stir into slow cooker. Cover and cook for additional 30 minutes or until mixture thickens. Serve in shallow soup bowls. Serves 6 to 8.

Juicy Chicken over Wild Rice

2 green bell peppers, seeded, cut into strips	
2 pounds boneless, skinless chicken thighs	910 g
1 (1 ounce) packet onion soup mix	30 g
1 (6 ounce) can frozen orange juice concentrate, thawed	175 ml
2 (6 ounce) boxes long grain-wild rice mix	2 (170 g)

- Place bell peppers in sprayed slow cooker. Cook chicken in skillet over medium-high heat for about 6 to 7 minutes or just until chicken is slightly brown. Place chicken over bell peppers.

- Combine onion soup mix, orange juice concentrate and 1½ cups (375 ml) water in bowl, mix well. Pour mixture over chicken. Cover and cook on LOW for 6 to 7 hours.

- Cook rice according to package directions, place on serving platter and top with chicken and sauce. Serves 6 to 8.

Glazed Pineapple-Chicken

2 red bell peppers, seeded, cut into strips	
6 boneless, skinless chicken thighs, halved	
1 (20 ounce) can pineapple chunks with liquid	570 g
½ cup honey-mustard grill-and-glaze sauce	125 ml
1 tablespoon cornstarch	15 ml
2 cups instant rice	190 g

- Place bell pepper strips in sprayed slow cooker and top with chicken. Combine pineapple with liquid, honey-glaze sauce, cornstarch and ½ teaspoon (2 ml) salt; mix well. Pour mixture over chicken. Cover and cook on LOW for 5 to 7 hours.

- Cook rice according to package directions and place on serving platter. Top with chicken mixture. Serves 4 to 6.

Sweet 'n Spicy Mexican Dinner

1 pound boneless chicken thighs	455 g
1 (1 ounce) packet taco seasoning	30 g
½ cup seasoned breadcrumbs	60 g
Canola oil	
1 (16 ounce) jar thick-and-chunky salsa	455 g
1½ cups peach preserves	480 g
2 cups cooked rice	315 g

- Cut chicken in ½-inch (1.2 cm) cubes and place in resealable plastic bag; add taco seasoning and breadcrumbs. Toss to coat chicken. Brown chicken cubes with a little oil in skillet and place in sprayed slow cooker.

- Combine salsa and preserves in bowl; mix well and spoon over chicken. Cover and cook on LOW for 5 to 6 hours. Serve over rice. Serves 4 to 6.

Chicken Alfredo

1½ pounds boneless, skinless chicken thighs, cut into strips	680 g
2 ribs celery, sliced diagonally	
1 red bell pepper, seeded, julienned	
1 (16 ounce) jar alfredo sauce	455 g
3 cups fresh broccoli florets	215 g
1 (8 ounce) package fettuccini or linguine	230 g
1 (4 ounce) package grated parmesan cheese	115 g

- Cut chicken into strips. Layer chicken, celery and bell pepper in sprayed slow cooker. Pour alfredo sauce evenly over all. Cover and cook on LOW for 5 to 6 hours.

- Turn heat to HIGH and add broccoli florets to chicken-alfredo mixture. Cover and cook for additional 30 minutes.

- Cook pasta according to package directions and drain. Just before serving pour pasta into cooker, mix and sprinkle parmesan cheese on top. Serves 4 to 6.

Surprise Chicken Thighs

2 pounds chicken thighs	910 g
¾ cup chili sauce	205 g
¾ cup packed brown sugar	165 g
1 (1 ounce) packet dry onion soup mix	30 g
¼ teaspoon cayenne pepper	1 ml
Rice, cooked	

- Arrange chicken pieces in sprayed slow cooker.

- Combine chili sauce, brown sugar, dry onion soup mix, cayenne pepper and ¼ cup (60 ml) water in bowl and spoon over chicken. Cover and cook on LOW for 6 to 7 hours. Serve over rice. Serves 4 to 6.

IF cooking a cut-up chicken, remember that dark meat cooks slower than white meat. Therefore, dark meat should be placed at the bottom of the cooker with light meat on top. This is true for everything placed in the slow cooker; those things that take longer to cook should be in the bottom where the heat is more intense and the things that are more tender should be on top. For example, root vegetables such as potatoes, carrots, onions, turnips, etc., actually cook slower than meat and should be placed at the bottom of the slow cooker.

Southern Chicken

1 cup half-and-half cream	310 g
1 tablespoon flour	15 ml
1 (1 ounce) packet chicken gravy mix	30 g
1 pound boneless, skinless chicken thighs	455 g
1 (16 ounce) package frozen stew vegetables, thawed	455 g
1 (4 ounce) jar sliced mushrooms, drained	115 g
1 (10 ounce) package frozen green peas, thawed	280 g
1½ cups biscuit mix	180 g
1 bunch fresh green onions, chopped	
½ cup milk	125 ml

- Combine cream, flour, gravy mix and 1 cup (250 ml) water in bowl, stir until smooth and pour in sprayed large slow cooker.

- Cut chicken into 1-inch (2.5 cm) pieces. Stir chicken, vegetables and mushrooms into slow cooker. Cover and cook on LOW for 4 to 6 hours or until chicken is tender and sauce thickens.

- Stir in peas. Combine biscuit mix, onions and milk in bowl and mix well. Drop tablespoonfuls of dough onto chicken mixture. Turn slow cooker to HIGH, cover and cook for additional 50 to 60 minutes. Serves 4 to 6.

Italian Chicken

1 small head cabbage	
1 onion	
1 (4 ounce) jar sliced mushrooms, drained	115 g
1 medium zucchini, sliced	
1 red bell pepper, seeded, julienned	
1 teaspoon Italian seasoning	5 ml
1½ pounds boneless, skinless chicken thighs	680 g
1 teaspoon minced garlic	5 ml
2 (15 ounce) cans Italian stewed tomatoes	2 (425 g)
Parmesan cheese	

- Cut cabbage into wedges; slice onion and separate into rings. Make layers of cabbage, onion, mushrooms, zucchini and bell pepper in sprayed large slow cooker.

- Sprinkle Italian seasoning over vegetables. Place chicken thighs on top of vegetables. Mix garlic with tomatoes in bowl and pour over chicken. Cover and cook on LOW for 4 to 6 hours. Sprinkle parmesan cheese over each serving. Serves 4 to 6.

Asparagus-Cheese Chicken

8 - 10 boneless, skinless chicken thighs	
2 tablespoons butter	30 g
1 (10 ounce) can cream of celery soup	280 g
1 (10 ounce) can cheddar cheese soup	280 g
⅓ cup milk	75 ml
1 (16 ounce) package frozen cut asparagus	455 g

- Place chicken in sprayed slow cooker. Combine butter, celery soup, cheddar cheese soup and milk in saucepan. Heat just enough for butter to melt and mix well. Pour over chicken thighs. Cover and cook on LOW for 5 to 6 hours.

- Place asparagus over chicken, cover and cook for additional 1 hour. Serves 4 to 6.

Arroz con Pollo

3 pounds chicken thighs	1.4 kg
2 (15 ounce) cans Italian stewed tomatoes	2 (425 g)
1 (16 ounce) package frozen green peas, thawed	455 g
2 cups long grain rice	370 g
1 (.28 ounce) packet yellow rice seasoning mix	10 g
2 (14 ounce) cans chicken broth	2 (395 g)
1 heaping teaspoon minced garlic	5 ml
1 teaspoon dried oregano	5 ml

- Combine all ingredients plus ¾ cup (175 ml) water in sprayed large slow cooker and stir well. Cover and cook on LOW for 7 to 8 hours or on HIGH for 3 hours 30 minutes to 4 hours. Serves 6 to 8.

Perfect Paprika Chicken

1¼ pounds boneless skinless chicken thighs, cut in ¾-inch pieces	570 g/1.8 cm
1 (16 ounce) package baby carrots	455 g
1 onion, halved, sliced	
1 green bell pepper, seeded, chopped	
3 teaspoons paprika	15 ml
½ teaspoon seasoned salt	2 ml
1 (10 ounce) can cream of chicken soup	280 g
1 (10 ounce) package frozen green peas, thawed	280 g
½ cup sour cream with chives	120 g
Noodles, cooked	

- Combine chicken, carrots, onion, bell pepper, paprika, seasoned salt and soup in sprayed large slow cooker. Stir to mix well. Cover and cook on LOW for 6 to 8 hours.

- Stir peas and sour cream into chicken mixture. Cover and cook for additional 10 minutes or until peas are thoroughly hot. This chicken is great served over noodles. Serves 6.

Reverse This Chicken Pie

1¼ pounds boneless, skinless chicken thighs	570 g
¼ cup finely chopped onion	40 g
1 (10 ounce) can chicken soup	280 g
1 cup milk, divided	250 ml
2 ribs celery, thinly sliced	
2¼ cups biscuit mix	270 g
1 (16 ounce) package frozen mixed vegetables, thawed	455 g

• Place chicken in sprayed slow cooker.

• Combine onion, soup, ⅓ cup (75 ml) milk and celery in small bowl, mix well. Spoon over chicken. Cover and cook on LOW for 8 to 10 hours.

• Prepare 8 biscuits using biscuit mix and remaining milk as directed on package. While biscuits are baking, gently stir vegetables into chicken mixture. Increase heat to HIGH, cover and cook for additional 15 minutes.

• To serve, split each biscuit and place bottoms in individual soup bowls. Spoon about ¾ cup (175 ml) chicken mixture on top of biscuits and place tops of biscuits over chicken mixture. Serves 8.

Expect Great Cacciatore

1 (1 pound 4 ounce) bone-in skinless chicken thighs	570 g
1 (4 ounce) jar sliced mushrooms, drained	115 g
1 (6 ounce) can Italian-style tomato paste	170 g
1 (14 ounce) can chicken broth	395 g
¼ cup white wine (can use cooking wine)	60 ml
½ teaspoon dried sage	2 ml
1 (12 ounce) package spaghetti	340 g
½ teaspoon dried basil	2 ml
1 tablespoon cornstarch	15 ml
1 (5 ounce) package grated parmesan cheese	145 g

• Place chicken thighs in sprayed slow cooker and top with mushrooms, tomato paste, broth, wine and sage. Cover and cook on LOW for 8 to 10 hours.

• Remove chicken from cooker and keep warm. Stir basil into sauce in cooker and increase heat to HIGH.

• Mix ¼ cup (60 ml) sauce from cooker with cornstarch in small bowl; stir into sauce in cooker. Cover and cook for 10 minutes, stirring several times.

• Cook spaghetti according to package directions and drain. Serve chicken and sauce over hot spaghetti and sprinkle top with parmesan cheese. Serves 6 to 8.

Mom's Easy Simmered Chicken

8 boneless, skinless chicken thighs	
2 tablespoon butter	30 g
1 (10 ounce) can cream of chicken soup	280 g
1 (10 ounce) can cream of celery soup	280 g
2 ribs celery, sliced	
2 teaspoons dried parsley	10 ml
1 (8 ounce) carton whole mushrooms	230 g
1½ cups white cooking wine	375 ml
1 - 2 cups instant rice	95 - 190 g

- Sprinkle chicken lightly with salt and pepper. Heat butter in skillet and cook chicken on medium-high heat for about 3 minutes, drain and place in sprayed slow cooker.

- Combine soups, celery, parsley and mushrooms in saucepan, stirring often and heat on medium heat just until mixture blends. Stir in wine and pour over chicken. Cover and cook on LOW heat for 8 hours.

- Cook rice according to package direction, drain and place on serving platter. Spoon chicken thighs and sauce on top of rice. Serves 6 to 8.

Crowd-Pleasing Chicken

1 onion, chopped	
4 medium potatoes, peeled, cut in thick slices	
1 green bell pepper, seeded, cut into strips	
1 red bell pepper, seeded, cut into strips	
½ cup pimento-stuffed olives	65 g
2 ribs celery, cut in 1-inch (2.5 cm) slices	
1 teaspoon Italian seasoning	5 ml
1 (15 ounce) can tomato sauce	425 g
½ cup white wine	125 ml
12 (about 3 pounds) boneless, skinless chicken thighs	12 (1.4 kg)

- Place onion, potatoes, bell peppers, stuffed olives and celery in sprayed slow cooker. Sprinkle Italian seasoning and ½ teaspoon (2 ml) pepper over vegetables and pour tomato sauce and wine over all. Top with chicken thighs.

- Cover and cook on HIGH for 5 hours or on LOW for 8 hours to 8 hours 30 minutes. Serves 8.

Chicken Tostadas

1 tablespoon minced garlic	15 ml
3 tablespoons chili powder	45 ml
2 tablespoons lime juice	30 ml
2 tablespoons olive oil	30 ml
2½ - 3 pounds boneless, skinless chicken thighs	1.1 - 1.4 kg
10 tostada shells	
1 cup shredded lettuce	55 g
1 (8 ounce) package Mexican 3-cheese blend	230 g
1 (16 ounce) jar thick-and-chunky salsa	455 g

- Combine garlic, chili powder, lime juice, oil and 1 teaspoon (5 ml) salt in sprayed slow cooker. Place chicken thighs in cooker, turning to coat each piece with a little of the garlic mixture. Cover and cook on LOW for 8 to 10 hours.

- Remove chicken to cutting board; shred chicken using 2 forks. Return to slow cooker and mix well.

- Place shells on individual plates, spoon in chicken mixture. Top with lettuce, cheese and salsa. Serve immediately. Yields 10 tostadas.

A Credit to This Citrus Chicken

1 (1 pound 4 ounces) package bone-in skinless chicken thighs	570 g
¼ cup fresh lime juice (2 limes)	60 ml
1 (14 ounce) can chicken broth	395 g
1 teaspoon minced garlic	5 ml
½ teaspoon dried thyme leaves	2 ml
¼ cup (½ stick) butter, melted	60 g
1 cup instant rice	95 g
1 (10 ounce) box frozen green peas, thawed	280 g
1 teaspoon dried parsley	5 ml

- Place chicken thighs in sprayed slow cooker.

- Combine lime juice, broth, garlic, thyme and melted butter in small bowl and mix well. Spoon over chicken thighs. Cover and cook on LOW for 8 to 10 hours.

- Increase heat to HIGH, stir in rice and green peas, cover and cook for additional 15 minutes.

- Remove chicken from cooker and keep warm; sprinkle with parsley. Spoon rice and peas on serving platter and top with chicken thighs. Spoon any remaining juices over chicken. Serves 6 to 8.

TIP: When you want chicken to keep its shape, bone-in chicken works best in slow cookers.

Chicken in Herbed Sauce

8 boneless chicken thighs, skin removed
2 onions, chopped
2 (10 ounce) cans cream of chicken soup   2 (280 g)
½ cup milk   125 ml
1 teaspoon Italian seasoning   5 ml
1 teaspoon dried tarragon   5 ml
¼ teaspoon dried rosemary   1 ml

- Place chicken thighs in sprayed slow cooker and top with onions. Combine soup, milk, Italian seasoning, tarragon, rosemary, a little pepper and ½ teaspoon (2 ml) salt in bowl; mix well and pour over chicken and onions. Cover and cook on LOW for 4 hours 30 minutes to 6 hours. Serves 4 to 6.

A Great Chicken Event

8 boneless, skinless chicken thighs, cut into 1-inch (2.5 cm) pieces
2 onions, halved, thinly sliced
1 (16 ounce) package baby carrots, cut in half   455 g
½ cup dried apricots, coarsely chopped   75 g
1 (14 ounce) can chicken broth   395 g
2 tablespoons tomato paste35 g
2 tablespoons lemon juice   30 ml
1 teaspoon seasoned salt   5 ml
2 teaspoons ground cumin   10 ml
1 teaspoon ground ginger   5 ml
1 teaspoon ground cinnamon   5 ml
2 tablespoons flour   15 g
2 (10 ounce) boxes couscous, cooked   2 (280 g)
Toasted pine nuts

- Layer chicken, onion, carrots and apricots in sprayed large slow cooker. Combine broth, tomato paste, lemon juice, seasoned salt, cumin, ginger, cinnamon and flour in medium bowl, mix well. Pour over chicken and vegetables. Cover and cook on HIGH for 5 hours or on LOW for 8 hours. Spoon chicken mixture over couscous and garnish with roasted pine nuts. Serves 8.

Tangy Chicken Legs

12 - 15 chicken legs
⅓ cup soy sauce   75 ml
⅔ cup packed brown sugar   150 g
Scant ⅛ teaspoon ground ginger   .5 ml

- Place chicken legs in sprayed slow cooker. Combine soy sauce, brown sugar, ¼ cup (60 ml) water and ginger in bowl and spoon over chicken legs. Cover and cook on LOW for 4 to 5 hours. Serves 6 to 8.

Cranberry Chicken

2 small chickens, quartered
1 (1 ounce) package onion soup mix   30 g
1 (16 ounce) can whole cranberry sauce   455 g
1 (8 ounce) bottle sweet-honey Catalina salad dressing   250 ml
2 cups instant rice   190 g

- Dry chicken with paper towels and place in sprayed slow cooker. Combine soup mix, cranberry sauce and salad dressing in saucepan on medium heat, stirring until mixture blends well. Pour over chicken. Cover and cook on LOW for 7 to 9 hours.

- Cook rice according to package directions and place on serving platter. Place chicken quarters over rice and spoon sauce over chicken and rice. Serves 8.

Honey-Glazed Chicken

1 red bell pepper, seeded, cut into rings
1 green bell pepper, seeded, cut into rings
1 broiler-fryer chicken, quartered
¼ cup (½ stick) butter, melted   60 g
⅓ cup packed brown sugar   75 g
½ cup honey   115 g
⅓ cup lemon juice   75 ml
1 tablespoon light soy sauce   15 ml
2 cups instant rice   190 g

- Place bell pepper rings in sprayed slow cooker and top with chicken quarters.

- Combine butter, brown sugar, honey, lemon juice and soy sauce in bowl and mix well. Spoon over chicken quarters. Cover and cook on LOW for 6 to 8 hours.

- Cook rice according to package directions, place on serving platter and add chicken quarters along with any liquid remaining in cooker. Serves 4.

Honey-Baked Chicken

2 small fryer chickens, quartered
½ cup (1 stick) butter, melted   115 g
⅔ cup honey   230 g
¼ cup dijon-style mustard   60 g
1 teaspoon curry powder   5 ml

- Place chicken pieces in sprayed large slow cooker, skin-side up and sprinkle a little salt over chicken.

- Combine butter, honey, mustard and curry powder in bowl and mix well. Pour over chicken quarters. Cover and cook on LOW for 6 to 8 hours. Baste chicken once during cooking. Serves 6 to 8.

Tangy Chicken

1 large fryer chicken, quartered
2 tablespoons butter   30 g
½ cup Heinz 57® sauce   125 ml
1 (15 ounce) can stewed tomatoes   425 g

- Wash chicken, dry with paper towels and place in sprayed large slow cooker.

- Combine butter, 57 sauce and stewed tomatoes in saucepan. Heat just until butter melts and ingredients mix well. Pour over chicken. Cover and cook on LOW for 5 to 6 hours. Serves 4 to 6.

Luau Chicken

1 whole chicken, quartered
½ cup plus 2 tablespoons flour, divided   75 g
½ teaspoon ground nutmeg   2 ml
½ teaspoon ground cinnamon   2 ml
2 large sweet potatoes, peeled, sliced
1 (8 ounce) can pineapple chunks with juice   230 g
1 (10 ounce) can cream of chicken soup   280 g
⅔ cup orange juice   150 ml
Rice, cooked

- Wash chicken and dry with paper towels. Combine ½ cup (60 g) flour, nutmeg and cinnamon in bowl and coat chicken. Place sweet potatoes and pineapple in sprayed large slow cooker. Arrange chicken on top.

- Combine chicken soup, orange juice and remaining flour in bowl and pour over chicken. Cover and cook on LOW for 7 to 9 hours or on HIGH for 4 to 5 hours. Serve over rice. Serves 4 to 6.

Tasty Chicken and Veggies

1 (2½ - 3 pound) whole chicken, quartered   1.1 - 1.4 kg
1 (16 ounce) package baby carrots   455 g
4 potatoes, peeled, sliced
3 ribs celery, sliced
1 onion, peeled, sliced
1 cup Italian salad dressing   250 ml
⅔ cup chicken broth   150 ml

- Rinse, dry and place chicken quarters in sprayed large slow cooker with carrots, potatoes, celery and onion.

- Pour salad dressing and chicken broth over chicken and vegetables. Cover and cook on LOW for 6 to 8 hours. Serves 4 to 6.

TIP: *When serving, garnish with sprigs of fresh parsley.*

Who Gets the Wishbone

2 carrots, peeled, cut in 1-inch (2.5 cm) pieces
3 ribs celery, cut in 1-inch (2.5 cm) pieces
2 onions, quartered
1 yellow bell pepper, seeded, cut in strips
6 medium red potatoes with peels, halved

1 (3 pound) chicken	1.4 kg
1 teaspoon dried basil	5 ml
1 teaspoon dried thyme	5 ml
1 teaspoon lemon pepper	5 ml

- Place carrots, celery, onion, bell pepper, potatoes and ½ cup (125 ml) water in sprayed large slow cooker. Place whole chicken on top of vegetables. Sprinkle basil, thyme, lemon pepper and 1 teaspoon (5 ml) salt over chicken.

- Cover and cook on LOW for 8 to 10 hours or on HIGH for 3 hours 30 minutes to 4 hours. Remove chicken to serving platter and place vegetables around chicken. Serves 6.

Sweetheart BBQ Chicken

1 chicken, quartered, skinned

1 (10 ounce) can tomato soup	280 g
¾ cup chopped onion	120 g
¾ cup white vinegar	175 ml
½ cup packed brown sugar	110 g
1 tablespoon Worcestershire sauce	15 ml
¼ teaspoon dried basil	1 ml

- Place quartered chicken in sprayed oval slow cooker. (If you like, you can use 3 chicken breast halves and 3 chicken thighs.)

- Combine tomato soup, onion, vinegar, brown sugar, Worcestershire, basil and ½ teaspoon (2 ml) salt in bowl; mix well. Pour over chicken, making sure mixture covers all pieces. Cover and cook on LOW for 6 to 8 hours. Serves 4 to 6.

TIP: This chicken is very good served with baked beans.

Do prep work ahead of time and seal chopped veggies, meats, etc., in plastic bags and refrigerate until ready to assemble the food in the slow cooker.

Savory Chicken Dinner for Four

1 cup chopped onion	160 g
1 (16 ounce) package baby carrots	455 g
3 ribs celery, cut into 1-inch (2.5 cm) slices	
3 large potatoes, peeled, sliced	
1 whole chicken, skinned, quartered	
1 teaspoon seasoned salt	5 ml
1 teaspoon poultry seasoning	5 ml
1 (14 ounce) can chicken broth	395 g
1 tablespoon cornstarch	15 ml

- Place onion, carrots, celery and potatoes in sprayed slow cooker and top with quartered chicken. Sprinkle with seasoned salt, poultry seasoning and a little pepper.

- Pour chicken broth over vegetables and chicken; cover and cook on HIGH for about 30 minutes; reduce heat to LOW and cook for 6 to 8 hours.

- Use slotted spoon to remove chicken and vegetables to serving platter and keep warm.

- Combine ¼ cup (60 ml) water with cornstarch in bowl and stir into liquid in slow cooker; stir until mixture thickens.

- Pour gravy over chicken and vegetables or place in gravy boat to serve with the chicken dinner. Serves 4.

Lemon Chicken

1 (2½ - 3 pound) chicken, quartered	1.1 - 1.4 kg
1 teaspoon dried oregano	5 ml
2 teaspoons minced garlic	10 ml
2 tablespoons butter	30 g
¼ cup lemon juice	60 ml

- Season chicken quarters with salt, pepper and oregano and rub garlic on chicken. Brown chicken quarters on all sides in butter in skillet and transfer to sprayed oval slow cooker.

- Add ⅓ cup (75 ml) water to skillet, scrape bottom and pour over chicken. Cover and cook on LOW for 5 to 7 hours.

- Pour lemon juice over chicken, cover and cook 1 additional hour. Serves 4 to 6.

Coq au Vin

1 large fryer chicken, quartered, skinned
Canola oil
10 - 12 small white onions, peeled
½ pound whole mushrooms   230 g
1 teaspoon minced garlic   5 ml
½ teaspoon dried thyme leaves   2 ml
10 - 12 small new (red) potatoes with peels
1 (10 ounce) can chicken broth   280 g
1 cup burgundy wine   250 ml
6 bacon slices, cooked, crumbled

- Brown chicken quarters in skillet on both sides.

- Place white onions, whole mushrooms, garlic and thyme in sprayed oval slow cooker. Add chicken quarters, potatoes, chicken broth and a little salt and pepper. Cover and cook on LOW for 7 to 9 hours or on HIGH for 3 to 4 hours.

- (If cooking on LOW, increase heat to HIGH.) Add wine, cover and cook for 1 additional hour. Sprinkle crumbled bacon over chicken before serving. Serves 4 to 6.

"Baked" Chicken

1 cup rice   200 g
2 (10 ounce) cans cream of chicken soup   2 (280 g)
1 (14 ounce) can chicken broth   395 g
1 (1 ounce) packet dry onion soup mix   30 g
1 chicken, quartered

- Place rice in sprayed large slow cooker. Combine soup, broth, 2 soup cans water and onion soup mix in saucepan and mix well. Heat just enough to mix ingredients. Spoon half over rice and place chicken quarters in slow cooker. Spoon remaining soup mixture over chicken. Cover and cook on LOW for 5 to 6 hours. Serves 4 to 6.

Russian Chicken

1 (8 ounce) bottle Russian salad dressing   250 ml
1 (16 ounce) can whole cranberry sauce   455 g
1 (1 ounce) packet onion soup mix   30 g
4 chicken quarters, skinned
Rice, cooked

- Combine salad dressing, cranberry sauce, ½ cup (125 ml) water and soup mix in bowl. Stir well to get all lumps out of soup mix. Place 4 chicken pieces in sprayed large slow cooker and spoon dressing-cranberry mixture over chicken. Cover and cook on LOW for 4 to 5 hours. Serve sauce and chicken over rice. Serves 4 to 6.

TIP: Use 6 chicken breasts if you don't want to cut up a chicken.

Chicken Cacciatore

2 onions, thinly sliced	
1 (2½ - 3) pound fryer chicken, quartered	1.1 - 1.2 kg
2 (6 ounce) cans tomato paste	2 (170 g)
1 (4 ounce) can sliced mushrooms	114 g
1½ teaspoons minced garlic	7 ml
½ teaspoon dried basil	2 ml
2 teaspoons oregano leaves	10 ml
⅔ cup dry white wine	150 ml

- Place sliced onions in sprayed oval slow cooker. Wash chicken quarters, dry with paper towels and place over onions.

- Combine tomato paste, mushrooms, garlic, basil, oregano and wine in bowl and pour over chicken quarters. Cover and cook on LOW for 7 to 8 hours or on HIGH for 4 hours. Serves 4 to 6.

Saffron Rice and Chicken

1 fryer-broiler chicken, quartered	
½ teaspoon garlic powder	2 ml
Canola oil	
1 (14 ounce) can chicken broth	400 g
1 onion, chopped	
1 green pepper, seeded, quartered	
1 yellow pepper, seeded, quartered	
1 (4 ounce) jar pimentos, drained	115 g
⅓ cup prepared bacon bits	20 g
2 tablespoons butter, melted	30 g
1 (5 ounce) package saffron yellow rice mix	145 g

- Sprinkle chicken with garlic powder and a little salt and pepper. Brown chicken quarters in little oil in skillet. Place chicken in sprayed oval slow cooker and pour broth in slow cooker.

- Combine, onion, bell peppers, pimentos and bacon bits in bowl and spoon over chicken quarters. Cover and cook on LOW for 4 to 5 hours.

- Carefully remove chicken quarters from cooker, stir in butter and rice mix and gently return chicken to cooker. Cover and cook for additional 1 hour or until rice is tender. Serves 4 to 6.

Chicken Casserole with Chips

1 (15 ounce) can garbanzo beans, rinsed, drained	425 g
1 (15 ounce) can pinto beans, rinsed, drained	425 g
1 (15 ounce) can whole kernel corn, drained	425 g
1 red onion, chopped	
1 green bell pepper, seeded, chopped	
1 teaspoon ground cumin	5 ml
1 teaspoon minced garlic	5 ml
4 cups cooked, cubed chicken	560 g
1 (16 ounce) jar salsa	455 g
1 (8 ounce) package shredded Velveeta® cheese	230 g
2 - 3 cups crushed tortilla chips	110 - 170 g
1 (8 ounce) carton sour cream	230 g

- Combine beans, corn, onion, bell pepper, cumin, garlic, chicken, salsa and cheese in bowl. Stir until blended well and spoon into sprayed slow cooker. Cover and cook on LOW for 6 to 8 hours.

- Top each serving with about ⅓ cup (20 g) chips and a dollop of sour cream. Serves 8.

Chicken-Sausage Extraordinaire

1 pound pork sausage	455 g
1 cup chopped celery	100 g
2 onions, chopped	
1 green bell pepper, seeded, chopped	
1 red bell pepper, seeded, chopped	
1 (4 ounce) jar sliced mushrooms, drained	115 g
5 boneless, skinless, chicken breast halves, cooked, sliced	
1 (14 ounce) can chicken broth	395 g
1 teaspoon poultry seasoning	5 ml
1 (6 ounce) box long grain-wild rice mix	170 g
¼ cup flour	30 g
1 (8 ounce) carton whipping cream, divided	230 g

- Brown and crumble sausage in skillet, remove with slotted spoon and set aside.

- Saute celery, onions and bell peppers in sausage fat until onion is transparent, but not brown. Drain. Stir in mushrooms, chicken, broth, poultry seasoning and sausage. Pour into sprayed slow cooker. Cover and cook on LOW for 5 to 7 hours.

- Cook rice according to package directions.

- Combine flour and about 3 tablespoons (15 ml) whipping cream; mix until they blend well; stir in remaining cream. Stir flour-cream mixture and cooked rice into cooker. Cover and cook for additional 30 to 45 minutes or until mixture thickens. Serve 8 to 10.

Chunky Chicken Casserole

1 (16 ounce) package frozen broccoli spears, thawed	455 g
1 (16 ounce) package baby carrots	455 g
1 red bell pepper, seeded, chopped	
3 ribs celery, sliced	
3 cups cooked, diced chicken	420 g
2 (10 ounce) cans cream of chicken soup	2 (280 g)
¼ cup milk	60 ml
1 tablespoon lemon juice	15 ml
¼ cup (½ stick) butter	60 ml
2 cups dry breadcrumbs	70 g

- Combine broccoli, carrots, bell pepper, celery and chicken in sprayed slow cooker.

- Combine soup, milk and lemon juice in bowl and spoon over broccoli-chicken mixture. Cover and cook on LOW for 6 to 8 hours.

- Melt butter in skillet on medium heat and stir in breadcrumbs. Cook, stirring constantly until breadcrumbs are crisp and light brown. Sprinkle hot breadcrumbs over each serving. Serves 8.

Chicken-Vegetable Medley

1 (16 ounce) package frozen broccoli spears, thawed	455 g
1 (16 ounce) package frozen cauliflower, thawed	455 g
1 red bell pepper, seeded, thawed	
1 cup sliced celery	100 g
4 cups cooked, cubed chicken	560 g
2 (10 ounce) cans cream of chicken soup	2 (280 g)
½ cup milk	125 ml
1 (8 ounce) package shredded Velveeta® cheese	230 g
1 cup instant brown rice	190 g
¼ cup (½ stick) butter, melted	55 g
1½ - 1 cups soft breadcrumbs	90 - 120 g

- Combine broccoli, cauliflower, bell pepper and celery in sprayed slow cooker.

- Combine chicken, soup, milk and cheese in bowl and mix well. Spoon over vegetable mixture. Cover and cook on LOW for 6 to 8 hours.

- Cook rice according to package directions. Stir into chicken-vegetable mixture. Cover and let stand for about 15 minutes or until hot.

- Melt butter in skillet on medium heat and add breadcrumbs; stirring constantly until crumbs are heated and light brown. Sprinkle over dish. Serves 8.

Not Just Chicken

1 (10 ounce) package frozen chopped bell peppers and onions, thawed	280 g
3 ribs celery, sliced	
1 (10 ounce) can diced tomatoes and green chilies	280 g
1 (15 ounce) can green peas, drained	425 g
3 cups cooked, cubed chicken	420 g
3 cups cooked, cubed ham	420 g
¼ cup cornstarch	30 g
1 pint half-and-half cream, divided	500 ml
1 (10 ounce) can cream of celery soup	280 g
1 (8 ounce) package shredded Velveeta® cheese	230 g
2 cups instant rice	190 g

- Combine bell peppers and onions, celery, tomatoes and green chilies, peas, chicken, and ham in sprayed slow cooker.

- Combine cornstarch and ¼ cup (60 ml) half-and-half cream; mix until mixture is smooth. Stir in remaining half-and-half cream, soup and cheese. Pour over chicken-ham-vegetable mixture. Cover and cook on LOW for 5 to 7 hours.

- Cook rice according to package directions, place on serving platter and spoon chicken-ham-vegetable mixture over rice. Serves 8 to 10.

Mr. Mozz's Spaghetti

1 bunch green onions with tops, chopped	
1 cup sliced celery	100 g
1 red bell pepper, seeded, chopped	
1 green bell pepper, seeded, chopped	
1 tablespoon dried cilantro leaves	15 ml
1 teaspoon Italian seasoning	5 ml
4 cups cooked, chopped chicken or turkey	560 g
1 (16 ounce) jar creamy alfredo sauce	455 g
1 (12 ounce) package shredded mozzarella cheese, divided	340 g
1 (12 ounce) package thin spaghetti	340 g
1 (10 ounce) box frozen green peas, thawed	280 g
1 (8 ounce) carton sour cream	230 g

- Combine onions, celery, bell peppers, cilantro leaves, Italian seasoning and chicken in sprayed slow cooker.

- Combine alfredo sauce and 2 cups (230 g) cheese in bowl and stir into slow cooker. Cover and cook on LOW for 5 to 7 hours.

- Cook spaghetti according to package directions, drain well.

- Stir in spaghetti, green peas and sour cream Cover and cook for additional 45 minutes to 1 hour or until mixture is thoroughly hot. Sprinkle remaining cheese on each serving. Serves 8.

Chicken-Spaghetti Ready

1 (16 ounce) package frozen chopped bell peppers and onions, thawed	455 g
3 ribs celery, sliced	
1 (15 ounce) cans Mexican stewed tomatoes	425 g
1 (4 ounce) can diced green chilies	115 g
1 (14 ounce) can chicken broth	395 g
4 cups cooked, cubed chicken	560 g
1 (8 ounce) package shredded Velveeta® cheese	230 g
1 (12 ounce) package spaghetti	340 g
1 (8 ounce) package shredded Monterey Jack cheese	230 g

- Combine bell peppers and onions, celery, tomatoes, green chilies, broth, chicken, and Velveeta® cheese in bowl; mix well and spoon into sprayed slow cooker. Cover and cook on LOW for 5 to 7 hours.

- Cook spaghetti according to package direction, drain and stir into slow cooker. Let stand for about 10 minutes for flavors to blend. Pour mixture into large serving bowl and sprinkle Monterey Jack cheese on top. Serves 8 to 10.

TIP: If you like, you could serve Jack cheese separately and let each person add cheese to individual servings.

Supper-Ready Chicken

1 large onion, sliced	
2 (15 ounce) cans whole new potatoes, drained, quartered	2 (425 g)
4 boneless, skinless chicken breasts, cooked	
1 (10 ounce) can cream of celery soup	280 g
½ cup milk	125 ml
1 cup shredded mozzarella cheese	115 g

- Place onion slices and potatoes in sprayed slow cooker. Slice chicken breasts and add to slow cooker.

- Combine soup and milk in bowl and spoon over chicken. Cover and cook on LOW for 4 to 5 hours. Top with shredded cheese. Serves 4 to 6.

Slow cooking does not require as much liquid as other cooking methods because the lid forms a seal with the cooker and does not allow moisture to escape. Therefore it is usually not necessary to add as much liquid. Use the amount specified in the recipe.

Chicken Dish, WOW!

2 (15 ounce) cans French-style green beans, drained	2 (425 g)
2 ribs celery, sliced	
1 (10 ounce) package frozen chopped bell peppers	
and onions, thawed	280 g
1 cup chow mein noodles	55 g
½ cup slivered almonds	85 g
4 cups cooked, diced chicken	560 g
1 (10 ounce) can fiesta nacho cheese soup	280 g
1 (10 ounce) can cream of chicken soup	280 g
1 (5 ounce) can evaporated milk	150 ml
1 (3 ounce) can french-fried onions	85 g

- Combine green beans, celery, bell peppers and onions, noodles, almonds, and diced chicken in sprayed slow cooker.

- Combine soups and evaporated milk in bowl, mix well and pour over vegetables-chicken mixture. Cover and cook on LOW for 8 to 10 hours.

- A few minutes before serving, place fried onions in pan and heat at 325° (160° C) oven for 5 minutes. Sprinkle over chicken dish or over individual servings. Serves 8 to 10.

Green Chili-Chicken Casserole

1 green bell pepper, seeded, cut into strips	
3 ribs celery, cut into 1-inch (2.5 cm) strips	
¼ cup (½ stick) butter, melted	60 g
1 (7 ounce) can diced green chilies	200 g
1 (10 ounce) can fiesta nacho cheese soup	280 g
3 boneless, skinless chicken breasts, cooked, sliced	
1 (10 ounce) can chicken broth	280 g
1 cup instant rice	95 g
1 (8 ounce) carton sour cream	230 g

- Combine bell pepper, celery, butter, green chilies, soup, chicken and broth in sprayed slow cooker. Stir until blended well. Cover and cook on LOW for 6 to 8 hours.

- Stir in rice, cover and cook for additional 15 minutes. Stir in sour cream. Serves 6 to 8.

Chinese Garden

1 (10 ounce) package frozen chopped bell peppers	
and onions, thawed	280 g
2 cups sliced celery	200 g
1 (15 ounce) can Chinese vegetables, drained	425 g
1 (8 ounce) can sliced bamboo shoots	230 g
3½ cups cooked, cubed chicken	490 g
1 (10 ounce) can cream of chicken soup	280 g
¼ cup milk	60 ml
2 tablespoons soy sauce	30 ml
½ teaspoon garlic powder	2 ml
1 (6 ounce) package fried rice with almonds	170 g
1 (8 ounce) carton sour cream	230 g
1 - 2 cups chow mein noodles	55 - 110 g

- Combine bell peppers and onions, celery, Chinese vegetables, and bamboo shoots in sprayed slow cooker and top with chicken.

- Combine soup, milk, soy sauce and garlic powder in bowl and pour over chicken-vegetable mixture. Cover and cook on LOW for 6 to 8 hours.

- Cook rice according to package directions; stir rice and sour cream into cooker. Sprinkle noodles over top. Serves 8.

TIP: If you would rather serve on individual plates, spread noodles on individual plates and spoon chicken-vegetable on top.

Chicken-Noodle Delight

3 ribs celery, sliced	
1 (10 ounce) package frozen chopped bell peppers	
and onions, thawed	280 g
1 (4 ounce) can sliced mushrooms, drained	115 g
3 cups cooked, cubed chicken breasts	420 g
1 (16 ounce) jar sun-dried tomato alfredo sauce	455 g
1 teaspoon chicken bouillon granules	5 ml
1 (8 ounce) package medium egg noodles	230 g
6 tablespoons (¾ stick) butter, melted	85 g
1 (8 ounce) package shredded cheddar cheese	230 g

- Combine celery, bell peppers and onions, mushrooms, and cubed chicken in sprayed slow cooker.

- Pour alfredo sauce over chicken mixture and sprinkle with chicken bouillon granules. Cover and cook on LOW for 5 to 7 hours.

- Cook egg noodles according to package directions, drain and stir in melted butter.

- Add noodles to cooker, stirring until ingredients blend well. Sprinkle with cheese. Serves 6 to 8.

Chicken and Rice Casserole

1 onion, chopped	
1 cup sliced celery	100 g
1 (4 ounce) jar pimentos, drained	115 g
2 (15 ounce) cans French-style green beans, drained	2 (425 g)
1 cup slivered almonds	170 g
4 cups cooked, diced chicken	560 g
¼ cup (½ stick) butter, melted	60 g
1 (10 ounce) can cream of chicken soup	280 g
1 (10 ounce) can cream of celery soup	280 g
½ cup milk	125 ml
1 (6 ounce) package long grain-wild rice mix	170 g
2½ - 3 cups lightly crushed potato chips	140 - 170 g

- Combine onion, celery, pimentos, green beans, almonds and chicken in sprayed slow cooker. Drizzle melted butter over chicken.

- Combine soups and milk in bowl and pour over all ingredients. Cover and cook on LOW for 6 to 8 hours.

- Cook rice according to package directions; gently stir rice into cooker. Cover and cook for additional 30 minutes for flavors to blend.

- Place lightly crushed potato chips in baking pan at 325° (160° C) oven for 10 minutes and sprinkle over dish. Serves 8.

Family Chicken Bake

1 (18 ounce) package frozen hash-brown potatoes, thawed	510 g
1 (10 ounce) package chopped frozen bell peppers and onions, thawed	280 g
2 ribs celery, sliced	
1 (7 ounce) can diced green chilies, drained	200 g
2 (14 ounce) cans chicken broth	2 (395 g)
¼ cup (½ stick) butter, melted	60 g
3 - 4 cups cooked, cubed chicken	420 - 560 g
1 (16 ounce) package shredded Velveeta® cheese, divided	455 g
1 (8 ounce) carton sour cream	230 g

- Combine potatoes, bell peppers and onions, celery, green chilies, broth, butter, chicken, and half cheese in bowl; stir until mixture blends well. Spoon into sprayed slow cooker. Cover and cook on LOW for 6 to 8 hours.

- Stir in sour cream, cover and let stand for about 15 minutes or until mixture is thoroughly hot. Sprinkle remaining cheese over top. Serves 8.

TIP: For a change of pace, heat some hot thick-and-chunky salsa to spoon over top of each serving.

Chicken-Sausage Casserole

1 pound bulk pork sausage	455 g
1 (16 ounce) carton mushrooms, sliced	455 g
1 onion, chopped	
2 red bell peppers, seeded, chopped	
3 cups cooked, cubed chicken	420 g
1 (10 ounce) can cream of chicken soup	280 g
1 (10 ounce) can chicken broth	280 g
2 cups buttery cracker crumbs, slightly toasted	120 g

- Combine broken-up sausage, mushrooms, onion, bell peppers, chicken, soup and broth in sprayed slow cooker. Cover and cook on LOW for 7 to 9 hours.

- Spoon mixture in large serving bowl and sprinkle heated crumbs over top. Serves 8.

Monterey Bake

6 (6 inch) corn tortillas	6 (15 cm)
3 cups cubed cooked chicken	420 g
1 (10 ounce) package frozen whole kernel corn	280 g
1 (15 ounce) can pinto beans with liquid	425 g
1 (16 ounce) jar hot salsa	455 g
¼ cup sour cream	60 g
1 tablespoon flour	15 ml
3 tablespoons snipped fresh cilantro	5 g
1 (8 ounce) package shredded 4-cheese blend	230 g

- Preheat oven to 250° (120° C).

- Cut tortillas into 6 wedges. Place half of tortillas wedges in sprayed slow cooker. Place remaining wedges on baking pan, bake for about 10 minutes and set aside.

- Layer chicken, corn and beans over tortillas in cooker. Combine salsa, sour cream, flour and cilantro in bowl and pour over chicken, corn and beans. Cover and cook on LOW for 3 to 4 hours.

- When ready to serve, place baked tortillas wedges and cheese on top of each serving. Serves 4 to 6.

Very high humidity can affect cooking time for a slow cooker. Time may need to be added when cooking in extreme humidity.

Chicken and Cornbread Stuffing

1 (10 ounce) can cream of chicken soup	280 g
2 stalks celery, sliced	
½ cup (1 stick) butter, melted	115 g
3 cups cooked, cubed chicken	420 g
1 (16 ounce) package frozen broccoli, corn and red peppers	455 g
1 (8 ounce) box cornbread stuffing mix	230 g

- Combine chicken soup, celery, butter, chicken, vegetables, stuffing mix and ⅓ cup (75 ml) water in large bowl. Mix well and transfer to sprayed large slow cooker. Cover and cook on LOW for 5 to 6 hours. Serves 4 to 6.

TIP: This is a great recipe for leftover chicken.

Chicken and Everything Good

2 (10 ounce) cans cream of chicken soup	2 (280 g)
⅓ cup (⅔ stick) butter, melted	75 g
3 cups cooked, cubed chicken	420 g
1 (16 ounce) package frozen broccoli, corn and red peppers	455 g
1 (10 ounce) package frozen green peas	280 g
1 (8 ounce) package cornbread stuffing mix	230 g

- Combine soup, butter and ⅓ cup (75 ml) water in large bowl and mix well. Add chicken, vegetables and stuffing mix and stir well. Spoon mixture into sprayed large slow cooker. Cover and cook on LOW for 5 to 6 hours or on HIGH for 2 hours 30 minutes to 3 hours. Serves 4 to 6.

Taco Chicken over Spanish Rice

1 cup flour	120 g
2 (1 ounce) packets taco seasoning mix	2 (30 g)
6 boneless, skinless chicken breast halves	
2 onions, sliced	
2 (15 ounce) cans Spanish rice	2 (425 g)
1 cup shredded Mexican 4-cheese blend	115 g

- Combine flour and taco seasoning in shallow bowl; add chicken and toss to coat.

- Place onions in sprayed slow cooker and top with chicken breasts. Spoon 2 tablespoons (30 ml) water into cooker; cover and cook on LOW for 6 to 8 hours.

- Place Spanish rice in saucepan over medium heat, stir constantly until rice is thoroughly hot. Stir in cheese. Place rice-cheese mixture on serving platter and top with chicken breasts. Serves 6.

As the Chicken Flies

1 (16 ounce) package frozen broccoli florets, thawed	455 g
1 (16 ounce) package frozen cauliflower, thawed	455 g
1 red bell pepper, seeded, cut into strips	
3 - 4 cups cooked, cubed chicken	420 - 560 g
1 (10 ounce) can cream of chicken soup	280 g
1 cup shredded cheddar cheese	115 g
1 (10 ounce) can cream of broccoli soup	280 g
1½ - 2 cups crushed cheese crackers	90 - 180 g

- Place broccoli, cauliflower and bell pepper in sprayed slow cooker and top with cubed chicken. Spoon cream of chicken soup, as evenly as possible, over chicken; top with shredded cheese. Spoon cream of broccoli soup over cheese. Cover and cook on LOW for 5 to 7 hours.

- Place crushed crackers in baking pan and heat in oven at 325° (160° C) for about 10 minutes. Sprinkle heated crackers over vegetable-chicken mixture. Serves 8 to 10.

A Deal of a Chicken Bake

1 (16 ounce) package frozen chopped bell peppers	
and onions, thawed	455 g
1 red bell pepper, seeded, cut into strips	
3 ribs celery, chopped	
1 (14 ounce) can chicken broth	395 g
1 (10 ounce) can cream of chicken soup	280 g
4 - 5 cups cooked, cubed chicken	560 - 700 g
1 (16 ounce) package Mexican Velveeta® cheese, divided	455 g
1 (18 ounce) package frozen hash-brown potatoes, thawed	510 g

- Combine bell peppers and onions, red bell pepper, celery, broth, soup, chicken, and a little pepper in sprayed slow cooker, mix well. Add half cheese and potatoes and stir until mixture is blends well. Cover and cook on LOW for 6 to 8 hours. Sprinkle remaining cheese over top. Serves 16 to 18.

Family Chicken Special

3 cups cooked, chopped chicken	420 g
1 (15 ounce) can green peas, drained	425 g
1 cup instant rice	95 g
1 red bell pepper, seeded, chopped	
1 (10 ounce) can cream of chicken soup	280 g
½ cup mayonnaise	110 g
¼ cup (½ stick) butter, melted	60 g
1 (4 ounce) can diced pimientos, drained	115 g

- Combine all ingredients in bowl; stir until they blend well. Transfer to sprayed slow cooker; cover and cook on LOW for 6 to 8 hours or on HIGH for 3 to 4 hours. Serves 4 to 5.

Family Night Chicken Casserole

1½ cups cooked rice	240 g
3 cups cooked, cubed chicken	280 g
1 red bell pepper, seeded, chopped	
1 (16 ounce) package frozen cut green beans, thawed, drained	455 g
1 (10 ounce) can cream of chicken soup	280 g
¾ cup mayonnaise	170 g
1 (3 ounce) can french-fried onions	85 g

- Combine rice, chicken, bell pepper, green beans, soup, mayonnaise and a little pepper in large bowl and toss to mix. Spoon into sprayed slow cooker. Cover and cook on LOW for 6 to 8 hours or on HIGH for 3 to 4 hours. Sprinkle with fried onions. Serves 4 to 6.

Veggie-Cheesy Chicken

1 (16 ounce) package frozen broccoli florets, thawed	455 g
1 (10 ounce) package frozen cauliflower, thawed	280 g
1 red bell pepper, seeded, cut into strips	
1 cup sliced celery	
2 cups cooked brown rice	390 g
1 teaspoon seasoned salt	5 ml
4 cups cooked chicken cut into strips	560 g
½ cup (1 stick) butter, divided	115 g
¼ cup flour	30 g
1 pint half and half cream, divided	500 ml
1 (10 ounce) can cream of chicken soup	280 g
1 (12 ounce) package shredded cheddar cheese, divided	340 g

- Combine broccoli, cauliflower, bell pepper, celery, brown rice, seasoned salt and chicken in sprayed slow cooker.

- Melt butter in medium saucepan on medium heat and stir in flour. Gradually add about 1 cup (250 ml) cream, stirring constantly; then add remaining cream and soup, stirring until mixture thickens. Pour this mixture over broccoli-chicken mixture and gently stir. Cover and cook on LOW for 6 to 8 hours.

- Stir in half cheddar cheese; cover and cook another 20 minutes or just until cheese melts and blends with the chicken-vegetable mixture. Just before serving, sprinkle remaining cheese over top. Serves 8 to 10.

Comfort Chicken and Cauliflower

1 (10 ounce) can chicken broth	280 g
1 cup rice	185 g
1 (10 ounce) can cream of chicken soup	280 g
2 cups cooked chicken breasts, cut in 1-inch pieces	280 g/2.5 cm
1 red bell pepper, seeded, chopped	
1 teaspoon seasoned salt	5 ml
1 cup shredded 4-cheese blend	115 g
1 (10 ounce) package frozen cauliflower florets, thawed	280 g

- Combine broth, rice, soup, chicken pieces, bell pepper, seasoned salt, cheese and 2 cups (500 ml) water in sprayed slow cooker, mix well. Cover and cook on HIGH for 1 to 2 hours.

- Stir in cauliflower florets, cover and cook for additional 20 to 25 minutes. Serves 6.

Chicken Lasagna

1 (16 ounce) package cooked Italian-style chicken sausage links, diced	455 g
1 (16 ounce) jar marinara sauce	455 g
2 (15 ounce) containers ricotta cheese	2 (425 g)
1 (8 ounce) package shredded mozzarella cheese, divided	230 g
¾ cup grated parmesan cheese, divided	75 g
1½ teaspoons Italian seasoning	7 ml
½ teaspoon dried basil	2 ml
2 teaspoons minced garlic	10 ml
1 (8 ounce) box no-cook lasagna noodles	230 g

- Combine chicken sausage, marinara sauce and ½ cup (125 ml) water in bowl, mix well.

- In separate bowl, combine ricotta cheese, 1½ cups (175 g) mozzarella cheese, ½ cup (50 g) parmesan cheese, Italian seasoning, basil, garlic and ½ teaspoon (2 ml) pepper.

- Spread one-fourth sausage-marinara sauce in sprayed slow cooker. Top with one-third noodles (you may need to break some of the noodles to fit slow cooker). Spread with one-third cheese mixture, covering noodles completely. Repeat layers of sauce, noodles and cheese twice. Spread with remaining sauce mixture. Cover and cook on LOW for 5 hours to 5 hours 30 minutes.

- Sprinkle with remaining mozzarella and parmesan. Cover and let stand for 10 to 15 minutes, letting cheese melt. Serves 8.

Smoky Turkey Supper

1 (24 ounce) package frozen hash-brown potatoes, thawed	680 g
1 (10 ounce) package frozen chopped bell peppers	
and onions, thawed	280 g
1 (10 ounce) can cream of chicken soup	280 g
1 (8 ounce) carton sour cream	230 g
3 cups cooked, cubed smoked turkey	420 g
1 (8 ounce) package shredded cheddar cheese	230 g
3 green onions, sliced	

- Spread hash-brown potatoes in sprayed slow cooker and top with bell peppers and onions, soup, sour cream, smoked turkey, and cheese. Gently stir until they blend well. Cover and cook on LOW for 5 to 6 hours. Sprinkle sliced green onions over each serving. Serves 6.

Turkey Cassoulet

2 cups cooked, cubed turkey	280 g
1 (8 ounce) package smoked turkey sausage	230 g
3 carrots, sliced	
1 onion, halved, sliced	
1 (15 ounce) can navy bean	425 g
1 (15 ounce) can white lima beans	425 g
1 (8 ounce) can tomato sauce	230 g
1 teaspoon dried thyme	5 ml
¼ teaspoon ground allspice	1 ml

- Cut turkey sausage in ½-inch (1.2 cm) pieces. Combine all ingredients in sprayed slow cooker. Cover and cook on LOW for 4 to 5 hours. Serves 4.

TIP: This is a great recipe for leftover turkey.

Turkey and Dressing

1 (6 ounce) package turkey stuffing	170 g
3 - 4 cups cooked, diced turkey	420 - 560 g
1 red bell pepper, seeded, chopped	
2 tablespoons dried parsley flakes	10 g
1 (10 ounce) can cream of chicken soup	280 g
1 (8 ounce) carton sour cream	230 g
½ cup (1 stick) butter, melted	115 g
1 teaspoon ground cumin	5 ml
1½ cups shredded mozzarella cheese	175 g

- Combine stuffing, turkey, bell pepper, parsley flakes, soup, sour cream, butter and cumin in sprayed slow cooker. Stir to blend well. Cover and cook on LOW for 5 to 7 hours. Sprinkle with cheese. Serves 8 to 10.

Colorful Rice and Turkey

1 (10 ounce) can cream of mushroom soup	280 g
1 (10 ounce) can cream of chicken soup	280 g
2 cups rice	370 g
3 ribs celery, sliced diagonally	
1 (16 ounce) package frozen Oriental vegetable mix	455 g
3 cups cooked, cubed turkey	420 g
1 teaspoon poultry seasoning	5 ml
2 (14 ounce) cans chicken broth	2 (395 g)

- Combine soups and 1 soup can water in saucepan. Heat just enough to mix well and pour into sprayed large slow cooker. Add remaining ingredients and mix. Cover and cook on LOW for 5 to 6 hours. Serves 4 to 6.

Turkey-Stuffing Casserole

3 - 4 cups cooked, chopped turkey	420 - 560 g
1 (16 ounce) package frozen broccoli florets, thawed	455 g
1 (10 ounce) can cream of chicken soup	280 g
¾ cup half-and-half cream	175 ml
1 (8 ounce) package shredded Swiss cheese	230 g
1 (6 ounce) package turkey stuffing mix	170 g
½ cup chopped walnuts	65 g

- Combine turkey and broccoli in sprayed slow cooker. Combine soup, half-and-half cream and cheese and spoon over turkey-broccoli mixture. In separate bowl, combine stuffing mix, walnuts and ¾ cup (175 ml) water and spread evenly over soup mixture. Cover and cook on LOW for 5 to 7 hours. Serves 8.

Delightful Turkey Breast

1 (3 pound) whole skinless turkey breast	1.4 kg
1 (16 ounce) can whole cranberry sauce	455 g
1 (1 ounce) packet onion soup mix	30 g
½ teaspoon dried basil	2 ml
⅓ cup orange juice	75 ml
3 cups instant rice	285 g
2 tablespoons butter	30 g

- Place turkey breast in sprayed slow cooker and sprinkle with 1 teaspoon (5 ml) pepper.

- Combine cranberry sauce, onion soup mix, basil and orange juice in medium saucepan. Bring to a boil, stirring constantly and heat just until mixture blends well. Pour over turkey breast. Cover and cook on LOW for 6 to 8 hours.

- Cook instant rice with 2½ cups (625 ml) water as directed on package, add butter when rice is done. Place rice on serving platter and place turkey breast on top. Serves 6 to 8.

Maple-Plum Glazed Turkey Breast

1 cup red plum jam	320 g
1 cup maple syrup	250 ml
1 teaspoon dry mustard	5 ml
¼ cup lemon juice	60 ml
1 (3 - 5 pound) boneless turkey breast	1.4 - 2.3 kg

- Combine jam, syrup, mustard and lemon juice in saucepan. Bring to a boil, turn heat down and simmer for about 20 minutes or until slightly thick. Set aside 1 cup (250 ml).

- Place turkey breast in sprayed slow cooker and pour remaining glaze over turkey. Cover and cook on LOW for 5 to 7 hours.

- When ready to serve, slice turkey and serve with heated set aside glaze. Serves 6 to 8.

Easy-Fixin' Turkey Supper

1 (6 ounce) package stuffing mix for turkey	170 g
3 ribs celery, sliced	
1 (16 ounce) package frozen mixed vegetables, thawed	455 g
1½ pounds deli turkey meat, cut into strips	680 g
2 (10 ounce) cans cream of chicken soup	2 (280 g)
½ cup milk	125 ml
¾ cup coarsely chopped walnuts	100 g

- Make stuffing according to package directions and place about ¾ cup (45 g) stuffing in sprayed slow cooker. Top with celery, mixed vegetables and turkey strips.

- Combine soup and milk in bowl and spoon over turkey and vegetables. Spread remaining stuffing over top. Cover and cook on LOW for 5 to 7 hours.

- Place walnuts in baking pan and heat in oven at 325° (160° C) for about 10 to 15 minutes. Sprinkle walnuts over mixture and serve immediately. Serves 6 to 8.

Quality Turkey Meat Loaf

2 pounds ground turkey breast	910 g
2 tablespoons poultry seasoning	30 ml
1 teaspoon instant chopped onion	5 ml
2 slices whole wheat bread, cubed	
1 large egg	
½ cup barbecue sauce	125 ml

- Make foil handles for meat loaf (see TIP on page 213).

- Combine all ingredients and ½ teaspoon (2 ml) pepper in bowl and mix well. Shape into loaf and place in sprayed oval slow cooker. Cover and cook on LOW for 6 to 7 hours.

- Remove from cooker and let stand for about 15 minutes before slicing. Serves 6 to 8.

Turkey Bake

1½ pounds turkey tenderloins	680 g
1 (6 ounce) package fried rice and vermicelli mix	170 g
1 (10 ounce) package frozen green peas, thawed	280 g
1 cup sliced celery	100 g
¼ cup (½ stick) butter, melted	60 g
1 (14 ounce) can chicken broth	395 g
1½ cups fresh broccoli florets	105 g

- Cut tenderloins into strips. Saute turkey strips in non-stick skillet until no longer pink.

- Combine turkey strips, rice-vermicelli mix plus seasoning packet, peas, celery, butter, chicken broth and 1 cup (250 ml) water in sprayed large slow cooker and mix well. Cover and cook on LOW for 4 to 5 hours.

- Turn heat to HIGH, add broccoli. cover and cook for additional 20 minutes. Serves 4 to 6.

Turkey Loaf

2 pounds ground turkey	910 g
1 onion, very finely chopped	
½ red bell pepper, very finely chopped	
2 teaspoons minced garlic	10 ml
½ cup chili sauce	135 g
2 large eggs, beaten	
¾ cup Italian seasoned breadcrumbs	175 ml

- Make foil handles for meat loaf (see TIP on page 213).

- Combine all ingredients plus 1 teaspoon (5 ml) salt and ½ teaspoon (2 ml) pepper in large bowl and mix well. Shape into round loaf and place in sprayed slow cooker. Cover and cook on LOW for 5 to 6 hours. Serves 4 to 6.

Turkey Spaghetti

2 pounds ground turkey	910 g
2 (10 ounce) cans tomato bisque soup	2 (280 g)
1 (14 ounce) can chicken broth	395 g
2 (7 ounce) boxes ready-cut spaghetti, cooked, drained	2 (200 g)
1 (15 ounce) can whole kernel corn, drained	425 g
1 (4 ounce) can sliced mushrooms, drained	115 g
¼ cup ketchup	70 g

- Cook ground turkey in non-stick skillet and season with a little salt and pepper. Place cooked turkey in sprayed large slow cooker. Add in soup, broth. spaghetti, corn, mushrooms and ketchup and stir to blend. Cover and cook on LOW for 5 to 7 hours or on HIGH for 3 hours. Serves 4 to 6.

Sausage and Rice

1 pound turkey sausage	455 g
1 (6 ounce) box flavored rice mix	170 g
2 (14 ounce) cans chicken broth	2 (395 g)
2 cups sliced celery	200 g
1 red bell pepper, seeded, julienned	
1 (15 ounce) can cut green beans, drained	425 g
⅓ cup slivered almonds, toasted	55 g

- Break up turkey sausage and brown in skillet. Place in sprayed slow cooker.

- Add rice, 1 cup (250 ml) water, chicken broth, celery, bell pepper and green beans and stir to mix. Cover and cook on LOW for 3 to 4 hours. When ready to serve, sprinkle almonds over top. Serves 4.

Western Pork Supper

6 (¾-inch thick) boneless pork chops	6 (1.8 cm)
1 (15 ounce) can chili beans	425 g
1 ½ cups salsa	
1 (16 ounce) package frozen seasoned corn with black beans, tomatoes, bell peppers, and onions, thawed	455 g
1 (4 ounce) can sliced ripe olives	115 g
2 cups instant brown rice	375 g

- Arrange pork chops in sprayed oval slow cooker and cover with chili beans and salsa. Cover and cook on LOW for 5 hours or on HIGH for 2 hours 30 minutes.

- (If cooking on LOW, increase heat to HIGH.) Stir in seasoned corn and olives. Cover and cook for additional 30 minutes.

- Cook brown rice according to package directions and place on serving platter. Spoon pork chops and vegetables over rice. Serves 6.

Stuffing over Pork Chops

1 (6 ounce) box savory herb stuffing mix	170 g
¼ cup (½ stick) butter, melted	60 g
1 (10 ounce) can chicken broth	280 g
8 center-cut pork chops	
2 onions, each cut in 4 slices	

- Prepare stuffing mix according to package directions with amount of water called for and melted butter.

- Pour broth in sprayed large slow cooker.

- Lightly brown pork chops on each side in skillet on medium-high heat and place in slow cooker. Top each pork chop with 1 slice of onion; use a large ice cream dipper to place a dip of stuffing mixture over each onion slice. Cover and cook on LOW for 6 to 8 hours. Serves 8.

Salsa Pork Chops

6 (¾ inch thick) boneless pork chops	6 (1.8 cm)
1 cup seasoned breadcrumbs	120 g
1 (10 ounce) package frozen chopped bell peppers and	
onions, thawed	280 g
1 (11 ounce) can Mexicorn®, drained	310 g
½ teaspoon dried sage	2 ml
1 cup chunky salsa, divided	265 g

- Cut pocket in each pork chop, cutting from edge almost to center and season with salt and pepper.

- Combine breadcrumbs, bell peppers and onions, corn, sage and 1 to 2 tablespoons (15 30 ml) salsa in bowl and mix well. Pack crumb mixture into pockets in pork chops and secure with toothpick. Place any remaining crumb mixture in sprayed slow cooker and top with pork chops. Spoon remaining salsa over pork chops.

- Cover and cook on LOW for 8 to 10 hours or on HIGH for 4 to 5 hours. Place pork chops on platter and spoon crumb mixture to one side. Serves 6.

Published Pork Chops

1 tablespoon canola oil	15 ml
6 (¾ inch thick) boneless pork chops	6 (1.8 cm)
1 (10 ounce) can fiesta nacho cheese soup	280 g
1 (10 ounce) can chicken broth	280 g
2 cups cooked instant rice	330 g

- Heat oil in skillet, brown pork chops and place in sprayed slow cooker. Combine cheese soup and broth in bowl and pour over pork chops. Cover and cook on LOW for 6 to 7 hours.

- Place rice on serving platter and top with pork chops. Serves 4 to 6.

Pork, Potatoes and Gravy

6 (½-inch thick) pork chops	6 (1.2 cm)
6 medium potatoes, peeled, cut into fourths	
2 (10 ounce) cans cream of onion soup	2 (280 g)
1 (4 ounce) can sliced mushrooms, drained	115 g
½ cup milk	125 ml
¼ teaspoon dried thyme	1 ml
1 teaspoon Worcestershire sauce	5 ml
3 tablespoons cornstarch	20 g

- Cook pork chops in sprayed non-stick skillet over medium-high heat, turning once, until light brown. Place potatoes in sprayed slow cooker.

- Combine soup, mushrooms, milk, thyme, Worcestershire and cornstarch in bowl and mix well. Spoon half soup mixture over potatoes; place pork chops over potatoes and cover with remaining soup mixture. Cover and cook on LOW for 6 to 7 hours. Serves 6.

Pork Chops in Salsa

1 (10 ounce) can chicken broth	280 g
6 boneless center-cut pork chops	
Lemon pepper	
½ teaspoon dried thyme	2 ml
1 onion, cut in 6 slices	
1 (16 ounce) jar mild (or hot) salsa	455 g
6 red potatoes, halved	

- Pour chicken broth in sprayed slow cooker and arrange pork chops in cooker. Sprinkle heavily with lemon pepper and dried thyme. Place onion slices over each pork chop.

- Spoon salsa over chops and onions and arrange potatoes around chops. Cover and cook on LOW for 5 to 6 hours. Serve salsa in bowl to spoon over pork chops. Serves 6.

Pork Chop Dinner

4 medium potatoes, peeled, sliced	
2 onions, sliced	
2 green bell peppers, seeded, cut in strips	
2 ribs celery, cut in 1-inch (2.5 cm) pieces	
6 (½-inch thick) boneless pork chops	6 (1.2 cm)
2 (10 ounce) cans cream of onion soup	2 (280 g)
½ cup milk	125 ml

- Place potatoes, onions, bell peppers and celery in sprayed slow cooker. Top with pork chops. Heat onion soup and milk in saucepan, mixing until well blended and pour over pork chops. Cover and cook on LOW for 6 to 8 hours. Serves 6.

Perfect Pork Chops and Potatoes

2 tablespoons canola oil	30 ml
6 - 8 boneless pork chops	
1 (10 ounce) can cream of chicken soup	280 g
1 tablespoon mustard	15 ml
½ cup chicken broth	125 ml
1 teaspoon minced garlic	5 ml
6 - 8 red potatoes with peels, sliced	
2 - 3 onions, sliced	

- Heat oil in skillet on medium-high heat and brown pork chops on both sides. Combine soup, mustard, broth, garlic and a little salt and pepper in sprayed slow cooker. Layer potatoes and onions over mixture; place browned pork chops on top. Cover and cook on LOW for 8 to 10 hours or on HIGH for 4 to 5 hours. Serves 6 to 8.

Indulge with Pork and Kraut

6 (¾-inch thick) pork chops	6 (1.8 cm)
1 (16 ounce) bag sauerkraut, rinsed, drained	455 g
1 pound small new (red) potatoes, scrubbed	455 g
1 cup apple juice	250 ml
½ (16 ounce) package baby carrots	½ (455 g)
½ onion, chopped	
1 teaspoon dried thyme	5 ml

- Place pork chops in sprayed large slow cooker without overlapping, if possible. Add sauerkraut, potatoes, juice, carrots, onion, thyme and 1 teaspoon (5 ml) pepper. Cover and cook on LOW for 8 to 9 hours or on HIGH for 4 hours to 4 hours 30 minutes. Serves 6.

Good-Time Chops, Taters and Peas

1 (10 ounce) can cream of mushroom soup	280 g
1 (4 ounce) can sliced mushrooms	115 g
5 - 6 boneless pork chops	
Lemon pepper	
2 (15 ounce) cans whole new potatoes, drained	2 (425 g)
1 (10 ounce) can frozen green peas, thawed	280 g

- Spoon soup and mushrooms in sprayed slow cooker and stir in ¼ cup (60 ml) water to thin soup slightly. Season each pork chop with lemon pepper and place in slow cooker. Cover and cook on LOW for 6 to 8 hours.

- Place potatoes and peas around pork chops; turn heat to HIGH, cover and cook for additional 1 hour 30 minutes. Serves 5 to 6.

Good Ol' Stand-By Chops

6 - 8 (½-inch thick) boneless pork chops	
1 cup orange juice	250 ml
2 tablespoons dijon-style mustard	30 ml
2 tablespoons lemon juice	30 ml
¾ cup packed brown sugar	165 g
⅓ cup Craisins®	40 g
¼ cup (½ stick) butter	55 g
2 cups instant rice	190 g

- Cut any fat off pork chops. In large skillet on medium to high heat, brown pork chops on both sides and place in sprayed slow cooker.

- Combine orange juice, mustard, lemon juice, brown sugar and Craisins® in saucepan on medium heat. Cook while stirring until mixture is hot and well blended. Pour sauce over pork chops. Cover and cook on LOW heat 6 to 8 hours.

- Cook rice according to package directions and place on serving plate. Top with pork chops and a little of the sauce. Serves 6 to 8.

Aloha Pork Chops

1 green bell pepper, seeded, julienned	
1 red bell pepper, seeded, julienned	
1 onion, sliced	
6 - 8 (½ inch thick) boneless pork chops	6 - 8 (1.2 cm)
1 (15 ounce) can pineapple chunks with juice	425 g
1 tablespoon mustard	15 ml
2 tablespoons white wine vinegar	30 ml
1 tablespoon brown sugar	15 ml
1 papaya, peeled, seeded, sliced	
Macadamia nuts	

- Place bell peppers and onion in sprayed slow cooker and place pork chops on top.

- Combine juice from pineapple, mustard, vinegar, brown sugar and ½ teaspoon (2 ml) salt in bowl; mix and pour over pork chops. Cover and cook on LOW for 5 to 6 hours.

- Place pork chops on serving plate and keep warm. Increase heat to HIGH and stir in pineapple and papaya; cook for additional 10 minutes. Pour over pork chops and sprinkle macadamia nuts on each serving. Serves 6 to 8.

Ginger Pork Chops

6 (1-inch thick) pork chops	6 (2.5 cm)
⅓ cup teriyaki sauce	75 ml
1 (10 ounce) can tomato bisque soup	280 g
⅓ cup packed brown sugar	75 g
1 teaspoon ground ginger	5 ml
2 cups instant rice	190 g

- Trim excess fat off pork chops, sprinkle with a little salt and pepper and place in sprayed slow cooker.

- Combine teriyaki sauce, soup, brown sugar and ginger in bowl; mix until they blend well. Pour mixture over pork chops. Cover and cook on LOW for 4 hours 30 minutes to 6 hours.

- Cook rice according to package directions and place on serving platter. Top with pork chops and sauce. Serves 6.

Promising Pork Chops

6 boneless pork chops	
1 (4 ounce) can sliced mushrooms	115 g
1 (7 ounce) can diced tomatoes and green chilies	200 g
1 (10 ounce) can cream of mushroom soup	280 g
1 (8 ounce) carton sour cream	230 g
1 (8 ounce) package penne pasta	230 g

- Place pork chops in sprayed slow cooker and layer mushrooms and tomatoes and green chilies over top. Spread mushroom soup over top. Cover and cook on LOW for 6 to 8 hours.

- Transfer pork chops to ovenproof contain and keep warm in oven. Stir sour cream into sauce in slow cooker and cook on HIGH for additional 10 minutes.

- Cook pasta according to package directions. Stir pasta into sauce and place pork chops on top. Or if you prefer, place pasta-sauce mixture on serving platter and top with warm pork chops. Serves 6.

Savory Pork Chops

6 (¾-inch thick) pork chops	6 (1.8 cm)
1 cup pineapple juice	250 ml
⅓ cup packed brown sugar	75 g
3 tablespoons cider vinegar	45 ml
Noodles, cooked	

- Brown pork chops in skillet on both sides and place in sprayed slow cooker.

- Combine pineapple juice, brown sugar and vinegar in bowl and mix well. Pour mixture over pork chops. Cover and cook on LOW for 4 to 5 hours. Serve over noodles. Serves 4 to 6.

Smothered Pork Chop Dinner

6 (¾-inch thick) bone-in pork chops	6 (1.8 cm)
8 - 10 medium red potatoes with peels	
2 onions, sliced	
1 (10 ounce) can cream of chicken soup	280 g
1 (10 ounce) can chicken broth	280 g
¼ cup dijon-style mustard	60 g
1 teaspoon dried basil leaves	5 ml

- Sprinkle pork chops with a little salt and pepper and brown in non-stick skillet. Place potatoes and onions in sprayed large slow cooker and add browned pork chops.

- Combine soup, mustard and basil leaves in saucepan. Heat just enough to mix well and pour over pork chops. Cover and cook on LOW for 7 to 9 hours. Serves 4 to 6.

TIP: To "dress-up" pork chops, sprinkle with 1 (3 ounce/85 g) can french-fried onions.

Pork Chops Deluxe

6 (1-inch thick) boneless pork chops	6 (2.5 cm)
1 teaspoon seasoned salt	5 ml
1 (11 ounce) can Mexicorn®, drained	310 g
1 (10 ounce) package frozen chopped bell peppers and onions, thawed	280 g
1 (4 ounce) can sliced mushrooms, drained, chopped	115 g
1¼ cups seasoned breadcrumbs	150 g
1 (8 ounce) can tomato sauce	230 g
1 (4 ounce) can diced green chilies	115 g

- Cut pocket in each pork chop, cutting from side almost to edge. Season pockets with seasoned salt.

- Combine corn, bell peppers and onions, mushrooms, and breadcrumbs in bowl. Pack vegetable mixture into pockets and secure along open side with wooden toothpicks. Spread any remaining vegetable mixture in sprayed slow cooker.

- Combine tomato sauce and green chilies in bowl and mix well. Moisten top surface of each stuffed chop with tomato-chilies mixture and place in slow cooker. Pour remaining tomato mixture on top of pork chops. Cover and cook on LOW for 8 to 9 hours or on HIGH for 4 to 5 hours.

- Remove pork chops to serving platter and mound vegetable mixture in center. Serves 6.

Stuffed Pork Chops

4 - 5 (1-inch thick) pork chops	4 - 5 (2.5 cm)
1 (15 ounce) can mixed vegetables, well drained	425 g
1 (8 ounce) can whole kernel corn, drained	230 g
½ cup rice	95 g
1 cup Italian-seasoned breadcrumbs	120 g
1 (15 ounce) can stewed tomatoes, slightly drained	425 g

- Cut pocket in each pork chop and season with a little salt and pepper. Combine vegetables, corn, rice and breadcrumbs in large bowl and stuff pork chops with mixture. Secure open sides with toothpicks.

- Place remaining vegetable mixture in sprayed slow cooker. Add pork chops and spoon stewed tomatoes over top of pork chops. Cover and cook on LOW for 8 to 9 hours. Serves 4 to 5.

Ranch Pork Chops

6 (¾-inch thick) bone-in pork chops	6 (1.8 cm)
1 (.04 ounce) packet ranch dressing mix	10 g
2 (15 ounce) cans new potatoes, drained, quartered	2 (425 g)
1 (10 ounce) can French onion soup	280 g

- Place pork chops in sprayed large oval slow cooker. Sprinkle with ranch dressing mix and ½ teaspoon (2 ml) pepper.

- Place potatoes around pork chops and pour French onion soup around potatoes and chops. Cover and cook on LOW for 4 to 5 hours. Serves 4 to 6.

Pork Chops with Orange Sauce

2 medium yellow squash, sliced	
2 onions, sliced	
6 - 8 bone-in pork chops	
½ cup chicken broth	125 ml
½ cup orange marmalade	160 g
1 tablespoon honey-mustard	15 ml
2 tablespoons cornstarch	15 g

- Place squash and onions in sprayed large slow cooker. Place pork chops over vegetables and sprinkle with a little salt and pepper.

- Combine broth, marmalade and mustard in bowl and spoon over pork chops. Cover and cook on LOW for 4 to 6 hours. Transfer pork chops and vegetables to serving platter and keep warm.

- For sauce, pour liquid from slow cooker into medium saucepan. Combine 2 tablespoons (30 ml) water with cornstarch and add to saucepan. Heat mixture and stir constantly until thick. Serve over pork chops and vegetables. Serves 6 to 8.

Pork Chops for Supper

6 (¾-inch thick) pork loin chops	6 (1.8 cm)
1 onion, halved, sliced	
1 (8 ounce) can tomato sauce	230 g
¼ cup packed brown sugar	55 g
1 tablespoon Worcestershire sauce	15 ml
1 teaspoon seasoned salt	5 ml

- Brown pork chops in skillet on both sides and place in sprayed slow cooker. Place onions over pork chops.

- Combine tomato sauce, brown sugar, Worcestershire sauce, seasoned salt and ¼ cup (60 ml) water in bowl and spoon over onions and pork chops. Cover and cook on LOW for 4 to 5 hours. Serves 4 to 6.

Pork Chops and Gravy

6 (½-inch thick) pork chops	6 (1.2 cm)
8 - 10 new (red) potatoes with peels, quartered	
1 (16 ounce) package baby carrots	455 g
2 (10 ounce) cans cream of mushroom with roasted garlic soup	2 (280 g)

- Sprinkle a little salt and pepper on pork chops. Brown pork chops in skillet and place in sprayed large slow cooker. Place potatoes and carrots around pork chops.

- Heat soup with ½ cup (125 ml) water in saucepan and pour over chops and vegetables. Cover and cook on LOW for 6 to 7 hours. Serves 4 to 6.

Pork Chops Pizza

6 (1-inch thick) boneless pork chops	6 (2.5 cm)
1 onion, finely chopped	
1 green bell pepper, seeded, finely chopped	
1 (8 ounce) jar pizza sauce	230 g
1 (10 ounce) box plain couscous	280 g
2 tablespoons butter	30 g
1 cup shredded mozzarella cheese	115 g

- Trim fat from pork chops and sprinkle with a little salt and pepper. Brown and cook pork chops in skillet on both sides for 5 minutes. Transfer chops to sprayed oval slow cooker. Spoon onion and bell pepper over chops and pour pizza sauce over top. Cover and cook on LOW for 4 to 6 hours.

- Cook couscous according to package directions except add 2 tablespoons (28 g) butter instead of 1 tablespoon (15 ml) and place on serving platter. Spoon chops and sauce over couscous and sprinkle cheese over chops. Serves 4 to 6.

Pineapple-Pork Chops

6 - 8 (½-inch thick) boneless pork chops	6 - 8 (1.2 cm)
Canola oil	
1 (6 ounce) can frozen pineapple juice concentrate, thawed	175 ml
¼ cup packed brown sugar	55 g
⅓ cup wine or tarragon vinegar	75 ml
⅓ cup honey	115 g
1 (6 ounce) package parmesan-butter rice, cooked	170 g

- Brown pork chops in a little oil in skillet and transfer to sprayed slow cooker.

- Combine pineapple juice concentrate, brown sugar, vinegar and honey in bowl. Pour over pork chops. Cover and cook on LOW for 5 to 6 hours. Serve over rice. Serves 6 to 8.

Peachy Pork Chops

6 - 8 (¾-inch thick) bone-in pork chops	6 - 8 (1.8 cm)
½ cup packed brown sugar	110 g
¼ teaspoon ground cinnamon	1 ml
¼ teaspoon ground cloves	1 ml
1 (8 ounce) can tomato sauce	230 g
1 (28 ounce) can peach halves with juice	795 g
¼ cup white vinegar	60 ml

- Brown pork chops in skillet on both sides and place in sprayed oval slow cooker.

- Combine brown sugar, cinnamon, cloves, tomato sauce, ¼ cup (60 ml) juice from peaches and vinegar in bowl. Pour mixture over pork chops and place peach halves over top. Cover and cook on LOW for 4 to 5 hours. Serves 6 to 8.

Italian Pork Chops

6 - 8 (1-inch thick) boneless pork chops	6 - 8 (2.5 cm)
½ pound fresh mushrooms, sliced	230 g
1 (10 ounce) package frozen chopped bell peppers and onions, thawed	280 g
1 teaspoon Italian seasoning	5 ml
1 (15 ounce) can Italian stewed tomatoes	425 g

- Brown pork chops in skillet and sprinkle with salt and pepper on both sides.

- Combine mushrooms, bell pepper and onions, and Italian seasoning in sprayed large slow cooker. Place pork chops over vegetables and pour stewed tomatoes over pork chops. Cover and cook on LOW for 7 to 8 hours. Serves 6 to 8.

Honey-Mustard Pork Chops

Try this sauce over rice. It is wonderful!

1 (10 ounce) can golden mushroom soup	280 g
⅓ cup white wine	75 ml
¼ cup honey-mustard	60 g
1 teaspoon minced garlic	5 ml
4 - 5 (¾-inch thick) pork chops	4 - 5 (1.8 cm)

- Combine soup, wine, honey-mustard, minced garlic and 1 teaspoon (5 ml) salt in large bowl and mix well.

- Place pork chops, sprinkled with a little pepper in sprayed slow cooker and spoon soup-honey-mustard mixture over chops. Cover and cook on LOW for 5 to 6 hours.

- When ready to serve, lift pork chops out of sauce and onto serving plate. Stir sauce to mix well and serve with chops. Serves 4 to 5.

TIP: For a "meat and potatoes meal", just slice 3 potatoes and place in slow cooker before adding pork chops.

Delicious Pork Chops

1¾ cups flour	210 g
2 tablespoons dry mustard	30 ml
8 boneless, thick pork chops	
Canola oil	
1 (10 ounce) can chicken and rice soup	280 g

- Combine flour and mustard in shallow bowl. Dredge pork chops in flour-mustard mixture. Brown pork chops in a little oil in skillet. Place all chops in sprayed large oval slow cooker.

- Pour soup over pork and add about ¼ cup (60 ml) water. Cover and cook on LOW for 6 to 8 hours. Serves 6 to 8.

"Baked" Pork Chops

6 - 8 (½-inch thick) pork chops	6 - 8 (1.2 cm)
Canola oil	
1 (10 ounce) can cream of chicken soup	280 g
3 tablespoons ketchup	50 g
1 tablespoon Worcestershire sauce	15 ml
1 onion, chopped	

- Brown pork chops in a little oil in skillet and season with a little salt and pepper. Place pork chops in sprayed slow cooker.

- Combine chicken soup, ketchup, Worcestershire and onion in bowl and pour over pork chops. Cover and cook on LOW for 5 to 6 hours. Serves 6 to 8.

Country Pork Chops

7 - 8 red potatoes with peels, sliced	
2 onions, sliced	
1 (10 ounce) can cream of celery soup	280 g
⅓ cup chicken broth	75 ml
3 tablespoons dijon-style mustard	45 ml
1 (4 ounce) can sliced mushrooms, drained	115 g
1 teaspoon minced garlic	5 ml
¾ teaspoon dried basil	4 ml
8 boneless pork chops	
Canola oil	

- Place potatoes and onions in sprayed large slow cooker. Combine soup, broth, mustard, mushrooms, garlic and basil in bowl, mix well and pour over potatoes and onions. Stir to coat vegetables.

- Sprinkle pork chops with a little salt and pepper. Brown pork chops on both sides in a little oil in skillet. Place chops over vegetables. Cover and cook on LOW for 6 to 7 hours. Serves 6 to 8.

Spicy Peach Pork Loin

1 (3 - 4 pound) pork loin	1.4 - 1.8 kg
2 tablespoons light soy sauce	30 ml
3 tablespoons dijon-style mustard	45 g
1 (16 ounce) jar peach preserves	455 g
1 (16 ounce) jar thick-and-chunky salsa	455 g
½ cup packed brown sugar	110 g

- Sprinkle pork loin with a little salt and pepper and place in sprayed slow cooker. Combine soy sauce, mustard, preserves, salsa and brown sugar in saucepan and cook on medium heat, stirring constantly until mixture blends well. Pour sauce over pork loin. Cover and cook on LOW for 5 to 7 hours.

- Spoon sauce over pork several times before slicing. Serves 8 to 10.

South-of-the-Border Supper

1½ pounds boneless pork loin, cut into 1-inch pieces	680 g/1.2 cm
1 (16 ounce) jar salsa	455 g
1 (10 ounce) can diced tomatoes and green chilies, drained	280 g
2 (15 ounce) cans pinto beans, rinsed, drained	2 (425 g)
2 cups instant rice	190 g
1 cup shredded Mexican Velveeta® cheese	115 g

- Combine pork pieces, salsa and tomatoes and green chilies in sprayed slow cooker. Cover and cook on LOW for 6 to 8 hours.

- Stir in beans, cover and cook for additional 20 minutes or until mixture is hot. Cook rice according to package directions and place in large serving bowl. Spoon pork mixture over rice and sprinkle with cheese. Serves 4 to 6.

Pork Roast with a Peach Treat

1 (4 pound) pork loin	1.8 kg
1 (15 ounce) can sliced peaches in heavy syrup	425 g
½ cup chili sauce	135 g
½ cup packed light brown sugar	110 g
3 tablespoons apple cider vinegar	45 ml
1 teaspoon pumpkin pie spice	5 ml
1 tablespoon cornstarch	15 ml
1 (16 ounce) package rotini (corkscrew) pasta	455 g
1 tablespoon dried parsley	15 ml

- Place roast in sprayed large slow cooker. Sprinkle with generous amount of salt and pepper.

- Drain peaches. Whisk peach syrup, chili sauce, brown sugar, vinegar and pumpkin pie spice in bowl; pour over roast. Scatter peach slices on top. Cover and cook on HIGH for 3 hours or on LOW for 6 hours.

- Remove roast to serving platter and let stand for about 10 minutes. Spoon out peach slices and set aside.

- Place liquid from cooker in small saucepan and bring to a boil. Stir 2 tablespoons (30 ml) water into cornstarch in bowl; add to saucepan, stirring constantly and cook until sauce thickens.

- Cook pasta according to package directions, drain and toss with parsley. Slice roast, place peach slices on roast and pasta on each side of roast. Serve sauce on the side. Serves 8 to 10.

Pork Loin Topped with Pecans

½ cup finely ground pecans	55 g
1 teaspoon mustard	5 ml
1 tablespoon brown sugar	15 ml
1(3 pound) pork loin	1.4 kg
1 (14 ounce) can beef broth	395 g
2 tablespoons chili sauce	35 g
2 tablespoon lemon juice	30 ml
1 (10 ounce) box plain couscous	280 g

- Place ground pecans, mustard and brown sugar in small bowl and mix well. Press pecan mixture into pork roast and place in sprayed slow cooker.

- Combine broth, chili sauce and lemon juice in bowl and pour into slow cooker. Cover and cook on LOW for 8 to 10 hours.

- Let stand for 10 minutes before slicing to serve.

- Cook couscous according to package directions and place in serving bowl. Serve with sliced pork roast. Serves 8 to 10.

Choice Pork Loin Slices

1 (3 - 4 pound) pork loin	1.4 - 1.8 kg
1 (16 ounce) jar apricot preserves	455 g
⅓ cup lemon juice	75 ml
⅓ cup ketchup	90 g
⅓ cup packed brown sugar	75 g
1 tablespoon light soy sauce	15 ml
2 cups instant rice	190 g

- Place pork loin in sprayed slow cooker.

- Combine preserves, lemon juice, ketchup, brown sugar and soy sauce in bowl and pour over pork loin. Cover and cook on LOW for 7 to 9 hours.

- Cook rice according to package directions and place on serving plate. Let pork loin stand for about 15 minutes before slicing. Place slices and sauce over rice. Serves 8.

Pork Roast, Apricots and Stuffing

2 (6 ounce) boxes cornbread stuffing mix	2 (170 g)
2 ribs celery, sliced	
1 onion, finely chopped	
1 egg	
1 (14 ounce) can chicken broth	395 g
¾ cup dried apricots, chopped	120 g
1 (3 pound) boneless pork loin roast	1.4 kg
½ cup apricot preserves	160 g

- Combine stuffing mix, celery, onion, egg, broth, apricots and 1 cup (250 ml) water in bowl. (Using kitchen scissors is an easy way to chop apricots.) Transfer to sprayed slow cooker and place roast on top of stuffing mixture. Brush preserves over roast. Cover and cook on LOW for 7 to 8 hours.

- Slice roast and serve with stuffing. Serves 8.

If adding herbs and spices at the beginning of cooking, you will find that whole spices and fresh herbs rather than ground and dried will retain flavor. Ground spices and dried herbs tend to "cook out" and lose flavor during the long cooking time. It is best to add these at the end of the cooking time. Always taste and adjust seasonings.

Praise This Pork Roast

2 onions, sliced	
1 (3 pound) boneless pork loin roast	1.4 kg
¾ cup dried apples	120 g
¾ cup dried apricots	120 g
⅓ cup sliced pitted ripe olives	45 g
½ cup chicken broth	125 ml
½ cup orange juice	125 ml
½ teaspoon ground nutmeg	2 ml

- Place onions in sprayed slow cooker and set roast on top of onions. Top roast with apples, apricots and olives.

- Combine broth, juice and nutmeg in bowl and pour over fruit and roast. Cover and cook on LOW for 7 to 9 hours. Serve fruit mixture with sliced roast. Serves 8.

Sweet-and-Sour Pork Loin

1 (4 - 5 pound) pork loin roast	1.8 - 2.3 kg
1 (10 ounce) can chicken broth	280 g
1 (12 ounce) bottle chili sauce	340 g
1 tablespoon lemon juice	15 ml
1 (16 ounce) jar apricot preserves	455 g
3 ribs celery, cut into 1-inch strips	
2 bell peppers, seeded, cut into strips	

- Season roast with a little salt and pepper and place in sprayed slow cooker. Pour ½ cup (125 ml) water around roast. Cover and cook on LOW for 7 to 9 hours.

- Combine broth, chili sauce, lemon juice and preserves in saucepan on high heat, stirring constantly, just until well mixed and hot.

- Place celery and bell peppers around roast and pour sauce over all. Turn heat to HIGH, cover and cook for additional 30 minutes.

- Let roast stand for about 15 minutes before slicing to serve. Serves 10 to 12.

While you can cook whole roasts or chickens in a slow cooker, you need to be sure the internal temperature reaches a safe level. It is easier to cut up the meat to ensure it is completely cooked.

Popular Pork Roast and Stuffing

2 (6 ounce) boxes herb-seasoned stuffing mix	2 (170 g)
1 (14 ounce) can chicken broth	395 g
½ cup dried peaches, chopped	80 g
1 small onion, chopped	
1 (3 pound) boneless pork loin roast	1.4 kg
⅓ cup peach preserves	110 g
1 tablespoon white vinegar	15 ml

- Combine stuffing, broth, 1 cup (250 ml) water, peaches and onion in bowl and mix well. (Use kitchen scissors to cut up dried peaches.) Transfer to sprayed slow cooker and place roast on stuffing mixture.

- Combine preserves and vinegar in bowl and brush over roast. Cover and cook on LOW for 7 to 8 hours.

- Place roast on cutting board and slice. Place slices at one end of platter and spoon stuffing at other end. Serves 8.

Our Best Pork Roast

1 (16 ounce) can whole cranberry sauce	455 g
½ cup quartered dried apricots	75 g
½ teaspoon grated orange peel	2 ml
⅓ cup orange juice	75 ml
1 large shallot, chopped	
1 tablespoon cider vinegar	15 ml
1 teaspoon mustard	5 ml
2 tablespoons brown sugar	30 g
¼ teaspoon dried ginger	1 ml
2 - 3 pound pork loin roast	910 g - 1.4 kg

- Combine cranberry sauce, apricots, orange peel, orange juice, shallot, vinegar, mustard, brown sugar, ginger and 1 teaspoon (5 ml) salt in bowl. Stir mixture until well blended and spoon into sprayed slow cooker.

- Trim roast of any fat and add roast to slow cooker. Spoon a little cranberry mixture on top. Cover and cook on LOW for 7 to 9 hours or until pork is tender.

- Skim off any fat from top of cranberry mixture; place roast on cutting board. Slice pork and top with sauce. Serves 6 to 8.

Golden Sweet Potatoes and Pork

4 - 5 medium sweet potatoes, peeled, cut into ½-inch (1.2 cm) slices	
1 (4 pound) pork tenderloin	1.8 kg
1 cup packed brown sugar	220 g
½ teaspoon cayenne pepper	2 ml
2 teaspoons seasoned salt	10 ml
½ teaspoon garlic powder	2 ml

- Place sliced sweet potatoes in sprayed slow cooker and place tenderloin on top.

- Combine brown sugar, cayenne pepper, seasoned salt and garlic powder in small bowl and sprinkle over pork and potatoes. Cover and cook on LOW for 8 to 10 hours.

- Remove pork from cooker and place on serving platter. Slice pork and spread sweet potatoes around pork. Spoon juices over top. Serves 8.

On-the-Border Pork Casserole

2 - 2½ pounds pork tenderloin, cut into 1-inch cubes	910 g - 1.1 kg (2.5 cm)
1 (10 ounce) package frozen chopped bell peppers and onions, thawed	280 g
2 (15 ounce) can black beans, rinsed, drained	2 (425 g)
1 (10 ounce) can fiesta nacho cheese soup	280 g
1 (15 ounce) can Mexican-style stewed tomatoes	425 g
1 (16 ounce) jar mild salsa	455 g
2 teaspoons ground cumin	10 ml
½ teaspoon garlic powder	2 ml
1 (16 ounce) package shredded Mexican-style Velveeta® cheese, divided	455 g
2 cups cooked brown rice	390 g

- Combine pork cubes, bell peppers and onions, beans, soup, tomatoes, salsa, cumin, garlic powder and half cheese in sprayed slow cooker. Cover and cook on LOW for 7 to 9 hours.

- Stir in rice, cover and cook for additional 15 minutes or until rice is thoroughly hot. Sprinkle with remaining cheese before serving. Serves 16 to 18.

Savory Tenderloin

1 - 2 pounds pork tenderloin	455 - 910 g
1 (12 ounce) bottle chili sauce	340 g
1 (16 ounce) can jellied cranberry sauce	455 g
¼ cup packed brown sugar	55 g
¼ teaspoon garlic powder	1 ml
½ teaspoon seasoned salt	2 ml
3 cups instant brown rice	565 g
2 tablespoons butter	30 g

- Trim pork tenderloin of any fat and place in sprayed slow cooker.

- Combine chili sauce, cranberry sauce, brown sugar, garlic powder and seasoned salt in saucepan and bring to a boil, stirring constantly and cook just until mixture is blended. Pour over tenderloin. Cover and cook on HIGH for 4 to 5 hours; reduce heat to LOW and cook for additional 3 to 4 hours.

- Cook brown rice with 2½ cups (625 ml) water as directed on package, adding butter when rice has cooked. Place rice on serving platter, slice pork tenderloin and place on top of rice. Serves 6 to 8.

Terrific Pork Tenderloin

2 - 3 (1 pound) pork tenderloins	2 - 3 (455 g)
1 teaspoon seasoned salt	5 ml
1 teaspoon garlic powder	5ml
1 (4 ounce) can diced green chilies	115 g
2 (10 ounce) cans cream of celery soup	2 (280 g)
Rice, cooked	

- Place tenderloins in sprayed oval slow cooker. Season with seasoned salt and garlic powder.

- Combine green chilies and celery soup in bowl and spoon over tenderloins, covering completely. Cover and cook on LOW for 8 hours. Serve over rice. Serves 6 to 8.

Be careful to layer ingredients according to the recipe's instructions. Different foods have different cooking times and those requiring the most cooking time generally are placed at the bottom of the cooker. Meat cooks faster than root vegetables and therefore is often placed on top of potatoes and onions, for example. Tender vegetables are sometimes added in the last hour or so of cooking.

Tender Pork Loin

1 (3 - 4 pound) pork loin	1.4 - 1.8 kg
2 teaspoons minced garlic	10 ml
½ teaspoon rosemary	2 ml
1 teaspoon sage	5 ml
1½ teaspoons marjoram	7 ml

- Place pork loin in sprayed slow cooker, rub with minced garlic and sprinkle with rosemary, sage and marjoram. Add about ¼ cup (60 ml) water to slow cooker. Cover and cook on LOW heat for 4 to 5 hours. Serves 6 to 8.

TIP: Sometimes it is hard to buy a small (3 to 4 pound/1.4 to 1.8 kg) pork loin, but they are available in (8 to 9 pound/3.6 to 4.1 kg) sizes. Because pork loin is such a good cut of pork (no bones – no fat), you can buy a whole loin, cut it into 2 or 3 pieces and freeze pieces for later use.

Spinach-Stuffed Pork Roast

1 (2 - 2½ pound) pork tenderloin	910 g – 1.1 kg
1 (10 ounce) package frozen chopped spinach, thawed	280 g
⅓ cup seasoned breadcrumbs	40 g
⅓ cup grated parmesan cheese	35 g
2 tablespoons canola oil	30 ml
½ teaspoon seasoned salt	2 ml

- Cut tenderloin horizontally lengthwise about ½-inch (1.2 cm) from top to within ¾-inch (1.8 cm) of opposite end and open flat. Turn pork to cut other side, from inside edge to outer edge, and open flat. If one side is thicker than other side, cover with plastic wrap and pound until both sides are ¾-inch (1.8 cm) thick.

- Squeeze spinach between paper towels to completely remove excess moisture. Combine spinach, breadcrumbs and cheese in bowl and mix well. Spread mixture on inside surfaces of pork and press down. Roll pork and tie with kitchen twine.

- Heat oil in large skillet over medium-high heat and brown pork on all sides. Place in sprayed oval slow cooker and sprinkle with salt. Cover and cook on LOW for 6 to 8 hours. Serves 4 to 6.

Do not "preheat" a slow cooker. This can result in cracking the ceramic insert.

Roasted Red Pepper Tenderloin

2 pounds pork tenderloin	910 g
1 (.04 ounce) packet ranch dressing mix	10 g
1 cup roasted red bell peppers, rinsed, chopped	90 g
1 (8 ounce) carton sour cream	230 g

- Brown tenderloins in large skillet and place in sprayed large oval slow cooker. Combine ranch dressing mix, roasted bell peppers and ½ cup (125 ml) water in bowl and spoon over tenderloins. Cover and cook on LOW for 4 to 5 hours.

- When ready to serve, remove tenderloins from slow cooker. Stir sour cream into sauce in cooker. Serve over tenderloin slices. Serves 4 to 6.

Garlic-Roasted Pork Loin

4 teaspoons minced garlic	15 ml
1 tablespoon ketchup	15 ml
2 tablespoons soy sauce, divided	30 ml
2 tablespoons honey, plus ½ cup honey, divided	215 g
1 (3 - 4 pound) pork loin	1.4 - 1.8 kg
2 tablespoons rice vinegar	30 ml

- Combine garlic, ketchup, 1 tablespoon (15 ml) soy sauce and 2 tablespoons (45 g) honey and rub evenly over pork loin. Place pork loin in sprayed slow cooker. Cover and cook on LOW for 7 to 9 hours.

- Combine remaining soy sauce, remaining honey and vinegar in saucepan and cook until hot, about 10 minutes. Slice pork diagonally and place on serving platter. Drizzle sauce over pork slices. Serves 8.

Show-Time Pork Roast

2 onions, sliced	
1 green bell pepper, seeded, sliced	
3 pound boneless pork roast	1.4 kg
2 tablespoons soy sauce	30 ml
1 tablespoon ketchup	15 ml
¼ cup sugar	50 g
3 tablespoons red wine vinegar	45 ml
1 teaspoon minced garlic	5 ml
1 (12 ounce) package egg noodles, cooked, buttered	340 g

- Arrange onion and bell pepper in sprayed slow cooker; then place roast on top.

- Combine soy sauce, ketchup, sugar, vinegar, garlic and a little salt in bowl; mix well and pour over roast. Cover and cook on LOW for 6 to 8 hours or on HIGH for 3 to 4 hours. Serve over noodles. Serves 8.

Honey-B Pork Roast

1 (3 pound) boneless pork roast	1.4 kg
1 (16 ounce) package baby carrots	455 g
6 - 8 small onions, halved	
½ cup barbecue sauce	130 g
½ cup honey	170 g
¼ teaspoon ground nutmeg	1 ml

- Place pork roast, carrots and onions in sprayed slow cooker.

- Combine barbecue sauce, honey, nutmeg and ½ teaspoon (2 ml) pepper in small bowl. Spoon over roast. Cover and cook on LOW for 8 to 10 hours. Let roast stand out of cooker for about 10 to 15 minutes before slicing. Serves 6.

Pork with a Cranberry Glaze

1 (3 - 4 pound) pork shoulder roast	1.4 - 1.8 kg
1 (16 ounce) package frozen stew vegetables, thawed	455 g
1 (16 ounce) can whole cranberry sauce	455 g
1 (4 ounce) can diced green chilies	115 g
¾ cup chili sauce	205 g
1 teaspoon dijon-style mustard	5 ml
2 tablespoons brown sugar	30 g

- Brown roast on all sides in sprayed skillet over medium heat. Place roast in sprayed slow cooker and top with stew vegetables.

- Combine cranberry sauce, green chilies, chili sauce, mustard and brown sugar in saucepan; heat just enough to blend ingredients. Pour mixture over roast and vegetables. Cover and cook on LOW heat for 8 to 9 hours or on HIGH for 4 to 4 hours 30 minutes.

- Transfer roast and vegetables to serving platter and keep warm. Strain cooking juices and skim off fat. Bring juices to a boil in medium saucepan; reduce heat and simmer for about 25 minutes or until mixture thickens. Serve sauce with sliced pork roast. Serves 6 to 8.

Because dairy products tend to curdle in long cooking times, it is best to add them in the last 15 to 30 minutes of cooking unless otherwise specified in the recipe.

Ginger Pork Roast

1 (2 - 2½ pound) boneless pork roast	910 g - 1.1 kg
1 cup chicken broth	250 ml
3½ tablespoons quick-cooking tapioca	50 ml
3 tablespoons soy sauce	45 ml
1 teaspoon grated fresh ginger	5 ml
1 (15 ounce) can pineapple chunks with juice	425 g
1 (16 ounce) package baby carrots	455 g
1 (8 ounce) can sliced water chestnuts, drained	230 g
Rice, cooked	

- Trim fat from pork. Cut pork into 1-inch (2.5 cm) pieces, brown in large skillet and drain.

- Combine broth, tapioca, soy sauce, ginger, pineapple juice, carrots and water chestnuts in sprayed slow cooker. (Refrigerate pineapple chunks until ready to include in recipe.)

- Add browned pork. Cover and cook on LOW for 6 to 8 hours.

- Turn heat to HIGH and stir in pineapple chunks. Cover and cook for additional 10 minutes. Serve over rice. Serves 4 to 6.

Barbecue Pork Roast

Use leftovers for great sandwiches.

1 onion, thinly sliced, separated into rings	
2 tablespoons flour	15 g
1 (2 - 3 pound) pork shoulder roast	910 g - 1.4 kg
1 (8 ounce) bottle barbecue sauce	230 g
1 tablespoon chili powder	15 ml
1 teaspoon ground cumin	5 ml

- Place onion in sprayed slow cooker. Sprinkle flour over onions. If necessary, cut roast to fit cooker and place over onions.

- Combine barbecue sauce, chili powder and cumin in bowl and pour over roast. Cover and cook on LOW for 8 to 10 hours.

- Remove roast from cooker and slice. Serve sauce over sliced roast. Serves 6 to 8.

TIP: *To make sandwiches, shred roast and return to cooker. Cook for additional 30 minutes to heat thoroughly.*

Pork Roast with Apricot Glaze

1 (3 pound) boneless pork roast	1.4 kg
⅓ cup chicken broth	75 ml
1 (18 ounce) jar apricot preserves	510 g
2 tablespoons dijon-style mustard	30 g
1 onion, finely chopped	
1 green bell pepper, seeded, finely chopped	
Rice, cooked	

- Trim fat from roast and, if necessary, cut roast to fit into sprayed slow cooker. Place in cooker.

- Combine broth, preserves, mustard, onion and bell pepper in saucepan and heat just enough to mix ingredients well and pour over roast. Cover and cook on LOW for 9 to 10 hours or on HIGH for 5 to 6 hours.

- Transfer meat to serving plate and keep warm. Sauce left in cooker is delicious as is or thicker. To thicken sauce, mix 1 tablespoon (15 ml) cornstarch and 2 tablespoons (30 ml) water. Place in saucepan and add sauce from cooker. Heat sauce and stir constantly until sauce thickens slightly. Sauce may be served on the side or just spoon over roast and rice. Serves 6 to 8.

Fruit-Stuffed Pork Roast

1 (3 - 3½ pound) boneless pork loin roast	1.4 – 1.6 kg
1 cup mixed dried fruit	160 g
1 tablespoon dried onion flakes	15 ml
1 teaspoon thyme	5 ml
½ teaspoon ground cinnamon	2 ml
2 tablespoons canola oil	30 ml
½ cup apple cider	125 ml

- Cut horizontally through center of pork almost to opposite side. Open pork like a book.

- Layer dried fruit and onion flakes in opening. Bring halves of pork together and tie at 1-inch (2.5 cm) intervals with kitchen twine.

- Combine ½ teaspoon (2 ml) salt, thyme, cinnamon and ½ teaspoon (2 ml) pepper in small bowl and rub into roast. Place roast in skillet with oil and brown roast on all sides. Place in sprayed slow cooker and pour apple cider in cooker. Cover and cook on LOW for 3 to 4 hours. Let stand 10 or 15 minutes before slicing. Serves 6 to 8.

Pork and Cabbage Supper

1 (16 ounce) package baby carrots	455 g
1 cup chicken broth	250 ml
1 (1 ounce) packet golden onion soup mix	30 g
1 (3 - 4 pound) pork shoulder roast	1.4 - 1.8 kg
1 medium head cabbage	

- Place carrots in sprayed slow cooker. Add chicken broth and 1 cup (250 ml) water. Sprinkle dry soup mix and lots of pepper over carrots.

- Cut roast in half (if needed to fit in cooker) and place over carrot mixture. Cover and cook on LOW for 6 to 7 hours.

- Cut cabbage in small-size chunks and place over roast. Cover and cook for additional 1 to 2 hours or until cabbage is tender. Serves 6 to 8.

Honey-Mustard Pork Roast

1 green bell pepper, seeded, chopped	
1 red bell pepper, seeded, chopped	
2 yellow onions, chopped	
3 tablespoons sweet and tangy honey-mustard	45 g
1 (2 - 2½ pound) pork loin roast	910 g - 1.1 kg

- Combine bell peppers and onions in sprayed slow cooker. Rub honey-mustard liberally over pork loin with most of honey-mustard on top; place in slow cooker. Cover and cook on LOW for 4 to 6 hours.

- Place on serving platter. Spoon bell peppers, onions and pan juices over slices of roast to serve. Serves 4 to 6.

Succulent Ham Supper

6 - 8 slices cooked ham	
1 onion, sliced	
2 ribs celery, cut in 1-inch (2.5 cm) pieces	
4 medium potatoes, peeled, sliced	
1 (11 ounce) can Mexicorn®, drained	310 g
1 (10 ounce) can cream of mushroom soup	280 g
1½ cups shredded mozzarella cheese	175 g
1 tablespoon marinade for chicken	15 ml

- Layer ham slices, onion, celery, potatoes and corn in sprayed slow cooker.

- Combine mushroom soup, cheese and marinade for chicken in bowl and spoon over ham-corn layers. Cover and cook on LOW for 8 hours. Serves 6 to 8.

Pineapple-Glazed Ham

1 (3 pound) cooked ham	1.4 kg
1 (15 ounce) can crushed pineapple, divided	425 g
⅔ cup packed brown sugar	150 g
⅓ cup orange marmalade, divided	110 g
1 teaspoon mustard	5 ml

- Place ham in sprayed slow cooker. Drain pineapple liquid from can into slow cooker. Refrigerate pineapple until ham is ready to serve.

- Combine brown sugar, 1 tablespoon (15 ml) marmalade and mustard in bowl and mix well; spread over ham. Cover and cook on LOW for 6 to 8 hours.

- When ready to serve, combine refrigerated pineapple and remaining orange marmalade in bowl and microwave on HIGH for about 1½ minutes or until thoroughly hot, stirring once halfway through cooking.

- Slice just the number of slices needed for this meal. You will have extra ham for ham sandwiches the next day. Serve ham with pineapple mixture. Serves 8.

Ham with a Spicy Sauce

1 (6 - 7 pound) cooked ham butt or shank	2.7 - 3.2 kg
Whole cloves	
1 cup apricot jam	320 g
1 tablespoon vinegar	15 ml
1 teaspoon dry mustard	5 ml
¼ teaspoon ground cinnamon	1 ml
Dash of hot sauce	

- Place metal rack in sprayed slow cooker and position ham in center of cooker. Cover and cook on LOW for 5 to 6 hours.

- Remove ham and pour off juices; then remove fat and skin. Score ham and stud with whole cloves. Remove metal rack and return ham to slow cooker.

- Melt jam with vinegar, mustard, cinnamon and dash of hot sauce in small saucepan. Spoon sauce over ham. Increase heat to HIGH; cover and cook for additional 30 minutes, brushing with sauce several times. Serve hot or cold. Serves 8 to 10.

Dinner Party Ham

1 (3 pound) fully cooked boneless ham	1.4 kg
2 onions, quartered	
2 (6 ounce) jars mango chutney	2 (170 g)
1 tablespoon balsamic vinegar	15 ml
2 (15 ounce) cans sweet potatoes, drained	2 (425 g)

- Trim any excess fat off ham and place ham in sprayed large slow cooker. Place onions around ham.

- Combine chutney and vinegar in small bowl and pour over ham. Cover and cook on LOW for 7 hours.

- Place sweet potato chunks around ham, cover and cook for additional 1 hour or until sweet potatoes are thoroughly hot. Let ham stand for about 10 minutes before slicing. Serves 8.

Much About Ham and Sausage over Rice

1 cup cooked, cubed ham	140 g
1 onion, chopped	
1 bell pepper, seeded, chopped	
1 (15 ounce) can kidney beans, rinsed, drained	425 g
1 (15 ounce) can pinto beans, drained	425 g
1 (15 ounce) can tomato sauce	425 g
1 (10 ounce) can diced tomatoes and green chilies	280 g
3 cups instant rice	285 g
2 teaspoons Cajun seasoning	10 ml
1 pound cooked smoked sausage, cut in ½-inch pieces	455 g/1.2 cm

- Place ham, onion, bell pepper, beans, tomato sauce, and tomatoes and green chilies in sprayed slow cooker. Cover and cook on LOW for 8 to 9 hours.

- About 20 minutes before serving, heat 3 cups (750 ml) water to boiling in large saucepan. Remove from heat and stir in rice. Cover and let stand for about 5 minutes. Fluff rice with fork before serving.

- Increase heat to HIGH on slow cooker and stir in Cajun seasoning and smoked sausage. Cover and cook about 15 minutes or until sausage is thoroughly hot.

- Place ½ cup (85 g) rice in individual soup bowls and top with ¾ cup (175 ml) ham-sausage mixture. Serves 8.

Ham-Potato Casserole

5 medium potatoes, peeled, sliced	
2 cups cooked, cubed ham	280 g
1 (15 ounce) can whole kernel corn, drained	425 g
1 (10 ounce) package frozen chopped bell peppers	
and onions, thawed	280 g
2 tablespoons flour	15 g
½ cup milk, divided	125 ml
2 (10 ounce) cans cheddar cheese soup	2 (280 g)

- Combine sliced potatoes, ham, corn, and bell peppers and onions in sprayed slow cooker.

- Mix flour and ¼ cup (60 ml) milk in bowl until smooth, stir in remaining milk and soup. Spoon mixture over potato-ham mixture. Cover and cook on LOW for 7 to 8 hours or until potatoes are tender. Serves 6.

Easy Creamy Ham and Potato Casserole

3 - 4 large potatoes, peeled, thinly sliced	
1 (8 ounce) package shredded cheddar cheese	230 g
½ cup chopped onion	80 g
½ cup chopped green bell pepper	75 g
2 ribs celery, sliced	
2 cups cooked, chopped ham	280 g
1 (10 ounce) can cream of chicken soup	280 g
⅔ cup milk	150 ml
1 teaspoon seasoned salt	5 ml

- Place potatoes, cheese, onion, bell pepper, celery and ham in sprayed slow cooker and mix well.

- Combine soup, milk and seasoned salt in bowl and pour evenly over potato-vegetable mixture. Cover and cook on HIGH for 4 hours. Serves 8.

Cheesy Scalloped Potatoes and Ham

5 medium potatoes, peeled, sliced, divided	
1 onion, chopped, divided	
2 cups cooked, cubed ham, divided	280 g
1 (8 ounce) package cubed Velveeta® cheese, divided	230 g
1 (10 ounce) can broccoli-cheese soup	280 g
¼ cup milk	60 ml

- Layer half each of potatoes, onion, ham and cheese in sprayed slow cooker and repeat layers. Combine soup and milk in bowl until fairly smooth and spoon over potato-ham mixture.

- Cover and cook on HIGH for 1 hour. Reduce heat to LOW and cook for 6 to 7 hours. Serves 4.

Brown Sugar Glazed Ham

1 (1 pound) cooked smoked ½-inch thick center cut ham slice	455 g/1.2 cm
⅓ cup orange juice	75 ml
⅓ cup packed brown sugar	75 g
2 teaspoons dijon-style mustard	10 ml

- Place ham slice in sprayed slow cooker. Combine juice, brown sugar and mustard in small bowl. Spread over ham slice. Cover and cook on LOW for 3 to 4 hours or until ham has glossy glaze. Cut ham into individual servings. Serves 4 to 5.

Home-Style Ham Loaf

3 cups cooked, ground ham	420 g
½ pound ground beef	230 g
½ pound hot sausage	230 g
½ cup finely chopped onion	80 g
¾ cup cracker crumbs	45 g
1 large egg, slightly beaten	
1 teaspoon sugar	5 ml
1 tablespoon dijon-style mustard	15 ml
¼ cup chili sauce	70 g

- Make foil handles for meat loaf (see TIP on page 213).

- Combine all ingredients in large bowl; mix well. Form into 9 x 5-inch (23 13 cm) loaf and place in sprayed oblong slow cooker. Cover and cook on LOW for 6 to 7 hours. Slice to serve. Slices are also good for making sandwiches. Serves 6.

TIP: If using leftover ham, grind ham in food processor.

Special Ham Supper

2½ cups cooked, ground ham	350 g
⅔ cup finely crushed cheese crackers	40 g
1 large egg	
⅓ cup hot-and-spicy ketchup	90 g
¼ cup (½ stick) butter	60 g
1 (18 ounce) package frozen hash-brown potatoes, thawed	510 g
1 onion, coarsely chopped	
1 (5 ounce) can evaporated milk	150 ml
1½ cups shredded Monterey Jack cheese	175 g
½ teaspoon paprika	2 ml

- Combine ground ham (you can use leftover ham), crackers, egg and ketchup in bowl and shape into 6 patties.

- Melt butter in skillet and cook potatoes and onion on medium heat for about 10 minutes, turning frequently to prevent browning. Drain and transfer to sprayed slow cooker.

- Combine evaporated milk, cheese, paprika and a little salt and pepper in bowl. Pour over potatoes and onions. Place ham patties on top; cover and cook on LOW for 3 to 5 hours. Serves 6.

Walnut Ham

½ pound cooked ham slices	230 g
2 (10 ounce) cans cream of onion soup	2 (280 g)
⅓ cup grated parmesan cheese	35 g
⅔ cup chopped walnuts	90 g
Linguine, cooked	

- Cut ham into ½-inch (1.2 cm) strips. Place soups, cheese, walnuts and ham strips in sprayed slow cooker. Cover and cook on LOW for 1 to 2 hours or until hot and bubbly. Serve over linguine. Serves 4.

Zesty Ham Supper

1 (28 ounce) package frozen hash-brown potatoes with onions and peppers, thawed	795 g
3 cups cooked, diced ham	420 g
1 (10 ounce) box frozen green peas, thawed	280 g
2 (10 ounce) cans fiesta nacho cheese soup	2 (280 g)
1 cup milk	250 ml
1 bunch fresh green onions, chopped	

- Place potatoes, ham and peas in sprayed large slow cooker and stir to mix. Combine soup and milk in bowl and mix well. Pour over potato mixture and mix well. Cover and cook on LOW for 6 to 8 hours. Sprinkle green onions over top when ready to serve. Serves 6 to 8.

Apricot Ham

1 (6 - 8 pound) butt or shank ham	2.7 - 3.6 kg
Whole cloves	
2 tablespoons dry mustard	30 g
1¼ cups apricot jam	400 g
1¼ cups packed light brown sugar	275 g

- Place ham, fat-side up, in sprayed slow cooker. Stick lots of whole cloves on outside of ham.

- Combine mustard, jam and brown sugar in bowl and spread all over ham. Cover and cook on LOW for 5 to 6 hours. Serves 8 to 10.

Saucy Ham Loaf

Great with sweet-and-hot mustard recipe below. Start this the night before.

1 pound ground ham	455 g
½ pound ground beef	230 g
½ pound ground pork	230 g
2 eggs, slightly beaten	
1 cup Italian-seasoned breadcrumbs	120 g
1 (5 ounce) can evaporated milk	150 ml
¼ cup chili sauce	70 g
1 teaspoon seasoned salt	5 ml

- Make foil handles for meat loaf (see TIP on page 213).

- Combine all ingredients in bowl and form into loaf in sprayed oval slow cooker. Shape loaf so it does not touch sides of cooker. Cover and cook on LOW for 6 to 7 hours. Serve with Sweet-and-Hot Mustard.

Sweet-and-Hot Mustard:

Use on Ham Loaf or ham sandwiches.

4 ounces dry mustard	115 g
1 cup vinegar	250 ml
3 eggs, beaten	
1 cup sugar	200 g

- Mix mustard and vinegar in bowl until smooth and let stand overnight.

- Add eggs and sugar to mustard-vinegar mixture and cook in double boiler for 8 to 10 minutes or until mixture coats the spoon. Cool and store in covered jars in refrigerator. Serve with Saucy Ham Loaf or with ham sandwiches. Serves 4 to 6.

Cherry Ham Loaf

Great for leftover ham.

1½ pounds cooked, ground ham	680 g
1 pound ground turkey	455 g
2 eggs	
1 cup seasoned breadcrumbs	120 g
2 teaspoons chicken seasoning	10 ml

- Make foil handles for meat loaf (see TIP on page 213).

- Combine all ingredients in bowl and mix well. Shape into short loaf that fits into sprayed oval slow cooker. Cover and cook on LOW for 4 to 5 hours. Serve with Cherry Sauce.

Cherry Sauce:

1 cup cherry preserves	320 g
2 tablespoons cider vinegar	30 ml
Scant ⅛ teaspoon ground cloves	.5 ml
Scant ⅛ teaspoon ground cinnamon	.5 ml

- Place cherry preserves, vinegar, cloves and cinnamon in saucepan and heat. Serve over slices of Ham Loaf. Serves 4 to 6.

Ham and Potato Dish

4 large baking potatoes, peeled	
3 cups cubed cooked ham	420 g
1 (10 ounce) box frozen whole kernel corn, drained	280 g
1 (10 ounce) package frozen chopped bell peppers and onions, thawed	280 g
1 teaspoon seasoned salt	5 ml
2 (10 ounce) cans fiesta nacho cheese soup	2 (280 g)
½ cup milk	125 ml
1 (3 ounce) can french-fried onions	85 g

- Cut potatoes into 1-inch (2.5 cm) cubes. Combine potatoes, ham, corn, onions and peppers and seasoned salt in sprayed slow cooker.

- Heat soup and milk in saucepan just enough to mix well. Add to slow cooker and mix well. Cover and cook on LOW for 5 to 6 hours or until potatoes are tender. When ready to serve, sprinkle fried onions over top. Serves 4 to 6.

Ben's Ham and Rice

1 (6.7 ounce) box brown-wild rice, mushroom recipe	170 g
3 - 4 cups cooked, chopped or cubed ham	420 - 560 g
1 (4 ounce) can sliced mushrooms, drained	115 g
1 (10 ounce) package frozen green peas	280 g
2 cups chopped celery	200 g

- Combine rice, seasoning packet, ham, mushrooms, peas, and celery plus 2⅔ cups (650 ml) water in sprayed slow cooker. Stir to mix well. Cover and cook on LOW for 2 to 4 hours. Serves 4 to 6.

Creamy Potatoes and Ham

1 pint half-and-half cream	500 ml
1 cup milk	250 ml
1 (10 ounce) can fiesta nacho cheese soup	280 g
2 (5 ounce) boxes scalloped potatoes mix	2 (145 g)
2 - 3 cups cooked, diced ham	280 - 420 g
2 ribs celery, sliced	
2 (11 ounce) cans Mexicorn®, drained	310 g
1 cup shredded cheddar cheese	115 g

- Combine half-and-half cream, milk, soup and contents of seasoning packets from potatoes in large bowl; mix until they blend well.

- Add potatoes, ham, celery and corn and mix well. Pour mixture into sprayed slow cooker. Pour 2 cups (500 ml) boiling water over potato mixture and stir to mix well. Cover and cook on LOW for 7 to 8 hours. Sprinkle 1 tablespoon (15 ml) cheese over each serving. Serves 8 to 10.

Creamed Ham with Spaghetti

2 (10 ounce) cans cream of mushroom with roasted garlic soup	2 (280 g)
1 cup sliced fresh mushrooms	70 g
2 - 2½ cups cooked, cubed ham	280 - 350 g
1 (5 ounce) can evaporated milk	150 ml
1 (7 ounce) box ready-cut spaghetti	200 g

- Combine soup, mushrooms, ham, evaporated milk and a little salt and pepper in sprayed slow cooker. Cover and cook on LOW for 2 hours and mix well.

- Cook spaghetti according to package directions and drain. Add spaghetti to slow cooker and toss to coat. Serves 4 to 6.

Ham to the Rescue

2½ cups cooked, ground ham	350 g
⅔ cup crushed white cheddar Cheez-Its® crackers	40 g
1 large egg	
⅓ cup chili sauce	90 g
4 medium potatoes, peeled, sliced	
Canola oil	
1 green bell pepper, seeded, julienned	
1 (8 ounce) package shredded cheddar-Jack cheese	230 g
1 (5 ounce) can evaporated milk	150 ml
1 teaspoon seasoned salt	5 ml

- Combine ham, crushed crackers, egg and chili sauce in bowl and mix well. Shape ham mixture into 6 patties.

- Saute potatoes in a little oil in skillet and turn several times to brown lightly on both sides. Place potatoes and bell pepper in sprayed large slow cooker.

- In separate bowl, combine cheese, evaporated milk and seasoned salt and pour over potatoes. Place ham patties on top. Cover and cook on LOW for 3 to 4 hours. Serves 4 to 6.

Ham-Vegetable Supper

2 (16 ounce) package frozen broccoli, cauliflower and carrots, thawed	2 (455 g)
1 (10 ounce) package frozen green peas, thawed	280 g
2 (10 ounce) cans broccoli-cheese soup	2 (280 g)
½ cup milk	125 ml
1 (8 ounce) package shredded Velveeta® cheese	230 g
1 tablespoon dijon-style mustard	15 ml
2 - 3 cups cooked, cubed ham	280 - 420 g
1 cup corkscrew pasta, cooked	105 g
1 - 2 cups slightly crushed potato chips	55 - 110 g

- Combine all vegetables, soup, milk, cheese, mustard and 1 teaspoon (5 ml) each of salt and pepper in sprayed slow cooker. Cover and cook on LOW for 6 to 8 hours.

- Stir in ham and pasta, cover and cook for additional 30 minutes or until mixture is thoroughly hot. Sprinkle with potato chips just before serving or sprinkle chips over individual servings. Serves 8.

Always read the manufacturer's instructions for your slow cooker. These will introduce you to each feature and use.

Sweet and Spicy Ribs

1 (10 ounce) package frozen chopped bell peppers and onions, thawed	280 g
2 teaspoons minced garlic	10 ml
2 tablespoons canola oil	30 ml
2 tablespoons tomato paste	35 g
1 (6 ounce) can frozen pineapple juice concentrate, thawed	175 ml
½ cup packed brown sugar	110 g
¼ cup plus 2 tablespoons soy sauce, divided	60 ml/30 ml
2 tablespoons rice vinegar	30 ml
¼ teaspoon cayenne pepper	1 ml
3 pounds pork baby back ribs	1.4 kg
1 tablespoon cornstarch	15 ml

- Pulse bell peppers and onions and garlic in food processor until finely chopped. Heat oil in skillet and cook on medium-high heat for about 5 minutes. Transfer to bowl and stir in tomato paste, pineapple juice concentrate, brown sugar, ¼ cup (60 ml) soy sauce, rice vinegar and cayenne pepper.

- Pat ribs dry with paper towels and season with salt and pepper. Arrange ribs in sprayed slow cooker and spoon sauce over ribs. Cover and cook on LOW for 4 to 6 hours.

- Place ribs on serving platter. Place liquid from slow cooker in saucepan and simmer over medium heat until reduced by half.

- Whisk cornstarch in remaining soy sauce in bowl and stir into sauce. Cook until sauce is glossy and thickened. Slice ribs between bones and pour sauce over ribs and toss until well coated. Serves 6.

Party Ribs

3 pounds lean pork baby back ribs	1.4 kg
1 (14 ounce) can beef broth	395 g
¼ cup soy sauce	60 ml
¼ cup honey	85 g
⅓ cup maple syrup	75 ml
⅓ cup barbecue sauce	75 ml

- Preheat broiler.

- Place ribs in shallow pan and broil for about 10 minutes to melt excess fat, then place ribs in sprayed slow cooker. Sprinkle ribs with a little salt and pepper.

- Combine broth, soy sauce, honey, maple syrup and barbecue sauce in bowl, mix well. Pour over ribs. Cover and cook on LOW for 6 to 8 hours or on HIGH for 3 to 4 hours. Serves 5 to 6.

Groovy Baby Backs

3 pounds pork baby back ribs	1.4 kg
¾ cup hot-and-spicy ketchup	205 g
½ cup teriyaki marinade and sauce	125 ml
½ cup apricot preserves	160 g
⅓ cup packed brown sugar	75 g
1 teaspoon minced garlic	5 ml
¼ teaspoon liquid smoke	1 ml

- Cut ribs between bones, making individual ribs and place in sprayed slow cooker.

- Combine ketchup, teriyaki, preserves, brown sugar, garlic, liquid smoke and ½ teaspoon (2 ml) salt; mix well and pour over ribs. Cover and cook on LOW for 6 to 8 hours.

- Skim fat off ribs. Cooked ribs can be held in slow cooker for 1 to 2 hours. Serves 4 to 6.

Absolutely Good Ribs

4 - 4½ pounds pork baby back ribs	1.8 - 2 kg
1 (16 ounce) jar salsa	455 g
⅔ cup honey	230 g
2 tablespoons brown sugar	30 g
1 teaspoon ground ginger	5 ml
1 tablespoon cornstarch	15 ml

- Preheat broiler.

- Cut ribs into 1-rib portions and place on broiler pan. Broil for about 10 minutes on each side. Place ribs in sprayed slow cooker.

- Combine salsa, honey, brown sugar, ginger and cornstarch in bowl and pour over ribs. Cover and cook on LOW for 6 to 7 hours or on HIGH for 3 hours to 3 hours and 30 minutes.

- Skim off fat from sauce and serve ribs as entree or appetizers. Serves 6.

Barbecue Ribs and Beans

3 medium onions, thinly sliced	
4 pounds country-style pork ribs	1.8 kg
1 cup hot-and-spicy barbecue sauce	265 g
2 (15 ounce) cans baked beans	2 (425 g)

- Place onions in sprayed slow cooker and cover with pork ribs. Pour barbecue sauce over top. Cover and cook on LOW for 7 hours.

- Spoon baked beans (you could use drained pinto beans, if you like) around sides of ribs, cover and cook for additional 1 hour. Serves 8.

Glazed Country Ribs

2 pounds boneless country-style pork loin ribs	910 g
1 small onion, sliced, separated into rings	
1 teaspoon minced garlic	5 ml
½ cup chopped bell pepper	75 g
⅔ cup orange marmalade	215 g
2 tablespoons soy sauce	30 ml
2 tablespoons cornstarch	15 g
½ teaspoon ground ginger	2 ml

- Place ribs, onion and garlic in sprayed slow cooker. Cover and cook on LOW for 8 to 9 hours.

- Five minutes before serving, remove ribs from slow cooker and place on serving platter and keep warm.

- Combine bell pepper, marmalade, soy sauce, cornstarch and ground ginger in medium saucepan. Stir in ¾ cup (175 ml) juices from slow cooker (discard remaining juices). Cook on high, stirring constantly, until mixture thickens. Pour sauce over ribs. Serves 6.

Barbecued Ribs

4 - 5 pounds pork spareribs, cut into 2-rib pieces	1.8 - 2.3 kg
1 cup spicy ketchup	270 g
¼ cup vinegar	60 ml
⅔ cup packed brown sugar	150 g
1 tablespoon Worcestershire	15 ml

- Preheat broiler.

- Place spareribs on rack in shallow baking pan and brown for 10 to 15 minutes on each side. Drain and place in sprayed slow cooker.

- Combine ketchup, vinegar, brown sugar, Worcestershire and ½ teaspoon (2 ml) salt in small bowl. Pour mixture over ribs; turning ribs to evenly coat. Cover and cook on LOW for 5 to 6 hours or until ribs are tender. Serves 6.

Stirring is not necessary in most recipes. Stir only if the recipe calls for it. This includes assembling the ingredients in the slow cooker as well as during the cooking time. Remember that lifting the lid loses a lot of heat and it will take at least 20 minutes for the cooker to recover its heat when the lid has been removed, even briefly.

Home-Style Ribs

4 - 6 pounds boneless pork spareribs	1.8 - 2.7 kg
1 cup chili sauce	270 g
1 cup packed brown sugar	220 g
2 tablespoons vinegar	30 ml
2 tablespoons Worcestershire sauce	30 ml

- Sprinkle ribs liberally with salt and pepper. Place ribs in sprayed slow cooker.

- Combine ½ cup (125 ml) water, chili sauce, brown sugar, vinegar and Worcestershire in bowl and spoon over ribs. Cover and cook on LOW for 5 to 6 hours. Serves 6 to 8.

Delectable Apricot Ribs

4 - 5 pounds baby back pork ribs	1.8 - 2.3 kg
1 (16 ounce) jar apricot preserves	455 g
⅓ cup soy sauce	75 ml
¼ cup packed light brown sugar	55 g
2 teaspoons garlic powder	10 ml
¼ cup apple cider vinegar	60 ml

- Place ribs in sprayed slow cooker.

- Combine preserves, soy sauce, brown sugar, garlic powder and vinegar in bowl and spoon over ribs. Cover and cook on LOW for 6 to 7 hours. Serves 8 to 10.

Tangy Apricot Ribs

3 - 4 pounds baby back pork ribs	1.4 - 1.8 kg
1 (16 ounce) jar apricot preserves	455 g
⅓ cup soy sauce	75 ml
¼ cup packed light brown sugar	55 g

- Place ribs in sprayed large slow cooker. Combine preserves, soy sauce and brown sugar in bowl and spoon over ribs. Cover and cook on LOW for 6 to 8 hours. Serves 6 to 8.

Finger Lickin' Baby Backs

2½ - 3 pounds baby back pork ribs	1.1 - 1.4 kg
½ cup chili sauce	135 g
⅓ cup apple cider vinegar	75 ml
½ cup packed brown sugar	110 g

- Cut ribs in serving-size pieces, sprinkle with pepper and place in sprayed large slow cooker.

- Combine chili sauce, vinegar, brown sugar and about ¾ cup (175 ml) water in bowl and pour over ribs. Stir to coat ribs. Cover and cook on LOW for about 6 to 7 hours.

- After about 3 hours, move ribs around in slow cooker so sauce is spread over all ribs. Serves 4 to 6.

Slow and Spicy Ribs

¾ cup plum preserves	240 g
¼ cup ketchup	70 g
½ cup soy sauce	125 ml
5 garlic cloves, crushed	
½ teaspoon cayenne pepper	2 ml
3 pounds baby back pork ribs	1.4 kg

- Combine plum preserves, ketchup, soy sauce, garlic, cayenne pepper, ½ cup (125 ml) water, and 1 teaspoon (5 ml) each of salt and pepper in slow cooker.

- Cut ribs into individual pieces. Add ribs to cooker and mix well to coat with sauce. Cover and cook on low for 8 to 10 hours. Serves 6.

Pizzeria Casserole

1½ pounds bulk Italian pork sausage	680 g
1 (16 ounce) package rigatoni	455 g
1 (16 ounce) package shredded mozzarella cheese	455 g
1 (10 ounce) can cream of mushroom soup	280 g
1 small onion, finely chopped	
1 (15 ounce) can pizza sauce	425 g
1 (8 ounce) can pizza sauce	230 g
1 (3 ounce) package sliced pepperoni	85 g
1 (4 ounce) can pitted ripe olives, drained, halved	115 g

- Cook sausage in skillet until no longer pink. Cook rigatoni pasta according to package directions; drain.

- Place half sausage in sprayed slow cooker and add half of each of remaining ingredients. Repeat layers. Cover and cook on LOW for 4 hours. Remove slow cooker bowl and serve right from cooker. Serves 6 to 8.

Celebrated Sausage and Rice

1 (16 ounce) Polish sausage ring, cut into ¼-inch slices	455 g/6 mm
2 (15 ounce) cans Italian stewed tomatoes	2 (425 g)
1 (16 ounce) package frozen chopped bell peppers and onions, thawed	455 g
2 ribs celery, sliced	
1 teaspoon Italian seasoning	5 ml
1 teaspoon dried basil	5 ml
½ teaspoon hot pepper sauce	2 ml
1½ cups instant rice	145 g

- Layer sausage, stewed tomatoes, bell peppers and onions, and celery in sprayed slow cooker. Sprinkle with Italian seasoning, basil and pepper sauce. Cover and cook on LOW for 7 hours.

- Stir in rice and ½ cup (125 ml) water and cook for additional 30 minutes. Serves 4 to 5.

Sweet-and-Sour Sausage Links

2 (16 ounce) packages miniature smoked sausage links	2 (455 g)
¾ cup chili sauce	205 g
1 cup packed brown sugar	220 g
¼ cup prepared horseradish	55 g

- Place sausage links in sprayed slow cooker.

- Combine chili sauce, brown sugar and horseradish in bowl and pour over sausage. Cover and cook on LOW for 4 hours. Serves 4 to 6.

TIP: This can be served as an appetizer or served over rice.

Italian-Style Tortellini

2 pounds bulk Italian sausage	910 g
1 (15 ounce) carton refrigerated marinara sauce	425 g
2 cups sliced fresh mushrooms, sliced	145 g
1 (15 ounce) cans Italian stewed tomatoes	425 g
1 (9 ounce) package refrigerated cheese tortellini	255 g
1½ cups shredded mozzarella cheese	170 g

- Brown and cook sausage in skillet for 10 to 15 minutes and drain well. Combine sausage, marinara sauce, mushrooms and tomatoes in sprayed slow cooker. Cover and cook on LOW 6 to 7 hours.

- Stir in tortellini. Cover and cook on HIGH for about 15 minutes or until tortellini is tender. When ready to serve, sprinkle with cheese. Serves 4 to 6.

Fiery Sausage and Rice

2 pounds hot sausage	910 g
1 tablespoon ground cumin	15 ml
1 teaspoon minced garlic	5 ml
1 (16 ounce) package frozen chopped bell peppers and onions, thawed	455 g
2 ribs celery, sliced	
1 (32 ounce) carton beef broth	910 g
2 (6 ounce) boxes long-grain-wild rice mix	2 (170 g)
½ teaspoon hot sauce	2 ml

- Cook sausage in skillet on medium-high heat until light brown, about 5 minutes, breaking up sausage with back of spoon while cooking. Drain and stir in cumin, garlic, bell peppers and onions, celery and cook for additional 10 minutes, stirring often.

- Spoon mixture into sprayed slow cooker and stir in broth and rice. Cover and cook on LOW for 4 to 6 hours or on HIGH for 1 to 2 hours. Serves 10.

Ready Rice and Beans

1 pound spicy smoked sausage, cut into ½-inch slices	455 g/1.2 cm
1 (15 ounce) can kidney beans, rinsed, drained	425 g
1 (15 ounce) can pinto beans, rinsed, drained	425 g
1 (15 ounce) can Mexican stewed tomatoes	425 g
1 (10 ounce) package frozen chopped bell peppers and onions, thawed	280 g
1 cup rice	185 g

- Combine sausage, beans, tomatoes and bell peppers and onions in sprayed slow cooker. Cover and cook on LOW heat 5 hours 30 minutes to 6 hours.

- A few minutes before serving, cook rice according to package directions. Spoon cooked rice into individual bowls and top with bean mixture. Serves 4 to 5.

Slow cookers vary in size from about 1-quart up to 7- or 8-quart sizes. Most recipes will be fine in a 5-quart slow cooker. The smaller sizes are great for hot dips and sauces while the larger ones are good for big families and for entertaining. Some cooks like to have two of regular size so they can cook a side dish or dessert at the same time they are cooking a main dish.

Harvest Vegetable Casserole

3 - 4 medium red potatoes with peels, sliced	
2 onions, sliced	
3 carrots, sliced	
2 cups chopped green cabbage	140 g
¼ cup Italian dressing	60 ml
1 (1 pound) kielbasa sausage	455 g
1 (15 ounce) can Italian stewed tomatoes	425 g

- Place potatoes, onions, carrots, cabbage and Italian dressing in sprayed large slow cooker.

- Cut sausage into 1-inch (2.5 cm) pieces and place on top of vegetables. Drizzle stewed tomatoes in even layer over sausage. Cover and cook on LOW for 6 to 8 hours or until vegetables are tender. Serves 4 to 6.

Sausage and Beans

1 (1 pound) fully cooked smoked link sausage	455 g
2 (15 ounce) cans baked beans	2 (425 g)
1 (15 ounce) can great northern beans, drained	425 g
1 (15 ounce) can pinto beans, drained	425 g
½ cup chili sauce	135 g
⅔ cup packed brown sugar	150 g
1 tablespoon Worcestershire sauce	15 ml

- Cut link sausage into 1-inch (2.5 cm) slices. Layer sausage and beans in sprayed slow cooker.

- Combine chili sauce, brown sugar, a little pepper and Worcestershire sauce in bowl and pour over beans and sausage. Cover and cook on LOW for 4 hours. Stir before serving. Serves 4.

Sauerkraut and Bratwurst

1 (28 ounce) jar refrigerated sauerkraut	795 g
¾ cup beer	175 ml
1 tablespoon marinade for chicken	15 ml
1 (1 ounce) packet onion soup mix	30 g
2 pounds precooked bratwurst	910 g

- Combine sauerkraut, beer, Worcestershire and onion soup mix in sprayed slow cooker and mix well.

- Cut bratwurst in diagonal slices and place on top of sauerkraut-beer mixture. Cover and cook on LOW for 5 to 6 hours or on HIGH for 2 hours 30 minutes to 3 hours. Serves 4 to 6.

Sausage-Potato Bake

3 medium potatoes, peeled, sliced	
1 (16 ounce) package frozen cut green beans, thawed	455 g
2 (10 ounce) cans cream of celery soup	2 (280 g)
½ cup milk	125 ml
1 cup shredded Velveeta® cheese	230 g
1 pound cooked Polish sausage, sliced	455 g
1 (3 ounce) can french-fried onions	85 g

- Place potatoes and green beans in sprayed slow cooker.

- Combine soup, milk and cheese in bowl and spoon over potatoes and green beans; top with sliced sausage. Cover and cook on LOW for 6 to 8 hours.

- Sprinkle fried onions over top and let slow cooker stand for about 15 minutes for fried onions to warm. Serves 8.

Kielbasa and Black Beans

2 (15 ounce) cans black beans	2 (425 g)
1 (15 ounce) can stewed tomatoes	425 g
1 (15 ounce) can whole kernel corn	425 g
1 tablespoon minced garlic	15 ml
1 teaspoon chili powder	5 ml
1 pound kielbasa sausage, cubed	455 g
Cooked rice	
1 cup shredded cheddar cheese	115 g

- Place beans, tomatoes, corn, garlic and chili powder in slow cooker; mix well. Place sausage on top of bean mixture. Cover and cook on LOW for 6 to 7 hours. Serve over rice and sprinkle with cheese. Serves 6.

Mama Mia Meat Loaf

1 (15 ounce) jar spaghetti sauce, divided	340 g
1 pound Italian pork sausage, removed from casing	455 g
1 pound ground beef	455 g
1 cup breadcrumbs	120 g
1 cup chopped onion	160 g
1 cup grated parmesan cheese	100 g
1 teaspoon minced garlic	15 ml
1 egg	

- Make foil handles for meat loaf (see TIP on page 213).

- Combine ½ cup (125 g) spaghetti sauce, 1 teaspoon (5 ml) each of salt and pepper, and all remaining ingredients in large bowl; mix well. Form into loaf in sprayed slow cooker. Pour remaining sauce over loaf. Cover and cook on LOW 5 to 7 hours. Serves 8.

Italian Sausage and Potatoes

1 (28 ounce) can whole tomatoes	795 g
1 tablespoon Italian seasoning	15 ml
1 pound Italian sausage	455 g
2 potatoes, peeled, cubed	
1 zucchini, sliced	
1 onion, diced	
¼ cup breadcrumbs	30 g
1 cup shredded pepper jack cheese	115 g

- Combine tomatoes, Italian seasoning, 1 teaspoon (5 ml) each of salt and pepper, sausage, potatoes, zucchini and onion in sprayed slow cooker. Cover and cook on HIGH for 4 hours.

- Remove sausage and cut into large chunks. Return sausage to cooker and add breadcrumbs; stir well. Top with cheese. Serves 6.

Crab Casserole

3 tablespoons butter	45 g
1 (10 ounce) package frozen chopped bell peppers and onions, thawed	280 g
3 tablespoons flour	20 g
2 (14 ounce) cans chicken broth	2 (395 g)
1 cup rice	185 g
2 (6 ounce) cans crabmeat, drained, flaked	2 (170 g)
1 cup shredded cheddar cheese	115 g
½ cup sliced almonds	95 g
1 cup seasoned breadcrumbs	120 g

- Melt butter in skillet on medium heat and lightly saute bell peppers and onions. While heat is still on, add flour and stir well. Slowly add chicken broth, stirring constantly and cook until slightly thick.

- Combine rice, crabmeat, cheese and almonds in bowl. Stir in sauce and transfer to sprayed slow cooker. Cover and cook on HIGH for 3 to 5 hours.

- Spoon into ovenproof serving dish. Sprinkle breadcrumbs over top. Place under broiler until crumbs are slightly brown. Serves 5 to 6.

Cheesy Veggie-Crab Casserole

3 tablespoons butter plus ¼ cup (½ stick) butter, divided	100 g
2 ribs celery, thinly sliced	
1 (10 ounce) package frozen chopped bell peppers	
and onions, thawed	280 g
¼ cup flour	30 g
2 (14 ounce) cans chicken broth	2 (395 g)
1¼ cups instant rice	145 g
2 (6 once) cans crabmeat, drained, flaked	2 (170 g)
1 cup shredded cheddar cheese	115 g
1 (4 ounce) can sliced mushrooms, drained	115 g
½ cup sliced almonds	95 g
1 cup seasoned breadcrumbs	120 g

- Melt 3 tablespoons (40 g) butter in skillet on medium heat and lightly saute celery and **bell peppers and** onions. Add flour and stir well. Slowly add chicken broth, stirring constantly and cook until slightly thickened.

- Combine rice, crabmeat, cheese, mushrooms and almonds in bowl. Stir in sauce and transfer to sprayed slow cooker. Cover and cook on HIGH for 3 to 5 hours.

- Spoon contents of slow cooker into ovenproof serving dish.

- Melt ¼ cup (½ stick) butter and combine with breadcrumbs in small bowl; sprinkle over contents of serving dish. Place under broiler until crumbs are slightly brown. Serves 5 to 6.

Yummy Tuna Bake

2 (6 ounce) cans white tuna, drained, flaked	2 (170 g)
1 (10 ounce) can cream of chicken soup	280 g
3 eggs, hard-boiled, chopped	
3 ribs celery, thinly sliced	
1 red bell pepper, seeded, chopped	
½ cup coarsely chopped pecans	55 g
½ cup mayonnaise	110 g
2 cups crushed potato chips, divided	110 g

- Combine tuna, soup, eggs, celery, bell pepper, pecans, mayonnaise, 1 teaspoon (5 ml) pepper, half potato chips and a little salt in bowl and mix well. Transfer to sprayed slow cooker. Cover and cook on LOW for 5 to 7 hours.

- When ready to serve, sprinkle remaining potato chips on top. Serves 4 to 5.

Mr. Mac and Tuna

1½ cups small shell macaroni	160 g
¼ cup (½ stick) butter	55 g
1 onion, chopped	
1 green bell pepper, seeded, chopped	
2 ribs celery, thinly sliced	
⅓ cup flour	40 g
2 cups milk	500 ml
1 (8 ounce) package shredded Velveeta® cheese	230 g
1 (12 ounce) can tuna in water, drained	340 g

- Cook macaroni according to package directions and drain. Melt butter in skillet and saute onion, bell pepper and celery until tender. On medium heat, add flour and slowly add milk, stirring constantly until mixture thickens. Reduce heat to low, add cheese and stir until cheese melts.

- Place macaroni, vegetable-cheese sauce and tuna in sprayed slow cooker. Cover and cook on LOW for 2 hours 30 minutes or until bubbly at edge. Serves 6.

Super Shrimp and Rice

1 (16 ounce) package frozen salad shrimp, thawed	455 g
¾ cup chicken broth	175 ml
1 red bell pepper, seeded, cut into strips	
1 teaspoon chili powder	5 ml
¼ teaspoon dried oregano	1 ml
¼ cup (½ stick) butter, melted	55 g
1 (10 ounce) package frozen green peas, thawed	280 g
¼ cup sun-dried tomatoes, sliced	15 g
2 cups cooked rice	315 g

- Combine shrimp, broth, bell pepper, chili powder, oregano and butter in sprayed slow cooker. Cover and cook on LOW for 2 hours.

- Stir in green peas, tomatoes and rice; cover and cook for additional 15 minutes or until mixture is thoroughly hot. Serves 4 to 6.

When choosing a slow cooker, you may want to take advantage of the programmable features of some models. This allows for greater flexibility in control of time and temperature. Many models also include a "warm" setting that will keep food warm after the cooking time has elapsed. This is also useful in using the slow cooker to serve from on a buffet or for hot dips, etc.

Desserts

Cobblers, Puddings
and
Other Sweet Treats

Slow-Cook Baked Apples

4 - 5 large baking apples
1 tablespoon lemon juice   15 ml
⅓ cup Craisins®   40 g
½ cup chopped pecans   55 g
¾ cup packed brown sugar   165 g
½ teaspoon ground cinnamon   2 ml
¼ cup (½ stick) butter, softened   60 g
Caramel ice cream topping

- Scoop out center of each apple and leave cavity about ½-inch (1.2 cm) from bottom. Peel top of apples down about 1-inch (2.5 cm) and brush lemon juice on peeled edges.

- Combine Craisins®, pecans, brown sugar, cinnamon and butter in bowl. Spoon mixture into apple cavities.

- Pour ½ cup (125 ml) water in sprayed oval slow cooker and arrange apples inside. Cover and cook on LOW for 1 to 3 hours or until tender.

- Serve warm or room temperature and drizzle with caramel ice cream topping. Serves 4 to 6.

Campfire-Baked Apples in a Pot

6 large green baking apples
2 tablespoons lemon juice   30 ml
¼ cup (½ stick) butter, melted   60 g
1 cup packed brown sugar   220 g
1 teaspoon ground cinnamon   5 ml
½ teaspoon ground nutmeg   2 ml
Vanilla ice cream

- Peel, core and cut apples in half; place in sprayed slow cooker. Drizzle with lemon juice and butter. Sprinkle with brown sugar and spices. Cover and cook on LOW for 2 hours 30 minutes to 3 hours 30 minutes or on HIGH for 1 hour 30 minutes to 2 hours. Serve with vanilla ice cream. Serves 4 to 6.

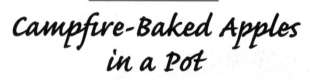

Whole and fresh spices, herbs, and seasonings hold up well and even intensify during long cooking times. Ground and dried herbs and spices tend to lose flavor and are best added at the end of cooking.

Cran-Apples Spectacular

1 (6 ounce) package dried apples	170 g
½ cup Craisins®	60 g
3 cups cranberry juice cocktail	750 ml
¾ cup packed brown sugar	165 g
2 cinnamon sticks, halved	
Pound cake or vanilla ice cream	

- Add apples, Craisins®, juice, brown sugar and cinnamon sticks to sprayed slow cooker. Cover and cook on LOW for 4 to 5 hours or until liquid absorbs and fruit is tender. Serve warm, at room temperature or chilled over slices of pound cake or over vanilla ice cream. Serves 6.

Yummy Cinnamon Apples

2 (20 ounce) cans apple pie filling	2 (570 g)
1 cup packed brown sugar	220 g
1½ teaspoons ground cinnamon	7 ml
1 (18 ounce) box yellow cake mix	510 g
½ cup (1 stick) butter, melted	115 g

- Spread apple pie filling evenly in sprayed slow cooker. Sprinkle with brown sugar and cinnamon. Top with cake mix and drizzle melted butter over cake mix. Cover and cook on LOW for 6 to 8 hours. Serve warm or at room temperature. Serves 16.

All About Apple Crisp

½ cup flour	60 g
1½ cups sugar, divided	300 g
½ teaspoon ground cinnamon, divided	2 ml
¼ cup (½ stick) butter, cut in pieces	55 g
½ cup chopped pecans	55 g
2 teaspoons lemon juice	10 ml
¼ teaspoon ground ginger	1 ml
5 - 6 Granny Smith apples, peeled, cut into wedges	
Vanilla ice cream	

- Combine flour, ½ cup (100 g) sugar, ¼ teaspoon (1 ml) cinnamon and butter pieces in bowl. Work butter into flour mixture with pastry blender or fork until mixture is like coarse crumbs. Stir in pecans.

- In separate bowl, whisk remaining sugar, remaining cinnamon, lemon juice and ginger. Add apple wedges and toss for mixture to cover apples; transfer to sprayed slow cooker and sprinkle flour-pecan mixture over apples.

- Cover and cook on LOW for 4 hours or on HIGH for 2 hours. Serve warm or at room temperature with a dip of vanilla ice cream. Serves 6 to 8.

Accent on Apples

1 (20 ounce) can pie apples (not pie filling)	570 g
¾ cup packed brown sugar	165 g
½ cup flour	60 g
½ cup quick-cooking oats	40 g
½ teaspoon ground cinnamon	2 ml
¼ teaspoon ground nutmeg	1 ml
3 tablespoons butter, softened	45 g
½ cup chopped pecans	55 g
Ice cream or whipped cream	

- Spoon pie apples into sprayed slow cooker.

- Combine brown sugar, flour, oats, cinnamon and nutmeg in bowl. Mix in butter with a fork until mixture is crumbly; stir in pecans. Sprinkle mixture over apples. Cover and cook on LOW for 5 to 6 hours.

- Serve warm or at room temperature with ice cream or whipped cream. Serves 6.

An Apple a Day!

5 Granny Smith apples	
⅓ cup finely chopped pecans	40 g
⅓ cup Craisins®	40 g
1 cup packed brown sugar	220 g
3 tablespoons butter	40 g
¾ teaspoon ground cinnamon	4 ml

- Core apples and peel 1-inch (2.5 cm) down from top and arrange in sprayed slow cooker. Combine pecans and Craisins® in bowl and fill apple center with mixture.

- Combine brown sugar, butter, cinnamon and ¾ cup (175 ml) water in saucepan and heat just until butter melts. Pour mixture over apples.

- Cover and cook on LOW for 2 to 4 hours. Check on apples after 2 hours; depending on the size, some apples will cook faster. Serves 5.

I Dream of Berry Cobbler

1 (16 ounce) package frozen mixed berries, thawed	455 g
1 (20 ounce) can blueberry pie filling	570 g
½ cup sugar	100 g
1 (7 ounce) package blueberry muffin mix	200 g
2 tablespoons canola oil	30 ml
Vanilla ice cream	

• Combine mixed berries, blueberry pie filling and sugar in bowl and place in sprayed slow cooker. Cover and cook on LOW for 3 hours.

• Increase heat to HIGH. Combine blueberry muffin mix, oil and ⅓ cup (75 ml) water in bowl and stir just until they blend well. Spoon muffin mixture over berry mixture. Cover and cook for additional 1 hour or until toothpick inserted into center of muffin mixture comes out clean.

• Let cooker stand uncovered for about 40 minutes before serving or until cobbler is slightly cooled. This cobbler is great with scoop of vanilla ice cream. Serves 8.

Peachy-Cranberry Delight

1½ cups quick-cooking oats	120 g
1 (1 pound) box brown sugar	455 g
⅔ cup sugar	135 g
¾ cup biscuit mix	90 g
2 teaspoons ground cinnamon	10 ml
½ cup orange juice	125 ml
1 (16 ounce) package frozen sliced peaches, thawed	455 g
1 (6 ounce) package Craisins®	170 g

• Combine oats, brown sugar, sugar, biscuit mix, cinnamon and orange juice in large bowl. Gently stir in peaches and Craisins®. Spoon into sprayed slow cooker. Cover and cook on LOW for 5 hours. Serve while still warm. Serves 10.

Fat conducts heat better than water so foods with more fat such as meats will cook faster than foods with less fat such as vegetables. Therefore, for more even cooking, fat should be trimmed from meats and meat should be browned and drained before cooking. Root vegetables should be at the bottom and sides of the cooker with the meat on top. Always follow the recipe's instructions for layering.

Cranberries Supreme

3 (20 ounce) cans pie apples (not pie filling)	3 (565 g)
2 (16 ounce) cans whole cranberries	3 (455 g)
3 cups sugar, divided	600 g
¾ cup packed brown sugar	165 g
⅓ cup (⅔ stick) butter	75 g
2½ cups crushed corn flakes	90 g
1 teaspoon ground cinnamon	5 ml
2 cups chopped pecans	220 g

- Combine pie apples, cranberries, 2 cups (400 g) sugar and brown sugar in large bowl and mix well. Spoon apple mixture into sprayed slow cooker.

- Melt butter in saucepan and add crushed corn flakes, cinnamon and pecans and mix well. Sprinkle over apples and cranberries. Cover and cook on HIGH 1 ½ to 2 hours. This dish can be served hot or room temperature. Serves 20.

TIP: Look for pie apples, not apple pie filling. They are with the pie fillings.

Fresh Peach Cobbler

1 cup sugar	200 g
¾ cup biscuit mix	90 g
2 eggs	
2 teaspoons vanilla	10 ml
1 (5 ounce) can evaporated milk	150 ml
2 tablespoons butter, melted	30 g
3 large, ripe peaches, peeled, mashed	
Peach ice cream	

- Combine sugar and biscuit mix in large bowl, stir in eggs, vanilla, evaporated milk and butter and mix well. Fold in peaches, pour into sprayed slow cooker and stir well. Cover and cook on LOW for 6 to 8 hours or on HIGH for 3 to 4 hours. Serve warm with peach ice cream. Serves 6.

Peach Crunch

¾ cup old-fashioned oats	60 g
⅔ cup packed brown sugar	150 g
¾ cup sugar	150 g
½ cup biscuit mix	60 g
½ teaspoon ground cinnamon	2 ml
2 (15 ounce) cans sliced peaches, well drained	2 (425 g)

- Combine oats, brown sugar, sugar, biscuit mix and cinnamon in bowl. Stir in drained peaches and spoon into sprayed slow cooker. Cover and cook on LOW for 4 to 5 hours. Serves 6 to 8.

Blueberry Goodness

1 (20 ounce) can blueberry pie filling	565 g
1 (18 ounce) box yellow cake mix	510 g
½ cup (1 stick) butter, softened	115 g
1 cup chopped walnuts	130 g
Vanilla ice cream	

- Place pie filling in sprayed slow cooker. Combine cake mix, butter and walnuts and spread over pie filling. Cover and cook on LOW for 2 hours. Serve over ice cream. Serves 8 to 10.

Slow Cooker Bananas Foster

5 bananas, sliced	
½ cup packed brown sugar	110 g
½ cup (1 stick) butter, melted	115 g
¼ cup rum (optional)	60 ml
Vanilla ice cream	

- Place all ingredients in slow cooker; mix well. Cook on LOW for 1 hour. Serve over ice cream. Serves 4.

Fruity Dessert Sauce

8 cups fresh fruit, thinly sliced	1.3 kg
1 cup orange juice	250 ml
⅓ cup packed brown sugar	75 g
⅓ cup sugar	70 g
2 tablespoons quick-cooking tapioca	35 g
1 teaspoon grated fresh ginger	5 ml
⅔ cup dried cranberries or cherries	65 g
Pound cake or ice cream	

- Combine fruit, orange juice, brown sugar, sugar, tapioca and ginger in sprayed slow cooker. Cover and cook on LOW for 4 hours.

- Add cranberries or cherries and mix well. Cover and let stand for 10 to 15 minutes. Spoon over slices of pound cake or over ice cream. Serves 6 to 8.

Delicious Bread Pudding

8 cups cubed leftover hot rolls, cinnamon rolls or bread	280 g
2 cups milk	500 ml
4 large eggs	
¾ cup sugar	150 g
⅓ cup packed brown sugar	75 g
¼ cup (½ stick) butter, melted	55 g
1 teaspoon vanilla	5 ml
¼ teaspoon ground nutmeg	1 ml
1 cup finely chopped pecans	110 g
Whipped topping, thawed	

- Place cubed bread or rolls in sprayed slow cooker.

- Combine milk, eggs, sugar, brown sugar, butter, vanilla and nutmeg in bowl and beat until smooth. Stir in pecans and pour over bread. Cover and cook on LOW for 3 hours. Serve with whipped topping. Serves 8.

Pineapple-Rice Pudding

1 cup cooked rice	160 g
¾ cup sugar	150 g
1 (1 pint) carton half-and-half cream	500 ml
1 tablespoon cornstarch	15 ml
3 eggs, beaten	
1 teaspoon vanilla	5 ml
1 (15 ounce) can crushed pineapple with juice	425 g
Toasted chopped pecans	

- Combine rice, sugar and half-and-half cream in bowl and mix well. Stir in cornstarch, eggs, vanilla and pineapple. Pour into sprayed slow cooker. Cover and cook on LOW for 2 to 3 hours.

- Top each serving with toasted chopped pecans as a special touch. Serves 6.

If you forgot to thaw the meat, you will need to add substantially to the cooking time in order for it to completely cook to a safe temperature. You may need to cook 4 or more hours longer at LOW and 2 hours longer at HIGH. It is a good idea to add at least 1 cup of warm liquid with the meat. Always check the internal temperature of meats with a cooking thermometer at the end of cooking.

Bread Pudding with Coconut and Nuts

1 cup sugar	200 g
½ cup (1 stick) butter, softened	115 g
1 teaspoon ground cinnamon	5 ml
4 eggs	
3 cups white bread cubes	105 g
⅓ cup flaked coconut	30 g
⅓ cup chopped pecans	40 g

- Beat sugar, butter and cinnamon in bowl. Add eggs and beat well until it blends. Stir in bread, coconut and pecans. Pour into sprayed slow cooker. Cover and cook on LOW for 3 to 4 hours or on HIGH for 1 hour 30 minutes to 2 hours or until knife inserted in center comes out clean. Serves 8.

TIP: Serve pudding warm with caramel ice cream topping, if desired.

Coconut Rice Pudding

¾ cup white rice	70 g
1 (15 ounce) can cream of coconut (not coconut milk)	425 g
1 (12 ounce) can evaporated milk	355 ml
¼ cup sugar	50 g
¾ cup sweetened flaked coconut	65 g
½ teaspoon rum extract	2 ml

- Place rice, cream of coconut, evaporated milk, sugar and 2¾ cups (675 ml) water in sprayed large slow cooker and stir until mixture blends well. Cover and cook on LOW for 4 to 5 hours or on HIGH for 2 hours 30 minutes to 3 hours.

- While pudding cooks, heat non-stick skillet over medium heat, add coconut and cook for 4 to 5 minutes or until light brown, stir constantly. Place coconut in small bowl and set aside.

- When pudding has cooked, remove bowl from cooker and stir in rum extract and let stand for about 10 minutes. Transfer pudding to individual serving bowls and top with coconut. Serves 8

TIP: If not serving right away, press sheet of plastic wrap over pudding so it will not form a "skin". Pudding can be refrigerated up to 2 days.

Rejoice with Rice Pudding

2½ cups cooked white rice	395 g
1½ cups evaporated milk	375 ml
¾ cup packed brown sugar	165 g
2 tablespoons butter, melted	30 g
2 teaspoons vanilla	10 ml
¾ teaspoon ground nutmeg	4 ml
3 eggs, beaten	
½ - 1 cup golden raisins	75 - 150 g

- Combine all ingredients in large bowl and stir until they blend well. Pour into sprayed slow cooker. Cover and cook on HIGH for 1 hour 30 minutes to 2 hours or on LOW for 4 to 6 hours. Stir during the first 30 minutes. Serves 6.

Gooey Chocolate Pudding

⅔ cup sugar	135 g
¼ cup cocoa	20 g
3 eggs, slightly beaten	
1½ cups milk	375 ml
1 teaspoon vanilla	5 ml
2 plain croissants, cut in 1-inch (2.5 cm) pieces, divided	
¾ cup chocolate chips, divided	130 g
1 (8 ounce) carton whipping cream	250 ml
2 tablespoons powdered sugar	15 g

- Combine sugar, cocoa, eggs, milk and vanilla in bowl and beat until mixture is well blended.

- Layer half croissants, chocolate chips and half egg mixture in sprayed 9-inch (23 cm) baking pan. Layer the remaining croissants and egg mixture.

- Add rack to slow cooker and pour in 1 cup (250 ml) water and place baking pan on rack. Cover and cook on LOW for 3 to 4 hours.

- Remove baking pan from slow cooker. Whip cream while adding powdered sugar in bowl. Place large spoonful of whipped cream on top of each serving. Serves 6.

Slow Chocolate Fix

1 (18 ounce) box chocolate cake mix	510 g
1 (8 ounce) carton sour cream 230 g	
4 eggs, beaten	
¾ cup canola oil	175 ml
1 (3.4 ounce) box instant chocolate pudding mix	100 g
¾ cup chopped pecans	85 g
Vanilla ice cream	

- Mix cake mix, sour cream, eggs, oil, pudding mix, pecans and 1 cup (250 ml) water in bowl. Pour into sprayed slow cooker. Cover and cook on LOW for 6 to 8 hours. Serve warm with vanilla ice cream. Serves 18.

Fudge Almighty

2 (16 ounce) jars slightly salted, dry-roasted peanuts	2 (455 g)
1 (12 ounce) package semi-sweet chocolate chips	340 g
1 (4 ounce) bar German chocolate, broken	115 g
2 (24 ounce) packages white chocolate bark	
or (3 pounds) almond bark, chopped	2 (680 g)/1.4 kg

- Place peanuts in sprayed slow cooker. Layer chocolate chips, German chocolate and white chocolate bark. Cover and cook on LOW for 3 hours without removing lid.

- Stir and cool in covered slow cooker. Stir again and drop teaspoonfuls of mixture onto wax paper. Yields 5 pounds (2.3 kg) fudge.

TIP: For darker fudge, use 1 white bark and 1 dark bark.

Chocolate Party Fondue

Use the slow cooker as a fondue pot.

2 (7 ounce) bars chocolate, chopped	2 (200 g)
1 (4 ounce) bar white chocolate, chopped	115 g
1 (7 ounce) jar marshmallow creme	200 g
¾ cup half-and-half cream	175 ml
½ cup slivered almonds, chopped, toasted	85 g
¼ cup amaretto liqueur	60 ml
Pound cake	

- Combine chocolate bars, white chocolate bar, marshmallow creme, half-and-half cream and almonds in sprayed small slow cooker. Cover and cook on LOW for about 2 hours or until chocolates melt.

- Stir to mix well and fold in amaretto liqueur. Use slow cooker as fondue pot or transfer chocolate mixture to fondue pot. Cut pound cake into small squares and dip into fondue. Serves 8 to 10.

Butterscotch-Spice Cake

1 (18 ounce) box spice cake mix	510 g
1 cup butterscotch chips	170 g
4 eggs, slightly beaten	
¾ cup canola oil	175 ml
1 (3.4 ounce) package butterscotch instant pudding mix	100 g
1 (8 ounce) carton sour cream	230 g
1 cup chopped pecans	110 g
Butter-pecan ice cream	

- Combine all ingredients and ¾ cup (175 ml) water in bowl. Pour into sprayed slow cooker. Cover and cook on LOW for 6 to 7 hours or on HIGH for 3 hours to 3 hours 30 minutes.

- Serve hot or at room temperature with butter-pecan ice cream. Serves 18.

Banana Nutty Bread

⅓ cup shortening	65 g
¾ cup sugar	150 g
2 eggs	
1¾ cups flour	210 g
1 teaspoon baking powder	5 ml
½ teaspoon baking soda	2 ml
1 cup mashed ripe bananas	230 g
½ cup chopped pecans	55 g
Place metal rack in oval slow cooker.	

- Cream shortening and sugar in bowl; add eggs and beat well. Stir in flour, baking powder, baking soda, bananas and ½ teaspoon (2 ml) salt, blending well. Stir in pecans and pour into sprayed, floured 9 x 4-inch (23 x 10 cm) foil loaf pan and cover with foil.

- Heat 2 cups (500 ml) water and pour in slow cooker. Place loaf pan on rack in cooker. Cover and cook on HIGH for 3 hours.

- Remove loaf from cooker and let stand for 10 minutes; then loosen edges with knife and invert on serving plate. Slice and serve warm or spread butter on slices and toast. Serves 6.

Index

Cookbooks Published by Cookbook Resources, LLC
Bringing Family and Friends to the Table

The Best 1001 Short, Easy Recipes

1001 Slow Cooker Recipes

*1001 Short, Easy,
Inexpensive Recipes*

1001 Fast Easy Recipes

1001 America's Favorite Recipes

Easy Slow Cooker Cookbook

Busy Woman's Slow Cooker Recipes

Busy Woman's Quick & Easy Recipes

365 Easy Soups and Stews

365 Easy Chicken Recipes

365 Easy One-Dish Recipes

365 Easy Soup Recipes

365 Easy Vegetarian Recipes

365 Easy Casserole Recipes

365 Easy Pasta Recipes

365 Easy Slow Cooker Recipes

Super Simple Cupcake Recipes

*Leaving Home Cookbook
and Survival Guide*

Essential 3-4-5 Ingredient Recipes

Ultimate 4 Ingredient Cookbook

Easy Cooking with 5 Ingredients

*The Best of Cooking
with 3 Ingredients*

Easy Diabetic Recipes

*Ultimate 4 Ingredient
Diabetic Cookbook*

*4-Ingredient Recipes
for 30-Minute Meals*

Cooking with Beer

The Washington Cookbook

The Pennsylvania Cookbook

The California Cookbook

Best-Loved New England Recipes

Best-Loved Canadian Recipes

*Best-Loved Recipes
from the Pacific Northwest*

*Easy Slow Cooker Recipes
(Handbook with Photos)*

*Cool Smoothies
(Handbook with Photos)*

*Easy Cupcake Recipes
(Handbook with Photos)*

*Easy Soup Recipes
(Handbook with Photos)*

Classic Tex-Mex and Texas Cooking

Best-Loved Southern Recipes

Classic Southwest Cooking

Miss Sadie's Southern Cooking

Classic Pennsylvania Dutch Cooking

The Quilters' Cookbook

Healthy Cooking with 4 Ingredients

*Trophy Hunters'
Wild Game Cookbook*

Recipe Keeper

Simple Old-Fashioned Baking

Quick Fixes with Cake Mixes

*Kitchen Keepsakes
& More Kitchen Keepsakes*

Cookbook 25 Years

Texas Longhorn Cookbook

Gifts for the Cookie Jar

All New Gifts for the Cookie Jar

The Big Bake Sale Cookbook

Easy One-Dish Meals

Easy Potluck Recipes

Easy Casseroles Cookbook

Easy Desserts

Sunday Night Suppers

Easy Church Suppers

365 Easy Meals

Gourmet Cooking with 5 Ingredients

Muffins In A Jar

A Little Taste of Texas

A Little Taste of Texas II

Ultimate Gifts for the Cookie Jar

**cookbook
resources** LLC
www.cookbookresources.com
Toll free 866-229-2665
Your Ultimate Source for Easy Cookbooks

1001
Slow
Cooker
Recipes

**Come home to
dinner – it's ready!**

*cookbook
resources* ® LLC

www.cookbookresources.com
Toll free 866-229-2665